PEACEMAKERS

PEACEMAKERS

American Leadership
and the End of Genocide
in the Balkans

JAMES W. PARDEW

UNIVERSITY PRESS OF KENTUCKY

Copyright © 2018 by The University Press of Kentucky

Scholarly publisher for the Commonwealth,
serving Bellarmine University, Berea College, Centre College of Kentucky, Eastern
Kentucky University, The Filson Historical Society, Georgetown College,
Kentucky Historical Society, Kentucky State University, Morehead State
University, Murray State University, Northern Kentucky University, Transylvania
University, University of Kentucky, University of Louisville, and Western
Kentucky University.
All rights reserved.

Editorial and Sales Offices: The University Press of Kentucky
663 South Limestone Street, Lexington, Kentucky 40508-4008
www.kentuckypress.com

Cataloging-in-Publication data available from the Library of Congress

ISBN 978-0-8131-7435-8 (hardcover : alk. paper)
ISBN 978-0-8131-7437-2 (epub)
ISBN 978-0-8131-7436-5 (pdf)

This book is printed on acid-free paper meeting
the requirements of the American National Standard
for Permanence in Paper for Printed Library Materials.

♾

Manufactured in the United States of America.

Member of the Association of
American University Presses

To Kathy with eternal love and respect

Contents

Maps

Abbreviations

ABiH	Army of the Republic of Bosnia-Herzegovina (Armija Republike Bosne i Hercegovine)
ASI	Acquisition Support Institute
CJCS	chairman of the Joint Chiefs of Staff
DOD	US Department of Defense
DPA	Democratic Party for Albanians (Demokratska Partija na Albancite)
EU	European Union
FRY	Federal Republic of Yugoslavia
HVO	Croatian Army in Bosnia (Hrvatsko Vijece Obrane)
ICTY	International Criminal Tribunal for the Former Yugoslavia
IFOR	Implementation Force in Bosnia
KDOM	US Kosovo Diplomatic Observer Mission
KFOR	Kosovo Force
KLA	Kosovo Liberation Army
KPC	Kosovo Protection Corps
KVM	Kosovo Verification Mission
LDK	Democratic League of Kosovo (Lidhja Demokratike e Kosoves)
MPRI	Military Professional Resources Incorporated
MTA	military-technical agreement
MUP	Special Ministry of Interior Police (Ministarstvo Unutrasnjih Poslova), Yugoslavia
NATO	North Atlantic Treaty Organization
NLA	National Liberation Army
NSC	US National Security Council
OSCE	Organization for Security and Co-operation in Europe
PDP	Party for Democratic Prosperity (Partija z Demokratski Prosperitet)

SACEUR	supreme Allied commander Europe
SDSM	Socialist Democratic Union of Macedonia (Socijaldemokratski Sojuz na Makedonija)
SFOR	Stabilization Force in Bosnia
SRSG	special representative of the UN secretary general in Kosovo
T&E Program	US Train and Equip Program for Bosnia
UAE	United Arab Emirates
UN	United Nations
UNMIK	United Nations Mission in Kosovo
UNPROFOR	United Nations Protection Force in Bosnia
UNSCR	United Nations Security Council resolution
VJ	Armed Forces of the Republic of Yugoslavia (Vojska Jugoslavije)
VMRO-DPMNE	Internal Macedonian Revolutionary Organization–Democratic Party for Macedonian National Unity (Vatreshna Makedonska-Revolutsionerna Organizatsiya–Demokratska Partija za Makedonsko Nacionalno Edinstvo)

Preface

After a reluctant start, American leadership of the international intervention in the former Yugoslavia ended the most destructive set of regional conflicts and humanitarian disasters in Europe since World War II.

A series of unexpected circumstances placed me at the heart of the US crisis-management process during the disintegration of Yugoslavia from 1995 until the independence of Kosovo in 2008. I left the US Army in 1994 as a colonel in the Pentagon, where I held the position of deputy J-2 (Intelligence) on the Joint Chiefs of Staff. As the end of my military career drew near, I began searching for follow-on work in Washington, DC, in the field of current intelligence or foreign policy. When Undersecretary of Defense for Policy Walter B. Slocombe hired me as a civilian to lead the Balkan Task Force in the Office of the Secretary of Defense, I never imagined the adventures ahead of me as the series of crises unfolded in the former Yugoslavia.

While I served as director of the Balkan Task Force, a major shift in US policy toward Bosnia and a tragic accident near Sarajevo propelled me into American diplomacy and policy development at the highest levels. I was to remain deeply involved in the US diplomatic and political-military policy in the Balkan region for the next thirteen years.

In that adventure, I saw American diplomacy and political-military policy making firsthand in a variety of situations, ranging from war termination in Bosnia to war prevention in Macedonia. This book is my account of those events, the leaders involved, the decisions they made, and how they made them as America and its allies struggled with the humanitarian tragedies and the security issues in the former Yugoslavia.

I thought carefully before using the word *genocide* in the title of this book. Genocide is a powerful term that recalls the horrific brutality against the Jews in Europe during World War II. After the war, the United Nations Convention on the Prevention and Punishment of the Crime of Genocide established genocide as acts committed with the intent to destroy, in whole or in part, a national, ethnical, racial, or religious group. Violence meeting those standards in the town of Srebrenica, Bosnia, in 1995 produced the US-led international intervention in Bosnia, which ended war crimes in Bosnia and brought many perpetrators of genocide to justice in a recognized international court. The intervention also prevented other war crimes in Kosovo and potentially Macedonia. I chose to highlight the term genocide because one of the most important legacies of the international intervention in the former Yugoslavia is the knowledge that those who commit genocide, including heads of state and government, military leaders and civilians, can be held legally accountable for their decisions and actions.

Crisis management and diplomacy do not lend themselves to set-piece doctrine or a uniform list of principles to apply to all situations because the circumstances in each are usually very different. However, the situations can involve similar patterns and some shared elements. One goal of this book is to identify some common themes and techniques that might be useful in future negotiations and some common pitfalls that might be avoided. In that regard, I make some judgments on American operational diplomacy—what worked, what didn't, how military operations and diplomacy meshed, and the strategic and tactical considerations that drove the process.

War and diplomacy are intensely human endeavors. National interests, power, and national strategy are at the core of national security, but the people involved—their vision, their will, and their character—play an important part in any negotiation. The breakup of the former Yugoslavia featured international intrigue, ambition, and a cast of colorful personalities on all sides—tyrants, genocidal thugs, heroes, and victims. On these pages, I tell the human story of the people engaged in this drama. I describe them as I saw them in the struggle for peace and stability as Yugoslavia broke apart.

I kept detailed personal journals throughout my experiences in the former Yugoslavia. Those journals, containing my observations of people, conversations, meetings, and decisions—recorded as events took place— are the primary sources for the details I give in this book. Except where I have cited other sources as references in the chapter notes, the quotations and descriptions on these pages are drawn from my journals or from my memory.

Throughout the text, I rely on shorthand titles to help move the narrative along. For instance, "the Balkans" refers to the territory of the former Yugoslavia, Albania, Greece, Bulgaria, Romania, and the Thracian region of Turkey. "Dayton" describes the location of the negotiations and resulting peace agreement for Bosnia, which was reached at Wright-Patterson Air Force Base, adjacent to Dayton, Ohio, in November 1995.

I make frequent reference to Bosnian Muslim political leaders as "Bosniaks." This awkward, nondescriptive term was developed somewhere along the line by those who wanted to separate the Bosnian Muslims' political movement from their religion. To those who coined this name, "Bosnian" was a geographic name used to refer to all ethnic groups in Bosnia. The name "Bosniak," as I use it, describes mostly Slavic Muslims whose home is Bosnia and who consolidated their political aspirations in a political movement led by President Alija Izetbegovic.

I have shortened the names of some countries for the readers' convenience. I refer to Bosnia and Herzegovina as "Bosnia"; Kosovo and Metokija as "Kosovo." I use "Macedonia" as a shorthand reference to the former Yugoslavia Republic of Macedonia. Each of the full names carries important regional, political, and cultural significance to various groups. This significance may be lost on readers not from the region or not knowledgeable in the nuances of Balkan issues. I intend no political message with this bit of editorial license.

I periodically mention "Europeans." These references collectively apply to senior leaders and policy makers and their representatives generally in major West European capitals when most of them have the same or a similar view.

The opinions and characterizations in this book are mine alone and do not necessarily represent official positions of the US government.

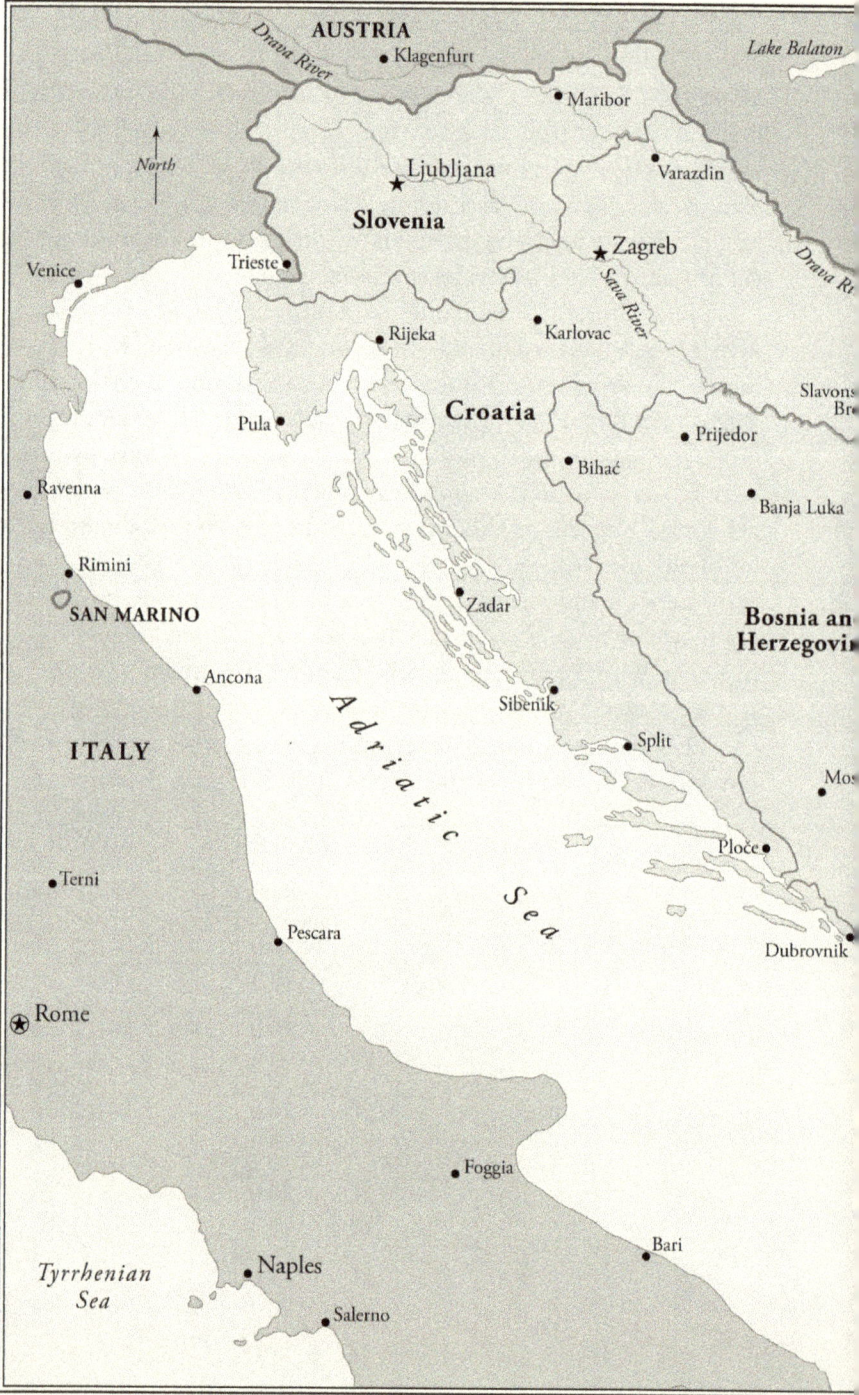

AUSTRIA

Klagenfurt

Lake Balaton

Drava River

Maribor

North

Ljubljana

Varazdin

Slovenia

Zagreb

Trieste

Sava River

Drava Rt

Venice

Rijeka

Karlovac

Croatia

Slavons
Bre

Pula

Prijedor

Bihać

Ravenna

Banja Luka

Rimini

SAN MARINO

Zadar

**Bosnia an
Herzegovi**

Ancona

A
d
r
i
a
t
i
c

Sibenik

Split

ITALY

Mos

Ploče

Terni

S
e
a

Pescara

Dubrovnik

Rome

Foggia

Bari

*Tyrrhenian
Sea*

Naples

Salerno

Socialist Federal Republic of Yugoslavia - 1989

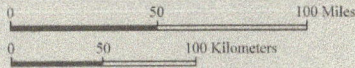

0   50   100 Miles

0   50   100 Kilometers

Kecskemet

HUNGARY

Danube River

Pecs

Szeged

Arad

Subotica

Kikinda

Timisoara

Sibiu

Osijek

Vukovar

Novi Sad

ROMANIA

a River

Sremska Mitrovica

Brčko

Sabac

Belgrade

Tuzla

Danube River

Serbia

Craiova

Kragujevac

Kraljevo

Danube River

Kruševac

★ Sarajevo

Niš

Leskovac

Montenegro

Mitrovicë

BULGARIA

Pristina

Podgorica

Kosovo

⊛ Sofia

Lake Scutari

Shkodër

Kumanovo

★ Skopje

Macedonia

⊛ Tiranë

Prilep

Lake Ohrid

ALBANIA

Lake Prespa

GREECE

Aegean Sea

Thessaloniki

Part 1

Bosnia
Shuttle Diplomacy

Old town Pocitelj, Bosnia-Herzegovina. (Shutterstock.com)

Welcome to the Balkans

The blast outside our apartment building jolted us awake. Someone had blown up an empty guard shack in front of our building in Izmir, Turkey, one night in early 1980. Kathy and I quickly sheltered the kids in the back of the apartment until the police arrived. At the time, I was a major in the US Army assigned to the US mission in the North Atlantic Treaty Organization (NATO) headquarters in Izmir. In Turkey in 1980, the political system was disintegrating, and political violence was common. A Turkish military coup was on the horizon. The blast in Izmir was my first direct exposure to political violence in the region. It would not be my last.

Twenty-two years later, in 2002, at a dinner at the residence of the Bulgarian ambassador in northwestern Washington, DC, Bulgarian guests around the table described the turbulent life of their new prime minister, Simeon Saxe-Coburg Gotha. The US Senate had just confirmed me as the US ambassador to Bulgaria, and the Bulgarian ambassador was hosting the dinner for Kathy and me before we left for Sofia.

The Bulgarians at the table discussed the book *Crown of Thorns*, which tells the story of Simeon's family.[1] His father, Boris, was czar of Bulgaria during World War II. Czar Boris resisted sending Bulgarian Jews to the extermination camps even though Bulgaria was an ally, albeit an unenthusiastic one, of Nazi Germany. Hitler summoned Boris to Berlin for a discussion. Shortly after returning to Bulgaria, Boris died under mysterious circumstances, generating widespread conspiracy theories of a Nazi assassination. He was buried at the Rila Monastery, and his six-year-old son, Simeon, assumed the Bulgarian throne.

Soviet sympathizers deposed young Czar Simeon in 1947 in favor of a Communist regime. The Communists dug up his father's body from the monastery and reburied it on the grounds of his palace near Sofia. Simeon spent most of his life in exile, first in Egypt, then Spain. When communism collapsed, Simeon, the last czar of the twentieth century, returned to Bulgaria as prime minister of an elected democratic government. Boris's body was never found, but his heart was recovered in the Bulgarian Academy of Science and reburied at Rila Monastery.

From 1995 until 2002, Kathy had kept a stable home in the Virginia suburbs for our sons as I bounced around the Balkans as a US official, engaged in the wars first in Bosnia, then in Kosovo, and finally in Macedonia.

"Nazis, czars, assassinations, Soviets, a body dug up from a monastery, a heart found in a science academy? What have you gotten me into this time?" Kathy said as we walked back to the car after the Bulgarian dinner.

"Welcome to the Balkans," I said.

From the Tides of Empires

The history of the Balkans is mingled with the history of the great powers of Western civilization. In fact, no other area in Europe has been exposed more to the ebb and flow of great powers important to the history of Western civilization than the Balkans.

It is the land of ancient Greek and Thracian cultures, of Phillip and Alexander the Great, and of Slavic tribes who came south across the Danube centuries ago. Rome expanded its empire into the region in the second century BCE. Trajan's magnificent triumphal column in the forum in Rome commemorates Rome's conquest of the Dacians in what is modern-day Romania. Roman emperor Constantine, born in Nis in today's Serbia, established the capital of the Eastern Roman Empire in Constantinople, now Istanbul. Byzantine armies occupied the Balkans and converted most of the population to Christianity.

After Constantinople fell to the Ottomans in 1453, Ottoman sultans gained control of the region and marched their armies from Istanbul through the captured territories in failed campaigns to seize Vienna. For centuries, the Balkans served as a transportation corridor between empires and a strategic buffer between East and West.

Russia liberated much of the region in the late nineteenth century when it pushed the weakened Ottoman Turks back toward Istanbul. Later, the Austria-Hungarian Empire exerted its influence on the region. Two regional wars were fought early in the twentieth century, and the area was drawn into both World War I and World War II, an involvement that included occupation by Nazi Germany. Large areas of the Balkans fell under the Soviet sphere of influence after 1945.

Each of the empires that occupied the Balkans left behind bits and pieces of its art, mythology, architecture, politics, and ethnic identity as its influence receded from the region. Today, festivals with roots in pagan ceremonies can be found in local villages. Monasteries, temples, churches, and mosques—some built on the remains of pagan temples—exist across the land. Ancient Roman ruins, Byzantine fortress walls, and Ottoman bridges and clock towers are interspersed around the Balkans as remnants of previous occupiers. Communities with clear links to Austro-Hungarian influences are common, and Communist architecture from the Soviet era can be found everywhere in old Soviet-dominated areas.

On a human level, villages, towns, and larger regions are populated by clusters of Turks, Bulgarians, Greeks, Orthodox Christians, Slavic Muslims, Roman Catholics, Serbs, Roma, Montenegrins, Jews, Albanians, Romanians, and many more groups. Despite periodic efforts to associate ethnic groups with specific geography, these diverse groups intermingle throughout the area.

As foreign occupations waxed and waned, each of the various cultural groups clung fiercely to its common cultural traditions, language, and histories as the core of its identity. For the group members, cultural identity was critical to the survival of the community when confronted by outsiders. For many, to compromise on ethnic or cultural identity was to put community survival at risk.

Yugoslavia

The Paris Peace Conference in 1919 created modern Yugoslavia when the leaders of the victorious powers in World War I defined the future of much of postwar Europe. In the deliberations, the conference accepted a Serb and Croat initiative to form a confederation of the region's ethnic groups into Yugoslavia, a power-sharing arrangement of mostly southern Slavs.[2] Two decades later, during World War II, Nazi Germany occupied the region despite the armed resistance by several nationalist insurgent groups. Marshall Joseph Tito, a Croat-Slovene by birth and a famous Communist partisan leader during the war, had the popular legitimacy to lead a unified postwar Yugoslavia. However, his leadership and his ability to suppress ethnic nationalism were personal. Tito's death in 1980 set the stage for the breakup of Yugoslavia; the end of Soviet communism accelerated the process.[3]

The World Changes

The wars, near wars, and human tragedies in the former Yugoslavia from 1991 to 2008 began at a time of historic upheaval in the international order as Russia discarded Soviet communism. In this period, the revolutionary changes in Russia, eastern Europe, and Eurasia were fraught with uncertainty for Washington and other Western capitals.

The fall of Soviet communism gave the United States during the 1990s an historic level of national power. But American leaders in the period had no concrete vision of America's role in the world after the doctrine of containment was no longer relevant.[4]

I was a "Cold Warrior" for the United States for most of my career, first as an armored cavalry platoon leader guarding West Germany's border with East Germany in 1966. Later, as director of foreign intelligence on the Army General Staff in Washington, I watched the Berlin Wall come down and the Soviet system disintegrate in eastern Europe.

Suddenly the Cold War was over. The international system that had been the focus of Western foreign and national security policy since 1945 had dissolved. The threat from the Warsaw Pact—the standard measure for US military strategy, force development, doctrine, and planning for almost fifty years—ceased to exist. Yugoslavia, where conflicts broke out as nationalist movements pressed for independence two years after the Berlin Wall came down, was a major exception to the mostly peaceful end to Soviet communism in eastern Europe.

The set of international crises in the former Yugoslavia from 1991 to 2008 took place on the Balkan fault lines between East and West. They were a clash of gods, of history, of national identity, of idealism, and of shameless ambition. Ultimately, only active US and international engagement in the former Yugoslavia could restore peace and stability to the Balkans. This engagement also would help define the nature of seven new nations and influence the character of international relations into the future.

2

Fools and Madmen

Fools and madmen are drawn easily to war—all glory and bravado in the beginning, tragedy and disaster at the end. Slobodan Milosevic, the president of the Republic of Serbia, in his military adventures in the former Yugoslavia overlooked one of the most important lessons of history: wars are easy to start, but once started they often take an unpredictable path.[1] Wars are almost never as short as expected. They generally cost more in lives and treasure than originally believed, and those who start wars are often consumed by them.

The end of communism in Yugoslavia set off a chain of violence that threatened the stability of the entire region. These ethnic conflicts in the Balkans killed tens of thousands of people and displaced millions more as Yugoslavia broke apart.

A Narrow Vision

The lack of vision by local leaders for a democratic, European future was a primary cause of the violence in the Balkans. Very few leaders in the post-Communist Yugoslavia could see beyond their local political ambitions and personal cultural identity to foresee their country as a modern European democracy. They had few models in their personal experience to draw from. These local political leaders viewed the solution of every political question as a zero-sum competition with other ethnic groups. Compromise, except under very specific—almost mathematical—conditions, was not their tradition.

The people of the region also shared the blame. The various populations in the region generally supported Milosevic and other nationalist leaders who chose war to pursue their objectives. I cannot recall one serious peace movement in any of the regions of the former Yugoslavia that placed restraints on leaders who favored war from 1992 to 2008.

People learned about life and politics as youngsters listening to stories at the feet of parents and grandparents and at local celebrations in their communities. In the Balkans, every group had been a victim of repression by some dominant master at some point in its history. This psychology of victimhood colored each group's outlook toward outside groups, even if they all had lived as neighbors for generations. Geography reinforced the narrow vision. The Balkan region was isolated from the European mainstream by geography, and in its isolation local ethnic identity was strong.

What Yugoslavia's unification effort failed to solve was how to integrate society into a national political culture in which the nation is the source of personal, political, economic, and legal identity. When Belgrade lost its grip and the political bands holding Yugoslavia together snapped with the fall of communism, Yugoslavia almost immediately fractured along ethnic lines.

Political Conversion

Self-interest is a powerful motivation for conversion. By 1989, many Communist leaders saw what was coming and began to change from ardent Communist bureaucrats to committed democrats and market capitalists, often stealing the nation's wealth in the process of conversion. Their primary political strategy to win and hold power was to stress extreme ethnic nationalism among their constituent populations.

Slobodan Milosevic was one such leader. In 1989, Milosevic was a successful Communist Party leader married to a woman with strong leftist credentials dating back to the Communist partisans of World War II.

For Milosevic, the conversion was rapid. In a series of speeches in Kosovo beginning in 1987, he called for unity among Serbs and declared never to give up Kosovo and to defend Serbs against violence.[2] He discovered that fear fuels hate and that fear and hate are potent political forces. As he transformed himself from Communist apparatchik to Serbian nationalist leader, his popularity grew among Serbs. Through his nationalist appeal as a Serb, Milosevic consolidated power when he became president of Serbia in 1990 and never looked back.

Religion and Politics—the Unholy Temptation

Political conversion was not the only personal transformation. After years of communism, many leaders in the region suddenly and conveniently discovered God.

Despite fifty years of Communist rule and religious repression, religion remained deeply ingrained in the people's cultural identity, but not so much in their faith. In general, Croats and Slovenes were historically Roman Catholic, and Serbs, Montenegrins, and ethnic Macedonians were Orthodox Christians. European Muslims, converted to Islam during the Ottoman period, formed the overwhelming majority population in Kosovo, the largest single group in Bosnia, and roughly one-third of the people in Macedonia.

As Yugoslavia broke apart, resurgent religion in the Balkans became an important political tool for ambitious leaders. Meanwhile, religious leaders, subservient to the Communist political establishment for decades, seemed happy to oblige.

I was raised a Southern Baptist in Arkansas, so I knew something about religious hypocrisy, and it was everywhere in post-Communist Yugoslavia. After communism fell, local leaders who had been atheists as good Communists suddenly flipped to become Christians of various types or Muslims when it suited their political ambitions. Down came the pictures of Lenin, up went religious symbols and pictures in political offices throughout the region. The clergy had access to the local leaders, and the latter appeared at religious ceremonies when it suited their ambition.

The mutual attraction of religion and politics is dangerous to any democracy. Rather than compete for believers without government help, religious leaders in post-Communist Yugoslavia could not resist the attraction of political power as a means to influence and sustain the faith. Likewise, political leaders wrapped themselves in a cloak of faith as an easy source of authority and legitimacy in their respective ethnic groups. In fact, the integration of religion and government corrupts both institutions, and when faith becomes a justification for war, the result can be particularly brutal and destructive. Such was the case in post-Communist Yugoslavia.

There were, of course, some exceptions to the cynical use of religion for political gain among national leaders. Of the primary leaders in the Balkans at the time, Bosnian president Alija Izetbegovic, a Muslim, and Macedonian president Boris Trajkovski, a Christian, struck me as serious men of faith.

History

The breakup of Yugoslavia was difficult psychologically for the Serbs. They had bought into the Croatian idea of a unified Yugoslavia in the peace talks in Paris in 1919, but Serbia was the heart of that nation for most Serbs.[3] Belgrade, which had been Yugoslavia's capital, was also the Serbs' capital, and the Serbs held key positions throughout the Yugoslavian government. The fragmentation of Yugoslavia beginning in 1991 was a historic blow to their esteem.

Milosevic, officially president of Serbia in 1989, resisted Yugoslavia's breakup most intensely in areas where large Serbian communities lived or where Serbia had historic ties: Croatia, Bosnia, and Kosovo. Serbian involvement in Bosnia and Kosovo was particularly brutal. Milosevic never believed Bosnia was a legitimate nation and plotted with Croatian president Franjo Tudjman to divide it between them. Kosovo carried a special status in Serbian history, and Milosevic had made an absolute commitment to ensure Serbian control of that region.

Peace negotiations are about the future. When negotiations center on debates about the past, they are likely to flounder. History and specific geography are important background information to understand the positions of the parties in the negotiations, but US negotiators in the Balkans learned quickly that any debate over historic maps and interpretations of the past led nowhere. All along, the US peace effort worked to keep the proposed solutions within existing Yugoslav provincial boundaries and to create institutions that would address the present and the future to avoid getting bogged down in the past.

Lines and Proportions

One traditional way of solving ethnic problems in Yugoslavia was to draw political borders to segregate ethnic entities geographically, and these Yugoslav models were well known to local leaders involved in the Balkan conflicts. During the peace talks over the post-Communist wars, West European participants also were inclined to seek segregated territorial solutions to help solve ethnic problems.

Richard C. Holbrooke and subsequent US envoys were committed to keeping the existing borders of Bosnia and other provinces of the former Yugoslavia rather than to trying to negotiate some type of territorial separation. Realistically, there was no place in the Balkans where a line could be drawn that would create a clear ethnic division without significant population relocation.

To the parties, territorial division among ethnic groups was a primary issue—what ethnic groups got to live where and who had political authority over that territory. Milosevic and Tudjman in particular wanted ethnicity, not birth location or residency, to be the source of national identity.

Proportional representation according to some type of agreed percentages of the various ethnic groups in the allocation of power and benefits was the second traditional way to deal with ethnic disputes in Yugoslavia. When forced to integrate, negotiating parties were adept at debating an agreed-percentage solution rather than considering individual merit. Once the percentage was set, then that percentage could be used for the allocation of positions and resources throughout the structure. In this way, ethnic leaders could ensure maximum separation and therefore vertical control from top to bottom in any structure. This type of phony integration was a constant theme of the Balkan negotiations, and these negotiated structures remained in place in many areas as major obstacles to development in the region.

3

The Inconvenient War

Slovenia, Croatia, and Macedonia declared independence from Yugoslavia in 1991. After first resisting secession with military force in Slovenia and Croatia, the government in Belgrade withdrew Serbian troops except in the border area of eastern Croatia. When a Muslim-dominated Bosnian government in Sarajevo proclaimed independence in 1992, fighting broke out between Serbs, Muslims, and Croats throughout Bosnia. Milosevic backed the Bosnian Serbs, who controlled most of the military facilities and equipment in Bosnia, in resisting independence. As Yugoslavia fractured, the United States joined other governments in recognizing Slovenia, Croatia, Macedonia, and Bosnia as sovereign nations.

The fighting in Bosnia was rarely conventional combat operations between competing armies. It was instead generally a punishing Serbian campaign against the Muslim and Croat civilian population. Bosnian Serb forces laid siege to Sarajevo, the Bosnian capital, isolating the city while using artillery and snipers to punish and harass its residents. Away from Sarajevo, Serbian forces and paramilitaries attacked smaller communities. Executions, rape, and torture were common.

Throughout the war, Bosnian Serb forces received considerable direct military assistance from Belgrade and from paramilitary groups originating in Serbia. Belgrade tried, with some early success, to portray the conflict as purely a local Bosnian Serbian resistance to independence rather than something sponsored and supported directly by Belgrade. Personally, I had no doubts that the Milosevic regime authorized and heavily supported all forms of Bosnian Serb activities. Establishing legal proof of Belgrade's control over Serbian atrocities in Bosnia was difficult, but the circumstantial evidence was overwhelming.

No "Dog in This Fight"

George H. W. Bush, after eight years as vice president in the Reagan administration, became the forty-first president of the United States in Janu-

Serbian military forces inflicted more than 1,000 days of shelling, sniping, and isolation on the people of Sarajevo from 1992 to 1995. (Shutterstock.com)

ary 1989. It fell to Bush to manage the US response to the unfolding demise of the Soviet Union that Mikhail Gorbachev, secretary-general of the Soviet Communist Party, had set in motion during the Reagan presidency. In Bush's first year, the Berlin Wall came down; in 1991, the Soviet Union ceased to exist. Every nation in the former Soviet sphere of influence in eastern Europe was in a state of political transformation as the Soviet Empire receded. Never in history had an empire as powerful as the Soviet Union collapsed as quickly and as peacefully. For Russia, the United States, and Europe, the stakes in this process were enormous.

In this period of revolution in world affairs, Yugoslavia was not a top priority for the Bush presidency, even after fighting broke out and spread to Bosnia in 1992. US leaders were absorbed with events throughout eastern Europe and Russia and with Gorbachev's position as leader of the transition in the Kremlin. The United States feared that supporting the breaking away of provinces in Yugoslavia might undermine Gorbachev.[1]

The Bush national security team also faced unrelated foreign problems. Close to home, Bush ordered an invasion of Panama in late 1989 to oust strong man Manuel Noriega. He also was concerned by a surge of refugees fleeing from Haiti to the United States after a military coup in 1991 removed the Aristide government. The most challenging military problem for Bush was the Iraqi invasion of Kuwait in 1990. The preparation and execution of the US-led allied Operation Desert Storm to expel Saddam Hussein's forces from Kuwait consumed the US government's attention and energy in 1990–1991 and beyond.[2]

The Bush administration deflected the nagging problem of war in Bosnia. US national security leaders were not personally interested in the conflict and did not see sufficient US interest in Bosnia to warrant anything more than humanitarian assistance. They felt that the Bosnian problem, although unfortunate, was Europe's to solve. In the military, General Colin Powell, chairman of the Joint Chiefs of Staff (CJCS), a public hero after his leadership in the Pentagon during Operation Desert Storm, was adamantly opposed to US military forces on the ground in the Balkans.

The trauma of Vietnam also was in the background of any discussion of sending US troops to Bosnia. Powell and other senior Bush administration officials saw a parallel between the Balkans and Vietnam, where the United States had become bogged down in an unwinnable civil war.[3] Republicans in Congress, also opposed to US troops on the ground in Bosnia, proposed a "lift and strike" policy. This plan would lift the international arms embargo to enable the arming of the Government of Bosnia while providing an international air strike to give support to civilians under attack. The Congress authorized the transfer of surplus US military equipment for Bosnian fighters to give substance to this policy proposal.[4]

Secretary of State James Baker summed up the administration's attitude toward the conflicts in Yugoslavia on returning from a trip to the region in June 1991: "We don't have a dog in that fight."[5]

In the summer of 1992, the Democratic Party chose former Arkansas governor William J. Clinton to oppose Bush, who was seeking a second term as president. Clinton and his campaign organization considered Bush to be vulnerable on the war in Bosnia and the humanitarian suffering in Somalia and so made them core foreign-policy issues during the campaign. Bush, even more vulnerable on the weak US economy, received no political boost from the military victory in Iraq, and on November 3, 1992, US voters elected Clinton as their president.

Despite all its objections to nation building, peacekeeping, and humanitarian operations, a lame-duck Bush administration, perhaps to compensate for a lack of action on Bosnia, deployed 35,000 US troops to Somalia in December 1992 to end starvation and relieve suffering in a lawless land controlled by local warlords.[6] I was one of those troops. As my last overseas deployment in the US Army, I served for six weeks on the intelligence staff of the US Joint Headquarters in Mogadishu.

International Failure in Bosnia, 1992–1995

The international response to the ethnic fighting in Bosnia from 1992 to 1995 was primarily in the hands of European governments, the European Union (EU), and the United Nations (UN). In confronting the war in Bosnia, the major European countries and Russia fell back on their traditional biases based on history, cultural ties, and national attitudes. Russia favored their Slavic cousins in Serbia; the French and British also were sympathetic to the Serbs; Germany leaned toward the Croats. The Muslims in the region were left to find friends in the United States, Turkey, and predominantly Muslim countries.

European leaders and institutions were not prepared to assume independent responsibility for a security problem as complex as Bosnia. For forty-five years after World War II, European nations had looked to the United States for security leadership. Further, many European leaders viewed the Balkans as a backwater of Europe populated by a hodge-podge of ethnic groups and out of the European mainstream.

The primary institution for responding to the violence in Yugoslavia was the UN. The UN deployed peacekeepers as the UN Protection Force (UNPROFOR) in Bosnia under a series of UN Security Council resolutions in 1992. The mission of UNPROFOR evolved from security of humanitarian activities to protection of innocent civilians in designated safe areas.[7] Between 1992 and November 1995, when the Dayton Agreement was completed, the UN Security Council issued almost fifty resolutions related to Bosnia.[8] Unfortunately, UNPROFOR was an organization with limited capability, unwieldy command and control, and no will to intervene forcefully to protect civilians.

Ethnic cleansing, the euphemism Serbian extremists used for their actions to kill or drive out non-Serbs from areas the Serbs claimed, entered the lexicon of history to describe the acts of genocide against the people of Bosnia. By 1995, about 100,000 Bosnians, an estimated 65 percent of them Muslims, had been killed.[9] Almost half of the 4.4 million people in Bosnia were uprooted from their homes. About 1.2 million people were internally displaced in Bosnia, and 900,000 became international refugees.[10]

In 1995, after years of failing to enable adequate humanitarian support

Bosnia and Herzegovina - 1995

to the civilian population, UNPROFOR and the UN had little credibility left in Bosnia.

From 1992 to 1995, the tragedy in Bosnia played out in full view of the international public. Areas of Sarajevo were in ruins, and public awareness of the brutality generated international outrage and sympathy for the people of Bosnia, especially in the Muslim world.

Help Where You Can Find It

Denied security assistance from the West, the Muslims in Bosnia turned as a matter of survival to other Muslims willing to violate the arms embargo and help with their self-defense. They found willing partners through-out the Islamic world. Funding and humanitarian aid flowed into Sarajevo from Iran, Saudi Arabia, and other predominantly Muslim countries. Others at the extremist edge of Islam also were eager to help by providing volunteer fighters and military equipment. A set of relationships developed between Bosnians and Muslims outside the region—some open, some not; some humanitarian; and some military.

Iran was the largest donor of direct military assistance to the Bosnian government, providing major shipments of arms to Bosnia through financial and shipping arrangements with Croatia. The United States took no action to interfere with these arrangements. In addition to arms, Iran deployed between 1,000 and 2,000 Iranian Revolutionary Guards Corps personnel to advise the Bosnian army. Foreign fighters—mujahedeen—numbering in the hundreds arrived to fight alongside the Bosnian army. Bosnian Muslim soldiers, with no chance to receive training in the West, went to Iran for military training.

Clinton Inherits Bosnia and Somalia

In January 1993, the Bush presidency handed over to the incoming Clinton administration a rapidly deteriorating humanitarian crisis in Bosnia and a significant American commitment to the UN humanitarian mission in Somalia.

The Democrats had been out of power in the White House for twelve years when Clinton was sworn in as president in January 1993, and it showed, particularly on foreign policy. The new administration was inexperienced as it settled in and wanted to avoid any unnecessary foreign commitments.[11]

Clinton was the first post–Cold War American president, and Yugoslavia was to be a major early international test of the post–Cold War period.[12] However, Clinton's personal interests concentrated on US domestic policy. He was not inclined to devote his time and energy to knotty foreign conflicts.[13]

The deteriorating international situation in Somalia, producing the loss of two US Black Hawk helicopters and eighteen US soldiers in Mogadishu in October 1993, and the Hutus' murder of one million Tutsis in Rwanda in April 1994 did nothing to encourage Clinton to engage directly in Bosnia.

The administration was initially fragmented internally on the issue of what to do about Bosnia. Vice President Al Gore and several key members of the National Security Council (NSC) Staff favored US leadership on Bosnia. Ambassador Madeleine Albright at the UN actively promoted the use of US military force in Bosnia.[14] At the State Department, several officials advocated US intervention, and a number of young Foreign Service officers wrote a dissent letter to the secretary of state openly calling for a US policy change on Bosnia. Some signers resigned in protest over the lack of US engagement there.

The Clinton administration also inherited a standing US policy and a US military leadership that actively opposed any US military engagement on the ground in Bosnia. At NATO headquarters in Brussels, the US government had promoted the traditional alliance policy that Bosnia was outside NATO's primary area of responsibility.

Led by General Powell, who carried over deep into the first year of the Clinton presidency, the Joint Chiefs of Staff remained against any US military mission that would put American troops on the ground in the Balkans. Powell in 1993 was at the height of his influence in Washington—a public hero after directing the US military victory in Iraq and an accomplished bureaucratic fighter from years in Washington policy making. In the new Clinton administration, he was the most experienced senior official in government on political-military issues.

I periodically briefed Powell on current intelligence when I served on the Joint Staff from 1992 to 1994. The hard-nosed generals and colonels on the Joint Staff universally respected him as an extremely bright, practical, and confident leader. I also quite frequently briefed Les Aspin, the new secretary of defense, but Aspin was not in Powell's league in any aspect of defense or military policy—not even close. Without White House leadership, the senior Clinton administration civilians in the Pentagon were not willing to directly oppose the generals' determination to stay out of Bosnia.

The NSC Staff in the White House looked for a way to fulfill the president's campaign promise to end the war in Bosnia but to do so without deploying US military forces there. US engagement became even more difficult for the Clinton administration when Republicans, who had consistently objected to US troops in Bosnia, took control of both houses of Congress in 1995.

By 1995, the ineffective international effort to end the violence was humiliating the UN and the European governments involved in Bosnia. The United States, criticizing European inaction from the sidelines, faced increasingly strained relationships with its traditional European allies. The

United States complied with the international arms embargo on Bosnia, but it was a restriction that favored the Serbs while offering only limited humanitarian assistance to the Bosnians. Inside the government, Albright and others agitated for greater US involvement. With Washington policy in a state of paralysis, UNPROFOR in Bosnia could do little to stop the savage attacks on civilians.

A massacre in a small, isolated town in Bosnia unknown to most Americans changed everything in the summer of 1995.

4

Genocide

The intelligence pictures showed women and girls boarding buses lined up on the streets in the center of town. The buses validated other reports that the men and boys were being separated from the females.

"God help those poor people in that miserable place," I thought as I looked at the pictures at my desk in the Pentagon in July 1995. Separating the men from the women and small children indicated that summary executions might be taking place. The town in the photos was Srebrenica, Bosnia, and US policy in the Balkans was about to take a dramatic turn from sideline criticism to active involvement.

Srebrenica was a small, isolated community in a valley of the forested mountains in eastern Bosnia near the border with Serbia. The UN designated it one of three "safe areas" in eastern Bosnia after negotiations between UNPROFOR and local Serbian officials. UNPROFOR deployed a small contingent of Dutch peacekeepers to Srebrenica to monitor the safe area.

The Dutch peacekeepers were in an untenable military situation. They had inadequate political and military guidance, and they lacked backup military support from UNPROFOR—or from anyone else for that matter. From a tactical military perspective, Srebrenica was not defensible with the available UN forces. But as bad as the Dutch peacekeepers' situation was, they should have done more to stop the slaughter.

For almost two weeks in July 1995, Srebrenica and surrounding communities were a human slaughterhouse. Bosnian Serb general Ratko Mladic and his staff were present as the Bosnian Serb army, along with Serbian paramilitary troops, evacuated women and then tortured and executed more than 8,000 Muslim men and boys in warehouses, factories, schools, and fields in and around Srebrenica. UNPROFOR took no effective action to stop the massacre.[1]

Eyewitness reports of the murders, killing fields, and mass graves very quickly generated new levels of international disgust at the UN's failure to

Commander of Bosnian Serb military forces General Ratko Mladic (*left front*) and Bosnian Serb political leader Radovan Karadzic (*right front*), 1995. (Associated Press)

prevent this latest savagery against civilians. Srebrenica destroyed the last small measure of UN and UNPROFOR credibility in Bosnia and forced Western capitals to reassess the international effort in Bosnia.[2]

Blaming the international failure in Bosnia on the UN was too easy, though. The UN is a convenient scapegoat when national governments fail to take effective action on difficult problems. That was the case in Bosnia from 1992 to 1995 as the UN became the focus of public frustration by governments that wished to complain but to take no real action to end the killing.

UN peacekeepers can be valuable assets in situations when the conflicting parties are willing to be separated by international forces, but they generally are not well suited to conduct coercive military operations against aggressive national forces. The UN was designed to be an institution to pursue peace, not to wage war. It has no operational military staff or other capacity to direct military operations, and its mandates frequently are the result of international compromises in which competing national interests hamper effective military actions. In Bosnia, UNPROFOR was doomed to failure.

The Srebrenica massacre was the turning point for US policy in the Balkans. After Srebrenica, the United States began to assume leadership of the international effort to restore peace and stability in Bosnia, Kosovo, and Macedonia. In the process, it commissioned major diplomatic missions, led NATO air strikes, and deployed thousands of military troops and civilian peacekeepers to the Balkans. Reaching the decision to engage directly in Bosnia was not a quick or an easy one, however.

The Clinton Team

At the time of the Srebrenica massacre, the key players involved in finding a solution to the crisis in Bosnia were Anthony Lake, national security adviser to the president, and Samuel R. "Sandy" Berger, his deputy. The low-key Lake was a former Foreign Service officer and African specialist. He joined the Clinton team late and did not have a particularly close relationship to the president. An internationalist and humanitarian, he favored active US leadership in Bosnia.[3] Berger, an attorney by trade, ran the day-to-day operations of interagency coordination, including an escalating number of Deputies Committee (made up of national security deputy cabinet secretaries) meetings on Bosnia in the White House Situation Room. Berger was close to the president personally but did not have Lake's foreign-policy experience. Alexander Vershbow, a Foreign Service officer detailed from the State Department to the NSC Staff, was the NSC Staff's director for Europe and responsible for Balkan policy development in the White House. Vershbow was a hawk on American engagement in Bosnia.[4]

The Clinton national security team hoped that Powell's replacement in September 1993, General John Shalikashvili, an immigrant of Georgian royal heritage who rose to four stars in the US Army, would be more flexible on Bosnia. They learned quickly that Shalikashvili, too, would resist US military deployment to the Balkans.

William J. Perry had replaced Les Aspin, who died in May 1995, as secretary of defense. Secretary Perry cast a gracious, unassuming image that belied an internal toughness. I never saw him take a confrontational position on an issue in policy debates. He relied instead on his intelligence and the strength of his arguments to win the day. On a personal level, I felt that Secretary Perry favored a stronger US military intervention in Bosnia, but he did not challenge tough military resistance head on.

Two other figures in the Office of the Secretary of Defense were critical to developing the Department of Defense (DOD) position on the Balkans. As undersecretary for policy, Walter B. Slocombe was an experienced Washington tax attorney with an interest in national security. His most trusted adviser on the Balkans was Joseph J. Kruzel, deputy assistant secretary of defense for Europe and NATO. Kruzel, an Air Force Academy graduate and Vietnam veteran with a doctorate from Harvard, was a young, rising star on foreign and national security policy in the Democratic Party.

Kruzel supervised the Balkan Task Force for the secretary of defense. He had recruited me to be director of the task force when I left the army in 1994 and was my boss.

Three players dominated Balkan policy at the State Department. Secretary of State Warren Christopher was morally outraged by the brutality the Serbs inflicted on the people in Bosnia. Always dressed in carefully tailored British suits, shirts, and ties, Christopher had been a longtime activist in Democratic Party causes from his law firm in California and had served as deputy secretary of state in the Carter administration. Like Perry, Christopher was publicly careful and low key but privately much more personable and congenial.

The point man for the Balkans within the European Bureau was Ambassador Robert C. Frasure, deputy assistant secretary of state for European and Canadian affairs.

And then there was Holbrooke.

Enter Holbrooke

In 1995, Richard Charles Albert Holbrooke, age fifty-four, was assistant secretary of state for European and Canadian affairs, a lower level at the State Department than his background and experience justified. His aggressive style and talent had made Holbrooke a powerful foreign-policy voice in Washington, but they had also created important enemies.

A graduate of Brown University, Holbrooke had served in Vietnam as a young Foreign Service officer. He later participated in the Paris Peace Talks as a staff officer. In those early days, he was a colleague of National Security Adviser Anthony Lake. Holbrooke left the Foreign Service, served in the Peace Corps in Morocco, and returned to the State Department to work in subsequent Democratic administrations. During the Carter presidency, at age thirty-six he was one of the youngest assistant secretaries ever in the State Department.[5]

After a period as ambassador to Germany early in the Clinton presidency, Holbrooke went back to Washington as an assistant secretary of state, a level he had held almost twenty years earlier. Watching Holbrooke interact with Lake and Christopher—both capable and cautious with low public profiles—I felt that they saw Holbrooke as a brilliant rogue, useful within the administration but very high maintenance.

By 1995, Holbrooke was an outspoken activist for stronger US and international intervention in Bosnia. In public, he described the situation as "the greatest collective security failure of the West since the 1930s."[6]

His open call for US action agitated senior military leaders and those who opposed US troops in Bosnia, but after Srebrenica they could no longer ignore the pressure. In Srebrenica, Holbrooke discovered a new reality in the strategic situation: faced with the continued humiliation of their peacekeeping troops in UNPROFOR after Srebrenica, European leaders were developing plans to withdraw from Bosnia. Allies in NATO, upset by US criticism of Bosnia without any US commitment on the ground, were about to demand US assistance in the withdrawal of their forces. One way or the other, US troops were going to Bosnia.

But before American forces were committed, the White House launched a major US diplomatic effort to find a way to peace. Holbrooke, the constant crusader, was its man to lead the effort. For his detractors, appointing Holbrooke was a win–win situation: he would either solve the administration's dilemma in Bosnia or fail and be off the national stage, and they could try something else.

Holbrooke grabbed the Bosnia challenge with both hands. He wasted no time in assembling a team from key US government agencies and scheduling his first trip to the region.

Holbrooke's original interagency negotiating team consisted of US Air Force colonel S. Nelson Drew of the NSC Staff; Bob Frasure from State; Joe Kruzel from DOD; and US Army lieutenant general Wesley K. Clark, J-5 (Strategic Plans and Policy) of the Joint Staff, representing the CJCS. Lieutenant Colonel Daniel Gerstein assisted Clark on the team.

Holbrooke and the negotiating team launched their first official visit to the Balkans in mid-August 1995, and my boss, Joe Kruzel, was on the trip.

5

Death on a Balkan Mountain

The driver maneuvered his heavy armored personnel carrier around a slower vehicle on the rain-soaked gravel road on the side of Mount Igman. He was trying to keep up with the lighter military vehicle ahead of him carrying Holbrooke and Lieutenant General Clark to Sarajevo.

The US negotiating team had broken into two groups for the overland trip to the capital of Bosnia. Holbrooke and Clark were in a military high-mobility multipurpose vehicle, or "Humvee." The rest of the group—Joe Kruzel, Bob Frasure, Colonel Drew, Lieutenant Colonel Gerstein, and security officer Peter Hargraves—traveled separately in the more cumbersome armored personnel carrier provided by the French contingent to UNPROFOR.

Mount Igman is one of several mountains dominating the horizon over Sarajevo from southwest to southeast. A narrow rock-and-gravel road curved over and around the mountain to connect the Bosnian capital with the world outside the conflict area. The road had no shoulder or guard rails and was only a single lane in some spots. Snow and rain made the route particularly treacherous. Because UNPROFOR patrolled and maintained the road, it was the only access to Sarajevo with any degree of security.

Not this Saturday, August 19, 1995. The telephone woke me up at 7:30 a.m. when I was at home in northern Virginia that day. The Pentagon Operations Center was calling to inform me that my boss Joseph Kruzel and others may have been injured in an accident on the way to Sarajevo. The armored personnel carrier transporting Kruzel and others from the US team had gone off the road on Mount Igman and flipped over several times. At first, Kruzel was reported to have survived.

By 10:00 that morning, I knew that Joe Kruzel was dead. Nelson Drew and Bob Frasure also were killed in the armored vehicle accident.[1]

The death of three respected professionals shocked official Washington and affected Holbrooke deeply. At the DOD, the loss of Joe Kruzel was a serious blow to the policy team. Someone who had become an effective player in the interagency policy process was gone. Undersecretary Slocombe was deeply upset by the loss of his friend and trusted adviser.

Those who knew Joe Kruzel recognized his potential as he guided European policy in the Pentagon. He was creative, he motivated his people in a positive way, and he had a great sense of humor. I felt especially close to him because when I left the army, he had helped me span the cultural divide between colonel and civilian senior executive service policy specialist in the Washington bureaucracy.

The New US Negotiating Team

Walt Slocombe summoned me to his office on the day the remains of the Americans killed on Mount Igman were returned to Washington. To my surprise, a tearful undersecretary said that he and the secretary wanted me to replace Kruzel on the Holbrooke negotiating team.

I was honored by the appointment. It was natural for me, as a former military officer, to step forward to fill the gap when the leader falls, and I knew the issues, the region, and DOD. What I did not have was direct experience with high-stakes diplomacy.

I soon concluded that there may not have been too many candidates for the job. Some of my civilian colleagues treated me as if the appointment were a death sentence, expressing condolences in advance for taking the job. DOD's insistence that I have an official photo and a new biography before leaving for the first mission reinforced that impression.

Following the memorial service at Arlington National Cemetery on August 24, the White House issued a public announcement of the composition of the reconstituted negotiating team.[2]

Richard Holbrooke remained the leader of the negotiating team, and although emotionally staggered by the deaths of three original team members, he was eager to return to the negotiating process.

Clark and Gerstein, who had survived the accident on Mount Igman, remained on the team. Although I did not know Clark well at the time, I discovered that he and I had grown up in Arkansas at about the same time. In the army, Clark was on a hyperfast track through the officer ranks to general. He was valedictorian of the West Point Class of 1966 and a Rhodes scholar. His army career was that of an officer on the way not just to the rank of general but to the most senior positions in the US military. As a three star on the Joint Staff, Clark was responsible for strategy and policy, a position that gave him close interaction with CJCS Shalikashvili and with the policy staff in the Office of the Secretary of Defense, the State Department, and the White House.

President Clinton, like Clark and me, had grown up in Arkansas at about the same time period. I had never met the president before joining the Holbrooke team, and I never saw anything to suggest that Clark had any close personal rapport with the president. His relationship with his professional peers was like Holbrooke's with his peers, albeit within the more closed military community. Clark was talented and tireless, but many peers and subordinates resented his ambition and determination to win every encounter no matter how minor.

Holbrooke relished the presence of a senior US military officer on his team—within limits. Clark, a year earlier, had created a controversy at a meeting with Bosnian Serb general Ratko Mladic in Banja Luka, Bosnia. In that meeting, Clark had accepted as gifts a bottle of brandy and an inscribed pistol from Mladic. The acceptance of these gifts upset the State Department and international observers, who considered Mladic a war criminal.[3] But what created the uproar in Washington was the photo of Clark and Mladic wearing each other's military hats during the meeting. Clark had to work hard to overcome the damage to his image created in the United States by this photo, which many European press outlets published.

Prominent Washington attorney Roberts B. Owen was a new addition to the team as the senior adviser on Yugoslavia to Secretary of State Warren Christopher. As a legal adviser at the State Department in the Carter administration, Owen brought practical international legal advice to the process. A friend of Christopher, he was someone the secretary could trust inside the negotiations. As a team member, Owen was a thoughtful, calming presence who presented clear solutions to tricky negotiating problems. His legal expertise in the volumes of documents associated with the Dayton Agreement was critical to the future legal framework in Bosnia.

Christopher R. Hill, office director for southern and central Europe at State, replaced Bob Frasure, his former boss, on the negotiating team. Hill, a career Foreign Service officer, had been a Peace Corps volunteer, like Holbrooke. He had worked closely with Holbrooke as a subordinate in the European Bureau, and Holbrooke had come to respect Hill's judgment and knowledge on the Balkans.

The one team member whom I knew from the past was US Army brigadier general Donald L. Kerrick, who was appointed to replace Nelson Drew as the NSC representative. Like me, Kerrick was a career army intelligence officer. Our professional paths had touched in the past, and we had served together on the Army Staff in the Office of the Deputy Chief of Staff for Intelligence in the Pentagon. National Security Adviser Lake respected Kerrick for his work on Bosnia at the NSC, where Kerrick had been assigned earlier in the Clinton administration.

Kerrick was in a sensitive position as the NSC representative on the team. Technically, he reported to Alexander Vershbow, but he also had direct access to Tony Lake and Sandy Berger. Like others, Kerrick was expected to keep an eye on the independent Holbrooke. Holbrooke was openly hostile toward Vershbow, whom he considered to be an irritating layer in his link to the president. But Kerrick overcame any early concerns Holbrooke may have had by being a productive member of the team throughout the negotiations.

As the replacement for Kruzel, I knew Bosnia and the issues of the negotiations from my position as director of the Balkan Task Force, but I had been out of the army for only a little more than a year. For me, membership on the Holbrooke team was a crash course in high-profile diplomacy.

The reconstituted US negotiating team went directly from the memorial ceremony at the Fort Meyer Chapel to an informal meeting in the chapel offices, where we were introduced to President Clinton and other members of the NSC.

The first meeting of the new negotiating team the next day was my real introduction to Holbrooke. Officers at many levels of the Pentagon mistrusted him and considered someone who would be aggressive and reckless in committing US forces to the Balkans. I decided to take my personal measure of the new situation before stepping forward. In the meeting with Holbrooke, I took note of his visible and vast personal ego.

The Essential Airplane

The first stage of the negotiations consisted of "shuttle diplomacy" in which Holbrooke and the team flew directly between capitals in the Balkans and in Central Europe to meet with the parties to the conflict and other national leaders. Transportation during the shuttle was provided by a DOD special-mission aircraft. Secretary of Defense Perry and the White House authorized Holbrooke to use the official secretary of defense plane for the shuttle. The C-20 was the military version of the Gulfstream III commercial jet available for long-distance transportation of senior government officials. DOD named US Air Force colonel Robert Lowe as the trip coordinator for the shuttle.

Holbrooke valued this aircraft for many reasons. The C-20 with "United States of America" displayed on the side gave him an elevated status as a US negotiator. It also allowed the team to move easily between European capitals. This was particularly important in the Balkans, where efficient commercial air service between capitals did not exist.

Holbrooke used the C-20's passenger configuration and the hours spent flying to establish his leadership of the negotiating team and to bond its individual members into a cohesive unit. He always rode in the back with the rest of the primary team, leaving the more comfortable executive cabin in the front to the administrative staff. During the shuttle, the team would spend hours talking, reading, and considering options in the privacy of this aircraft.

In the cramped, uncomfortable space of the aircraft, Holbrooke talked with us about options and difficult decisions ahead. He asked our opinions and seemed to listen. He accepted differences of opinion, no matter how much they varied from his, as long as they stayed within the team.

Years later in his office as US ambassador to the UN, Holbrooke pointed to a picture of the negotiating team standing alongside the C-20 during the shuttle.

"For me, you are either in that picture, or you are not. If you are in the picture, you are special to me," he said. I felt that he meant it, but, like so much about Holbrooke, you never knew for sure how much was real and how much was for effect.

The Sunday following the funerals, August 27, 1995, I joined the others at Andrews Air Force Base near Washington to board the C-20 for the first shuttle by the reconstituted team. For me, this was a thrilling, if uncertain, adventure that was to change the direction of my life forever.

6

The Godfather

Unlike many US leaders, especially in the Pentagon, I believed that Bosnia was important. I felt that the situation there was a defining moment for the United States in Europe and in NATO in the post-Soviet era and that the United States could no longer avoid active engagement in the war.

I wrote in my private notebook as the new negotiating team prepared to leave Washington that this conflict violated America's most basic values. In Europe, fifty years after World War II, the fighting in Bosnia stemmed from extreme ethnic bigotry and cultural chauvinism, producing a level of genocide not seen in Europe since the Holocaust. I did not see how the United States could remain on the sidelines in a war in Europe, the region most critical to US national security.

Since these personal opinions diverged from the general view in the Pentagon, I largely kept them to myself. I was excited to be a part of this great adventure. After my career in the military, the risks seemed more than reasonable.

Presidential Guidance

The American negotiators operated under guidance developed by the Washington interagency process and approved by President Clinton. The presidential guidance, prepared with no direct input from Holbrooke, contained seven goals:

1. A comprehensive peace settlement
2. Three-way recognition of Bosnia-Herzegovina, Croatia, and the Federal Republic of Yugoslavia (Serbia and Montenegro)
3. Support for the Contact Group plan separating Bosnia into two entities, 49 percent of the territory going to the Bosnian Serbs and 51 percent to the Muslim-Croat Federation
4. The peaceful return to Croatia of Eastern Slavonia, which had been seized by the Serbs

5. An all-out effort to achieve a cease-fire or an end to all offensive operations
6. A comprehensive program for regional economic reconstruction
7. Lifting of all economic sanctions against Yugoslavia and an American-backed program to equip and train the Federation military if a settlement were reached[1]

The seven points made no mention of the deployment of US ground forces if Holbrooke were to achieve an agreement.

The Contact Group

The Contact Group was essential to international coordination during the Holbrooke negotiations and the later engagement in Kosovo and Macedonia. It was an ad hoc collection of representatives from important countries with a high interest in the international response to the breakup of Yugoslavia. It consisted of senior officials from the foreign ministries of the United States, Great Britain, France, Russia, Germany, and later Italy.

Russian participation in the Contact Group was especially important. Membership in the Contact Group drew Russia inside the important international deliberations on the Balkans and into a cooperative partnership with Western powers on a difficult international problem. Having Russia inside the Contact Group also reduced problems in the coordination of policy with the UN and other international organizations.

The Contact Group had no formal structure, leadership, or headquarters. Its small size, informality, and lack of organizational protocols made it an efficient way to coordinate international policy on high-level issues between senior leaders in these critical countries.

Holbrooke typically negotiated privately between the United States and the parties in the Balkans. He kept the Contact Group informed as he went along and asked for its members' assistance when required. In coming months, his coordination of his actions with the Contact Group at the level of national political director guaranteed his direction over the negotiating process.

Diplomatic Energy

At the outset, I was skeptical that the Holbrooke mission would succeed. I had followed the situation in Bosnia closely for the past four years. I also had watched a series of notable international figures come and go, trying but failing to reach some rational conclusion to this war. None came close. Why, I wondered, would Holbrooke do any better?

One of Holbrooke's first tasks as he left Washington for the region was to gain control of the international negotiating process. The international effort to solve Bosnia had many senior players—too many. Former president Jimmy Carter and his foundation were talking to Bosnian Serb president Radovan Karadzic and the Bosnian Serb leadership. Former Swedish prime minister, the young and active Carl Bildt, also was negotiating with the Serbs in Bosnia on behalf of the EU. Others from various European capitals and international organizations dabbled on the periphery of the crisis, trying to help.

Diplomatic energy is an important force in a peace negotiation, and Holbrooke brought focused intensity and momentum to the process. He immediately dominated the international agenda and put the parties in the reactive mode. He moved more quickly and with more certainty and determination than others. Combined with a tight control on information from inside the talks, the speed with which he took action meant that detractors, competitors, and skeptics could not keep up with him.

With Washington now in the game, the warring factions quickly concluded that Holbrooke's negotiations were the best hope for success. He also brought the Contact Group nations into a close but outer ring of his negotiations.

As the shuttle resumed, the US team stopped first in Paris to meet the Bosnian Muslim leaders and the Contact Group before moving on to Belgrade to see Milosevic. Holbrooke wanted the Paris meetings to help him decide how to structure the negotiations.

If Holbrooke had anything more than a general plan on how to proceed, it was not apparent to me in August 1995. He studied the Camp David negotiations during the Carter administration as the most recent model for concepts on how to proceed during the early stages of his negotiating process for Bosnia. He saw shuttle diplomacy in the region as a first step in a process leading to some form of proximity talks away from Bosnia, in which the parties would be isolated from domestic political pressures and focused on the negotiations.

Holbrooke needed to stop the fighting and then concentrate on a political settlement. What a final agreement might look like was not clear in August 1995. He had the seven US goals given to him before the tragic first trip as a guide. Otherwise, he saw Milosevic as the key to Serbian decision making and a convenient cutout to dealing with Karadzic, Mladic, and other Bosnian Serbs directing the war from the mountain town of Pale. Whether Milosevic could control them was not clear.

Paris, August 28–29, 1995

Paris was the site of the conference in 1919 that had established Yugoslavia as a nation.[2] In 1995, the city would once again be important, but this time in the dismemberment of Yugoslavia and the settlement of the war in Bosnia. The French capital, specifically the residence of the US ambassador to France, became the unofficial hub in central Europe for Holbrooke's shuttle diplomacy.

Paris was special for Holbrooke. He was a longtime friend of Pamela Harriman, the US ambassador to France in 1995. He had served there as a young diplomat during the Vietnam War and had met Kati Martin there. The two were married in May 1995, less than three months before Holbrooke began the Bosnia shuttle.

At about 10:00 a.m. on August 28, the overnight C-20 flight from Andrews Air Force Base to Paris arrived at Le Bourget, the French military airfield near Paris and the site of Charles Lindbergh's landing after the first transatlantic flight in 1927. Ambassador Harriman met the delegation and escorted us to her residence in central Paris.

The American ambassador's residence sat behind a high wall along a section of the rue du Saint-Honore near the Élysée Palace, the home of the president of France. The Rothschild family had owned the property, constructed in the nineteenth century, until the Nazis requisitioned it to serve as an officers' club for Hermann Göring's Luftwaffe after the fall of Paris. The United States bought the building in 1948 and converted it to the ambassador's residence in 1971. At first glance, it looked a little frayed by the intensity of its history.

The charm of the residence soon overcame that first impression. The State Department was careful to restore and furnish the building with a few American touches, including a Charles Wilson Peale painting of George Washington. The ambassador added personal works from the Harriman art collection over the Louis XIV, XV and XVI furnishings in the residence. Along with several small French pictures, she hung Van Gogh's magnificent painting *Roses* (1890) in one of the three first-floor salons. The painting, now in the National Gallery of Art in Washington, DC, is of white roses just past their peak in a vase with wisps of white on a pale green background. Harriman kept a vase of cut white roses on a table near the painting.

Harriman was a skilled host for the first meetings of the negotiations. The former daughter-in-law of Winston Churchill and reputed international courtesan of considerable notoriety, Pamela Harriman had loved and married well. In 1971, she had wed W. Averell Harriman, with whom Holbrooke had served as a staff member of the US delegation to the Vietnam peace talks in 1968–1969.

On the day the American diplomats arrived in Paris, Serbian gunners launched artillery attacks on downtown Sarajevo. This latest shelling killed thirty-seven Bosnian civilians and wounded another one hundred. Right after the recent slaughter of Muslim men and boys at Srebrenica and new threats to the UN safe area at Gorazde, these latest attacks on Sarajevo demanded an international response. Bosnian Serb artillery continued to shell Sarajevo over the next two days as Holbrooke held his preliminary meetings in Paris.

Getting from Sarajevo to Paris to meet Holbrooke was difficult for Bosnian Muslim authorities. Normal road and air transportation out of Sarajevo was closed to them. To meet with Holbrooke and the new negotiating team, Bosnian president Alija Izetbegovic had to ride a cart through a clandestine tunnel under the Sarajevo airport runway, then travel over the treacherous Mount Igman road before reaching aircraft connections to central Europe. His foreign minister, Muhamed Sacirbey, accompanied him on the trip.

The stress of the travel to Paris and the years of enduring the misery of life in a city under siege showed on Izetbegovic. On first meeting him, I saw the Bosnian president as thoughtful but aloof. A political activist and leader of the Muslim community, Izetbegovic had written extensively on Islam and politics before Bosnia's independence. The Serbs had labeled him an Islamic fundamentalist and jailed him from 1983 to 1988 on charges of conspiracy to create a Muslim state. As Yugoslavia began to break apart, however, he formed a political party and became president of a coalition government. Following a referendum, Izetbegovic led Bosnia's declaration of independence from Serbia, and the war in Bosnia began.[3]

The seventy-year-old Izetbegovic had endured the months of shelling, sniping, and deprivation with the people of Sarajevo since the war began. To them, he was a symbol of resistance and sacrifice, and this shared suffering made him a singular authority for the Bosnian Muslims in the negotiations.

Sacirbey was the public face of the beleaguered Bosnians in the American and international media. He was the son of a close confidante of Izetbegovic. However, "Mo," as he was called, had played football for and earned a degree from Tulane University in New Orleans. Afterward, he had successfully built a career in finance in New York City. Articulate and effective in the media, Sacirbey had become an important public spokesman for the plight of the Bosnians in Sarajevo. Holbrooke did not like Sacirbey's erratic style, but he used him as one means to gauge Izetbegovic's flexibility and to serve as a negotiating conduit to the Bosnian president.

As the negotiations proceeded, Sacirbey's influence declined. In a late September 1995 note to the secretary of defense, I described him as "inconsistent, free-lancing without the authority of his government, seized with the public limelight for its own sake and immature. In Sarajevo, Sacirbey is an outsider."

Izetbegovic and his party arrived in Paris livid about UNPROFOR's failure to protect civilians. They demanded massive NATO military strikes in response to the ongoing shelling of Sarajevo.

Holbrooke was sensitive to the extreme difficulty facing the Bosnian leaders. He was eager to talk to them before he met with Milosevic in Belgrade, but the shelling in Sarajevo had delayed the US meeting with President Izetbegovic in Paris.

Around 11:00 p.m. on August 28, Holbrooke, his team, and the Bosnian guests dined among the antique Belgian tapestries of the American residence's formal dining room. The first day of the new shuttle was over at 1:00 a.m.

This rapid series of meetings and extended hours on the first day set the pace for the rest of the shuttle. Intensity was a characteristic of Holbrooke's negotiating style. He generated as much pressure as possible and attacked several issues at once. The rhythm of the negotiations was often frantic, with the team flying overnight to face a full day of meetings and events until late in the night, then getting up early the next morning to start the process again. This tempo put pressure on the negotiating parties while keeping Holbrooke and the team as the driving force in the process. He thrived on such intensity, but after a while I calculated that Holbrooke could sustain such a pace with little or no sleep for about three days before he would collapse for several hours and then start over.

On our second night in Paris, Harriman hosted another dinner for Holbrooke and the Bosnians. This time she invited some French intellectuals. On meeting them, I wondered if they were compelled to follow some nonconformist bohemian dress and behavior code to be validated as French intellectuals.

One guest at the dinner was Mabel Wisse-Smit. This twenty-seven-year-old Dutch beauty and humanitarian activist was working for the Soros Foundation in Bosnia while maintaining a personal relationship with Mo Sacirbey. This connection continued through the negotiations in Dayton, Ohio. In 2004, Mabel's relationships with Sacirbey and an assassinated drug lord became a major public controversy in the Netherlands when she married Prince Friso, second son of Queen Beatrix, and became Princess Mabel of Orange-Nassau.

While authorities in Washington, New York, and Brussels considered NATO airstrikes against Serb artillery around Sarajevo, Holbrooke canvassed the negotiating team and reported to Washington an opinion favoring airstrikes to assist in decision making at NATO. At its headquarters in Brussels, NATO decided to launch sustained airstrikes against Bosnian Serb military targets in retaliation for Serbian attacks on Sarajevo and the UN safe areas.

The first NATO attack aircraft in Operation Deliberate Force crossed into Bosnia at 1:40 a.m. on August 30.[4] Thirty-two minutes later the first bombs struck Serb targets. With that attack, the great Western alliance, which had deterred Soviet military expansion into western Europe since the end of World War II, launched the first sustained combat operations against hostile enemy forces in NATO history. As the US negotiators left Paris, it was understood that the discussions there had revealed several points important to Holbrooke's negotiations:

1. The basic US principles Lake delivered to Holbrooke were acceptable as a basis for negotiations with the Bosnian Muslim leaders in Sarajevo.
2. The negotiations in the early stages would be conducted during active combat on the ground between Croats, Muslims, and Serbs and in the air by NATO airstrikes.
3. Bosnian Serbs had to be a part of the Belgrade delegation. A separate negotiation with the Bosnian Serbs was unacceptable.
4. Izetbegovic would not engage in direct talks with either Bosnian Serb president Radovan Karadzic or General Ratko Mladic.

The ongoing NATO airstrikes in Bosnia raised an immediate problem for the US negotiators. Could the negotiating team continue to Belgrade as planned while NATO bombs fell on Serbian forces? After considerable deliberation, at 3:00 a.m. on August 30 Holbrooke and Washington agreed to allow the American team to go on to Belgrade later that morning.

The Arsonist and the Fireman—Belgrade, August 30, 1995

As the air force C-20 left Paris midmorning on August 30, bound for Belgrade, I was curious about Milosevic. What kind of man would he be? I knew the basics. Both parents reportedly had committed suicide. He had risen through the ranks in the Yugoslav Communist Party to become a senior apparatchik in the government.[5] Like so many in eastern Europe after the collapse of communism, he had rebranded himself as a democratic leader. Milosevic's public conversion from Communist to Serbian nationalist had begun in Kosovo, and he had never looked back.[6]

Although elected in a popular vote as president of Serbia, Milosevic had assumed vast powers in Belgrade, but he struggled to hang on to a rapidly diminishing Serbian miniempire as Tito's Yugoslavia disintegrated around him. He ran Serbia using a combination of extreme nationalism, control of the security services and the military, and a corrupt economic patronage system that dominated the economy.

I had never met a man with so much innocent blood on his hands. I knew something about killing after years in the US Army, including a tour in Vietnam. I had visited Auschwitz, the killing fields of Cambodia, and mass graves in Somalia. Yet I had never met the perpetrators. Milosevic had at a minimum tolerated or encouraged ethnic cleansing and genocide. In August 1995, he was the key figure in bringing the killing in Bosnia to an end.

The situation for Milosevic and the Serbs was going from bad to worse. The international embargo on Serbia had devastated the country's economy, and Serbia had become an isolated international pariah for its support of the Bosnian Serb campaign in Bosnia. A Croatian military offensive had the Bosnian Serb fighters in retreat in western Bosnia, and NATO airstrikes were targeting Serbian artillery around Sarajevo and other areas of the country.

Holbrooke's goals for the meeting with Milosevic in Belgrade were ambitious. He wanted to limit the composition of the Serbian delegation in the negotiations to one group led by Milosevic. He wanted to test several

aspects of a settlement, including territorial arrangements, constitutional proposals, and the status of Sarajevo. He also wanted agreements on
opening Sarajevo Airport and a land corridor into the city as confidence-
building measures for the negotiations. During the meeting, we expected
Milosevic to push hard for an end to NATO airstrikes against Bosnian Serb
military positions.

We landed a little after noon at a military airfield outside Belgrade. The
motorcade followed an aggressive Serbian police escort with lights flashing
along the expressway into the capital. The police cars cut in front of civilian vehicles at high speed. Serb policemen with sticks tipped with round
traffic-control circles leaned out of the police car windows. They banged
their traffic sticks on the windshields of frightened civilian drivers, often
forcing them to the shoulder of the road as the motorcade raced across the
Sava River into the center of Belgrade.

Belgrade, located where the Danube and Sava Rivers converge, should
have been a beautiful capital city. It was not. In the autumn of 1995, Belgrade, like many eastern European capitals, was as gray as Leonid Brezhnev
in a suit.

After a brief discussion with US chief of mission Rudolph Perina, the
team arrived at the Serbian presidential palace in central Belgrade at 1:30
p.m. to begin what was to be a familiar format for meetings with the Serbian leader in weeks to come.

The president's stocky *chef de cabinet,* Goran Milinovic, met us at the
entrance and escorted us past security guards to a meeting room, where
President Milosevic greeted us. Like many buildings in post-Soviet eastern
Europe, the presidential palace had seen better days. The walls of the large
meeting room were made of green-and-pink marble and decorated with
Communist-era paintings. A large brown marble statue of a woman with
one arm over her head stood in one corner. The furniture was in the over-
stuffed Soviet-era style. All in all, the setting was drab. We sat in chairs
and a couch in a semicircle, with Milosevic at one end and Holbrooke next
to him.

Goran was discreetly out of the circle but close enough to take notes
of the meeting. Goran's English seemed very limited, and all conversations
with Milosevic were in English, so we wondered how those notes could
possibly be accurate. Nevertheless, Goran was a silent staple of every Milosevic meeting.

In subsequent meetings, Milosevic sometimes brought Milan Milutinovic, his foreign minister, into the discussion, but he generally ran the meetings alone. The Serbian president spoke effective if somewhat broken English, and he used his errors in English to humorous effect when it suited him. He obviously enjoyed the intellectual debate with Holbrooke.

The local US chief of mission often attended the meetings with Milosevic, but not always. Holbrooke and Milosevic would occasionally drift away for private conversations, but this was rare.

These meetings were Holbrooke's show for members of the US team. We were stage props for his performance and played our roles as determined beforehand. In the meetings with Milosevic, we spoke when necessary or when worked out in advance with Holbrooke.

Milosevic began by expressing his condolences for the diplomats killed on Mount Igman. He then shifted to introductions and pleasantries to establish some rapport with the new team as a waiter served pre-prepared drinks. Milosevic teased anyone who took a glass of anything other than alcohol as a "juice drinker."

As for Holbrooke, I never saw him turn down a drink when offered, but I never saw him, unlike Milosevic, do more than raise the glass to his lips when appropriate. He and Milosevic verbally sparred for hours over various issues, Milosevic smoking and drinking, Holbrooke doing neither.

Milosevic was always a correct European host, but he also used a kind of macho humor—the kind he probably used in drinking with buddies and subordinates—to break the ice and to create a more informal atmosphere for discussions. He once described the risk of a presidential summit on Bosnia as being like "launching Evel Knievel over the Grand Canyon," referring to the failed rocket-cycle launch by daredevil showman Evel Knievel over the Snake River Canyon in Idaho in 1974. Apparently, even the most goofball elements of American popular culture in the 1970s had penetrated deeply into the world of the ambitious Communist apparatchiks in eastern Europe. But Holbrooke was not interested in a spectacular failure.

Physically, Milosevic looked like a heart attack in the making. With his puffy face and combed-back shock of silver hair, he had the appearance of so many Communist leaders of his generation. Over the course of many hours with Milosevic, I concluded that he was a functioning alcoholic. He was heavy and looked older than his fifty-four years. He drank a great deal and occasionally would get tipsy and then sober up several times in the course of a long day. He probably wanted us to do the same. However, I never thought that he was not in control of his senses or his strategy. In the beginning, he heavily smoked a Dutch brand of cigarillos but later quit for a time.

Milosevic could change in a second from jovial host to raging tyrant, then back again. He was adept at spinning a completely bogus but somewhat logical tale to support his position or to avoid responsibility. He generally could stay consistent with his story. He constantly probed for soft spots in Holbrooke's position or arguments. Holbrooke did the same to him.

After the first meeting with Milosevic, I wrote a memorandum to Secretary Perry and Undersecretary Slocombe titled "Dining with the Godfather."

"Having spent hours watching Holbrooke and Milosevic, I wouldn't buy a used car from either one of them," I added in a handwritten note at the bottom of the memo. Years later, after Holbrooke saw my private memos to Secretary Perry, he called me from Kuala Lumpur, Malaysia, to joke, "This is Holbrooke—one of two people you wouldn't buy a used car from."

Serbia was a case in which international economic sanctions as leverage on a nation worked. Serbia was hurting, and it was clear from the start that Milosevic was looking for a solution as he sized up his negotiating opponent.

Milosevic was aware that the Americans wanted a single negotiating team to represent the Serbs in the negotiations. He produced an internal agreement known as the "Patriarch Letter" because it had been witnessed by Pavel, patriarch of the Serbian Orthodox Church. The letter established a Serbian negotiating delegation of six persons, to be determined by Milosevic. Three of the six would be representatives of the Bosnian Serbs—specifically Momcilo Krajisnik, Radovan Karadzic, and General Ratko Mladic. The others included Milosevic and two Serbs whom Milosevic was to appoint. In a tie within the delegation, Milosevic would cast the deciding vote, essentially giving him control over the delegation's decisions.[7]

Milosevic engaged in similar theater to create the illusion that he did not control Serbian actions in Bosnia. In Bosnia, he declared that Bosnian Serb political leaders, military forces, and Serbian paramilitary groups operated independently from Belgrade. This fiction allowed him to claim that he had no responsibility for the atrocities committed in Bosnia. He was careful to ensure that no trail of evidence could be traced back directly to him to expose this ruse, and he maintained it until the end. But I was convinced by his dominance of the Bosnian Serbs in the negotiations and by the overwhelming circumstantial evidence that he was responsible for the genocide and crimes against humanity in Bosnia.

Communist leaders in the old Soviet system valued political theater to avoid accountability, and Milosevic was skilled at the practice. This technique of creating the fiction of independent groups and rogue elements had served him in the past, and they continued to be a part of his repertoire in dealing with the international community. Vladimir Putin would use the same type of theater during the Russian occupation of Ukraine in 2014–2015.

The Milosevic fiction of influence without control was also useful to international negotiators, who needed a negotiating authority to speak for the Bosnian Serbs. As long as doubt existed about whether Milosevic was directly responsible for the Serbian atrocities in Bosnia, Holbrooke could negotiate with him with less controversy at home and abroad.

Milosevic seemed eager for a deal. He wanted to move quickly to an international conference. He wanted Croatian president Franjo Tudjman, Bosnian president Alija Izetbegovic, and himself to represent the parties at the conference, with the United States serving as the lead negotiator. He did not favor three-way direct talks without the United States as an intermediary.

"The history of the Balkans is the history of Serbs and Croats, not Muslims," Milosevic said about the participation of President Tudjman in the negotiations. Milosevic surely calculated that Tudjman would be a potential negotiating ally. He preferred to ignore five hundred years of Ottoman control of the region and the reality of millions of Muslims living in the modern Balkans.

Milosevic made other concessions during the discussions. "We accept the Contact Group plan as the basis for negotiations," he said.

"And the 51/49 percent territorial split contained in the Contact Group plan?" Holbrooke asked, referring to an earlier Contact Group proposal that created an internal split within Bosnia of 51 percent for the Federation and 49 percent for the Serbs. This internal division of territory would become a rigid bargaining position for the Serbs and the most difficult issue in the negotiations at Dayton.

"Yes, we accept that as a starting point for negotiations," Milosevic said.

Milosevic rejected the idea of placing the city of Sarajevo under UN control. To our surprise, he was forthcoming immediately on Sarajevo as the capital for the Bosniaks.

"The Muslims must have a viable capital in Sarajevo," he said without prompting. His primary concerns were the Serbian suburbs surrounding Sarajevo.

"What about Kosovo?" Holbrooke diverted the flow of conversation momentarily.

"That's an internal issue," Milosevic responded, then launched into a long explanation of the rights of Kosovars in Yugoslavia.

"Is an immediate cease-fire possible in Bosnia?" Holbrooke said, returning to the subject of Bosnia.

"Yes," Milosevic responded.

"It is possible only if you can control the Bosnian Serb army. We need some confidence-building measures," Holbrooke stated.

Then for the first time in an hour and a half of discussions, Milosevic raised the NATO bombing campaign.

"You should stop the bombing now," Milosevic asserted.

"I can make no guarantees, but Lieutenant General Clark may be able to stop it," Holbrooke said, quickly diverting responsibility to the military.

This little maneuver was classic Holbrooke. Over the next several hours, the US diplomat would declare that he had no authority whatsoever over the NATO bombing campaign, but he did so in a way that convinced Milosevic, also a gamesman, that he really did have considerable control of the bombing campaign. Holbrooke then used the possibility—but uncertainty—of his authority to squeeze as much from the Serbian president as possible. In fact, neither Clark nor Holbrooke had direct control over NATO operations. That authority resided in Brussels, Washington, and other NATO capitals, but Holbrooke did have influence in the decision-making process.

Milosevic arranged for a late lunch to continue the discussions. As we began moving toward the dining room, he seized the opportunity to press the point again.

"This NATO bombing is not helpful. Please stop the bombing," he almost pleaded.

"We will call Washington for a pause in the bombing if Mladic will stop shelling Sarajevo," Holbrooke offered.

"Will you stop the bombing now without [a commitment from] Mladic?"

"Let's have lunch, Mr. President," Holbrooke said, dismissing the idea.

These meals were to be a common feature of the meetings with Milosevic. They took place around a large table in the dining room in the presidential palace, where waiters in tuxedos served each guest from large trays containing mounds of hearty Balkan food. The people in the Balkans often exhibit hospitality toward guests by serving extra large quantities at meals, especially grilled meats. Milosevic was obviously a meat-and-potatoes guy.

Milosevic sat in the center of the table. Behind him on the wall was a large tapestry of Serbian peasant women. Holbrooke sat across from him, and the rest of us filled in the seats around the table. Milosevic returned to the idea of an international conference as the hors d'oeuvres were served with the first of several Serbian wines. Milosevic wanted to move quickly to an international conference on Bosnia.

Aides entered the room with a note for Milosevic, supposedly containing a message from General Mladic.

"Mladic promised that he will stop actions against Muslims if NATO and the Muslims are not firing on him. A facsimile to that effect will follow," Milosevic said.

"We will wait for the fax," Holbrooke responded. The fax from Mladic never arrived.

One problem other than Bosnia that Holbrooke could not avoid was Serbian occupation of Eastern Slavonia in Croatia. The Croatian leadership in Zagreb was a third regional power essential to reaching a settlement in Bosnia. For the Croats, Eastern Slavonia was the primary issue, and they insisted that it be included in the Bosnia negotiations.

Eastern Slavonia is a sliver of territory along the Danube River that forms the border between Croatia and Serbia. When war broke out between Serbia and Croatia in 1991 after Croatia declared independence, this strip of land declared its independence from Croatia and aligned itself with Serbia. Heavy fighting largely destroyed the river town of Vukovar and created thousands of refugees from the region. In 1995, the status of Eastern Slavonia was unresolved, and Zagreb demanded a solution to this issue in any discussion on Bosnia. Milosevic resisted any inclusion of Eastern Slavonia in the Bosnia negotiations, and the conversation then returned to Bosnia.

"What about [diplomatic] recognition of Bosnia?" Holbrooke asked.

"Not yet," Milosevic said. "I am ready to accept a union in Bosnia-Herzegovina, but Bosnian Serbs are not ready." He then laid out his ideas for a future Bosnia:

- Bosnia would be a union of the Croat-Muslim Federation and the Republika Srpska.

- The two states within Bosnia—the Federation and the Republika Srpska—would receive equal treatment.
- Each would have special rights with its respective national neighbors (Croatia and Serbia).
- The union of Bosnia would have an international legal personality.

The waiters arrived with platters piled high with grilled lamb, pork, and beef as well as with potatoes and other vegetables.

The team then left the presidential palace to report to Washington on Milosevic's apparent willingness to negotiate a cease-fire and to open Sarajevo in exchange for a suspension of the NATO airstrikes.

Holbrooke worked the telephones constantly between negotiating sessions. He reported by telephone to Secretary Christopher, National Security Adviser Lake, and others when required. No level of US government except President Clinton seemed off limits for a direct connection. He also interacted frequently with the media and foreign government by telephone.

Holbrooke set rules within the team. He demanded that he personally approve all negotiation reports being sent from the team to home agencies in Washington. Although I understood his rule, I violated it constantly. In my view, Secretary Perry and Undersecretary Slocombe deserved my unfiltered opinion about the status of the talks. I often returned to my hotel room to write a short memo of the day's activities, which was sent through military channels to my leaders in DOD.

A few weeks into the shuttle, Holbrooke confronted me about my memos sent to DOD without his preapproval. By that time, a lecture from Holbrooke about stretching the rules rang a bit hollow, and I never stopped writing them. I later gave him the memos to use in his book *To End a War*. I declined, however, to give him the journals I kept during the negotiations.

After contacting Washington on the potential to suspend the airstrikes in exchange for a cease-fire and the opening of land access to Sarajevo, the team returned to the presidential palace in the center of Belgrade around 7:00 p.m. for another meeting with Milosevic.

Holbrooke appointed Clark and me to head the map discussions. We soon learned that any discussion of territory or lines on a map instantly ignited emotional outbursts from the parties involved.

This first long day of talks between Holbrooke and Milosevic left several impressions. First, Holbrooke and Milosevic, the two men in the center of the Bosnian storm, were crafty, tough, and determined competitors.

This high-stakes dance between these two men would have a huge effect on the outcome of the peace process. Second, Milosevic was eager for a deal and wanted it soon. It was not clear, however, just how far he would go to bring peace to Bosnia or to recognize Bosnia as an independent nation. And, finally, Milosevic was much more flexible on Sarajevo than we ever imagined.

At the hotel after the last meeting with Milosevic, Holbrooke spent most of the night discussing with Washington the potential deal to suspend the airstrikes. After another abbreviated night, the team left Belgrade mid-morning for Zagreb to meet with Croatian leaders.

Leverage

A negotiator can influence the will of the parties to reach agreement through the skillful use of available leverage. Each of the parties in this particular negotiation—Belgrade, Sarajevo, and Zagreb—wanted a settlement in Bosnia on its own terms. Holbrooke had the experience, the diplomatic creativity, and the stature of the United States behind him. He also had a burning, tireless determination to succeed. With firm backing from the United States, Europe, Russia, NATO, and the UN, he had an array of military, economic, and political incentives at his disposal to influence the parties to reach a deal.

Holbrooke was a master at using both incentives and penalties to leverage the negotiating parties to reach an agreement. Any desire by the parties was a source of leverage for the US negotiator, and he used them all. He leveraged every advantage, big or small, all the time with almost everyone.

His leverage with Milosevic was considerable. Holbrooke had influence on the NATO air campaign punishing Serbian forces in Bosnia and on the Croatian military offensive in western Bosnia. More broadly, the American-led negotiations offered Milosevic the opportunity to extract Serbia and himself from the costs of supporting the war in Bosnia.

The Bosniaks had even more powerful incentives to negotiate. Their people, territory, and infrastructure had suffered enormously from four years of war. The American-led negotiations gave real hope of ending the bloody fighting on terms that recognized Bosnia as a sovereign and independent country. The negotiations might produce a constitution for Bosnia that held out hope of a democratic government. Success also might produce desperately needed economic assistance for the country and military assistance to help with its future self-defense.

Croatia, too, had important incentives to assist in achieving a peace agreement. It saw an opportunity to throw its primary issue—the dispute with Serbia over Eastern Slavonia—into the negotiating mix. The Croats also needed the war to end to improve the potential for economic development and to begin the process of integration into NATO and the EU. By cooperating with the international community in finding an end to the war in Bosnia, Croatian leaders also had an opportunity to strengthen the country's relationship with the United States and western Europe.

Deadlines can amplify leverage, and Holbrooke loved to use deadlines to pressure the parties. He employed real and artificial deadlines at every opportunity in the negotiations.

All the parties understood that these talks were a unique opportunity to resolve their problems. They had red lines they could not cross in the negotiations, but none of them, with the possible exception of the Bosnian Serbs, had an interest in these negotiations' failure. Such failure could produce a dark and uncertain future for them all.

The Essential Third Party—Zagreb, August 31, 1995

US ambassador to Croatia Peter Galbraith met the plane and escorted the team to the embassy in Zagreb, where Holbrooke continued to discuss suspension of the airstrikes by telephone, this time with the NATO secretary-general Willy Claes and US general George A. Joulwan, NATO's supreme Allied commander Europe (SACEUR).

A little after noon we arrived at the presidential palace in Zagreb, where we scampered to catch up with Holbrooke as he led the delegation past the presidential guard of the palace, who were dressed in bright-red ceremonial costumes rumored to be personally designed by Croatian president Franjo Tudjman.

President Tudjman had been a Croat partisan in World War II. Despite rising to the rank of general in the Yugoslav army, he had retained his nationalist impulses and became an agitator against Serbian rule after leaving the army. Tudjman was as much a Croat nationalist as Milosevic was a Serb nationalist. Tudjman was craftier, however, and avoided the kind of international condemnation leveled at Milosevic for the war in Bosnia.

Unlike Milosevic, who favored small, informal meetings, discussions with Tudjman were formal, with several key national security ministers and advisers in the room. Tudjman emphasized the optics and ceremony of his presidency.

The Croatian leaders were well organized and well prepared for the talks. They knew what they wanted and were unified behind Tudjman, who was clearly in charge. They also negotiated from a position of strength. Their army was pushing the Serbs out of western Bosnia, and Croats were a critical partner for the Bosniaks in the Federation in Bosnia.

All three men—Milosevic, Tudjman, Izetbegovic—knew each other well and understood each other's political ambition and respective culture. But Izetbegovic was the odd man out. Like Milosevic, Tudjman was dismissive of Bosnia and the Muslim population there, seeing the issues in the region's political dynamics as being between the Croats and the Serbs.

The Croatian president and his cabinet were eager to talk to Holbrooke, but not about stopping the violence around Sarajevo. Tudjman focused on Croatian interests. The Croats had their own issues, including Serbia in Eastern Slavonia and the ongoing Croat military offensive in Bosnia. Holbrooke already had Eastern Slavonia on his list of problems to solve.

The Croatian leaders, like Milosevic, favored some form of NATO forces to assist in implementation of any peace deal in the region. However, they were concerned about Russian participation in peace implementation. Tudjman specifically said that Zagreb would accept Russian forces in the region only as part of a NATO implementation force.

Holbrooke also met with the highest UN official in the region, Yasushi Akashi, the UN secretary-general's personal representative for Bosnia-Herzegovina, in his hotel suite in Zagreb. Holbrooke learned that Milosevic had been trying to negotiate separately with Akashi and French lieutenant general Bernard Janvier, commander of UNPROFOR, to find a way to end the NATO bombing. Holbrooke did not overreact to this effort to go around him. He never seemed surprised at the duplicity of others.

The process to suspend the airstrikes in return for progress on lifting the siege of Sarajevo was moving forward. NATO in Brussels delegated authority to suspend the air strikes to subordinate commanders of NATO forces to facilitate progress on Sarajevo. Holbrooke and the team left Zagreb and flew back to Belgrade for further talks with the Serbs.

Agreed Basic Principles: Belgrade to Skopje and Geneva, September 1–8, 1995

"Jim, give me your tie," Holbrooke said as we began the day in Belgrade.

"Sure, Dick, but can I ask why?" I responded.

"Kati said that I've been wearing the same tie on television for three days in a row, and she wants me to change." We exchanged ties.

This small episode says much about Holbrooke. Kati was Kati Martin, his recent bride. She was clearly the center of his personal life, and he valued her opinion even on simple things. This high-energy public figure who delighted in going nose to nose with presidents was no tough guy around Kati. He obviously adored his wife and listened to her advice. At one point on the shuttle, Holbrooke announced that he preferred to be called "Richard" rather than "Dick" because Kati felt that "Richard" was more dignified. Holbrooke was to make the same request to President Obama years later, and Obama had a similar reaction, but in that case the tale was used to belittle Holbrooke.[8]

Holbrooke had some time to kill, and Chris Hill had an affinity for the new nation of Macedonia. Hill and I were dispatched to Skopje for the day to update Macedonian president Kiro Gligorov on the Bosnia negotiations. Gligorov was another former Communist turned nationalist who had led his country to independence from Yugoslavia. In this case, the Serbs did not seem to care, but the Greek government was furious that this new country was claiming the heritage of the ancient Macedonians. In protest, Greece was blocking its border with Macedonia and causing the new country as much international trouble as it could.

Gligorov and some Europeans wanted to include Macedonian issues in the talks, but Holbrooke was reluctant to broaden the Bosnia negotiations. He decided to intervene separately on the Macedonia–Greece dispute.

Chris Hill was later to become US ambassador to Macedonia. I had no idea then that I would become deeply involved in a negotiation to prevent another Balkan war in Macedonia in 2001.

Hill and I flew back to Belgrade to link up with Holbrooke and the team, who had spent much of the day with Milosevic discussing ideas on structural arrangement for postwar Bosnia. This meeting with Milosevic took place at the Dobanovci presidential villa, a more rustic lodge in a hunting preserve near Belgrade. The Dobanovci villa, with its fountains, patios, and walking paths through the woods eighteen miles or so from Belgrade, was one of several presidential retreats left over from the Tito days.

Milosevic was drunk when Hill and I joined the meeting at the villa. He was holding forth with the group and punctuating his points with American obscenities. A late lunch for the group at 4:30 sobered him up.

Joining Milosevic and the team at lunch were Serbian foreign minister Milan Milutinovic, Bosnian Serb vice president Nikola Koljevic, and Bosnian Serb "foreign minister" Aleksa Buha. Milutinovic struck me as a Milosevic sycophant and crony. Neither of the two Bosnian Serbs was powerful within the Serb leadership at Pale, but their presence broke the ice on Bosnian Serbs' participation in the discussions. Holbrooke liked having the mild-mannered Koljevic around because it served his own flair for drama.

Holbrooke often referred to Koljevic as a Shakespearean scholar who taught English literature at the University of Michigan. In fact, Koljevic spoke English and had been a Shakespearean scholar at Sarajevo University. He may have held a limited teaching position in a US college at some point.

While we were in Belgrade, French officials and Carl Bildt were trying to engage Milosevic directly around Holbrooke, but Milosevic had moved them to the margins in favor of the American negotiator.

One of the most important elements of any international negotiations is the authority of the international negotiator. Multiple voices speaking for the international community in a negotiation can destroy the process. The parties are delighted to have one international voice in the negotiations— until something does not go their way. At that point, like small children with a stern parent, they will seek a friendlier alternative. Similarly, many alternative voices will leap into a high-visibility negotiating process, especially if it is floundering.

The atmosphere of the discussions at this stage was one of agreement. The Serbs resisted slightly on certain points but seemed to be going through the motions. Milosevic ordered a light dinner at 9:30 p.m. At the table, he looked the caricature of a mafia boss holding court.

Holbrooke held a press conference before a mass of international reporters following meetings with the Contact Group and German officials in Bonn on September 2. His interaction with the media was impressive.

Careful management of information from negotiations to the media is essential for any negotiator. In a negotiation with high public interest, the media require information. They must be fed, or they will gather information elsewhere. Yet the audience for anything said in public is so diverse that any misstep can be a disaster.

Holbrooke knew the media in detail and had exceptional skill in handling public affairs. He worked hard to use public information as a tool to support the negotiations and to ensure that the media did not damage the process. He devoured piles of media reports during the day. He knew the top American television and print journalists by name and reputation. He knew their political orientation and their deadlines, and he carefully culti-vated his relationship with them.

Holbrooke also recognized that the senior parties in the negotiations had their own press to inform. At the end of important meetings, he spent a few moments reaching an agreement with the senior official on the press line that should come out of the meeting. I cannot recall him ever making a serious mistake in a press interview in the months we spent traveling with him. Inside the negotiating team, no member dared conduct a press inter-view unless Holbrooke authorized it.

This level of media attention elevated his personal public stature. He enticed them with little tidbits of information or gave them access to us or the chance to travel with us. They coveted these little goodies and in return were careful not to antagonize him unnecessarily.

After Bonn, the team flew to Brussels for a meeting with NATO. Hol-brooke updated the North Atlantic Council, the political authority in NATO headed by the NATO secretary-general and made up of ambassa-dors from the various NATO member countries. Clark and I also briefed the council on the need for a NATO peace-implementation force to replace UNPROFOR if the negotiations were successful.

NATO suspended bombing on September 1 but issued an ultimatum to the Serbs that further shelling in Bosnia would restart the NATO air campaign. The Serbs remained defiant, and so bombing recommenced on September 5.

Holbrooke gained considerable influence over the NATO airstrikes. By the first week of September, the NATO air campaign was calibrated close-ly with the diplomatic effort. Although Holbrooke did not have personal authority to start or stop the airstrikes, he demonstrated that the air cam-paign had significant effect on the negotiations, and his recommendations about when to pause or restart airstrikes often carried dominant weight in deliberations in Washington and Brussels.

While Holbrooke took a brief side trip to Athens, the rest of us met with Milosevic at the presidential palace in Belgrade in the early evening of September 3. In a discussion of NATO bombing, Milosevic understood that the NATO decision to bomb was not just a tactical military decision but a reflection of the larger attitude of major European nations and the United States toward Serbs and Serbia. He was somber, thoughtful, and subdued over the likelihood of more bombing. He left the room several times to talk with Mladic on the phone during the meetings.

Holbrooke arrived in time for another dinner in the palace dining room. Fish—a welcome alternative to the heaping platters of grilled red meat—was also on offer.

On Labor Day, September 4, the team left Belgrade for three stops in Balkan capitals. On the way to Athens, Holbrooke laughed that he had been shameless in a private meeting with Greek prime minister Andreas Papandreau the previous day.

"Absolutely shameless. I am glad no one saw it," he said, laughing, but did not elaborate. I presumed that Holbrooke had been absurdly flattering, pandering to Papandreau's ego regarding his importance to world affairs to get the solution he wanted.

In Athens, Holbrooke updated the Greek government on the negotiations and finalized the agreement he had reached with Papandreau to open the border with Macedonia.

A stop in Skopje for a meeting with President Gligorov and his team was next. Holbrooke pressed the Macedonians to complete the agreement with Greece. Gligorov asked for more concessions but backed off when Holbrooke became aggressive and threatened to leave. Finally, the Greek and Macedonian leaders reached an agreement, which was signed in New York the following week.

The last stop for the day was Ankara, Turkey, where the team met with President Izetbegovic and Mo Sacirbey at the residence of US ambassador Marc Grossman. The Bosniaks pressed for the team to go to Sarajevo with or without NATO bombs falling. But as much as Holbrooke would have liked to go to Sarajevo, he declined to go if NATO was still bombing.

The next day, September 5, began in Ankara and ended back in Belgrade. Holbrooke brought in Clark and me to talk territory in Bosnia with Milosevic. We had developed a list of principles to go over with the Serbian president, including a proposed Contact Group internal border for a Serbian political entity within Bosnia and a provision that Sarajevo would be the capital of the Federation and administered by the government of Bosnia. As with any discussion of maps, Milosevic reacted strongly, accusing me of being "pro-Muslim."

Another long day came to a close. By my calculations, the negotiation team had spent a total of about thirty hours with Milosevic since leaving Washington.

On the last day of this round of the shuttle, Friday, September 8, Holbrooke hosted an early-morning meeting of the Contact Group at the US embassy in Geneva. The Russians again complained about NATO bombing, proposed a meeting in Moscow, and asked to join the shuttle. Holbrooke let them talk and debate process questions but deflected every proposal that he did not support.

After the Contact Group completed its deliberations, the three foreign ministers from the Balkans joined the meeting to consider a set of principles to reach a settlement.

The principles that the parties and the Contact Group agreed to in Geneva were important for their content, but they also represented an official investment by the Contact Group countries, in particular Russia, in the Holbrooke process.[9] Among the agreed provisions, Belgrade and Zagreb recognized the legal existence of Bosnia in its present borders, removing doubt about the future sovereignty of Bosnia as a nation. The price for that recognition was high. The principles also agreed that Bosnia would consist of two separate entities, the Federation and the Republika Srpska, a Serbian entity within Bosnia. The principles authorized the two entities to have "parallel special relationships with neighboring countries," thus giving the Republika Srpska a special relationship with Belgrade.

Territory was always an issue in Bosnia. Before the Croat-Muslim military offensive in western Bosnia, the Serbs were estimated to control 70 percent of the territory in Bosnia. Croatian military pressure, however, was reducing the Serbs' area of control. The Geneva principles formally accepted the previous Contact Group recommendation of a territorial split between the parties: 51 percent for the Muslim-Croat Federation and 49 percent for the Republika Srpska.[10]

The Contact Group's superstructure over the negotiations was working. It kept the Europeans and Russia both informed and on board at critical points in the negotiations and helped at the UN.

Holbrooke was careful to engage the Europeans and Russians to help prevent complications during important negotiations. He told me once that the Europeans would concentrate on process—where meetings were to be held, level of attendance, protocol, agenda—but would not be a problem on substance. He was right. In general, they seemed agreeable to letting Holbrooke carry the heavy load on substance. That certainly suited Holbrooke.

The Contact Group was helping make Russia a cooperative partner in the negotiations. At this stage in Russia's post-Communist development, Boris Yeltsin was in the final year of his first term as president. His foreign policy was a dramatic shift to a cooperative relationship with the United States and western Europe. Although the Russians were sympathetic regarding the current difficult position of their Slavic cousins in Serbia, the Yeltsin government was not willing to damage its relationship with the West to protect Milosevic. Russian policy was particularly critical in the UN. There, Russia held veto power on any Security Council resolution important for international action to stop the fighting in Bosnia, including UN authorization for NATO deployment and combat operations.

The Russian negotiators were vocal but manageable in the Contact Group. They were not a factor in Belgrade. Milosevic privately was cynical about Russia throughout the negotiations. In part, he was playing to an American audience by saying what he thought we wanted to hear. However, he also had no illusions about Russian interests. As I wrote Secretary Perry on September 10, Milosevic knew full well that the future of Serbia was with Europe, not with Russia. He also must have calculated that Russia was not about to trade its relations with the West to protect the Serbs.

After the Geneva meeting, the US negotiating team left Europe for Washington. As I looked back on the past thirteen days, I felt that the shuttle had been a whirlwind of productive activity, thanks largely to Holbrooke's energy and the C-20. In travel alone, the team had hopped between the capitals of ten different countries, including four stops in Belgrade, three in Zagreb, and two in Paris. Each stop led to meetings with the head of state, ministers, and senior officials of the local government and with leaders of international organizations.

Holbrooke seemed to be charming all the snakes in the pit and drawing them in his direction. With the authority of the United States, he had seized the opportunity to negotiate an end to the war in Bosnia. He was in charge and had the diplomatic wind at his back. Every door in Europe and the region was open to him, and no one could keep pace with him as he maneuvered according to his own agenda among the various parties to the conflict and at various European capitals. Russia, which could have been a major obstacle to an agreement, pressed for the Serbian position within the Contact Group, but not very hard because it did not seem willing to torpedo the peace process.

No matter how skilled the negotiator, the most critical element in any negotiation is the will of the parties to reach a settlement. The parties themselves may not know for certain if they have the will to reach an agreement because for them the stakes are so extreme if they make a mistake. On the war in Bosnia, Holbrooke found a willing negotiating partner in Milosevic, and the relationship between these two men would be the one essential link in reaching the Dayton Agreement and implementing it in coming months. In early September 1995, Milosevic's determination to reach an agreement seemed firm. Although he was eager to move the process forward, the devil would be in the details: How far would he and the Bosniaks go to end the war?

The US envoy did not yet have a cease-fire or an end to the siege of Sarajevo, but he had a significant start. In these thirteen days in August and September, Holbrooke had created a tangible negotiating instrument in the set of principles the parties had agreed to in Geneva. The Dayton Agreement at the end of November would be an expansion of this brief list of principles.

With the momentum Holbrooke created, he had linked the negotiation to a NATO bombing campaign and had helped generate NATO planning for a force in Bosnia during the implementation phase of a negotiated settlement.

Holbrooke was always careful to have an escape route if the process were to fail. One such mechanism was to ensure that the success or failure of the negotiations lay with the parties. The negotiations were theirs, not his, and he always characterized them this way. In fact, Holbrooke was taking a huge risk to his professional and personal reputation by engaging himself so deeply in these talks.

Holbrooke could be a shameless manipulator and an overbearing bully, but I came to respect his drive, creativity, and willingness to take serious risks in a very uncertain situation. He had a keen sense of opportunity and how to seize it. My own opinion at the end of this trip had moved from deep skepticism that Holbrooke could achieve a negotiated settlement to flickers of optimism that he could pull it off.

Washington, September 9–11, 1995

On the first day back in Washington, I briefed Secretary Perry, CJCS General Shalikashvili, and Walt Slocombe in the Pentagon on the negotiations as I saw them. The military continued to resist any further involvement in the Balkans, but the situation was closing in around them as Holbrooke made progress. In the meeting, Shalikashvili was clearly unsettled by the negotiation's success.

The CJCS asked a question, then made two points. Could the United States avoid participating in the implementation force? The answer I gave was no. The US military would be expected to be an essential component of any NATO force. He then laid down two markers for the future: first, US helicopters should not be used to fly the negotiating team in Bosnia, and, second, the CJCS would resist any use of American military forces to arm and train the Bosnian military in the future.

After the meeting, Secretary Perry took me back to his office to thank me for taking on this job and for sending timely reports of the negotiations. This gesture did much for my morale as his representative on the negotiating team.

On September 10, US cruise missiles struck military targets near Banja Luka, the largest Serbian town in Bosnia. The next day President Clinton joined the Principals Committee (made up of national security cabinet secretaries) in the White House Situation Room as they discussed Holbrooke's progress and the effects of the bombing campaign on the negotiations. Holbrooke favored a continuation of bombing at least until the next round of talks in Belgrade.

With less than ninety hours on the ground in Washington, the team left Andrews Air Force Base once again for Belgrade on September 12.

7

Lifting the Siege

Holbrooke wanted an agreement to end the siege of Sarajevo, but he had to move quickly. NATO was running out of targets and could not sustain the air campaign much longer.

He again passed up the comfortable front cabin of the plane to stuff himself in the back with the rest of us. As he frequently did on flights shortly after takeoff, he removed his shoes and socks due to some sort of foot issue. Even locked in a small aircraft cabin, the barefooted Holbrooke was a flurry of multitasking activity. His assistant in the front of the plane fed him a stream of government cables, press clippings, intelligence reports, and information papers. As he ripped through those, we talked about the approach he should take with Milosevic and the sequence of topics in the discussion.

The C-20 landed at the usual Serbian air force base near Belgrade on Wednesday, September 13, and after an embassy update we traveled to the hunting lodge to meet Milosevic. This time Milosevic had a surprise waiting for us.

Night of the War Criminals: Dobanovci Villa outside Belgrade, September 13–14, 1995

Milosevic was not interested in pleasantries or light banter. The chain-smoking Serbian president was all business and went straight to the NATO air attacks. The recent cruise missile strikes near Banja Luka had grabbed his attention, and he immediately raised the issue.

"This bombing problem must be stopped immediately," Milosevic said. "Women and children are being killed. In Banja Luka, the missiles hit people who are opposed to Karadzic."

"General Mladic can stop the bombing any time he wants. He just must comply with the conditions in General Janvier's letter," Holbrooke responded, referring to a letter with conditions sent recently to Mladic by the UNPROFOR commander General Bernard Janvier.

Milosevic then proposed the development of a "concrete plan" for a general cease-fire in Bosnia, including the withdrawal of heavy weapons from Sarajevo. This was the opening Holbrooke was waiting for.

Milosevic made only one significant condition. He wanted Bosnian Serb leaders, including Bosnian Serb president Radovan Karadzic and General Ratko Mladic, to take part in the cease-fire negotiations.

This condition presented Holbrooke with a serious dilemma. A month earlier the International Criminal Tribunal for the Former Yugoslavia (ICTY) in The Hague had indicted both Karadzic and Mladic for genocide and crimes against humanity in Bosnia.[1]

Holbrooke and Milosevic had previously agreed that Milosevic would represent all Serbs in the negotiations to avoid the possibility of dealing with the Bosnian Serbs charged with war crimes. Now Holbrooke faced the prospects of negotiating directly with indicted war criminals. His choice was to allow the war criminals into the meeting or to risk missing an opportunity to end the fighting in Bosnia. The political dangers of negotiating with war criminals were obvious. I felt fortunate not to be in Holbrooke's shoes at that moment.

A debate on the nature of the cease-fire ensued while Holbrooke pondered his options. Milosevic wanted a cease-fire before heavy weapons were withdrawn. He wanted a Russian battalion to monitor and verify the agreement, and he demanded assurances that the "Muslims" could be restrained in the wake of an agreement.

Holbrooke rejected all of those demands and criticized Mladic for attacks on civilians.

Unknown to us, the Bosnian Serb delegation was two hundred yards away, waiting for approval to join the talks. Pressed again to allow the Bosnians to join the discussion, Holbrooke agreed but reiterated that he was negotiating with Milosevic as the official representative of the Serbs. Holbrooke also agreed to assist the Serbs in producing a Serbian statement that could end the bombing. The statement was not to be an agreement with the United States but a Serbian commitment that Holbrooke would provide to the UN and NATO. Holbrooke again had placed responsibility for the outcome of his diplomacy on the Serbs, not on himself.

Milosevic left the meeting to talk to the Bosnian Serbs while the US team walked through the nearby woods. We could see the black Mercedes driving to the lodge and unloading the passengers as we waited. After Milosevic talked to them for about fifteen minutes, we were asked to join the Serbs at 6:15 p.m.

In the dusk of an early autumn evening, the men who had perpetrated the greatest crimes against humanity in Europe since the Holocaust gathered on the patio of the lodge.

Former psychiatrist Radovan Karadzic, the nationalist president of the Bosnian Serbs, led the group. The stocky General Ratko Mladic was with him. As commander of the Bosnian Serb army, Mladic was responsible for the sniping and shelling of civilians in Sarajevo and the massacre at Srebrenica.

Karadzic, in a deep-maroon suit, was instantly recognizable by the bushy mop of hair that from the front somewhat resembled a gray coonskin cap of the Davy Crockett era. He was smaller than I expected. Mladic was in his fatigue uniform and smelled like a soldier who had been in the field too long.

They were not alone. Bosnian Serb vice president Nikolai Koljevic, whom we had met in Geneva, was in the group. One face I did not recognize was that of Momcilo Krajisnik, who ultimately became one of the most important figures in the negotiations. Krajisnik was the cofounder, with Karadzic, of the nationalist Serbian Democratic Party in Bosnia and was president of the Bosnian Serb Assembly. The more I dealt with Bosnian Serbs, the more I realized that Krajisnik was the real political backbone of the Bosnian Serb nationalist movement. He was a true believer in their cause, more so than the others, including Karadzic. Krajisnik was tough, determined, and unbending in his attitudes toward the negotiations. When others were ready to compromise, when others were intimidated, Krajisnik would stand alone in opposition.

A second Bosnian Serb general, Zdravko Tolimir, accompanied Mladic to the lodge. The thin, balding Tolimir, although less well known than Mladic, was directly responsible for war crimes in Bosnia. Technically, he was chief of intelligence and security for the army, reporting directly to Mladic. He was reported to be the onsite commander overseeing the detention, mass executions, and burial of those slaughtered after Srebrenica had fallen.

I watched them with curiosity. These men represented the brutal acts they had sanctioned or committed in Bosnia. They were not insane, nor were they particularly cunning. Rather, they struck me as a somewhat shabby group of provincials who were passionately committed to a brutal and deadly cause from a time gone by. For them, the ends justified the means.

Had Milosevic launched and supported this group for his own political purposes and then lost control of them? He certainly influenced them directly in the Holbrooke talks. How much control he had over them was hard to tell. Holbrooke set these questions aside for the time being. For him, the objective was to get them to agree to stop the killing in Bosnia.

The group went into the lodge and sat on one side of a table covered in green felt. The Americans faced them on the other side of the table. Milosevic spoke in English, which was translated into Serbian for the Bosnians. Karadzic, who spoke English reasonably well, took notes with his black Mont Blanc pen.

Mladic glared across the table like a sullen teenager. He seemed most concerned with being humiliated by an agreement. He had already had one defiant outburst that evening. "No matter how much you bomb us, you will never humiliate us," he had railed earlier. Perceived humiliation seemed to be these men's major concern as the discussions progressed.

Milosevic immediately proposed a cease-fire around Sarajevo. Holbrooke responded with ideas on what needed to be done to arrive at an agreement. Karadzic, speaking in English, called for a cease-fire throughout Bosnia. The Serbs also were concerned about Muslim exploitation of any withdrawal.

Holbrooke assured them that the United States would use its influence to restrain the Bosniaks. He went on to demand a complete withdrawal of all heavy weapons around Sarajevo, the opening of the Sarajevo Airport to all flights, and uncontested travel on the road corridor from Kiseljak to Sarajevo.

After much back and forth over the next several hours, including an allegation by Milosevic that NATO was directly supporting the Croatian offensive in Bosnia, the group drafted a rough statement for the Serbs.

Following more debate, Karadzic agreed in principle with the statement. Mladic reluctantly concurred if the conditions applied to both sides.

Clark proposed a seventy-two-hour suspension of the bombing to begin the substantial and verifiable withdrawal of heavy weapons. If compliance were verified, bombing would continue to be suspended until withdrawal was complete. Once the weapons were withdrawn, a cease-fire would apply throughout Bosnia, and the airport and highway to Sarajevo would be opened. Holbrooke and the Serbs took a break while we drafted a proposed final statement.

Sometime after midnight, we finished the draft statement. The Serbs were waiting outside on the patio. In the most surreal moment of the negotiations, Clark stood beneath a lamp on the patio of the hunting lodge and read the document that would end the siege of Sarajevo to the gaggle of Serb politicians and generals gathered around him.

Holbrooke sensed the Serbs' desire to conclude an agreement. He pressed them directly: "Do we have an agreed document or not? If not, I see no need to talk further."

"Let us look at the document carefully," Karadzic responded. I did not sense any objections that would prevent their agreement. At this point in the discussion, it seemed that the major issues were settled. The Serbs wanted two things from the statement: the NATO bombing to stop and a complete cease-fire in Bosnia. They were prepared to give up a great deal to achieve those objectives.

A few of us went back into the lodge, where Clark reviewed the document in detail as it was translated for Mladic. At one point, Mladic launched another emotional outburst, but Karadzic settled him down.

Throughout the evening, Karadzic was the facilitator looking for compromise within the Bosnian Serb delegation. The most difficult hard-liners, Krajisnik and Tolimir, in the end stepped aside in favor of Milosevic and Karadzic.

Mladic was trapped. He hated the conditions set forth in the statement, but he had no leverage to block an agreement. His army could not tolerate the bombing, and the situation on the ground was rapidly deteriorating as the Croatian army made progress in its offensive in western Bosnia.

The statement signed by the Serbian leaders agreed to

1. cease all offensive operations in the Sarajevo area and withdraw heavy weapons to 12.5 miles away from the city under international monitoring;
2. consolidate heavy weapons;
3. open the Sarajevo Airport and two land corridors to the city to enable delivery of humanitarian relief supplies.[2]

The detailed talks ended around 2:30 a.m. when the Serbs signed the statement. We later discovered that a mistake had been made in the definition of smaller heavy weapons, but that detail was resolved. Given the conditions for the negotiations, this problem was minor.

On that climactic night, Holbrooke had achieved his goal of completing an agreement to end the siege of Sarajevo and remove the heavy weapons surrounding the city. Milosevic had also achieved his goals. Conditions to suspend the NATO bombing were set, and he had maneuvered Holbrooke into direct discussions with Karadzic and Mladic.

Milosevic sold out the Bosnian Serb army that night. These Serbian men obviously knew each other very well. In addition, they had lived their entire lives in a hierarchical, top-down system. They might not like what Milosevic wanted, but in the end they complied. As the agreement took shape, the Bosnian Serbs became downcast and began behaving like losers. I noted in my journal that night, "The general atmosphere is one of the collapse of the Bosnian Serb Army."

The result of this night's work also was a historic achievement for Holbrooke. He still had a difficult process ahead, but with this document he had concentrated the power of NATO military operations, the UN, and the governments in the United States, Russia, and Europe at a critical moment to stop the shelling and isolation of Sarajevo and to begin to end the misery that the people of that city had suffered for years. Holbrooke would go on to complete the Dayton Agreement, but, for me, the night with the war criminals outside Belgrade was one of his finest diplomatic moments.

Peace or Vengeance: Zagreb and Mostar, September 15, 1995

The team left Belgrade after a couple of hours sleep to deliver the agreement to General Janvier, the UN commander in Zagreb. Before landing, Clark had arranged by phone with Washington and Brussels a technical pause in the bombing. Janvier was delighted with the deal. He interpreted the Serbian statement as meeting the conditions necessary to suspend the bombing. NATO and the UN would jointly announce the agreement and the suspension.

After updating UN special envoy Akashi in Zagreb, the team called on Croatian president Franjo Tudjman, who was ecstatic over the progress of Croatian forces against Serbs near Banja Luka, Bosnia. No doubt the battlefield situation was a primary reason the Bosnian Serbs were so eager for a total cease-fire throughout Bosnia.

Selling the statement to President Izetbegovic and the Bosniaks was a far more difficult proposition. Holbrooke and the team flew to Split, Croatia, then traveled by car to Mostar, Bosnia. In passing through the city, we could see that the relatively undamaged Croatian section of Mostar was a sharp contrast to the severely damaged Muslim area. We crossed the Neretva River at Mostar on a temporary bridge replacing the sixteenth-century Ottoman bridge destroyed during the war.

Joining President Izetbegovic in the discussion were the Bosnian prime minister, Haris Silajdzic, and Kresimir Zubak, the senior Croatian leader of the Federation, the perpetually strained coalition of Bosniaks and Croats in Bosnia. Bosnian Muslim soldiers in a hodgepodge of uniforms and weapons guarded the meeting.

The Bosnians were in high spirits from the NATO bombing and the looming Serbian military defeat in western Bosnia. After years of suffering, these men wanted revenge, not compromise. Holbrooke briefed them on the Serb statement and underscored that it was a Serb product, not an American one.

The Muslim leaders blew up.

"Do not suspend the airstrikes. We are a small step from total success," Silajdzic argued.

Silajdzic, former professor in Arabic language and Islamic studies at Sarajevo University, was the most rigid and outspoken of the Bosniak leaders. Compromise or conciliation was not in him. He wanted the Serbs defeated and justice for all those lost in the war.

The Bosnians' rage at the Serbian statement intensified.

"NATO airstrikes are not attacking weapons and fortifications around Sarajevo," one Bosnian said.

"This statement makes things worse than before. This just buys them time," said another.

"Janvier cannot accept this."

Janvier had already accepted it in Zagreb, and Clark had called British lieutenant general Rupert Smith, Janvier's subordinate UNPROFOR commander in Sarajevo, to explain the statement and to report that the road to Sarajevo would be opened.

Holbrooke tried to interpret the statement in a way that gave it the best outcome for the Bosniaks. His arguments were not working, and the situation was delicate. He couldn't be seen as pushing the long-suffering Bosniaks around, but he couldn't be seen as being a Serb stooge, either.

We spent the night in the Pax Hotel in Medugorje, the location of a reported religious miracle that drew thousands of Catholic pilgrims to the town each year. Holbrooke could have used his own miracle at this point. He was walking through a Balkan diplomatic minefield.

"This is terrible," Silajdzic continued to rant in Mostar the next morning.

Meanwhile, Izetbegovic wanted to return Muslim refugees to their homes before future elections could be held. He wanted international forces to replace Serbs around Sarajevo, and he wanted the northern border town of Brcko under international supervision.

Suddenly, over small cups of strong, sweet Turkish coffee, the Bosniaks were raising new conditions that the Serbs should accept, or, they argued, the bombing should continue, but it was too late to change the agreement. They expected more than lifting the siege of Sarajevo.

After his diplomatic triumph in Belgrade, Holbrooke was verbally hammered by the Bosniaks, who seemed to want revenge more than peace. He was working to help them, yet they refused to be grateful. Next to the accident on Mount Igman, this was the low point in the negotiations during the shuttle.

We left the Bosnian leaders fuming in Mostar as most of the team headed for Geneva and meetings with the Contact Group. Hill and Owen broke off to go to Sarajevo to work on constitutional issues with the Bosniaks. In Belgrade, major demonstrations were taking place near the US embassy as tens of thousands of Serb refugees were reported to be fleeing the Croatian offensive in western Bosnia. Meanwhile, the international media were in a frenzy after the announcement of the Serbian statement and the suspension of bombing,

The practical wisdom of keeping expectations low in the press and in Washington was a valuable diplomatic lesson I learned from Holbrooke. It was easy to see why he wanted to control information coming from the team, considering the swirling nature of the press and various leaders' eagerness to find a solution to Bosnia. Highlighting accomplishments and raising expectations are so tempting when you can claim credit for making progress in the negotiations. However, an experienced diplomat such as Holbrooke knew that a claim of major success is fool's gold early in the talks. The wise negotiator keeps hope alive but expectations low in case things go awry. A positive outcome of these negotiations, although a possibility, was very far from certain. The negotiations could go off the rails at any point along the way.

The Sarajevo Airport reopened on September 15, and humanitarian supplies began to arrive in the beleaguered city for the first time in five months.[3]

Refining the Sarajevo Cease-Fire: Belgrade, September 16, 1995

Two days after the Serbian statement on Sarajevo was signed, it needed some adjustments. The press in Sarajevo was criticizing it for exempting eighty-two-millimeter mortars from weapons to be withdrawn from around Sarajevo. Shelling by these mortars had caused significant casualties and had terrorized the civilian population in Sarajevo.

To correct the statement, the Americans met again with Milosevic at the lodge outside of Belgrade, which allowed the team to avoid demonstrations in the capital, and Milosevic seemed to prefer this more informal atmosphere to talk. The Serbian president was most interested in which Bosniaks had attended the meeting with Holbrooke on the Serbian statement because participation in the meeting indicated the seriousness of the group.

For this session, Milosevic brought in his senior general, chief of the General Staff of the Yugoslav army General Momcilo Perisic. Mladic reportedly had been seized with a case of kidney stones and was indisposed in the hospital. It was not clear if his malady was real, if he could not stand the humiliation of retreat, or if authorities had removed him as an ineffective leader. Regardless of the reason, his deputy, General Manojlo Milovanovic, replaced Mladic on the ground to deal with the withdrawal from Sarajevo and the Croatian offensive.

Perisic arrived at the lodge in the early evening to work out the details directly with Clark and the American team. Slight of build, trim, rigid in military bearing, and polished in his service dress uniform, Perisic showed the confidence of someone experienced in the stress of authority and pressure. He was better prepared and presented a more professional image than Mladic, the emotional thug, but he also had a view of the world heavily colored by Balkan prejudices.

Holbrooke laid out a set of points from his discussions in Zagreb and Mostar to be defined if the bombing were to remain suspended. The Serbian leaders gave Holbrooke acceptable answers to his required modifications. This meeting, following the Serb statement on September 14, showed just how the combination of NATO bombing and the Croatian ground offensive had disrupted the Serbian military position in Bosnia. The Serbs wanted a deal and were compliant with Holbrooke's demands.

For Perisic, the discussion was a platform to deliver his theory that the Bosniak demand for control of the town of Gorazde and eastern Bosnia was a plot to create a "Muslim road" that would physically link Bosnia through the Balkans to Tehran and Baghdad. I later heard this same Muslim conspiracy theory of a "Green Road" to the Middle East from a senior Croatian adviser to President Tudjman in Zagreb. Despite the geographic gaps and the lack of a shred of evidence, this theory was nonetheless widely held among senior officials in the region.

After the war, the ICTY in The Hague convicted Perisic of war crimes in Bosnia and sentenced him to twenty-seven years in prison. On appeal, the court ruled that prosecutors had failed to prove that his actions were directed as criminal activities in Bosnia. His conviction was reversed by the tribunal, and he was set free in 2013.[4]

Stopping the Croatian Offensive in Bosnia: Zagreb, Sunday, September 17, 1995

Holbrooke and the team had an unwelcome message to deliver in Zagreb after leaving Belgrade. We had concluded that the Croatian offensive pushing Serbs out of western Bosnia should be stopped. The offensive was a Croatian military operation conducted by the Zagreb government and assisted by Bosniak forces. Washington had neither promoted nor supported the offensive but also had taken no steps to interfere or stop it up to this point. The offensive had been a US decision by inaction.

In the Serbs' minds, this offensive was linked to the NATO bombing and therefore tied to their cooperation around Sarajevo. If the Croatian offensive continued, cooperation by Serb leaders in Belgrade and Pale would be more difficult.

Continued military operations also could generate hundreds of thousands of Serb refugees flooding out of western and northern Bosnia and into Serbia, which would end any hope of a multicultural society or an agreed political settlement in Bosnia. The press was reporting that thousands of Serb refugees already were fleeing the major western town of Banja Luka as the Croat–Bosniak offensive moved forward.[5]

In addition to creating more refugees, the defeat of the Bosnian Serb army might destabilize Milosevic politically and remove the one Serb who seemed interested in negotiating a solution. Further, the Yugoslav army might intervene with regular units into Bosnia in the event of a full collapse.

The team drafted a letter to President Tudjman calling for a halt to the offensive. We split up on arrival in Zagreb on Sunday morning, September 17. Clark and I went to the Croatian Defense Ministry to issue the US position to Minister of Defense Goiko Susak. Holbrooke and others delivered the news to President Tudjman.

Susak was gleeful when he greeted us in his ministry office at 9:00 a.m. that morning. He took us to a map in his office and pointed to a place on it.

"Do you see this hill overlooking Banja Luka [the second largest city in Bosnia]?" he said. "Our forces have occupied this hill. It is the last defensible terrain between us and Banja Luka. In twenty-four hours, we will capture Banja Luka and then drive the Serbs from western and northern Bosnia."

The history of the Serbs in Bosnia was in his hands. Susak was a man on the verge of an epic victory for Croatia. But now was the time to give him the bad news.

"Minister, the United States demands that Croatia stop your offensive. You are not to take or clear Banja Luka," I said.

Susak was visibly shocked. I may as well have punched him in the gut. He regained his composure.

"The Muslim army is near. They will take Banja Luka," Susak said.

"Do not clear Banja Luka. You are responsible for military operations in this area. The Bosniaks alone cannot continue without Croatian assistance," I replied. I went on to emphasize the importance of the Federation in the future of Bosnia.

"We won't take it, and we will restrain the Bosniak army," Susak said. He then launched into a tirade. "The Muslims attacked us in Petrovac. We have supported the Federation and will continue to do so. We supply arms, support their goals with military operations. The Federation is in our interest."

After his outburst ran its course, we took our leave from an angry, fuming Susak. We then called on General Janvier, who was struggling with determining the Serbs' compliance with the conditions of their statement. Fighting would continue until a complete cease-fire was agreed, but the United States had stopped the Croat–Bosniak offensive to seize Banja Luka and push Serbs out of northern and western Bosnia

Years later, frustrated by constant Serbian obstruction to the implementation of the Dayton Agreement, Holbrooke privately pondered whether stopping this offensive had been the right decision. It was a good question, especially since the Serbs gave him no credit for saving the lives and property of countless Serbs with this decision. However, I felt that it ultimately was the right thing to do. The alternative meant more misery, more refugees, and an uncertain situation in Belgrade.

After the brief stop to update General Janvier, the team flew to Ancona, Italy, to switch planes for the team's first flight to Sarajevo. This trip was being taken to check the status of Serb compliance as the basis for a recommendation to NATO on whether to continue the suspension of or resume the bombing. Holbrooke wanted the suspension to remain in place but would accept resumption if necessary.

The Sarajevo airport was open for military aircraft, and as our C-130 spiraled into its steep tactical landing approach, we took off the helmets and flak jackets we wore over our suits so that we would have a somewhat normal appearance for the press waiting at the airport.

At the Bosnian presidential building, Holbrooke informed President Izetbegovic that the United States did not believe capturing Banja Luka was in the interest of peace. The irritable Bosnians grumbled for a while but accepted the news because they had no real capacity to continue the offensive without the Croats.

The difference in styles between Belgrade and Sarajevo was stark. In Belgrade, Milosevic alone spoke for the Serbs, occasionally bringing others into the discussions but only to support his specific purpose.

In Sarajevo, the Bosniaks sat eight people across the table from the US team. Although Izetbegovic was the leader, the discussion included a freeflowing divergence of opinions from the Bosnians. They seemed not to have arrived at a unified position before the meeting but rather sought to work it out at the table.

I had written Secretary Perry on September 10 that the Bosnian government authorities were the most erratic party in the negotiations. They were split into many factions with many constituencies, and they seemed confused by the conflicting inputs they received from us, from NATO, from support in the Islamic world, and from the many voices in various capitals. President Izetbegovic was the most rational, but the group generally lacked discipline and a coherent position until forced to a decision.

At UNPROFOR headquarters not far from the presidency, Lieutenant General Rupert Smith reported that he had met with the Bosnian Serb military representative earlier in the day. In Smith's view, the Serbs were complying with the statement. Weapons were moving away from Sarajevo, and the Serbs had agreed to open the two roads into the city to nonmilitary traffic without hindrance, although compliance had not been tested. The Serbs were fearful and had military command-and-control issues. Smith also had to deal with his own multinational military command that was unwieldy and resistant to outside instructions. Holbrooke wanted a level of certainty from Lieutenant General Smith that was difficult to determine in such a fluid situation.

Before 10:00 p.m., Smith at UNPROFOR in Sarajevo formally recommended to UN authorities that the suspension of the NATO bombing continue.

I felt that we were shaping very fluid events on the fly as Holbrooke adjusted to new realities day by day, minute by minute. Somehow, it all seemed to be working.

Later on September 17, NATO suspended bombing for three days. Major fighting in Bosnia had stopped. Now the diplomatic process turned to sustaining the peace through a political agreement between the parties.

Setting the Stage for Dayton: Belgrade and Zagreb, September 17–19, 1995

The fighting on the Bosnian battlefields subsided as Milosevic waited for us at the Serbian presidential palace in Belgrade, where his table was set for a 10:00 p.m. dinner on September 17. Only Milosevic, Foreign Minister Milutinovic, and Goran the scribe were present for this discussion.

Although the fighting in Bosnia was winding down, economic sanctions remained in place on Serbia. Milosevic expected a reward for helping to end the fighting and to lift the siege of Sarajevo. He proposed a presidential summit to allow sanctions to be removed, and he wanted it immediately. Holbrooke was cautious.

"I told Tudjman and Izetbegovic not to take Banja Luka. They assured me that they would not attack it," Holbrooke said to Milosevic.

"Tudjman will take everything he can, but I do not think he will succeed. General Milovanovic is a very good general," Milosevic said. "It is time to arrange a conference on Bosnia and to pick a date. I want it as soon as possible. You should not discuss the conference with Tudjman or Izetbegovic. Just announce it."

Over dinner, Holbrooke identified several elements that he considered essential for an agreement and set some ground rules for an international conference. Milosevic used the meeting to push for opening the conference on Bosnia right away.

"When are you proposing a conference?" Holbrooke asked.

"The last week in September, less than ten days from now. We should bring Mladic and Karadzic."

Milosevic had maneuvered Holbrooke into meeting with the Pale Serbian leadership several days earlier, but the US negotiator knew that those indicted by the ICTY could not participate in a peace conference in Europe or the United States.

"If [General] Mladic comes to New York, he will be arrested on the spot, but that's not my issue," Holbrooke said. "Their attendance is out of the question. It will destroy your delegation, and President Clinton cannot participate."

"Diplomats are always suffering from protocol. I don't have that disease," Milosevic said.

"Please never mention The Hague tribunal outside of this room," Milosevic added. The ICTY was a topic too hot for him to negotiate. He and the Serbian leaders were extremely sensitive to any mention of the ICTY in The Hague. They knew the potential dangers that the court presented to their legitimacy and did everything possible to discredit it in Serbia.

Milosevic did not challenge Holbrooke's extensive list of objectives for a conference, but the team knew that a conference in ten days was not practical.

We returned to the presidential palace the next morning for a working breakfast. Holbrooke, who always prepared to dominate the agenda for these meetings, wanted to talk about preparation for the conference, but Milosevic preferred to talk territory. He took a map of Bosnia that we had brought with us and began to draw lines on it. His scribbling modified the known areas of control in several spots and outlined what was important to the Serbs.

He proposed that Sarajevo be open for travel but that the suburbs Ilidza and Grbavica and the airport be under Serbian administration.

He wanted a wide corridor in Bosnia under Serbian control along the northern border with Croatia and was willing to let some areas formerly controlled by the Serbs in the western and central regions of Bosnia go to the Federation. Former UN safe areas in Srebrenica and Zepa would be under Serb administration. The third safe area in Gorazde could be connected to the Federation by a single new highway.

This was not a basis for a territorial settlement, but the team had no territorial negotiating position to take seriously until Milosevic produced his map. The Milosevic map was at least a place to start for one side.

The team made a run to Zagreb to complete military discussions with the Croatians. The next morning, Tuesday, September 19, President Izetbegovic joined President Tudjman in Zagreb for the meeting with the team. The offensive had stopped short of Banja Luka but was succeeding else-where in western Bosnia, and Tudjman was full of himself. He was postur-ing, lecturing Izetbegovic, and trying to dominate the Bosniaks.

Holbrooke let the verbal poison fly uninterrupted. So much for Federa-tion cooperation on this day. We left the two presidents and flew back to Belgrade for the last meeting with Milosevic before going home.

Milosevic was animated and confident in greeting us. Bosnian Serb fighters had caught the Croatian forces crossing a river and had inflicted heavy losses. The Serbian president continued to urge a decision for a quick international conference.

"We must have a peace conference soon. When can we have one?"

"Maybe before Christmas," Holbrooke responded.

"We must settle this in a fortnight. *Periculum in mora* [There is danger in hesitation]," Milosevic said.

Holbrooke pivoted to another topic, the constitutional principles nec-essary for a settlement in Bosnia. Milosevic carefully read a paper on the constitution Holbrooke handed him.

"I agree with it," Milosevic said. "We must talk this over with the Bos-nian Serb leaders. Don't show them the agreement. Take a harder line and fall back to this. We need a kind of drama. There is a place for a 'certain kind of technology.' We have to argue first," he explained.

Milosevic then guaranteed that in the end the document he had ap-proved would be completed. He had virtual dictatorial powers and could have simply forced the outcome on the Bosnian Serbs, but he wanted to draw them in. His Communist past had taught him the value of politi-cal theater, but I had concluded by then that he would rather manipulate people than dictate to them. With Milosevic in such a positive mood at this point, Holbrooke asked for one more assurance—the Serbs would not in-terfere with the reestablishment of utilities in Sarajevo.

"OK. Let's do it," Milosevic said.

With that, the team left the presidential palace to board the flight back to Washington. As we arrived at Andrews, the UN and NATO suspended the bombing campaign in Bosnia indefinitely.

Momentum

The progress made in the shuttle negotiations was stunning. Only one month after the accident on Mount Igman, Holbrooke had achieved real momentum toward a settlement. Although an agreed cease-fire throughout Bosnia would not be completed for another two weeks, the air campaign was suspended, and major fighting would not resume. The siege of Sarajevo was gradually being lifted. The negotiators had met with the Bosnian Serbs and started preliminary negotiations on a map. The Contact Group was behind the Holbrooke process, and starting the proximity talks was in Holbrooke's hands.

Holbrooke maintained momentum in the negotiations through the pace of his engagement and the intensity of the talks. On the shuttle, the team often leaped between multiple European capitals each day. Visiting two capitals in one day was not unusual, and on September 17 the team had met three presidents in three capitals. In each meeting, Holbrooke pressed for agreement on previous proposals and left homework—a paper, a set of proposals, or ideas to be decided in the next meeting. This approach placed constant pressure on the parties and kept them somewhat off balance as he stressed their decision-making apparatus with important issues.

The team landed in Washington on Wednesday, September 20, in time for an update to the Joint Chiefs of Staff in the Pentagon and to the Principals Committee in the White House Situation Room. Two days later, three of us—Chris Hill, Bob Owen, and I—were off again to Belgrade to meet with the Bosnian Serbs.

With the prospects for a settlement improving, Republicans in Congress sided with the US military on the desire to keep American troops out of Bosnia. A group of senators wrote a letter to the president raising questions on the possibility of US troops being deployed in the Balkans. The following week President Clinton and Secretaries Perry and Christopher began engaging Congress specifically on the need for US troops in the NATO force to deploy to Bosnia in conjunction with a peace agreement.

8

A Certain Kind of Technology

Belgrade and Sarajevo, September 23–25, 1995

We had more room and the environment was less frantic without Holbrooke on the flight to Belgrade. Milosevic was waiting for Chris Hill, Roberts Owen, and me at the presidential palace for a strategy session before we met with the Bosnian Serbs. This meeting was to hear his advice on how the US negotiators should present their proposals to best bring the Bosnian Serbs to the position Holbrooke and Milosevic had already agreed on—what Milosevic referred to as political "technology."

When Hill and Owen were out of the room, Milosevic picked up a paper on territorial proposals I laid next to him. He reacted strongly to the idea that Sarajevo would be a unified city.

"No. This is not possible. The Republika Srpska must control Ilidza and Grbavica [two Sarajevo suburbs]. Sarajevo is not to be like Berlin, but the Federation cannot control the [whole] city," Milosevic demanded.

I argued that if he was to get the Serbian corridor in northern Bosnia connecting east and west, the Serbs would have to negotiate seriously on Sarajevo.

"Without a territorial agreement, we will reach no real agreement," I said.

Milosevic warned that a discussion of Sarajevo would get a very strong reaction from the Bosnian Serbs.

"We have to cross that bridge at some point. Why not now?" I said.

He nodded, but he was not about to give away a prize as valuable as Sarajevo at that point.

Then Milosevic turned to a future NATO presence in Bosnia and why the force should be small.

"No one will challenge NATO," he argued. He kept returning to this point.

"NATO will carry its own guarantee. The US concept today is overwhelming force, but they can reduce the size rapidly depending on the situation," I said.

Milosevic later urged us to describe the political superstructure in the new Republic of Bosnia-Herzegovina as a "tin roof" to the Bosnian Serbs—a term we would hear again in the future.

The Bosnian Serb Map

We departed the Belgrade presidential palace for the villa in the hunting preserve at Dobanovci where Karadzic, Koljevic, Krajisnic, and other Serbs waited for us.

Karadzic was in the same dark-maroon suit. I noted a small Orthodox cross pin he was wearing on his lapel. He took it off and offered to give it to me. I declined.

The talks did not go well as Hill and Owen laid out their proposals. I could envision Milosevic back in Belgrade with a glass of whiskey and a cigarillo chuckling to himself about the Americans at the villa verbally wrestling with the obstinate and confrontational Serbs from Bosnia.

On the political superstructure of a future Bosnia, Krajisnic said, "The Muslims want an iron roof [i.e., strong central government in Bosnia]. We can accept a paper roof. I want no roof."

The Bosnian Serbs wanted an extremely weak government for the nation, in which they would have a veto on any decision that government made. The republic they favored was one in which the Serbs would have virtual independence.

"We are not making a state here. We should never have accepted the Agreed Basic Principles in Geneva," Krajisnik asserted.

After a break, we came back to the territorial discussion. It went no better than the constitutional discussion. Krajisnik quickly sketched the Bosnian Serbs' position for Sarajevo on a map. They claimed flexibility, then showed none. Krajisnik, who was the point man on this subject, came with a stack of maps and presented a hard set of demands.

Krajisnik was a meticulous man who cared about his appearance. He was always neatly dressed in a conservative suit. His hair was carefully trimmed, and his hands manicured. Below the bushy eyebrows, he occasionally smiled, but there was no mirth in his eyes.

Karadzic and Mladic were the public face of the Bosnian Serbs, but Krajisnik was their leader. I judged that if the Bosnian Serbs were to be convinced to negotiate a settlement, Krajisnik must be convinced, and that might not be possible. He was the steel in the Bosnian Serb delegation.

Krajisnik laid out their territorial position:

1. Sarajevo was to be a divided city with the Muslim-Croat Federation in the North. The Republika Srpska would control the South and approaches from the east and west. Sarajevo was to be the capital of the Republika Srpska.
2. The Serbs would control a large corridor in the North connecting the eastern and western Republika Srpska.
3. The Muslims could have Gorazde and a road connecting it to the Federation.

The essential subjects were broached with the Bosnian Serbs. The meeting with them was mostly theater, but whose theater?

Milosevic Intervenes

The team returned to the villa late morning on September 24 after a short meeting with Milosevic, who would come to the villa later to check on progress with his clients from Bosnia.

Karadzic brought his wife, Ljiliana, to the villa to meet us. Otherwise, all the Bosnian Serbs from the previous day were present. The Serbs caucused over a revised paper while we waited in the crisp, bright Sunday morning.

Milosevic arrived as lunch was served. The discussions proceeded outside at a table by the fountain after lunch. Milosevic took the Bosnian group away for private discussions. When they returned, he delivered the final compromises to the paper in question. With a shove from him, the Bosnian Serbs had approved the constitutional principles with a few superficial changes, just as he had assured Holbrooke they would. Political "technology" had worked.

The C-20 stopped in Shannon, Ireland, to refuel on the flight home. As we waited in the airport snack bar around 10:00 p.m., a crew member came to tell us that US Air Force authorities in Washington had ordered the plane not to leave Shannon. We looked at each other and almost said in unison, "Holbrooke!"

Holbrooke had learned that the Bosniaks were rejecting the paper we had just negotiated with the Serbs. Izetbegovic had issued a public statement saying his delegation would not go to an imminent meeting at the UN in New York because of the unacceptable language worked out in Belgrade. We spent the night making our way not to New York but back to the Balkans and Sarajevo.

A hostile Bosniak leadership greeted us in the Sarajevo presidential building the next morning. Haris Silajdzic was furious that the document was modified in Belgrade without coordinating the change in a stop at Sarajevo before the US team headed home. Silajdzic demanded immediate proximity talks, claiming that the process of flying about was too cumbersome at this stage.

"For you, this is prestige. For us, this is the future," he said.

We discovered that we had not received some modifications that had been proposed by the Sarajevo group and therefore were not in the document that eventually came out of Belgrade.

We returned to the presidential building in the afternoon to meet with President Izetbegovic. The tattered building showed much wear from the war and the city's isolation.

Izetbegovic launched into an attack on changes to the document and the team's failure to stop in Sarajevo on the way back to the United States. After Izetbegovic and company vented, they calmed down and committed to joining the meetings in New York. They did not agree to the document, however.

The team reversed the travel route from Sarajevo to Shannon—this time without further interruptions. We landed at LaGuardia Airport in New York early in the morning on Tuesday, September 26. Kathy was waiting for me at the Waldorf Astoria in Manhattan. After a few hours of sleep, we joined Holbrooke and others at the US Mission to the UN.

Holbrooke took it from there. Using the pressure applied by the Contact Group, the UN spotlight, and the momentum of the process, he obtained an agreement on the "Further Agreed Principles."[1] These principles committed to elections and the creation of national institutions, which would form the foundation of the constitutional provisions of the Dayton Agreement that would eventually be signed in November. But the Bosniaks could not agree to the cease-fire the Serbs were seeking.

9

Sarajevo

September 28–October 6, 1995

Holbrooke wanted to broker a total cease-fire in Bosnia and to set up proximity talks for the middle of October 1995 during this trip to the region. But a conference in mid-October, given the time available, seemed unlikely.

The approach to the Sarajevo airport by the military cargo plane was another steep downward spiral. As we descended, the aircraft popped flares to deceive any potential missiles fired at the plane. Once on the runway, we again took off the military helmets and flak jackets in favor of suit coats. We departed the aircraft wearing suits and carrying briefcases as if we were getting off a commercial shuttle flight at LaGuardia.

Before the war, Sarajevo was an attractive cosmopolitan city in a valley surrounded by lush mountains. The main boulevard parallels the Miljacka River, which runs through the center of town. Yugoslavia had upgraded Sarajevo's infrastructure and buildings for the Winter Olympics in 1984, but many of the Olympic venues were destroyed or heavily damaged during the war. Sarajevo's population in September 1995 was mostly Muslim, with concentrations of Serbs and some Croats on the periphery.

Sarajevo was a seriously wounded city. Bosnian Serb forces had blocked or restricted delivery of humanitarian supplies by land and air for forty-four months. To keep Sarajevo alive, international relief flights brought more essentials to the city during the siege than were delivered during the Berlin Airlift in 1948–1949.[1] Gas, water, and electricity were sparse to non-existent for the population.

The city was shelled periodically, and sniper fire from the hills was a constant threat. Bomb and mortar fragments gouged holes in the sidewalks and streets and structures. Serb gunners had shot up buildings in Muslim areas of the city, including the virtual complete destruction of the historic library. Makeshift graves had sprouted up in Sarajevo's parks after Serb shelling and sniping killed more than 11,000 civilians in Sarajevo from 1992 to 1995.[2]

One of the most touching events of the negotiation occurred when Holbrooke arrived at the presidency in Sarajevo on September 29. As he was conducting an impromptu press conference at the entrance to the presidency, a crowd gathered across the street to watch. When they saw that it was Holbrooke, the people broke into spontaneous applause. That simple gesture of public appreciation for helping to relieve their misery made all the frustration and risk of the negotiations worth it for me.

Inside the presidency, the Bosniak leaders remained as grumpy and difficult as ever. They were in no hurry to sign a cease-fire agreement, probably hoping that NATO bombing would resume. Izetbegovic attacked Holbrooke over the lack of natural gas for heat and the UN's failure to open roads into the city or to make progress on the airport.

The weather in Sarajevo was wet and cold as winter approached. The mountains hovering over the city would have snow soon. Holbrooke and Clark were quartered in the embassy for the night. The rest of us were taken to the Sarajevo Holiday Inn, a Communist-era architectural monstrosity clad in yellow and located along "sniper's alley." Its provenance to the international Holiday Inn chain of hotels was suspect. The hotel was pockmarked by sniper bullets on the side facing the Serbs in the hills, which forced us to enter through a makeshift main door at the back of the building. Inside, $200 per night got you no heat, no water, no lights, bullet holes, and possibly dried blood on the floor.

One disconcerting feature of my room was the single, large-caliber bullet hole in the window, the curtain, and the headboard of the bed. The previous day a sniper had killed someone on the south side of the hotel, so I planned to keep the room dark to avoid creating a silhouette in the window. I was prepared to sleep on the floor. The embassy security people decided later that the hotel was too risky and brought us back to the embassy, where folding cots and army sleeping bags were provided.

High-level international diplomacy suddenly began to look like a military deployment from my army days. Ambassador-designate John K. Menzies, a couple of Foreign Service officers, a communications team, and some security people lived and worked in the embassy building when they were not moving about the very dangerous city doing embassy business.

We began drafting a cease-fire agreement for the parties to complete while we were in the region. General Rupert Smith at UNPROFOR invited us for dinner at his headquarters next to the embassy, so we joined him.

General Smith was a tough, experienced, and capable British general officer. He was reserved but polite and had the trim, chiseled features of a serious professional combat commander. The general had a vase of fresh-cut roses on a table and a bird feeder in the window of his office. Despite the common language, the cultural differences between Americans and the British can be vast, and this was one such instance. I could not imagine an American general deployed or in garrison with cut roses and a bird feeder in the office. I admired General Smith for this touch of personal confidence and a symbolic example of the differences between two committed allies.

Holbrooke stormed into the dinner. He was incensed by the slow progress of the UN and UNPROFOR on opening the roads into Sarajevo and the airport and took his complaints directly to the UNPROFOR commander. Holbrooke verbally attacked Smith and his civilian UN counterpart for failure to make progress. When the two UN officials attempted to defend themselves, Holbrooke blew up.

I stared at my shoes in horror. Smith did not deserve this treatment. I had never in my career seen a civilian official berate a senior military officer as Holbrooke attacked Smith that evening. Smith took his tongue-lashing well. His jaw was set, and you could tell that he was furious, but he maintained his professional composure. Holbrooke stomped off, and the rest of the team finished dinner with the general, who continued to be a gracious host.

After US embassy officers drove the Kiseljak-to-Sarajevo road for the first time to ensure that it was open, Holbrooke turned his attention to getting a cease-fire. The team made a quick stop in Zagreb before moving on to Belgrade for the night.

Over time, US intelligence had collected evidence of a close association between and support by the Serbian army and the Bosnian Serb army. Holbrooke asked Don Kerrick and me to put together a list of things the Serbian army was doing to support the Bosnian Serb army but to hide the sources because he wanted to confront Milosevic on supporting the latter. To help cover precisely what we knew, Kerrick and I dreamed up some feasible support possibilities and added them to the list. The paper was a direct challenge to the fiction that the Milosevic government did not control events in Bosnia.

At the Serbian presidential palace in Belgrade that evening, Milosevic was in a joking mood. Holbrooke was not. The US envoy laid out a string of complaints, some regarding Sarajevo, others related to Serbian misbehavior on the international stage. Milosevic agreed to let natural gas go through to Sarajevo.

Holbrooke provided Milosevic a copy of the draft cease-fire agreement for Bosnia. While Milosevic was reading the draft, Holbrooke raised the sensitive issue of Serbian military support of the Bosnian Serb army. He then handed Milosevic the paper that he said I had given to him.

Milosevic's mood darkened. He looked at the list and then began a verbal dance to avoid responsibility for events in Bosnia. After some lively discussion, he denied some of the items on the list and admitted to others, including some that we had made up. He then dropped the topic and the paper and turned to another topic.

On territory, Milosevic continued to press for a broad Serbian-controlled corridor in northern Bosnia, but he was showing flexibility on Sarajevo.

"I told Karadzic that Izetbegovic has earned Sarajevo. 'He took your shells for three years and is still there,'" Milosevic offered to our surprise.

That night he also confirmed my opinion that Krajisnik, not Karadzic, was the key Serb leader in Bosnia.

"Krajisnik uses Karadzic as cover," Milosevic explained.

As we were leaving the presidency, I left the paper on Serbian military support to Bosnia on the table. Milosevic picked it up and returned it to me.

"No, you keep it," I said, and we left for our regular rooms in the Hyatt.

National intelligence can be a critical component of diplomatic negotiations, and this vignette on the Serbian military support to the Bosnian Serbs was one example of the use of intelligence during the Bosnia negotiations. Holbrooke took intelligence as a matter of course. For him, it was one tool. I was impressed that he had no preconceived notions about intelligence as a function and had neither a positive nor a negative bias about it. He consumed intelligence reports as voraciously as he did diplomatic cables, press reports, and other sources of information. He was open to ideas on intelligence but did not have unrealistic expectations about what intelligence could provide.

The team stopped briefly the next day in Zagreb to press the Croats for more cooperation within the Federation and to push the UN in Zagreb for quicker action on the Sarajevo Airport. Word of Holbrooke's outburst to General Smith had made the rounds, and the UN civilian leadership was becoming more responsive.

Holbrooke had decided that he would take a break from the negotiations and travel to Sofia, Bulgaria, a country he had never visited before. The Bulgarians were delighted to host Holbrooke and his traveling circus as their new democracy struggled to recover from its postwar Communist past. They made it a major event, including dinner with President Zhelyu Zhelev and meetings with the prime minister and members of the cabinet. Unforeseen at the time, I would return to Sofia seven years later as the US ambassador to Bulgaria.

After this short stop, the team headed back to Sarajevo, where the Bosniaks were rejecting the cease-fire in the delusion that their forces were making progress against the Bosnian Serb army. After a night off in Sarajevo, we woke up the next morning to news that Macedonian president Kiro Gligorov, whom we had visited a few weeks earlier, had been the target of an assassination plot. Gligorov survived the bomb directed at his motorcade in Skopje, but he was severely wounded, losing a portion of his face in the explosion. The assassination attempt essentially ended his public political career.

Milosevic was off the nicotine during this stop, but Holbrooke did nothing to calm his nerves. The envoy again pushed for a cease-fire as he continued to accuse the Serbian government of supporting the Bosnian Serb army. Milosevic complained again about his limited control over the Bosnian Serbs.

"Serbs and Muslims in Bosnia are basically the same. We always think of them the same—stupid," Milosevic said.

Bully for Peace: Sarajevo, October 4–5, 1995

The US Senate had recently confirmed John Menzies as ambassador to Bosnia. Holbrooke's first order of business in Sarajevo on October 4 was to swear in Menzies as US ambassador, the position he had courageously but unofficially held for weeks. The Bosnian government offered the Konak House for the ceremony. The body of Archduke Ferdinand had been taken to this building to lay in state prior to its return to Austria after the assassination in Sarajevo. Menzies was honored by the availability of this building from the Ottoman period because it had not been used recently for official ceremonies. President Izetbegovic and members of the Bosnian government, delighted to have an official American ambassador resident in the capital city, attended the swearing in.

The group then moved to a Bosnian military facility, where Clark decorated six Bosnian soldiers with US Achievement Medals for assisting the Americans injured and killed in the Igman Road accident. As with the Menzies ceremony, this was a prominent event in Sarajevo. Formal recognition of Bosnian soldiers had been rare during the stress of war in recent years.

The ceremonies did not produce more flexibility in the Bosniaks' negotiating position, however. Later in the presidency, Izetbegovic continued to complain that the UN was not moving fast enough to open the roads and the airport or to ensure that utilities in Sarajevo were restored. Further, the Bosniaks, buoyed by the earlier Croatian military success in western Bosnia, did not want to rush to endorse the cease-fire. They feared that they were being pressured into ill-considered agreements that they would regret later. They knew that the Serbs were eager for the fighting to end and that Milosevic wanted to escape economic and other sanctions. The fractious Bosniaks wanted to get everything they could from the negotiations. Who could blame them?

We had an assessment from Washington to give to them, describing the military risks of continued fighting. Holbrooke also informed them that further airstrikes would not be forthcoming if they got into military trouble because they delayed an agreement.

On the proximity talks, Izetbegovic warned Holbrooke that they would make no guarantees that such a conference would succeed.

"Nothing is settled until everything is settled," Izetbegovic cautioned. "All of this [the preliminary agreements] is for nothing if we [Bosniaks] do not get what we want in territory and the structure of government."

Holbrooke and most of the party flew off to Belgrade to meet with Milosevic and the Bosnian Serbs on the cease-fire, while Chris Hill and I stayed behind in Sarajevo. With Holbrooke gone, we had a little time to see something of the crippled city.

After sundown, the streets in Sarajevo were mostly dark, with people moving about as shadowy figures in the night. Electricity and basic utilities were sporadic at best during the siege. The city had become a society of hunter-gatherers who worked out what arrangements they could for subsistence and survival. Through their agony, the people of Sarajevo did their best to retain their dignity.

Ambassador Menzies took us out to dinner at the Jez (Yez) Restaurant in a cellar in the center of the city, patronized mostly by international officials and press. Only a very few locals could afford a relatively safe, temporary escape from the misery of the streets. A string trio entertained as decent food and drink were served.

We ended the evening at a coffee bar on an interior street where young people gathered in the evening for some social contact amid all this danger and poverty. I thought that many European cities must have been something like this during World War II.

At about 2:00 a.m. on October 5, the Serbs signed the agreement with Holbrooke. The envoy flew back to Sarajevo later that morning to finish the cease-fire deal with the Bosniaks.

The most difficult event in a negotiation is the point of closure, and one of the most important diplomatic lessons for me from the Dayton process was about closing—getting authoritative signatures on an agreement. Among his many diplomatic talents, Richard Holbrooke had a fierce determination to close the deal.

For the cease-fire in Bosnia, Holbrooke would not be denied in Sarajevo. As often happens in negotiations, the diplomat saved the most difficult point for last to allow the momentum of the process to add pressure. He hit town with one signature to get—Izetbegovic's—to conclude the cease-fire, and he was hell bent on getting it. He also used an imminent departure from the city that afternoon to add the pressure of time.

We arrived at the presidential building at 1:00 p.m., with the cease-fire document signed by Milosevic and the Bosnian Serbs the previous night and negotiated by phone with Mo Sacirbey in Sarajevo.

Izetbegovic stalled. He complained that because the Serbs had already signed the document, he could no longer make changes to it. He refused to sign the same document as the Serbs, so we had to produce a clean copy for him. He grumbled about the Serbian public statement and demanded to write the joint statement with Holbrooke. He wanted an impossible assurance that NATO bombing would resume if gas and electricity were not restored to Sarajevo soon. The Bosnian Muslims neither liked nor trusted Holbrooke, but they could not escape him, and he did not seem to care what they thought of him personally.

A frustrated Holbrooke had had enough. As a nervous Izetbegovic watched, Holbrooke turned into an overbearing, threatening tyrant. I had seen this posturing with Gligorov in Macedonia, but I could hardly watch this time.

Finally, Izetbegovic took the agreement, looked at it, and said, "I don't see your signature on this document, Mr. Holbrooke."

Holbrooke grabbed the agreement and signed vigorously as a witness. He glared at the Bosnian president, slid the paper back across the table, slammed the pen down on the paper in front of Izetbegovic, and said, "Now you, Mr. President."

With his hand shaking, his place in Bosnian history and the future of his people at stake, the pale, seventy-year-old Bosnian president signed the cease-fire agreement. Holbrooke grabbed the signed document and gave them a copy, and we bolted for the airport and a flight to Rome.

The fighting in Bosnia was to stop immediately at midnight on October 10, 1995. After a two-day delay demanded by the Bosnian government, the agreement took effect on October 12.

The cease-fire agreement terminated all hostile military activities throughout Bosnia to allow for the negotiation of a comprehensive peace agreement. It called for an exchange of prisoners and opened the roads between Sarajevo and Gorazde to nonmilitary traffic. UNPROFOR was to monitor the cease-fire and supervise the prisoner exchange.[3]

The team stopped in Rome for the night. Everyone except me went back to Washington on the C-20 the next day, but I was to link up with Secretary Perry in Geneva for a meeting with the Russian minister of defense to discuss Russian participation in the NATO force deployed to Bosnia.

I had a full day to myself in Rome—a city both glorious and gritty, as it probably always has been. Rome, as usual, was full of American students and tourists determined to absorb as much culture as their time in Rome would allow. I spent the day wandering the streets. I stopped for a long lunch alone at an outdoor café near the Spanish Steps to reflect on recent events. I had found myself caught up in a diplomatic whirlwind of immense importance to so many people, and I was becoming accustomed to it.

We had spent so much time in Belgrade meeting with men whose hands were covered in the blood of a tragic and brutal war and in Sarajevo with Muslims who were so difficult to engage effectively. Despite these difficulties, we could not lose sight that the Muslims were the primary victims in this war.

I bought an *International Herald Tribune* on the Via Veneto after noticing a large picture of Holbrooke and Chris Hill on the front page. Later at dinner in the hotel, I chatted about Rome with some tourists from California, but I avoided the subject of the Balkans for the evening.

Arming the Bosnian Muslims

As Holbrooke engaged the warring parties in the Balkans, President Clinton and his national security team were locked in a political battle in Washington with Republicans in the Congress over sending US troops to Bosnia in the event of a peace agreement.

One year in advance of the US presidential elections, the Republicans were attacking the president's commitment to NATO to send US troops to assist in the implementation of a peace agreement.

With the military resistant to any engagement in Bosnia, the Republicans saw President Clinton as politically vulnerable on this subject. As a settlement became increasingly likely, Republicans in Congress, led by future Republican presidential candidate Senator Robert Dole, threatened to block the deployment of US troops to Bosnia if the president tried to do so without congressional approval.

The Republicans had put forth a simple solution to the war in Bosnia: lift the international arms embargo on the region and let the Muslims defend themselves. This strategy recognized the inherent unfairness of the embargo. The Serbs had plenty of arms to fight the war. The Bosniaks did not have enough to defend themselves. However, the Republican proposal raised more problems that it solved. The United States did not have the votes in the UN to lift the international embargo. Lifting the arms embargo unilaterally would increase the fighting in Bosnia with only European troops on the ground, which would further split the United States from its traditional allies. In fact, the Europeans made it clear to Washington that lifting the arms embargo would cause their immediate withdrawal from Bosnia.

The Bosniaks demanded a removal of the arms embargo as a condition for a settlement, and they wanted arms and training from the United States. These demands gave Holbrooke leverage in the negotiations but did not resolve the various US military issues.

As Holbrooke maneuvered the parties toward a peace settlement, the Clinton administration adopted a composite strategy to deal with the thorny issues of political resistance to US deployment: the arms embargo and the growing influence of extremists in Sarajevo.

At the meeting of NATO defense ministers at Williamsburg, Virginia, on October 6, Secretary of Defense Perry informed his NATO colleagues that the Clinton administration was prepared to organize and assist in a multinational effort to arm and train Muslim military forces if a peace accord were achieved. The purpose of this program would be to level the military playing field with the Serbs and thus to ensure a lasting military stability in the region. He further announced that US forces would not be involved but that the United States might hire private security contractors to do the job. This approach appealed to the Republicans and offered the added advantage of creating the conditions for sufficient stability as an exit strategy for US forces in Bosnia.[4] The Europeans were quietly horrified. Their preferred option was to disarm the region.

I should have paid more attention to this debate. Three months later I would find myself in charge of implementing the US policy to arm and train the Bosnians.

Negotiating the Unthinkable: Russia and NATO Together, Geneva, October 8, 1995

A million combat-ready military forces armed with nuclear weapons from NATO and the Warsaw Pact stared at each other across central Europe for fifty years until communism collapsed in the Soviet Union after 1989. No serious analyst could have predicted that five years later NATO and Russia would deploy soldiers together and share military responsibilities in a common task.

US secretary of defense William Perry and Russian minister of defense Pavel Sergeyevic Grachev, who was a former Soviet general and veteran of Afghanistan, met in Geneva to complete preliminary arrangements for just such a combined operation if a peace agreement were reached in Bosnia.

At first, Grachev wanted to deploy a Russian division to Bosnia, and the Russians wanted considerable say in the political situation in Bosnia as well. In the end, they insisted on two points: political cover by the UN for the NATO deployment and hard currency to offset their deployment costs.

Russia consistently tried to weaken NATO through the UN. If it could force NATO operations into a UN mandate and command structure, the process would give Russia greater influence on NATO actions. Although many US allies were sympathetic to the Russian view, NATO ultimately deployed to Bosnia with a UN mandate but not under UN command.

In the end, Grachev agreed to reduce the size of the Russian contingent and to assign a Russian general to the NATO staff to enable Russian forces to operate within the NATO structure. Any association with NATO was extremely sensitive to Russia. As the meeting concluded, Grachev inquired about NATO enlargement.

"We oppose NATO expansion to the east," Grachev asserted.

"I will speak to you directly and honestly," Secretary Perry said. "NATO will get bigger and do so in this century."

More negotiating would ensue in coming weeks, but the basic deal between the United States and Russia on NATO and Russian military cooperation in Bosnia was done.

With that, on an October day in 1995 in Geneva, Switzerland, the enormous military confrontation that had existed in Europe since 1945 was set aside in favor of military cooperation between Western and Russian forces. At the same time, the North Atlantic Alliance was being transformed from an institution with a single focus to one with broader international security responsibilities and greater cooperation with forces outside the alliance.

Competing Objectives

The Holbrooke team's latest shuttle to the Balkans had given new momentum to the peace process. A cease-fire was in place in Bosnia. Sarajevo, Belgrade, Zagreb, and the Contact Group agreed on proximity talks to complete the negotiations. NATO was busy planning for an implementation force, and Russia was a constructive partner in the process. Specialists in Washington and European capitals worked on a variety of constitutional and legal proposals for a future Bosnian state. The way forward to a sustained peace and a viable Bosnian state had plenty of serious obstacles, but the general direction was very positive.

The upcoming proximity talks offered the parties in the region a chance to achieve most of their objectives. The question would be how much they were willing to give up to accomplish those objectives.

In Belgrade, Milosevic had to feel that the process was moving in a favorable direction. The negotiations held out the hopes of removing Serbia's international isolation and lifting the smothering economic sanctions. His personal international stature as an essential and agreeable negotiating partner was improving. The Bosnian Serbs were manageable, and he had avoided a military disaster in Bosnia. For Milosevic, the question was how much he could weaken a future Bosnian state in the negotiations and therefore retain Serbia's dominant influence over the Serbs in Bosnia.

In Sarajevo, Muslim leaders were troubled. They worried that they were paying a heavy price for agreeing to a cease-fire, even though the agreement meant that the siege of Sarajevo had been lifted. They wanted the NATO bombing to continue to allow Bosniak and Croatian forces on the ground to finish the job against the Serbs. They did not trust the international community. The UN had done little to stop the killing since the war had started. The Muslims had instead been hampered by arms embargos, which had restricted their ability to defend themselves. Their mistrust of Holbrooke was clear. They saw him as insufficiently committed to their cause, too close to Milosevic, and too willing to give away political structures important to a viable central government in Bosnia.

Further, the Bosniaks saw their Croatian partners in Bosnia as untrustworthy subordinates of the Tudjman government in Zagreb. From a Bosnian Muslim perspective, no one but them was interested in an independent Bosnia with a strong central government.

Zagreb was indeed focused on Croatian interests, including the conflict in Eastern Slavonia and the protection of Croatian equities in Bosnia. The Croats wanted the war to end so the country could develop normally. Europe and the United States needed Croatia to assist in reaching an agreement, and Tudjman saw an opportunity to use that leverage to Croatia's advantage. Like Milosevic, Tudjman was not supportive of a strong central government in Sarajevo. A weak Bosnia, independent of Serbia, was the best outcome for the Croats.

US objectives were straightforward: end the war and achieve a negotiated, comprehensive settlement that recognized Bosnia as a sovereign nation and provided for a Bosnian government based on Western democratic principles.

As Holbrooke moved the peace process forward, its structure was becoming unwieldy. He was encountering a bandwagon effect as more and more senior national leaders in Europe wanted a piece of the action when proximity talks became more likely. Holbrooke had more help than he wanted or needed.

10

The Last Shuttle

October 15–19, 1995

Holbrooke and the team had almost a full week in Washington before returning to the region for the last shuttle before the proximity talks. This gave us time to tidy up the details to ensure the process was moving on all fronts.

The administration had made a major decision. The proximity talks would be held at Wright-Patterson Air Force Base near Dayton, Ohio. Holbrooke, again influenced by Camp David, looked at several alternatives before settling on this base. The site needed to be large enough to accommodate five major delegations: the Bosniaks, the Serbs, the Croats, the Americans, and the Contact Group. Each of these delegations would bring with them various senior advisers and experts on the range of topics to be negotiated. Just the logistics of housing and feeding this number of delegates were considerable. The site had to be secure from threats, from the media, and from outside intrusion. And it had to be reasonably isolated to keep the parties from playing to their own constituencies while negotiating.

The State Department gave the task of finding and preparing the site to Assistant Secretary of State for Administration Patrick F. Kennedy. Holbrooke preferred a genteel setting as a comfortable venue for presidents, ministers, and international diplomats. Several locations were considered, including grand estates in New England, the Navy War College in Rhode Island, and high-end resorts. In the end, Kennedy convinced Holbrooke that Wright-Patterson Air Force Base was the best, most practical answer.

By now, we were comfortable with the shuttle, its independence, and the cast of characters in various capitals. In Washington, though, we were caught in the swirl of the big national policy apparatus with all its voices and interests. Getting away from Washington was a relief and a way to shape events on the move.

Holbrooke had become testy from the constant pressure, the expectations he had created, and the grand scope and complexity of what must be negotiated. He knew that serious procedural and substantive challenges were before him when the parties faced the reality of the issues to be decided.

Paris: October 15–16, 1995

The Quai d'Orsay, the French Foreign Ministry, was a splendid setting for the gathering of senior Contact Group representatives in Paris. The meeting room on the first floor of the ministry was a grand hall with red-satin wall covering, gilded mirrors, crystal chandeliers, and attendants in white tie and tails. Contact Group representatives were seated at a large table. Holbrooke and his team were on one side opposite senior diplomats from the United Kingdom, France, Germany, Italy, Russia, and the EU.

Holbrooke's message to them was in sharp contrast to the luxurious Paris venue. He struck a serious tone as he broke the news that the best place to hold proximity talks to end a war in Europe was a US Air Force base near a medium-size city in the heartland of the United States.

The representatives of the great powers of Europe appeared politely shocked.

Holbrooke touted the quality of the tennis courts, the bowling alley, and officers club at Wright-Patterson. They were going to love it, he assured them. It was a tough sell.

The venue for the talks was not the only topic of the meeting. Several countries wanted a piece of the action. Paris wanted to host a conference to sign any agreement reached at Dayton. The British wanted to host a reconstruction conference. Most troubling, Yeltsin wanted a meeting in Moscow before the parties convened in the United States. No one wished to offend Russia over a conference, and Paris and Berlin were particularly supportive of a Moscow meeting. In the end, Holbrooke decided to let leaders in Sarajevo, Belgrade, and Zagreb decide the fate of the Moscow proposal.

Moscow: October 16–17, 1995

Ambassador Thomas Pickering, among the most experienced career diplomats in the American Foreign Service at the time, met our plane when the team arrived in Moscow. Most of us had a night off in the Russian capital while Pickering took Holbrooke to a dinner with the Contact Group representatives. On the surface, Moscow appeared much more commercial than when I was last there in 1990—more colorful, more energetic.

The next day we met with the Contact Group members in the secure area of the British embassy to coordinate a common approach before meeting with the Russians. This meeting was difficult. Holbrooke wanted some ground rules, but the Europeans wanted more flexibility.

The full Contact Group meeting in the Russian Foreign Ministry, one of the massive Stalinist buildings dominating the Moscow skyline, was a major event for the Russians. Foreign Minister Andrey Kozyrev opened the session before a throng of media people. Once they were shooed away, Holbrooke laid out an aggressive agenda for the proximity talks.

The meeting decided that the Contact Group would be a part of the negotiations at Dayton. Bosnia was a European conflict, and European participation was essential to give continental legitimacy to the outcome and to gain support for the implementation that would follow any agreement.

With the Contact Group meeting out of the way, attention turned to the implementation forces and the Russians. The senior State Department policy expert on Russia, Deputy Secretary Strobe Talbott, and Undersecretary Walt Slocombe from DOD arrived to nail down the Russian participation in the NATO force in Bosnia.

The Russian General Staff was heavily represented in this meeting and was much more confrontational in the Russian approach to cooperating with NATO in Bosnia. But the Kremlin had made the policy decision, and the General Staff did not block progress in the end.

In Washington the next day, October 17, Secretaries Christopher and Perry told the Senate Armed Services Committee that the administration would deploy US troops to Bosnia with or without congressional support if an agreement were reached.[1]

Arkan's Tigers: Belgrade, Sarajevo, Zagreb, October 17–19, 1995

The team left Moscow for a stop in Belgrade before continuing to Zagreb. I tried without success to convince Holbrooke to spend the night in Sarajevo instead of in Zagreb. I counted around thirteen stops in Belgrade compared to a very few in Sarajevo, and this difference was having a negative impact on the Bosniaks' attitude toward Holbrooke and the negotiations.

At one point, Holbrooke and Milosevic broke away from the group for a private discussion. The next day at the hotel in Zagreb, Holbrooke told the team that during that conversation, the Serbian president had said that the reason that he did not have Karadzic killed was that it set a bad precedent for Serbian politics in the future. I thought to myself that Milosevic was thinking of his own security when he made that judgment.

Milosevic was disappointed about the decision to hold the talks at Wright-Patterson Air Force Base. He preferred a civilian venue. He still held to the fantasy of a White House meeting and insisted on meeting President Clinton as the talks started.

Any goodie, large or small, was leverage to Holbrooke. He constantly restocked his supply of leverage for the parties—everything from the invitation to a meeting to the lifting of sanctions. A meeting with an American president is leverage of the highest form, and Holbrooke would retain this one until the very end.

"That's possible only after an agreement is concluded," Holbrooke told Milosevic when the topic of a meeting with the US president came up.

Milosevic also argued for suspension of sanctions at the start of the conference and then a formal lifting of them when an agreement was reached. Holbrooke knew that economic sanctions were the ultimate leverage with Milosevic and would not accede to Milosevic's request. He also was aware that economic sanctions, once lifted, might be impossible to reimpose.

Holbrooke then raised with Milosevic the serious problem of "Arkan."

"You can expect no sympathy for sanctions relief with Arkan running around Bosnia committing atrocities," Holbrooke asserted.

"Arkan" was the Serbian nom de guerre of Zeljko Raznatovic, a career criminal who led a paramilitary force known as "Arkan's Tigers." It was the most vicious of the nationalist criminal bands operating in Bosnia and Croatia throughout the war.

Although the Serbs were largely complying with the terms of the cease-fire in Bosnia, Arkan and his Tigers, faces covered by balaclavas, conducted periodic forays into Bosnia, killing, raping, and generally plundering isolated Muslim communities. Izetbegovic and the government in Sarajevo increasingly complained about Arkan, demanding that Holbrooke and the international community do something to stop him.

Raznatovic had spent his youth in and out of jails in the Balkans and western Europe. At one point, he was on the Interpol list of the ten most-wanted criminals in Europe. He had developed ties to the Serbian Secret Services as a hit man for Yugoslavia in Europe in the 1970s. He had used those connections for protection of his growing criminal empire in Serbia.

Zeljko Raznatovic, known as "Arkan" (*center*), poses with masked members of Arkan's Tigers, a Serbian paramilitary group accused of war crimes in Bosnia, Croatia, and later Kosovo. (Associated Press)

After Milosevic came to power, Raznatovic had fit nicely into the corrupt structure that ruled Serbia.[2]

Milosevic's success in national elections gave his regime a semblance of legitimacy as a semidemocratic government. Extreme Serbian nationalism was his path to power, and he employed it liberally to generate public support for his leadership. He also ruled Serbia through a national hierarchy of corruption, patronage, and intimidation. Raznatovic was on the darkest fringe of this system, yet he did not hide in the shadows. The flamboyant Arkan was a visible man about town in Belgrade, with a mansion in an elite neighborhood of the city, an association with a national soccer club, and close ties to the Orthodox patriarch. He relished his public image and inflated his reputation as a patriotic Serbian hero among nationalist elements of society.

Arkan's wedding to popular celebrity Svetlana "Ceca" Velickovic, a sultry Serbian turbo folk singer twenty-one years his junior, was a national event in February 1995. The wedding began at dawn with automatic-weapons fire and lasted deep into the night. All events were videotaped and broadcast on national television as the couple changed into various national costumes for the separate events throughout the day. One Belgrade newspaper described Ceca's wedding dress at the formal matrimonial ceremony as "cocaine white."[3]

"This guy Arkan is out of control. He threatens thousands," Holbrooke said to Milosevic.

"No, I have checked it. Only volunteers are fighting. I will prosecute any criminals. I will not tolerate their acts, but others are doing this kind of thing—even worse. No one cares about the Serbs who are victims of terror," Milosevic said. "Arkan is a marginal issue. This is small compared to what Croatia has done. You are underevaluating the Nazis in Croatia. The question of Arkan is a marginal issue."

The Serbian president was trying to deflect our attention to the Croatian Ustashi fascists who had murdered hundreds of thousands of Serbs, Jews, and Roma while allied with Hitler in World War II.

Milosevic continued to push his top priority.

"Sanctions [on Serbia] are the most important question. We must have the suspension of sanctions before the conference. You can lift them on signature [of the agreement]."

After meeting with Milosevic, Holbrooke and the team made short stops in Sarajevo and Zagreb. In those discussions, Presidents Izetbegovic and Tudjman opposed a meeting in Moscow before Dayton, as Holbrooke expected. That meeting was dead.

We were very accustomed to the Serbian presidential palace, where we returned for yet another dinner meeting with Milosevic, this time to nail down preparations for the Dayton talks. Holbrooke invited Milosevic and his wife to arrive in New York a day or two before the talks in Ohio.

The Serbian president's wife, Mirjana Markovic, was a mystery to us. We had spent so much time with Milosevic in official and casual settings in the past few weeks, yet the Serbian contingent in these meetings always remained very small except when the Bosnian Serbs were present. We had never met Mrs. Milosevic despite several hints by Holbrooke that he would like to meet her.

Mirjana Markovic was committed to her husband. Their personal relationship went back to childhood, and she was a visible political activist in Belgrade in support of her husband during his presidency. She had impeccable Communist credentials. She was the illegitimate daughter of a wartime Communist partisan, and her aunt reportedly had been Tito's mistress. She had become a professor at Belgrade University as Milosevic worked his way up the ranks of the party. While Milosevic was president, Markovic wrote a column in a Communist weekly and was reported to be more authoritarian than her husband.[4]

Markovic did not accompany Milosevic to the United States. Holbrooke and the team never met her. After Milosevic's death in 2006, Markovic fled Serbia for exile in Russia and was later officially charged with murder in her home country.

Milosevic gave Holbrooke a letter accepting the invitation to participate in the conference, but with the condition that sanctions be suspended at the beginning of the conference.

The discussion then became a debate between sanctions relief and Arkan's activities in Bosnia. Milosevic said that Arkan could not be doing all that he was accused of doing in Bosnia. He launched into another comparison to "Nazis" in Croatia and atrocities by Bosnian Muslims against Serbs.

At one point, Holbrooke directed me to give a US paper on Arkan to Milosevic. I laid it on the table between us, but Milosevic never touched it.

"Serbia was not part of the war in Bosnia," Milosevic asserted.

I felt that Milosevic feared that this paper was another bit of evidence linking him to war crimes. The paper did not establish that link, but it was close enough to scare him. We left the paper on the table. The pressure worked. The following Monday, October 23, 1995, US information indicated that Arkan had pulled out of Bosnia.

A little more than four years later, in January 2000, a masked gunman shot Raznatovic in the left eye, killing him, in the lobby of the Intercontinental Hotel in Belgrade. More than 2,000 mourners attended his funeral.[5] It was widely believed but never proven that Milosevic or someone close to him had ordered the execution because Raznatovic knew too much about the war in Bosnia.[6]

The diplomatic shuttle phase of the negotiations to end the war in Bosnia was over. During the shuttle, Milosevic and Holbrooke had reached a personal accommodation. It was a relationship based not on trust or mutual respect but on the proven ability to deliver. They had come to know each other's personal characteristics, and both had demonstrated the ability to influence conditions that had the potential to achieve their respective interests. Theirs was a relationship based on pragmatism. Each man was betting he could maneuver the other to an acceptable outcome.

Final Preparations: Washington, DC, October 20–31, 1995

Washington was busy at all levels preparing for the proximity talks as the negotiating team returned from the last shuttle. The period leading to the opening of the peace conference on November 1 was spent refining constitutional and other documents for the parties to consider, developing US policy on sanctions relief for Serbia, and defining the US military mission for US participation in a future implementation force.

I decided to check out the preparation for the conference at Wright-Patterson Air Force Base. I heard much grumbling in Europe, and I was concerned about putting three national presidents, assorted ministers, and a gaggle of high-level international officials on an American air base, possibly for weeks. If the talks flopped, the delegations' accommodations should not be one of the excuses. Secretary Perry was also concerned and provided a plane for me to fly down on Saturday to check things out.

I discovered that Assistant Secretary of State Pat Kennedy and the air force had performed miracles at the base since the decision to hold the talks there. They were quickly converting Wright-Patterson into a functional venue. It would not meet European standards for high diplomacy, but it was practical and should get the job done.

Two security zones surrounded the negotiating venue, one the outer perimeter of the air base itself and a second fenced zone that would contain the figures involved in the talks. Security was heavy, and special passes would be required for the delegations inside the negotiating zone.

Kennedy and the air force transformed the Hope Center, a large conference facility at the air base, into the central negotiating venue for group discussions, meetings, and press conferences. The main conference center contained a sports bar named "Packy's," which would be the cafeteria-style dining facility for the delegations, presidents and all.

Near the Hope Center, four bachelor officer quarters located inside the secure area around a large parking lot were converted into billeting for the delegations: one building each for the Serbs, Croats, Bosniaks, and the American delegation. The Contact Group and EU representatives shared a fifth set of quarters nearby.

Each set of quarters contained rooms with a private bath, minibar, and TV. In each building, two rooms on the ground floor were combined into a suite for the president or head of delegation. Kennedy rented comfortable furniture for the presidential suites from venders in Dayton.

I reported back to Secretary Perry that the accommodations were not grand but would do. While I was visiting facilities at Wright-Patterson, the Principals Committee was considering suspension of sanctions on the opening of the conference, as Milosevic requested. Despite Holbrooke's preliminary opposition in Belgrade, Milosevic had finally convinced him that sanctions should be suspended on the opening of the conference at Dayton.

The US national security leadership met often in the Situation Room in the West Wing of the White House in the days leading up to the Dayton negotiations. Three issues dominated the discussion: whether to suspend sanctions against Serbia on the opening of the talks, as Milosevic wished; the nature of Russian military participation in a post-settlement international military force; and the US military role in the implementation and stabilization force.

A series of Deputies Committee and Principals Committee meetings starting on October 24 flip-flopped on the issue of suspending the sanctions at the opening of the talks. Finally, the Principals meeting on Friday, October 27, decided to retain economic sanctions on Serbia until the parties completed an agreement.

Cold War Heresy

Moscow continued to struggle with the radical idea of participating in a military mission with NATO. Cooperating with NATO was heresy for the conservative Russian Armed Forces.

Four years earlier, in 1991, after a failed coup against Gorbachev, his senior military adviser, General Sergei F. Akhromeyev, marshall of the Soviet Union and former chief of the Soviet, had hanged himself from the ceiling of his Kremlin office. A veteran of Stalingrad who had known nothing but the Soviet system in his life, Akhromeyev had left behind a note that read, "Everything I have worked for is being destroyed."[7]

He represented an institution of leaders who had been taught their entire lives that the United States and NATO were intent on destroying the Soviet Union and their way of life. Now Yeltsin was asking them to cooperate fully with the armed forces of their sworn enemy. Yeltsin, like Gorbachev in 1991, survived an attempted coup in 1993. For the moment, civilian control of the Russian military was holding, but Yeltsin and his people must have known that Russia's armed forces were under tremendous stress.

Yeltsin saw improved relations with the United States and the countries of central Europe as critical for the development of a new Russia. Russian cooperation with the Contact Group and NATO in Bosnia was a manifestation of that vision.

The Perry–Grachev meeting in Geneva on October 8 established the Russian agreement to participate in a NATO force deployed to Bosnia in conjunction with a peace agreement. A series of meetings with Deputy Secretary of State Talbott, Undersecretary of Defense Slocombe, and Lieutenant General Clark in Moscow carried the discussion further.

A summit between Presidents Clinton and Yeltsin at Hyde Park, New York, completed the decision on Russian participation. Yeltsin still wanted a preconference meeting in Moscow, and he wanted to ensure that Russian pride would not be offended in the deployment to Bosnia. Soviet experts in the United States maintained their own wariness of Russian intentions and resisted a larger Russian participation. Yeltsin finally agreed to a smaller deployment to Bosnia than he originally wanted. The summit, however, avoided the troubling issue of command and control of Russian forces in the NATO force.

At week's end, Secretary Perry and Minister Grachev formally agreed on the level of Russian participation in the NATO force in Bosnia. Russia would deploy "special-operations units" that would perform engineering, transportation, and construction missions throughout Bosnia. Russia ultimately accepted a compromise that created a parallel chain of military command for NATO and Russian forces in Bosnia. The SACEUR was the overall commander. However, a Russian general officer and a headquarters staff were collocated with the NATO military command in Belgium. Through this headquarters, Russia maintained national operational control of Russian troops on the ground in Bosnia in coordination with NATO activities there. The arrangement worked adequately for both sides during the Russian military presence in Bosnia.[8]

Resistance at Home

Completing arrangements for the Russian military relationship with NATO in Bosnia was easier for the US administration than arranging to deploy US forces. Military leaders in the Pentagon and Republicans in Congress continued to resist the commitment of US military forces to Bosnia, and briefings by Secretaries Christopher and Perry were difficult.

The relationship between the US military leaders and their commander in chief was an added difficulty. Senior military leaders were not particularly warm to President Clinton, nor was the president very comfortable with them. Further, the senior flag officers in the Pentagon continued to resist the use of US troops in what they perceived to be a messy civil war. They also wanted to avoid peacekeeping and nation-building commitments.

Strained Command Relationships

US military leaders were wary of the Clinton administration after a series of incidents shortly after they took office. Clinton's first secretary of defense, Les Aspin, with little or no consultation with senior military officers, announced soon after he took office that DOD would drop the long-standing prohibition of homosexuals in the US military. The Aspin declaration, overturning centuries of legal standing and tradition in the military, came as a shock to the services and their leaders in uniform.

Anyone who served for any time in the US Armed Forces knew that gays served honorably in virtually every organization, but Aspin's announcement created a political storm.

General Colin Powell, CJCS in 1993, brokered a compromise based on an unwritten understanding that had existed since the military services were founded—the "Don't ask, don't tell" policy—which got the administration off the hook, but the damage to the relationship between the White House and military leaders was done.

At about the same time, a public controversy broke out when the media reported that one of America's most decorated generals from the Vietnam War, Lieutenant General Barry R. McCaffrey, had been insulted by a member of the White House staff.[9] Subsequently, Secretary Aspin's opposition to the military request for tanks to be deployed to Mogadishu, Somalia,[10] and the "Blackhawk down" debacle further strained military leaders' confidence in the new administration and made them suspicious of anything but the most straightforward and conventional military commitments.

Vietnam's Legacy

The specter of Vietnam also affected US policy toward Bosnia. The leaders who directed US diplomatic and military policy in 1995 were members of the Vietnam generation. They had seen the negative consequences of decisions to use force in Vietnam: severe damage to a president's legacy, public hostility to the military as an institution, the human and financial costs to the nation, and the harm done to the readiness of US forces.

Virtually every senior military officer in a position of authority in Washington in 1995 was a Vietnam veteran. They all had experienced firsthand the war's devastating effect on US military capability. Most of them had been involved in the lengthy process of restoring the strength and character of the military after Vietnam. None of them wanted to repeat any aspect of that experience, certainly not on their watch.

As a Vietnam veteran, I, too, had early doubts that the Balkans were worthy of serious US military engagement. But by 1995 I was convinced that US leadership in Europe, US security interests in the Balkans, and the US commitment to human rights and dignity were important enough to warrant a direct and significant US military commitment to end a humanitarian disaster and restore stability to the region.

On October 30, just before the parties gathered at Dayton, the US House of Representatives passed a nonbinding resolution warning the administration not to deploy troops to Bosnia without congressional approval.[11]

The Volunteer Military

Bosnia in early 1995 was a political and moral dilemma for the Clinton administration as it continued to avoid direct engagement on the ground to stop the agonizing humanitarian disaster unfolding in Europe. Committing US forces to Bosnia should not have been as difficult for the administration as it turned out to be.

The decision to deploy US combat forces abroad carried less political risk for a president after the United States abandoned compulsory military service in response to the public reaction to the Vietnam War. By ending selective-service conscription in 1973 in favor of the all-volunteer force, the government lifted much of the direct public burden of military deployment. American society, except for volunteers and their families, was removed from the direct sacrifices and costs of combat operations. Gone were the large public demonstrations of the 1960s and early 1970s opposing a war waged by an army of draftees. With the end of the draft, presidents committed US forces to combat operations in Grenada, Panama, the Persian Gulf, and Somalia without serious public controversy.

In the wars in Iraq and Afghanistan after September 11, 2001, the George W. Bush administration, through tax cuts and a reliance on volunteer military forces, further shielded the general public from the immediate costs and consequences of war. The most privileged in society were less willing to serve and resistant to paying for the costs of war. Except for military volunteers in the combat zone and their families, life went on undisturbed for most Americans.

The volunteer military is more professional and more capable than the conscript force, but it has major limitations. The all-volunteer force is more expensive and therefore smaller and more reliant on civilian contractors. It was adequate for modest missions such as Bosnia and Kosovo, but the wars in Iraq and Afghanistan years later showed that it was not of sufficient size to sustain even medium-scale operations.

The dangers to US national security caused by the isolation of American society from military experience and sacrifice are serious. Fewer American leaders in positions of authority have any personal military experience. Those who do not understand the pain and uncertainty of war are more likely to favor it, but war without consequences—often unintended—is a fantasy.

Some type of automatic benchmarks set in law to trigger taxes to pay for military operations or to activate the selective service might help avoid these dangers. But implementing such measures would require a level of political will not present today in or out of government.

The growing momentum in Washington policy debates toward the deployment of US troops to Bosnia was wearing down military resistance. Holbrooke and the team saw the replacement of the discredited UNPRO-FOR by a capable NATO force with US participation as critical to implementation of any peace agreement. The Europeans wanted US participation and knew that NATO was the mechanism to achieve that goal. The parties to the negotiations, including Milosevic, wanted US troops on the ground in Bosnia as well. NATO leaders in Brussels had approved a concept for an implementation force, and even Russia was committed to participating.

Lieutenant General Wes Clark was the point man for defining the military role in Bosnia within the Holbrooke team, but Holbrooke took a personal interest in the subject. Prior to the opening of the Dayton negotiation, the Deputies Committee debated the military annex on October 24, as did the Principals Committee on October 25 and 27 and the NSC offsite at Warrenton, Virginia, on October 26.

Tension in these debates was high between the White House, the Pentagon, the State Department, and Holbrooke. The US envoy wanted the NATO force to take a more robust posture throughout Bosnia, but the military continually pushed to limit the mission and the scope of the operation.

If the US military had to go to Bosnia, the Joint Chiefs wanted a clear mission statement, precise rules of engagement, achievable objectives, and an exit strategy. They insisted that the negotiating parties agree to suitable military conditions as part of the settlement. Therefore, much time between the last shuttle trip to the region and the opening of the proximity talks at Dayton was spent drafting a military annex to a settlement agreement that would satisfy US and NATO military requirements for a future NATO force in Bosnia.

The administration still had serious work to do with the Pentagon and the Republican Congress. Otherwise, the only thing missing was a peace agreement.

Trick or Treat

Holbrooke did not have a final plan for the talks and was thinking through just how to handle them before we arrived at Dayton. I pushed for early map discussions below the level of the presidents, but Holbrooke was concerned about the volatile nature of any territorial talks and fearful that they might derail other areas of discussion. He was right.

Midmorning on October 31, we joined President Clinton, Vice President Gore, and members of the NSC, who were seated around the large oval mahogany table in the Cabinet Room of the West Wing overlooking the rose garden. A painting of a young George Washington by Rembrandt Peale and another painting of Theodore Roosevelt overlooked the discussion.

US negotiating team at the White House before departing for the Bosnia peace negotiations at Wright-Patterson Air Force Base, Dayton, Ohio. *Left to right:* Christopher Hill, Brigadier General Donald Kerrick, Lieutenant General Wesley Clark, Richard Holbrooke, President Bill Clinton, Vice President Al Gore, James Pardew, and Roberts Owen. (William J. Clinton Presidential Library)

President Clinton assessed the situation and issued guidance to the negotiating team.

"Congress would vote against us if a vote were held today. A successful agreement will change their attitude," he said. "There should be no mission creep, and you must have an exit strategy for [US forces deployed to Bosnia], but it [the mission] must deal with human rights violations and attacks on UN elements. Do not be tied to a time deadline in the negotiations. An intermediate agreement may be acceptable. Do not divide Sarajevo."

"We should not suspend sanctions on Serbia until we have an iron-clad agreement," Vice President Gore added. I had never met the vice president before and noted that he was a more powerful presence in the meeting than I expected.

The meeting concluded with a discussion of the venue for signing the agreement. Holbrooke proposed that any agreement should be signed in Paris to ensure Contact Group recognition and support.

After the morning excitement, we left the White House for Andrews and the flight to Wright-Patterson, where the conference would open the following day. The presidents of Serbia, Bosnia, and Croatia and their delegations were also arriving for the conference.

Holbrooke took Milosevic to Packy's for dinner that evening at Wright-Patterson. It was Halloween, and the Dayton peace talks were about to start. Trick or treat?

Part 2

Bosnia
The Dayton Agreement

The Old Bridge, Mostar, Bosnia-Herzegovina. (Shutterstock.com)

11

High Stakes in Ohio

Richard Holbrooke carried the burden of success or failure of the Dayton talks. Others contributed, but Holbrooke was the ringmaster, and he liked a disorderly and stressful show. In disorder and pressure, he found opportunity.

Success was no sure bet as the parties gathered for the twenty-one days of negotiations in the fenced compound inside Wright-Patterson Air Force Base near Dayton, Ohio. Proximity talks between heads of state and international negotiators are very high-risk endeavors, especially when they are as concentrated, isolated, and open-ended as they were at Dayton. The Dayton talks carried no guarantee of success, but failure to achieve a settlement would damage everyone involved and might well return Bosnia to war. Holbrooke saw the gathering as "a high-wire act without a net."[1]

The stakes were great in every camp. For the three presidents at Dayton, the talks would define the future of their countries and their personal place in their national history. The White House had put the reputation of the Clinton administration on the line by sponsoring the talks in the United States. NATO and the US military had large equities in the outcome of the talks. In Europe, the governments represented in the Contact Group had invested heavily in the entire international effort in Bosnia, but without success so far. The Europeans wanted no part of another failed effort to bring peace to Bosnia. Russia, too, wanted to be a contributing partner in a successful diplomatic effort with the United States and western Europe.

Holbrooke directed multiple layers of negotiations, many taking place at the same time. The three Balkan presidents—Milosevic, Tudjman, and Izetbegovic—brought a flock of advisers, experts, and lawyers to assist them in the negotiations. The European representatives wanted a say in the details of the negotiations. Finally, with the US administration's reputation at stake, the national security and foreign-policy establishments in Washington demanded input on important decisions.

Richard Holbrooke meets President of Serbia Slobodan Milosevic as Milosevic arrives for the peace talks at Wright-Patterson Air Force Base, Ohio, to end the war in Bosnia. (Associated Press)

The Dayton talks were the dominant event on the international agenda. Tensions were high among participants, and tempers frequently flared throughout. Holbrooke, as the senior negotiator, had to maintain order to keep the process from unraveling. But he faced auxiliary issues, such as the Serbs' holding of an American journalist in Bosnia and the ICTY's demands. Because of these competing pressures, Holbrooke was always in triage mode with respect to his time, energy, and attention.

To help him, Holbrooke had the full support of the State Department's foreign-policy and legal expertise. Several US ambassadors from the region, senior officials, and staff in the legal and specialized bureaus at State were present or on call to assist as needed.

The Dayton negotiations had a complicated agenda. The talks considered a range of proposals to create the structure, territory, and procedures for a new country. The negotiations involved a constitution for Bosnia, territorial boundaries, elections, refugee returns, the nature and authority of the international military force, NATO's status of forces, international police activities, and more.

In several cases, the size and scope of the proposed agreements overwhelmed the parties. Their leaders focused on the issues they cared most about: territory, in particular the status of Sarajevo and Eastern Slavonia, and the structure and authority of the future governments of Bosnia. Other proposals were left for subordinates to consider.

The negotiating process was hectic. Holbrooke allocated the various areas for negotiation to his primary team members, with support from Washington.

My job was the map. The external national boundary of Bosnia was not contested. The territorial problem to be resolved was the internal boundary between the Federation and the Republika Srpska within Bosnia. As an associated task, Holbrooke made me the US handler for the Bosnian Serb delegation. I engaged them often, but Milosevic had cut them out of substantive discussions. Mark Sawoski, a political appointee serving as a staff officer in DOD, joined me at Dayton to help with my tasks. Lieutenant General Clark was involved in the map, but he also focused on the military annex of the proposed agreement. Roberts Owen, Chris Hill, and Don Kerrick handled the constitutional, political, and policy aspects of the agreement.

Holbrooke planned for the negotiations at Dayton to consist of simultaneous discussions on a range on issues—all under US control. He wanted to keep the delegations separated for talks except when essential.

Holbrooke needed the Contact Group but wanted its representation small. The presence of senior representatives of the Contract Group and the EU, acting as advisers to the process, added legitimacy to the talks. Carl Bildt of Sweden had engaged in Bosnia as the EU special envoy for some time. Other senior Europeans at Dayton were career diplomats Pauline Neville-Jones, political director of the UK Foreign and Commonwealth Office; Jacques Blot, political director of the French Foreign Ministry; Wolfgang Ischinger, political director of the German Foreign Ministry; and Igor Ivanov, first deputy foreign minister of the Russian Federation.

The governments of each of the Contact Group delegations at Dayton expected their representatives to provide direct input into the process and to produce timely reporting on the progress of the negotiations. Their position was difficult. As the senior negotiator, Holbrooke tried to keep them informed and involved without creating disruptions in an already unwieldy negotiating structure. But they were rarely his top priority. As career diplomats, they generally understood the dilemma and tried to be helpful without disruptive intrusion. In some cases, their intervention was important. In others, their frustration with Holbrooke rose to the surface.

Meetings on various subjects and levels took place day and night. Holbrooke normally held a morning staff meeting with his augmented team. He occasionally called the staff together in the evening or when events required deliberations or guidance. Meanwhile, the parties and the Europeans would bring forth their own proposals for consideration. Holbrooke personally concentrated on the critical negotiating authorities at the talks—the Balkan presidents and Washington—and on the steady stream of high-level visitors to the negotiations. He engaged in the process tirelessly. By the last week, he was exhausted.

Holbrooke again was careful to control the flow of public information. He extracted a commitment from the parties not to negotiate through the media because use of the public media by one or more of the parties could disrupt sensitive points. The State Department set up a press center for the media, where its spokesman, Nicholas Burns, issued daily statements from the talks. The parties agreed that they would not independently report to the media but would go through the press center. For the most part, this arrangement held up.

Just prior to the opening of the talks in Ohio, the *New York Times* and the *Washington Post* ran extensive accounts of Serbian atrocities in Bosnia in their Sunday editions on October 29.[2]

Opening the Proximity Talks: November 1, 1995

Milosevic brought an important new personality to the talks: Jovica Stanisic, head of the State Security Service in the Serbian Ministry of Interior, arrived at Dayton with the Serb delegation. Stanisic had never attended any meetings with Milosevic in Serbia during the shuttle negotiations, but at Dayton he was a key figure in the Serbian delegation. He had a quiet, unobtrusive manner yet an air of authority. At Dayton, Milosevic used him to monitor the Bosnian Serb delegation, and his presence at meetings intimidated them.

You would never notice Stanisic in a room full of midcareer accountants, yet I felt that he knew the darkest Serbian secrets of the war in Bosnia. The State Security Service, led by Stanisic, was linked to special Serbian units and the vicious paramilitary groups fighting in Bosnia,[3] and it had the clandestine means to secretly funnel funds, equipment, and other support to the Bosnian Serbs. Although the evidence for this connection was mostly circumstantial, I suspected that Stanisic was the essential link between Milosevic and the atrocities committed by paramilitary forces such as Arkan's Tigers during the war.

Milosevic had to contend with the Bosnian Serbs accredited to his delegation. As arranged, two men indicted for war crimes, Radovan Karadzic and General Ratko Mladic, stayed in Bosnia. I was the handler of the Bosnian Serbs at Dayton, so my group of isolated and unhappy campers included Momcilo Krajisnik, head of the Bosnian contingent within the Serbian delegation; the meek little professor Vice President Nikola Koljevic; "Foreign Minister" Aleksa Buha; General Zdravko Tolimir; and Jovan Zamititsa, a particularly vitriolic little man who was the Bosnian Serb propaganda chief. Milosevic isolated the Bosnian Serbs in a set of rooms on the second floor of the Serb delegation building and cut them off from information as the negotiations progressed.

Secretary of State Warren Christopher and the European representatives opened the conference with public statements, after which the three Balkan presidents performed the symbolic handshake for the cameras. As an early sign of a conflict to come, protesters outside the negotiating venue demanded independence of Kosovo from Serbia.[4]

In a bilateral meeting with Secretary Christopher after the opening ceremony, Milosevic was testy. He bemoaned the damage done to Serbia by the sanctions. He groused about the recent American press reports on Srebrenica. He complained that his opening speech in English had not been broadcast by the media. Finally, he threatened to leave if Croatian president Tudjman departed the talks.

As usual, the Croatians set forth straightforward objectives and were better organized for the talks. They exploited the American need for their participation in the talks to get their primary issue—Eastern Slavonia—on the table. After a few days, Tudjman left the conference to his foreign and defense ministers and their experts, but not until after he and Milosevic engaged in heated face-to-face arguments.

Within the Bosniak delegation, some, Izetbegovic among them, had little inclination to compromise. Izetbegovic became especially difficult when Milosevic and Tudjman tried to bully him, as they did in direct meetings. His group was fragmented by independent senior advisers, each vying for prominence in the Bosniak delegation and for dominance of his own position on the various issues.

The Bosniaks were unified in one consistent demand on the Americans. As a condition for an agreement at Dayton, they expected the United States to assist them with arming and training a future army that would enable them to defend against the kind of military attacks they had endured over the past four years. They knew the US Congress supported them, and they demanded American military assistance on the completion of a peace deal. This issue became extremely challenging as the negotiations proceeded—not with the Serbs or Croats, oddly enough, but with the US military.

Generally, face-to-face talks between the Balkan presidents degenerated into verbal fireworks and made no negotiating progress. They could be collegial on occasion, but they often launched into angry attacks. When their teams or the other negotiators were present to give them an audience, the debate was especially hostile. In the proximity talks, as in the shuttles, progress usually was achieved when the international negotiators met separately with delegation leaders.

I spent the first few days trying to extract territorial positions from the parties. Control of territory and the status of NATO military forces in Bosnia after an agreement were the most difficult issues at Dayton. These issues would take the negotiation to the edge of collapse on multiple occasions.

The territorial debate focused on several points:

1. The status and control of Sarajevo.
2. The nature of the internal boundary between the Republika Srpska and the Federation. This boundary had several subordinate issues. The first was the requirement to meet the 51 percent Federation, 49 percent Republika Srpska territorial split. The second was the width of the northern territory along the Bosnian border with Croatia. Federation access to Gorazde and other Muslim enclaves in eastern Bosnia was a third problem.
3. The status of the multiethnic town Brcko on the Sava River, separating Bosnia and Croatia in the North.

The most challenging military issues were the size, authority, and status of the NATO security force as well as the separation of the combatants in Bosnia.

"Boogie Woogie Bugle Boy": November 3, 1995

The opening dinner for the delegations, hosted by the United States at the Air Force Museum in the first days at Dayton, was one of the most surreal events of the negotiations. The United States had selected Wright-Patterson Air Force Base as the venue for the negotiations for purely practical considerations. But after the NATO air campaign in Bosnia, the parties and the Europeans were not so sure the Americans were not sending a message with the location.

The National Museum of the Air Force outside the base contained a collection of aircraft and weapons from across the history of military aviation in the United States, presented on the level of the National Air and Space Museum in Washington, DC. On arrival at the museum, delegates to the negotiations were greeted with cocktails and a tour of the museum's collection before they were seated for dinner. A string quartet played as guests gathered at tables in one of the museum's great halls. The hall displayed a variety of combat aircraft and cruise missiles around the floor or dangling from the ceiling.

Several spouses of US team members attended the dinner, including Holbrooke's wife, Kati, who was seated between Milosevic and Izetbegovic. Milosevic and other presidents dined beneath a B-52 bomber and in sight of a cruise missile. The seating arrangement was not lost on the attendees. After dinner, an air force band and singers in period uniforms entertained with "Boogie Woogie Bugle Boy" and other music from the World War II era.

I do not know if Holbrooke had picked the museum as the site for the dinner because it was an interesting setting or because it served as a less than subtle message to the parties. But most of the attendees saw the dinner's setting as a raw expression of US military power.

Spinning in Place: Week One, November 1–7, 1995

The first several days of talks showed just how difficult the negotiations would be. As the delegations settled into their quarters, the US staff issued draft negotiating documents, and the parties held preliminary meetings. But no results were produced on two essential questions—territory and the status of international military forces.

The Bosniak delegation members held any map discussion hostage to their demand to work out a suitable arrangement between themselves and the Croats inside the Federation. The Croatians conditioned everything on their demand to negotiate the Eastern Slavonia issue at Dayton.

The Pentagon had specific language it wanted in the military annex. The Serbs could not accept the proposed NATO mandate and status of forces. Belgrade and Pale wanted a small NATO force with a weak authority, like the one they had with UNPROFOR. The Pentagon and Brussels would approve no such arrangement and insisted on specific language in the military annex to the negotiating document. The US generals also wanted to minimize the possible expansion of their carefully defined tasks, a process known as "mission creep."

"Next Halloween I'm going to dress up as a mission creep," a frustrated Holbrooke said.

President Clinton had made the decision to provide equipment and training to the Bosnian military. The decision was a bilateral commitment, not discussed with the other parties or the Europeans. Holbrooke decided not to include this incendiary topic in the negotiations.

If the US military leadership was disenchanted with the concept of going to Bosnia to secure the implementation of a peace deal, they were in quiet rebellion at any hint of US troops arming and training the Bosnian Muslim military. Rumors came from the White House staff that two members of the Joint Chiefs of Staff had threatened to go public in their opposition to the arm-and-train program for the Bosnians if they were required to participate in the program. The US military remained hostile to this commitment for the entire period of the US deployment to Bosnia, although they were unable to stop it.

The early optimism about the negotiations began to fade as progress stalled. I started the territorial discussion with a meeting at the delegations' staff level. Mark Sawoski and I learned very quickly that territory was too important to discuss below the most senior delegation level. Holbrooke tried direct private talks on territory between the regional presidents. But in the early stages at Dayton, these private sessions produced no progress either.

After I examined map options with the Serbs for two days, they agreed on a position to present to the Bosniaks. The Bosnian Serb proposal was nothing new: Sarajevo was to be a divided city; the Serbs would control the airport and a wide corridor in Serb territory in the North (Posavina Corridor). The Federation would have limited access to Gorazde, the former UN safe area in the East, and some areas on the margins of the internal Republika Srpska boundary.

I held off the Europeans, who were very curious about the progress on territory, when they pressed for participation in the map discussions. More parties in these talks would have made the discussions even more difficult, and, frankly, nothing of significance was happening anyway.

I knew that the Serbian proposal would not be acceptable to the Bosniaks, but we were looking for a starting point to explore options and potential ideas for compromise. The Bosniaks exploded when I presented the proposal to them. Their delegation never got past a divided Sarajevo. I carried the Bosniak rejection back to the Serbs, who tinkered with their proposal but made no substantive changes to it.

The future status of Sarajevo was the nuclear issue for the Bosnian Serbs in the territorial discussions. They wanted the city divided physically between Federation and Serb control, like Berlin during the Cold War. Izetbegovic would not accept any plan that did not place Sarajevo in Federation territory. We began looking for ideas. The Europeans liked the concept of Sarajevo as a federal city, like Washington, DC, or Brussels, but when Holbrooke broached the idea with Milosevic, he rejected it immediately. Holbrooke then decided to set the territorial discussions aside for a while.

As the pressure on him to deliver increased, Holbrooke's frustration with Washington was also on the rise. Meddling by those in Washington with equities in the talks was a constant distraction. They wanted to influence the talks but could not understand the dynamics or keep up with the events as they took place.

A Grinding Frustration: Week Two, November 8–14

The Bosniaks came forward with their own map proposal, and Holbrooke decided to convene a joint meeting with the Serbs to discuss territory. In that meeting, Milosevic provoked the group by drawing his own interior boundary for consideration. The conversation quickly turned to Sarajevo. Krajisnik again proposed to split control of the city between the two parties. Tempers flared. Holbrooke fell back on the federal city proposal.

Emotional outbursts turned the discussion into a disaster. After a break, Holbrooke blasted the parties for their inflexibility. Milosevic departed, leaving Krajisnik to speak for the Serbs. In a few minutes, a fed-up Holbrooke also left. I kept things going for another thirty minutes, but it was a waste of time.

Two new elements appeared on the scene in the second week. The first was Richard N. Perle, the controversial conservative specialist in US national security, who arrived to provide badly needed negotiating advice to the Bosnian Muslim delegation. The second was a team from the US Defense Mapping Agency, which came with technical and graphic equipment to help us render detailed terrain aspects of the negotiation.

Perle's appearance elevated the credibility of the Bosniak input at Dayton and in Washington. Perle was one of several Americans who served as informal advisers to the Bosniak delegation, but he was a special case, having made his reputation in strategic-arms-control debates. I was aware of him only superficially, but I would come to know him well in the next two years. Holbrooke referred to him at Dayton as the "Prince of Darkness," which seemed to fit Perle's physical appearance, demeanor, and assertive approach to negotiating.

Perle concentrated on the draft military annex to the agreement, a document deeply important to the US and allied governments. The Bosniaks had no negotiating capacity to adequately address military subjects, but Perle immediately reversed that condition. The negotiations on military issues were suddenly caught between the negotiators, the parties, NATO, Congress, the White House, and Richard Perle. This was a tough place to be.

The Defense Mapping Agency could produce detailed maps quickly. It also brought the technical means to electronically adjust the interior boundary between the Federation and the Republika Srpska as proposals were put forth. It could help find the agreed 51/49 percent territorial split. The Serbs and the Bosniaks were at first skeptical of the Mapping Agency process, but after a while they accepted the system's output.

With the technical ability to produce maps quickly, the exchange of map proposals was happening at a faster rate. Finally, late one evening, after a day of back and forth, I took a map to Izetbegovic for consideration. It produced another verbal tongue lashing from the Bosniak president and another complete rejection. Ten days into the talks, I felt that we had never had a serious, sustained map discussion that could lead to a compromise arrangement. Holbrooke was not concerned. He saw the Bosniak position as pure theater.

As the Dayton talks moved in circles, the assassination of Itzak Rabin in Israel days earlier by a religious zealot opposed to Rabin's peace initiatives had shocked Milosevic.

"You have your professional reputations at stake here. If I do as I am willing to do—give away key Serb suburbs around Sarajevo—they [the Bosnian Serb nationalists] will try to kill me," Milosevic said to Clark, Kerrick, and me on November 10. "They will try to kill me, I know it. What is at risk for me is my head."

Secretary of State Christopher returned to Dayton on November 10. Holbrooke had been using Christopher's return to press the parties to show progress. The Christopher effect worked on two issues: the Muslims and Croats agreed on the Federation structure in Bosnia, and the Serbs and the Croats reached an agreement on Eastern Slavonia. Yet the parties made no progress on the core issues for Bosnia.

Holbrooke privately warned his boss that success may not be achievable. "We need to face the reality that we may only get an interim agreement on Bosnia here," he confided to Christopher.

Clark was frustrated with the map discussion and decided to take over the process. Holbrooke had warned me not to clash with Clark, and I stepped aside. But the Clark effort fizzled, too.

The Bosniaks realized that their rigid position was producing nothing, so Izetbegovic presented the US delegation with the first serious proposal from their delegation. In their plan, the Bosniaks gave up to the Serbs the enclaves in Srebrenica and Zepa and some areas near Sarajevo and inside their area of control. They considered the idea to let NATO control Brcko in the North for a time. But Clark immediately opposed that idea as an expansion of the military mission.

We were nowhere on territory. The process had become a grinding frustration.

The Europeans were fuming. In a difficult meeting where they were updated on the status of territorial talks, they criticized the process and agitated about being outside the map deliberations. I offered maps and pens for their suggested solutions to our dilemma. I had no takers.

"Do Not Worry, Mrs. Pardew"

Personal commitments at home prevented Kathy from attending the dinners with the presidents at Dayton. I did not care about the other personalities, but I wanted my wife to meet Milosevic. She should see what kind of man could launch and sanction the savagery seen in Bosnia. I opted not to tell Holbrooke. Instead, I made an appointment to call on the Serbian president directly through Goran Milinovic, the chief of his cabinet.

Milosevic was gracious, as I expected. During the conversation, we mentioned that our son, Paul, a captain in the US Army, was preparing to deploy to Bosnia.

"Our son, Paul, is going to Bosnia with the US Army if an agreement is reached. I want him to be safe," Kathy said.

"Do not worry, Mrs. Pardew," Milosevic said. "Your son should bring his skis to enjoy the winter snow in Bosnia. There will be no problems."

Holbrooke suddenly entered the suite and interrupted the conversation. When the surprised senior American diplomat gave me a harsh look, we said our farewell and left.

After that meeting, my relationship with Milosevic was more personal and cordial. Milosevic began to call me "Jim." He later mentioned the meeting to others, especially to visiting US and NATO generals and defense officials. The next day Milosevic dispatched Goran to our room in the US delegation to present Kathy with a note and an engraved fountain pen as a token of her visit. Holbrooke was initially upset by my independent decision to call on Milosevic, but he later told me that Milosevic was touched by the visit. Holbrooke later found ways to use my newfound personal relationship in diplomatic activities.

Map Day

President Izetbegovic declared Sunday, November 12, "Map Day" and gave us a new map only minimally adjusted from the one previously rejected by the Serbs. Milosevic reviewed the Bosniak map and modified it. The Bosniaks immediately rejected Milosevic's proposal even though it contained a significant change from previous Serb offers—a road connecting the Federation territory to the eastern enclave of Gorazde. "Map Day," like so many others, flamed out.

Holbrooke needed leverage with the Bosniaks and presented a reconstruction finance package, including $500 million of US funding. The package seemed to increase their negotiating flexibility at least temporarily. The positive atmosphere did not last long, though.

Richard Perle, by then deep into the details, had heavily marked up the military annex of the draft agreement in areas the Joint Staff considered sacred. I told Holbrooke that these changes were so serious that they must go back to Washington for review. He agreed and tasked me with getting the annex into shape for presentation.

12

Get an Agreement or Shut It Down

Week Three, November 14–22

Warren Christopher stopped at Dayton early on November 14 before continuing to Japan. The secretary of state would come back to the talks when he returned from Asia at the end of the week. The message to Holbrooke was short and clear: "Get initials on an agreement or close down the talks," Christopher told the US negotiator. Washington was willing to give the process one more week.

After fourteen days of isolated negotiations, agreement seemed beyond reach. The talks yielded progress on some issues, but the basic problems with territory and the military annex remained stuck. The map seemed impossible. The parties' positions had moved very little since the first day. Still not resolved were the control of Sarajevo, the percentage differences in territory as defined by the boundary between the Federation and the Republika Srpska, the status of Brcko, and the width of the northern corridor in Serbian territory.

Holbrooke was feeling the pressure. He deployed all the negotiating leverage he had, and he presented the best compromise solutions he and the team could conjure up. But success eluded him on vital points. He also knew that he could not keep this massive, high-profile international operation going much longer without a deal.

The stress of the talks was taking its toll on everyone. The older Izetbegovic was especially showing the strain. One factor for the US team to consider was how much to stress the Bosniaks without causing a collapse of the talks. The negotiations were no longer a matter of substance. Adequate compromise solutions were available on every issue. The parties simply lacked the will to a reach a settlement. Only courage or fear would break the deadlock.

Bosnian Serb vice president Nikola Koljevic, whom I had been avoiding for days, caught me in my room to complain that Milosevic had cut the Bosnian Serbs completely out of the process. I listened and sympathized, but I could not help him and was not inclined to get involved.

I sent Richard Perle's changes to the military annex to Washington and then faced a secure video teleconference with the Deputies Committee to go over them. The Joint Staff wanted no changes to the original military draft, but after two and a half hours of debate we reached an agreement that I thought the Bosniaks and Perle could accept.

The military annex of the Dayton Agreement seemed largely settled. The Serbs continued to ask for a small NATO presence with a weak mandate in Bosnia, but their objections were halfhearted. The West Europeans softly promoted settlement language that retained an arms embargo on Bosnia, but this language in the agreement had no chance of approval, and the Europeans were not going to stop the process over this issue. The Russians remained concerned about the military command relationship with NATO, but they were not a serious problem.

I had come to respect Igor Ivanov, the Russian head of delegation, on a personal level. He was reserved and professional, but he had a quick wit and excellent sense of humor. I teased him that his work on the military annex and flying on a US Air Force plane qualified him to be an honorary member of NATO.

Ivanov could have caused considerable trouble at Dayton, but he never did. He displayed no particular empathy for the Serbs and was a contributing member of the Contact Group discussions. In his generation of Russian diplomats, none participated more closely with US negotiations from inside the process than Ivanov at Dayton. This level of US-Russian cooperation would be brief, however—on the Balkans and on other foreign-policy issues after 1999.

The only remaining issue was territory. With the success or failure of the negotiations at a decisive stage, Holbrooke took personal control over the map discussions. He used Secretary Christopher's return to Dayton on Friday evening, November 17, as a milestone for the parties to show progress. Holbrooke focused on midnight Sunday, November 19, as the deadline for an agreement. Under the pressure of the clock, he looked for any opportunity, no matter how small, to build pressure on the parties to settle.

After dinner one evening, Holbrooke decided to take Milosevic to see the technology of the Defense Mapping Agency operation, which allowed a person to digitally "fly" over the terrain on a computer screen. The whiskey was flowing, and the Serb president was having a blast. I left the group to get some sleep. The next morning, those who had stayed said the party had carried on until 2:30 a.m. Some kind of deal was made using the technology, which Holbrooke labeled "the Scotch Road to Gorazde." Not surprisingly, nothing of consequence came of the evening.

I spent Friday, November 17, escorting the secretary of defense; the SACEUR, General George Joulwan; and Major General William Nash, commanding general of the First Armored Division, which was the army force designated to deploy to Bosnia. The generals' presence at Dayton put faces to the NATO and US military commitment to an agreement and again put pressure on the parties.

In the generals' meeting with Milosevic, the Serbian president personalized the discussion by bringing up the discussion with Kathy about the impending deployment of our son, Paul, to Bosnia. Secretary Perry had met Paul at a training site in Germany.

I felt it important to take the two American flag officers to see the Bosnian Serbs because the latter were the men responsible for their government's attitude and actions in any implementation arrangement. The meeting with the Pale leaders was held in Serb foreign minister Milutinovic's room under his watchful eye. Krajisnik, as expected, was confident and seemed pleased to meet the generals. General Tolimir, however, looked intimidated. He greeted us with sweaty palms and never said a word during the meeting. He pulled out a ledger and pen, put his head down, and wrote down every word of the conversation. I presumed that he had to report the discussion to General Mladic in Bosnia. The ICTY would later convict Tolimir of war crimes.

The parties also were feeling the heat from the stalled negotiations. Mo Sacirbey announced his resignation as Bosnian foreign minister on CNN. The president of the Federation also resigned over some negotiating point within the Bosnian delegation. Neither resignation took effect.

"It Will Be a Brutal Clash"

Saturday, November 18, 1995

The decisive struggle for an agreement started on Saturday of the third week at Dayton. Secretary Christopher had returned the previous evening, and overnight the Bosniaks had come forward with some map proposals. Hill, Clark, and I took these proposals to Milosevic, who immediately rejected them because they did not provide the 51/49 percent territorial split that had been a standard since August. Meanwhile, Holbrooke and Christopher met with Izetbegovic and company. Izetbegovic angrily rejected the map proposals put forth by these two top US diplomats. Holbrooke closed the meeting with the Bosniaks by threatening to shut down the Dayton talks.

Christopher and Holbrooke had to resolve a serious question amid all this uncertainty: Should President Clinton come to Dayton on Monday, November 20? He wanted to be a part of the ceremony if an agreement were reached. Unfortunately, an agreement seemed remote that Saturday.

Clark and I separately sat down with the Serbs to go over final changes that Perle had agreed to on behalf of the Bosniaks and the Pentagon.

"This document constitutes NATO occupation of Bosnia because the implementation force commander is given almost absolute military decision-making authority," Stanisic said during the discussion.

He was right about the NATO commander's authority. The military annex contained a section that the US military often referred to as "the silver-bullet clause." This clause gave the NATO commander absolute authority over security matters in Bosnia. Although no Bosnian Serbs were in the room, this meeting with the Belgrade Serbs essentially completed the military annex of the Dayton Agreement. Holbrooke was relying on the Milosevic commitment that he could impose his will on the Bosnian Serbs to fulfill the agreement.

I pointed out to Holbrooke that the Bosnian Serbs also had to support the NATO deployment. Holbrooke was convinced that their support would not be a problem. Milosevic had assured him again and again that he would guarantee their cooperation.

"It will be a brutal clash," Milosevic told Holbrooke. I took that to mean Milosevic would take whatever measures were necessary to get their cooperation.

Elsewhere, Holbrooke and Christopher were roving between delegations on the map and other issues. National leaders in Europe were mobilized to make telephone calls to put pressure on the parties. British prime minister John Major and Turkish president Süleyman Demirel called Izetbegovic, and German Chancellor Helmut Kohl sent a message as well.

Milosevic came to the US delegation around 10:00 p.m. in a cooperative mood. He needed the 51/49 percent territorial split and a wide corridor in the Serb territory in the North. Otherwise, he was flexible. Haris

Silajdzic in the Bosniak delegation joined the discussion on the map, and some progress seemed possible. But hopes were dashed as the results of the discussion made their way through the Bosniak leadership. Another map deal fell through.

Sunday, November 19

I sat aside frustrations over maps for a while on this clear, crisp Sunday morning when I learned of the birth of Joshua Daniel Pardew, Paul's first child and Kathy's and my first grandchild.

In the negotiations, the situation was not so joyous. By noon, all significant issues were resolved except for the map. Holbrooke, still agitated by the failure of the maps talks the previous night, decided that the conference would end at noon on Monday, November 20. At this point, the chance of success seemed too remote to recommend that President Clinton come to Dayton on Monday.

In the early afternoon, Milosevic, now smoking again, walked across the parking lot to talk to Holbrooke. He was still tinkering with the line on the map to get his precious 51/49 percent deal.

Christopher and Holbrooke had lunch with Izetbegovic and a follow-on meeting with Milosevic, but no deal was possible. Every meeting with the Bosniaks was bitter and indecisive. Holbrooke was never able to develop a relationship of trust with them. They were a very difficult negotiating party as the process reached a climax.

Holbrooke was exhausted, increasingly emotional, and confrontational. His wife, Kati, who had returned to Dayton, gave him some moral support for the final frantic diplomatic phase.

Secretary Christopher was equally tireless in the final two days at Dayton, but he brought calmness and steady judgment to the frantic, final scramble for a deal. His presence may have been essential to bringing the negotiations to an agreement.

Monday, November 20

Negotiations continued through Sunday evening without much movement. However, sometime around 4:00 a.m. on Monday, November 20, a tentative deal was reached between Bosnian prime minister Silajdzic and Milosevic. Unfortunately, the deal involved land seized by the Croats in western Bosnia during the recent offensive. When the Croats saw the deal, they flew into a rage. A pale, sullen Izetbegovic joined the Croats in their objections, and the agreement collapsed.

"I can no longer work with that man," Silajdzic said of his compatriot, Izetbegovic, storming out of the discussion.

Milosevic had become flexible on major issues. He had given up Sarajevo to Federation control. He had accepted a corridor in the North that was narrower than he wanted, and he had agreed to a link between Gorazde and the Federation that was considerably wider than in previous iterations of the agreement. What remained was Milosevic's demand for a 51/49 percent split of Bosnian territory and the retention of Brcko under Serbian control.

Tudjman and Izetbegovic sensed weakness in Milosevic and saw an opportunity to press for an advantage with the Serbs. The latest failure turned the US negotiators' attention to the Croats. Christopher and Holbrooke met with President Tudjman the next morning to encourage the flexibility in western Bosnia that was critical for an agreement. A call from President Clinton to Tudjman also was lined up to add pressure on the Croatian president.

I updated Walt Slocombe, who was in the Pentagon fending off pressure from "sixty-seven stars" who opposed any US involvement in arming and training the Bosnians. The map issues were going in circles. One problem would be resolved and then reopened when we moved to other points.

"There is no hope of a settlement without a miracle," I told Slocombe and others later that afternoon. Secretary Perry, traveling in the Baltics, sent word that he supported ending the talks because no deal was better than a bad deal.

Under US pressure, the Croats gave up enough ground in western Bosnia to meet most of the Serbian territorial requirement in exchange for concessions by Milosevic. More was still needed, however, and it would have to come from the Bosniaks.

In the early evening, President Clinton called Secretary Christopher to say that if the parties did not want American help, the talks should be shut down. Christopher then made one more run at Izetbegovic.

Later that evening, Wolfgang Ischinger and Michael Steiner of the German delegation found the US team, less Holbrooke and Christopher, in a state of depression in the US delegation conference room. From the US team's demeanor, Ischinger and Steiner saw that the rumored end to the negotiations was not a diplomatic stunt. The two Germans immediately took the reality of the situation to the parties.

Multiple deadlines had come and gone without an agreement. A conference on this scale could not go on much longer. Years of tragedy in Bosnia, the lives of three promising, young American diplomats, all this work and travel seemed lost in a negotiation that was apparently impossible to settle. By the end of the evening, the team drafted a public statement to be issued on November 21 that the negotiations had failed. The three parties were notified of the decision.

Tuesday, November 21

Around 8:30 a.m. on Tuesday, Milosevic trudged through the morning snow on the parking lot separating the delegation buildings. He came to make a final offer to Christopher and Holbrooke. He would accept binding arbitration on Brcko if he got the final 1.5 percent needed to meet the 51/49 percent territorial criteria.

Clark and I went into a frantic territorial review with the Bosniak territorial expert to find the precious 1.5 percent on the Bosniak side of the internal boundary. This was more difficult than it should have been, but finally the Bosniaks transferred a small sliver of land to the Republika Srpska side of the internal boundary. With that small sliver, the Dayton Agreement was complete.

The boundary between the Republika Srpska and the Muslim-Croat Federation within Bosnia agreed to before the signing ceremony was shown on a small map about twenty-four by thirty inches covered in acetate. The boundary was drawn by hand to reveal the details of the territory, including the placement of Sarajevo in Federation territory. The isolated Bosnian Serbs did not yet know the specifics of the territorial agreement.

Holbrooke gave me the final map to deliver to Milosevic. He was not around when I arrived, but Foreign Minister Milutinovic accepted the map, and I left. Milutinovic told me later that the Bosnian Serbs were visibly stunned—one even falling to the floor in agony—when he showed them the map.

No Bosnian Serb initialed any negotiated document at the Dayton Agreement signing ceremony at 4:00 p.m. that afternoon. Serbian foreign minister Milutinovic initialed on their behalf.

CJCS Shalikashvili, who flew to Wright-Patterson for the closing ceremony, was not pleased. If the Dayton Agreement went into effect, the mission that the US military had resisted for years—deployment to Bosnia—would be unavoidable.

"I cannot in good faith recommend to the president that we commit troops to this operation without at least a public statement of support from the Bosnian Serbs," he told the negotiators privately.

Secretary Christopher admitted to the CJCS that the agreement was not perfect but suggested that Shalikashvili meet with Milosevic after the ceremony to get the necessary assurances from him. In the end, subsequent Serbian assurances in separate letters became sufficient to allow the deployment of US forces to Bosnia.

The closing ceremony, organized by the State Department on very short notice, went off without a hitch before a massive media presence at the Hope Center.

President Izetbegovic, weakened by the stress of the process, slowly took the platform. His demeanor was sour, and he scowled throughout the proceedings. In his speech, he described the Dayton Agreement as a bitter and unjust peace.

Maybe it was, but I felt that it was the best we could do under the circumstances.

More detailed negotiating took place after the primary participants at Dayton initialed the document and flew away. The precision of the territorial agreement still had to be worked out on a map. Lieutenant General Clark, Mark Sawoski, and I stayed behind with the Serbian, Bosniak, and Croatian territory experts to complete the task of reconciling a small hand-drawn map with a much more detailed, 1:50,000-scale official map. Clark worked all night with the parties and the Defense Mapping Agency to precisely define the internal boundary in Bosnia on this detailed map. I stayed out of his way. The Clark map became the official map of the Dayton Agreement.

The last of the negotiators departed on Wednesday, November 22. The three-week diplomatic extravaganza was at an end, and the process of restoring normal life to Wright-Patterson Air Force Base could begin.

The critical element of the negotiations at Dayton was Holbrooke's relationship with Milosevic, yet Holbrooke had no illusions about the Serbian leader. Rather, his approach to Milosevic was a practical one.

"It may seem odd to some people, given Milosevic's role in starting the war, but he remains the single most important person to the success of the Dayton Agreement," Holbrooke wrote after the agreement. "This does not make him a nice man or a trustworthy one, merely an essential one."[1]

Holbrooke assessed that Milosevic had originally thought he could steal most of Bosnia quickly and cheaply from the Muslims through the Bosnian Serbs. Instead, he had unleashed a war that he could not control and that included ethnic cleansing and other actions by leaders who were eventually indicted as war criminals. Ultimately, he abandoned the Bosnian Serbs bit by bit in the negotiations.[2]

President Tudjman was a major winner at Dayton: not only did the Croats get an acceptable settlement to their problem in Eastern Slavonia, but they also received considerable international credit for their territorial flexibility in helping achieve a settlement.

The situation for the Bosnian Muslim leaders was different. Other parties wanted a peace agreement. The Bosniaks, too, wanted peace, but they also wanted a viable government and justice. They got peace. President Izetbegovic was resistant to compromise after they had lost so much during the war. Holbrooke was frustrated by Izetbegovic and his team from start to finish, but he also admired their toughness during the war and their tenacity.[3]

In the end, Izetbegovic and his delegation must have concluded that they could not do better than what the Americans and Europeans offered at Dayton. For them, the failure of the Dayton talks would return their people to uncertainty. Haris Silajdzic said it best: "This is the last great chance for us. Failure at Dayton will end the US attempt to achieve peace, and the process will be turned over to others."

Maybe Holbrooke felt elation or a sense of great accomplishment at the end of the Dayton talks. I did not. I was mostly relieved that the negotiations were over. Every phase of the talks was fascinating, but the whole business was a nonstop process of grinding through issue after issue while wondering if the parties had the strength and the will to reach an agreement and then implement it.

The Last Team Trip to the Region, December 7–10, 1995

"The war is over," Milosevic said as he greeted the US negotiating team in Serbia on its last trip to the region between completion of the agreement at Dayton and the official signing in Paris on December 14.[4]

Once the parties initialed the agreement, a flurry of associated activity began in Washington and international capitals leading up to the signing ceremony. Holbrooke, the secretaries of state and defense, and the CJCS made several appearances on the hill as Congress conducted hearings on the US military commitment to the agreement. In Brussels, NATO preparations for deployment to Bosnia moved forward. In New York, the United Nations approved a timetable for lifting economic sanctions against Serbia. Amid all the activity, Holbrooke decided to make one last team trip to Sarajevo, Zagreb, and Belgrade before the signing ceremony in Paris.

The meetings with the presidents in the three regional capitals were upbeat and positive. Milosevic was on holiday at the large presidential lodge near the Danube River. Izetbegovic and Tudjman were as animated and jovial as I had ever seen them. Their attitude was reassuring.[5]

In Sarajevo, we pressed President Izetbegovic on the presence of the mujahedeen and his government's military relationship with Iran. He promised that foreign fighters and trainers were being demobilized and would be removed and that the arms shipments from Iran would be stopped.

As the team lounged around the aircraft on the flight to the region, a relaxed Holbrooke began teasing me about heading the program to arm and train the Bosnians. Holbrooke and the White House had a serious problem on this topic: the president had made a commitment to assist the Bosniaks with their defense, but the Joint Staff remained adamant in refusing to participate in such an effort. They argued that NATO was supposed to be "evenhanded" in implementing the Dayton Agreement, but how could it be evenhanded if it was arming one side?

After the subject came up a couple of times on the plane, I suggested to Holbrooke that we adjourn to the front cabin for a private chat if he were serious about my involvement in arming and training the Bosnians. He proposed that I come to the State Department to head up a team to assist the Bosnians in an international effort. I would have the full backing of the White House and the State Department and informal support from DOD, but not from the military. I told him that I would consider the offer seriously. I had no illusions about the difficulty of the job.

With the approval of Undersecretary Slocombe, I told Holbrooke a few days later that I would accept the appointment at State if ambassadorial rank came with it. He agreed.

Paris: Signing the Dayton Agreement, December 13–14, 1995

President Jacques Chirac of France was the host of the official ceremony to sign the international agreement on Bosnia in Paris. When Secretary Perry designated me to represent him at the Paris signing event, I was honored by his gesture. Holbrooke and the team arrived the day before the ceremony. Paris in mid-December was decorated for the holidays with greenery and thousands of small clear lights. As before, Ambassador Pamela Harriman's residence was the center of US activity, and she was in her element as hostess.

Early on the gray, chilly morning of December 14, we waited for the arrival of President Clinton. The movement of an American president creates a stir of activity ahead of him and a wake as he departs. Around 8:30 a.m., the embassy residence began to swirl with staff and security people arriving before the president.

President Clinton first met with the three Balkan presidents as a group and then with Milosevic and Izetbegovic individually. In the general meeting, the three Balkan presidents pledged their full support of the agreement. Each assured the US president of full support of American troops deployed to Bosnia.

President Clinton and Secretary Christopher used the bilateral meeting with Izetbegovic to warn the Bosnian Muslim leader about the Islamic extremists—various mujahedeen volunteers, Iranian Revolutionary Guards Corps, and others—who had come to Bosnia during the fighting to help the Muslims defend themselves. Izetbegovic committed to demobilizing these fighters. However, he opened the door for some to stay in Bosnia under humanitarian circumstances. Izetbegovic also pledged to encourage Serbs to stay in Sarajevo and to work to make the Federation successful as one of the two governing entities in Bosnia.

Milosevic finally got his bilateral meeting with President Clinton. This meeting was the incentive that Holbrooke had dangled beyond the Serbian president's eager reach until the agreement was complete. Milosevic used the meeting to lavish praise on Warren Christopher for his work at Dayton. The absence of similar praise for Holbrooke was an obvious message by omission.

The signing ceremony took place in late morning in the splendor of the Élysée Palace, the residence of the French president, just down rue Saint-Honore from the American residence. Attendees included the head of government from each Contact Group country: Chancellor Helmut Kohl of Germany, Prime Minister John Major of the United Kingdom, Prime Minister Viktor Chernomyrdin of Russia, and other senior leaders in addition to Chirac and Clinton. The three Balkan presidents signed the formal peace agreement, and speeches by President Clinton and other senior attendees followed the signing.

Clinton's speech described the agreement as an opportunity for the

Three Balkan presidents formally sign the Dayton Agreement in Paris, December 14, 1995. *Seated left to right*: President of Serbia Slobodan Milosevic, President of Croatia Franjo Tudjman, and President of Bosnia Alija Izetbegovic. *Standing, starting third from the left*: President of the United States Bill Clinton, President of France Jacques Chirac, Chancellor of Germany Helmut Kohl, Prime Minister of Great Britain John Major, and Prime Minister of Russia Viktor Chernomyrdin. (William J. Clinton Presidential Library)

parties to establish real long-term peace for their people. He encouraged them to look to the future and not to let their children down. For the Balkans, this was American idealism and a very tall order.

The event moved to the Quai d'Orsay, the French Foreign Ministry, where President Chirac hosted a lunch of lobster, turkey, and other courses, all supported by carefully selected wines for two hundred attendees. After lunch, the group moved to an adjoining hall for coffee, cognac, and cigars.

Milosevic, who had quit smoking again after Dayton, was delighted by this moment that he had wanted so badly. The Serbian president was Cinderella at the ball, schmoozing with the heads of government of the great powers of the West and Russia. I spoke with him briefly and encouraged him to have a cigar on this occasion. He gladly fired one up.

"President Clinton is a great man," Milosevic said as I moved away.

On the margins of the event, I ran into Nikola Koljevic, the accommodating and malleable vice president of the Bosnian Serbs. Koljevic, caught in a squeeze between Milosevic the tricky opportunist and Krajisnik the tough Serbian nationalist, had the dubious duty of signing the peace agreement for the Republika Srpska. He said that he had been harassed in his hotel room all night by telephone calls from Serb leaders in Bosnia giving him instructions that he could not carry out.

This was the last time I was to see the little professor. After signing the Dayton Agreement in Paris, Koljevic returned to Bosnia and faded from sight. A little more than a year later, he shot himself in the head and died a few days later in a Belgrade hospital.

After the Paris signing, Holbrooke arranged for the team to fly back to Washington on Air Force One with the president.

Four days before Christmas, the Clinton administration announced publicly that I would head an interagency task force in the State Department to help fulfill the commitment to equip and train the Bosnian Muslim army.[6]

Lead elements of the US Army cross the Sava River to enter Bosnia on December 31, 1995, as part of the NATO force to provide a secure environment for the implementation of the Dayton Agreement. (US Department of Defense. The appearance of US Department of Defense visual information does not imply or constitute department endorsement.)

Holbrooke went back to the State Department as assistant secretary for European, Canadian, and NATO affairs after delivering the most important foreign-policy achievement of the Clinton administration. He stayed in that position for only a couple more months, until late February 1996, when he left government. Holbrooke remained a special envoy for the Clinton administration while out of government. He returned to the Clinton administration in 1999 as the US ambassador to the United Nations.

Soldiers from the US First Armored Division, overcoming ice, snow, and deep mud, crossed the swollen Sava River and entered northern Bosnia on December 29, 1995, to take part in the NATO implementation force, Operation Joint Endeavor. They were augmented by troops from Russia and other non-NATO countries. At their high point, the number of NATO troops in Bosnia approached 60,000. The US contingent deployed initially to Bosnia was about 24,000.

Among the US First Armored Division soldiers crossing the Sava into Bosnia was Captain Paul Pardew, commander, B Company, 501st Military Intelligence Battalion, attached to the First Brigade.

Despite the US military's resistance to the mission before deployment, not one American soldier was killed by directed enemy action between 1995 and 2004, when US troops withdrew, turning security responsibility for Bosnia over to the EU.[7]

The Dayton Agreement: Promise and Limitations

The Dayton Agreement brought peace to Bosnia and in the process influenced important international relationships at a time of great change. Dayton also set the stage for the independence of Kosovo and the ultimate integration of Balkan nations into NATO and the EU.

In Bosnia, the Dayton Agreement put in place the constitutional structure to help Bosnia become a viable national state. It

1. ensured that Bosnia was recognized as an independent sovereign nation within its existing boundaries;
2. set the boundary line between the two entities in Bosnia—the Federation and the Republika Srpska;
3. established a democratic constitution for governance of Bosnia;
4. recognized the fundamental rights of citizens;
5. promoted the return of refugees and displaced persons;
6. preserved national monuments;

7. granted authority and status of forces for NATO and associated military forces in Bosnia;

8. authorized international organizations to function in Bosnia with significant authority to assist in implementation;

9. authorized an international police presence in Bosnia, which was to serve in advisory capacity only, with no authority to arrest or use force.[8]

Holbrooke stepped aside in 1996 to let others implement the agreement he had negotiated. He remained engaged from the margins, but primary responsibility for implementation fell to international institutions and national capitals.

The United States and the Contact Group reinforced the international authority of the Dayton Agreement through a UN Security Council resolution (UNSCR). The day after the agreement was signed in Paris, the Security Council passed UNSCR 1031 in New York. This resolution authorized NATO—without designating NATO by name—to use "all necessary means" under the enforcement provisions of Chapter VII of the UN Charter to implement military aspects of the agreement. The resolution also authorized an international high representative with the authority to oversee civilian aspects of the agreement.[9]

After Dayton, Bosnia was a sovereign nation with a democratic constitution. But its sovereignty was limited for years by the authority given to international institutions put in place by the Dayton Agreement.

The parties at Dayton agreed to a senior civilian international authority designated the high representative in Bosnia to oversee implementation of the nonmilitary aspects of the agreement. The "high rep," as this person was called, reported to the international Peace Implementation Council and was the final authority for interpreting the agreement. That authority allowed the high rep to overturn actions by the Bosnian political institutions if they were judged to violate the agreement. Carl Bildt, who had represented the EU at Dayton, was appointed the first international high representative.

The Dayton Agreement also gave responsibility and authority for creating a secure and stable environment for implementation of the agreement to the augmented NATO Implementation Force. NATO later changed the name to Stabilization Force (SFOR). Once deployed, SFOR became the absolute military authority in Bosnia.

CROATIA

Sava River

North

Danube River

Prijedor

Bosanski
Brod

**Republika
Srpska**

Bihać

Brčko

Banja Luka

Tuzla

Serbia

Zenica

Srebrenica

CROATIA

Kiseljak

Zepa

**Federation of
Bosnia and
Herzegovina**

Livno

Sarajevo

Pale

Goražde

Split

**Republika
Srpska**

YUGOSLAVIA

*Adriatic
Sea*

Mostar

Montenegro

Ploče

**Republic of Bosnia
and Herzegovina - 1996**

Trebinje

Dubrovnik

ALBANIA

| 0 | 25 | 50 Miles |
| 0 | 25 | 50 Kilometers |

Podgorica

The Dayton Agreement first and foremost was a peace agreement to end the agony of a brutal ethnic war in Europe. Like any negotiated settlement reached under the pressure of war, it contained many compromises and was far from a perfect solution to the deep political and social issues that plagued Bosnia. At best, it gave local leaders of good will a chance to move forward in the common interest of their people.

The greatest flaw in the Dayton negotiations was the weak central government it created. The Dayton constitution did not grant the government sufficient power to effectively govern the country and to overcome the individual parties' divisive strategies.

The Serbs at Dayton had not completely neutered the national government in the negotiations, but they had come close. The new central government was to be led by a tripartite ethnic presidency, each with essentially a veto over the government's actions. The country had no national military or police and very little authority to govern the two autonomous entities. After Dayton, existing Serb, Croat, and Muslim political parties continued to fight each other without regard for the country's common interest. Serbia and Croatia saw a weak Bosnia as in their interest and continually meddled in Bosnian politics.

Correcting critical flaws in the agreement is possible. Bosnian leaders have the authority to improve their country if they can find sufficient commitment to Bosnia as a nation and the will to make it a fully functional democracy.

Months after the agreement was signed, Holbrooke lamented the continuing influence of the wartime nationalist leaders and their political parties, which persisted in obstructing Dayton implementation and blocking political integration at every turn. Elections in Bosnia in September 1996 gave new legitimacy to these leaders and their parties. Holbrooke wondered later if he should have pushed to have them banned from participation in the first elections.

Dayton ended the war in Bosnia, but it did not end ethnic conflicts in the region as the former Yugoslavia continued to disintegrate. More threats to Balkan peace would play out over coming years.

13

Richard Holbrooke

Dayton was a historic accomplishment, and overall credit for the peace agreement in Bosnia belongs to Richard Holbrooke, the diplomatic engine of the Dayton Agreement. The negotiations produced a powerful performance in a major international crisis by this senior American diplomat at the top of his game. His focus, his drive and energy, his ability to adjust to new conditions and to handle the variety of military and political forces constantly bombarding the process made the agreement possible.

Holbrooke used a full array of diplomatic tools. He understood the nature of American power, and he used it to great effect. He enticed, he charmed, he bullied, he manipulated, and he pressured as necessary to push through resistance to get a suitable agreement. For Holbrooke, the agreement was the objective. How his personal techniques might be perceived or how his personal image might be affected seemed not to matter to him. Could the job have been done more gracefully? Probably. Could he have achieved a better settlement? I do not think so, given the conditions he faced.

Holbrooke steered this process through war-torn areas in Bosnia, major capitals of Europe, and a midwestern American city. He engaged a cast of characters ranging from the noble to the despicable. His work was dangerous and frequently teetered on the brink of failure. In the end, Holbrooke succeeded, bringing peace to Bosnia and new opportunities for what remained of Yugoslavia.

As a member of the US negotiating team in 1995, I worked closely with Holbrooke day in and day out for months in high-pressure situations. Members of that team were special to him. Like others on the team, I kept in touch with him for the rest of his life. I had an open, accessible relationship with him. I felt I could give him my personal views freely, even when they were uncomfortable for him or contradicted his opinion.

Holbrooke's character and personality had so many angles, layers, and contradictions that he is difficult to describe. He could be brilliant and compassionate at one moment, ruthless and ambitious the next.

On Bosnia, Holbrooke was fearless. He spoke an uncomfortable truth to his own administration about the failure of policy and the need for American leadership to end a genocide. He then took personal responsibility for American engagement in Bosnia, with no certainty that he could end the war—a task with a high failure rate for previous international figures.

As a diplomat, Holbrooke was a calculated gambler who bet everything that he could manipulate Milosevic to achieve peace in Bosnia. The gamble paid off. He constantly took physical and professional risks in the negotiations. His courage over the war in Bosnia contrasted sharply with the common image of him as a man consumed by self-interest.

Holbrooke combined his diplomatic experience with the pragmatism of a realist tempered by American idealism. He grasped the fundamental conditions of right and wrong and of guilt and innocence in Bosnia. I always felt that he had a stable moral core to help him navigate through the muck of Balkan politics.

Holbrooke operated from a broad strategic plan. Along the way, he kept his options open and adjusted his plan as conditions changed and opportunities arose. His overall plan had a sequence of components: integrate his negotiation with critical capitals and international institutions, focus on Milosevic, reach agreement with the parties on a set of key principles, achieve a cease-fire, and lift the siege of Sarajevo as a prelude to a comprehensive agreement negotiated in proximity talks.

Holbrooke's leadership of the negotiating team was an important aspect of the Dayton experience. Those of us on the inside of the team knew that we were a part of something special, something historic. Morale was high on the team as we learned to respect Holbrooke's talent and the difficulty of the negotiations. He was our leader, and we deferred to him in public.

In private, Holbrooke was inclusive. He endured the long flights at the back of the plane with us. He sought our advice. He seemed to listen to contrarian views, and he developed a personal bond with each of us over time. In private settings with the team, Holbrooke showed a vulnerable element to his personality that was appealing. Whether this hint of vulnerability was sincere or not was always a question, though.

Holbrooke was tireless and everywhere in the public eye as the drama of the negotiations played out in the media. His was a classic story to match the American self-narrative: a bold and tough American encounters a chaotic conflict between good and evil, protects the innocent, and restores law and order. Those of us accompanying Holbrooke on the Bosnia adventure could not help but enjoy our small moments of reflected glory.

Holbrooke's understanding of the media worked in his favor. He created a public image of hard-won success and increased momentum from the early days of the shuttle through to the Dayton negotiations. All the players were drawn into the positive swirl of his negotiating process. This momentum placed important pressure on everyone involved to conclude an agreement.

By the time the settlement was signed, Holbrooke was one of the most recognized American officials in the world, probably second only to President Clinton. Many Americans may not have known who the US secretaries of state and defense were, but they knew Holbrooke.

The public Holbrooke described in countless articles, interviews, and television specials became a cliché that amplified his more obvious flaws over his ability. The cliché Holbrooke was a capable diplomat but a shameless self-promoter with a gigantic ego and unlimited ambition, who bulldozed his way through any resistance to get what he wanted. And what he wanted was to be secretary of state or higher. In reality, he was a more complex figure.

Unfortunately, Holbrooke often reinforced his cliché image. He seemed to care a great deal about the eternal scramble for status in Manhattan, and he made no effort to hide his attraction to celebrity and public attention. He cultivated the media, and they could not resist him or the controversy he generated along the way.

He had plenty of irritating personal traits. Almost everyone who had a conversation with Holbrooke in a room full of people had the same experience: as you chatted, you saw him look beyond you to see if someone more important or powerful was a better option for his time.

He could be domineering and manipulative, and he stretched the truth when it suited his purpose. A negotiation is a process of competitive influence. Manipulation and political theater are tools of the trade. As I told Michael Kelly, who characterized him for the *New Yorker* during the peace talks, Holbrooke's diplomatic tools included a certain amount of theater, drama, and manipulation. He could not have achieved the Dayton Agreement without those skills.[1]

His overbearing and occasionally bombastic nature was legendary. He made snap decisions about people and could be harsh, even unnecessarily cruel. He would intimidate when it suited his purpose. He generally dominated a room, often to the displeasure of other big personalities in senior positions.

Of course, he was ambitious. Ambition kindles the political fires in Washington. He was a senior official of the US government, with unique skills and a track record of success at the highest levels of international diplomacy. Some in Washington conceal their ambition better than others, but Washington is a magnet for the ambitious.

Holbrooke was fully aware of his reputation but did little to correct it. At least outwardly, he had a very thick skin about his professional reputation. He seemed to subscribe to the philosophy that any notoriety is better than none. He also may have felt that he could not do much to change his image, so why bother?

Holbrooke never confided his personal ambitions to me. I never heard him say that he wanted to be secretary of state, but, like others, I just knew it. He was certainly qualified and had paid his political and professional dues. But the position of secretary of state was a goal that escaped him. His personality was too strong, his profile too high, and the insecurity in Washington too pervasive to give him such a platform.

In the end, I was conflicted about Holbrooke. I recognized his unique talent, creativity, and energy, but I also saw his flaws.

On a personal level, I am forever indebted to Richard Holbrooke. The experience on the negotiating team changed my life and opened opportunities for me I could never have had otherwise. Certainly, I would never have had the chance to negotiate the Ohrid Agreement in Macedonia in 2001 or to succeed in doing so.

I had no illusions about Holbrooke, either. Anyone involved with him could be manipulated, used, undermined, and dismissed. I never felt that he trusted or that he could be completely trusted.

My relationship with Holbrooke deteriorated as the years passed. In 1996, I denied his request to turn over to him my personal journals from the shuttle and the Dayton negotiations, although I gave him the associated memoranda. I turned him down on other requests as well, most notably in 2005, when he asked me to take the senior US negotiating position for Kosovo in the Bush administration. After I said no to the Kosovo offer, our relationship became more distant.

Holbrooke stayed connected with issues in the Balkans long after the

Dayton Agreement. He promoted independence for Kosovo and closely monitored developments in the former Yugoslavia.

In 2009, fourteen years after negotiating the Dayton Agreement, Holbrooke re-entered government as special representative for Afghanistan and Pakistan working for Secretary of State Hillary Clinton.

Holbrooke came late to the Afghanistan–Pakistan problem. By 2009, US policy on Afghanistan was dominated by military policy. The Obama administration's brain trust on Afghanistan consisted primarily of entrenched retired and active-duty generals, carryovers from the Bush administration, and former spooks with a very shallow record of lasting success in Afghanistan. For them, Holbrooke was an unwelcome intruder. But, in fact, when he entered the White House Situation Room to discuss Afghanistan, the diplomatic talent and foreign-policy experience in the room increased by orders of magnitude. Tragically, Holbrooke never connected with President Barack Obama or achieved any degree of authority over the policy.[2] Without the president's backing, he never had a chance, although he never stopped trying.

At his best, Richard Holbrooke was a remarkable American foreign-policy talent—a unique, once-in-a-generation diplomat for the United States. In a crisis, he had to be among the very best operational American envoys ever. Unfortunately, his personality and his contradictions undermined his potential. Holbrooke reached the cabinet level as the US ambassador to the UN; however, he never became secretary of state, and he never received the Nobel Peace Prize or the national recognition he deserved for bringing peace to Bosnia and stability to the Balkans.

Richard Holbrooke died on December 13, 2010, in Washington, DC, while working on the Afghanistan–Pakistan portfolio at the State Department.

Part 3

Bosnia
Military Stability

The reconstructed Vijecnica, the National Library and former city hall, Sarajevo, Bosnia-Herzegovina. (Shutterstock.com)

14

A President's Commitment

In January 1996, the people of Sarajevo were just beginning to clear away the rubble and the barricades from the war. I flew there quickly to give confidence to the Muslim leaders that the United States would follow through on its commitment to arm and train their military. In Washington, the Train and Equip (T&E) Program team was just beginning to become functional.

Sarajevo was dreary in winter. The temperature hovered around freezing, with alternating periods of snow, fog, and drizzle. I was back in the Communist-era Holiday Inn. Snipers were no longer a menace, so guests now could enter through the front door.

Basic services were slowly being restored in Sarajevo, but chimneys from makeshift wood stoves still poked through some apartment windows. Candles provided light in many homes. Most buildings in the center of the city were damaged by shelling, rifle bullets, and fire. Street signs and street lights were riddled by bullet holes. Handmade signs from the war still warned of the threat of sniper fire at vulnerable points in the city.

In the Bascarsilja, the old Ottoman area of the city near the main mosque, a few small, dark shops, most without heat, offered local crafts and antiques from the region. Some sold engraved brass shell casings as sad mementos of the recent fighting.

Near the open food market in the center of town, the pavement was scarred by the shrapnel from the impact of a mortar shell that had killed more than thirty people and triggered the NATO airstrikes when the negotiating team was in Paris the previous August. Someone had marked the spot of the carnage by filling in the shrapnel scars of the blast pattern in the pavement with a permanent material colored blood red.

The Sarajevo National Library, the Vijecnica, was a burned-out shell. Built originally as a city hall a hundred years earlier during Austro-Hungarian rule in Bosnia, the library had contained rare books and manuscripts going back to the Ottoman times. Most of the collection was destroyed when Serbian artillery shelling demolished and set ablaze the interior of the library on August 25 and 26, 1992.

After the attack, Bosnian theater director Gradimir Gojer called the shelling of the library "a triumph of barbarism."[1] But a careful restoration of this distinctive building, a combination of Austrian architecture and Moorish flourishes, was completed and the building rededicated in May 2014.[2]

A walk around Sarajevo reinforced my view that the US decision to help the Bosnian victims of the war defend themselves in the future was correct.

Commitment and Controversy

The task of building a Bosnian military force capable of defending the population against attacks by Serbian armed forces was as daunting as it was controversial. The project was a US presidential commitment, but in January 1996 the T&E effort was mostly on paper. It also faced serious opposition in the United States and abroad.

Even with a presidential mandate and the support of the national security staff and the secretaries of state and defense, many figures within the US government remained wary of the program. The intelligence community consistently projected the worst outcome for the effort, and top US military officials believed it threatened their image of neutrality in Bosnia.

US and NATO actions were hardly neutral. The United States had done nothing to prevent the Croatian offensive that drove Serbs out of western Bosnia. US and NATO aircraft had engaged Serb targets in Bosnia, while using the threat of more attacks in negotiating with Belgrade. The entire Dayton process was designed to stop a genocide against the Muslims perpetrated by Serbs. But attacking the pretense of neutrality would consume valuable time and energy and would only generate more hostility from the opponents of the T&E Program, so I wasted no time challenging it.

Outside the United States, only countries with majority Muslim populations approved of giving the Muslims in Bosnia the means to defend themselves. Other governments, particularly in Europe, saw equipping and training the Army of Bosnia and Herzegovina (Armija Republike Bosne i Hercegovine, ABiH) as a bad idea at best and a potential disaster at worst.

Many Americans and Europeans believed that because the Bosniaks were Muslims and received support from Iran and Muslim countries, they were Muslim extremists. In reality, the Bosnians in 1995 were post-Communist secular Muslims who saw themselves as Europeans and wanted to join the European mainstream. They wanted decent jobs, education for their children, and travel—not jihad. Their religious commitment was moderate at most.

The European alternative to the T&E Program—regional disarmament—was naive, if not cynical. At some point, NATO and allied military forces would leave Bosnia. When they departed, a military vacuum, like the one that had caused so much damage in the war, could not be left behind. A stable military balance, if not a cooperative relationship, should be the legacy of the peace effort in Bosnia.

Helping the Bosnian Muslims defend themselves was a just action by my country and would help stabilize the region if done right. The controversy over the T&E Program was of little concern to me if the president and key senior officials in the administration kept the will to follow through on their commitment. Once I accepted the job, I was determined to succeed.

The wartime ABiH was proud and brave, despite its limitations. It consisted of a motley assortment of people and military equipment. It had been thrown together in a crisis and had been unable to lift the siege of Sarajevo or adequately defend the population in the countryside against better-organized, better-trained, and better-equipped Serbian conventional and paramilitary forces supported by Belgrade.

The ABiH had numbered about 70,000 troops during the war. It had been led by a few officers with some military experience in the Yugoslav national army but not at a high level. Units had consisted of everything from mujahedeen volunteers to female infantry units. They had no aircraft, heavy weapons, or effective artillery. They had fought mostly with infantry weapons of every description, much of it supplied in a less-than-covert program by Iran through Croatia. Training had been rudimentary. Some selected personnel had gone to Iran for training; otherwise, an estimated 1,500 trainers and fighters from the Iranian Revolutionary Guards Corps had gone to Bosnia to help with training. Money from Iran, Saudi Arabia, and other Muslim countries sympathetic to the Muslims in Bosnia had provided funding to keep the ABiH and Bosnian government afloat.

In the beginning, the United States and the Bosniaks had different views of the new security assistance relationship. The Bosniaks thought weapons alone would solve their problem. They wanted weapons and lots of them from the T&E Program.

After the United States made the T&E commitment, the DOD dispatched a group of security assistance specialists from the Institute of

Defense Analysis to Bosnia to assess the ABiH and its needs. The study concluded that its primary needs were organization and training. Equipment in certain categories was important, but equipment would not be effective if not accompanied by proper organization and training. The institute's study formed the blueprint set of requirements for the T&E Program in its early stages.

Crossing the Potomac

I cleaned out my desk in the Pentagon in late December 1995 and crossed the Potomac River for a temporary assignment to lead the T&E Program from the Department of State. This temporary assignment at State was to last thirteen years and would involve more ethnic tensions, political intrigue, Balkan wars, and negotiations. But before all of that, I had a job to do in Bosnia.

"They are going to drive you crazy at State when you come over," Holbrooke told me after I accepted the appointment. "Don't worry, you will work it out," he said.

State and DOD are complementary national security organizations. Yet they are natural bureaucratic competitors because foreign policy and national security policy often overlap. The White House and the interagency process in Washington are the primary arbitrators between the two departments. Difficult or contentious decisions between them are coordinated by the staff of the various national security departments and are considered for decision in the White House by the Deputies Committee, the Principals Committee, and the president.

Since to that point I had been an army officer or a DOD civilian, coming to State from DOD involved considerable culture shock. The adjustment was relatively quick, though, and the experience at State gave me deep respect for the Foreign Service and for the impact the State Department has on world affairs.

The cultures of the two executive departments are very different. DOD is objective oriented; State often accepts process as success. DOD loves precision; State is often very comfortable with vagueness and some ambiguity. It can see negotiating flexibility and opportunity in "creative ambiguity." *Nuance*—a common term of art at State—is not a word I recall ever hearing in the Pentagon. The resource differences are vast. State operates on a shoestring budget compared with DOD and looks with envy at the massive DOD resources.

The generals are often suspicious of diplomats and the diplomats' potential to maneuver them into what they consider misguided military operations. Conversely, diplomats often become nervous when the generals get too close to politics and foreign policy. Some diplomats at State were very comfortable and effective at working with senior military and DOD officials. Others were a disaster. The same can be said for senior DOD and military people working with the diplomatic community. The relationships always carry a degree of tension and must be worked out by the individuals involved.

In DOD, only the senior political officials—not the uniformed military—supported the T&E Program. At State, the program received general backing from the entire organization. A considerable number of Foreign Service officers strongly believed in the program. Some of them, however, saw it as just an unfortunate obligation to be fulfilled by a token commitment.

The T&E Task Force

The first order of business was to build an interagency task force and prepare a policy concept for the T&E Program.

The State Department had two ad hoc organizations dedicated to implementing the Dayton Agreement. The one headed by Ambassador Robert Gallucci was responsible for the civilian implementation aspects of Dayton; the T&E Program was the other. State, through its European Bureau, provided office space and administrative support to both.

My new job needed a title, and I chose a bureaucratic one: "US special representative for military stabilization in the Balkans." The DOD lent me and several other people to State to run the T&E effort. Undersecretary Walt Slocombe dispatched Christopher Lamb, a member of the Senior Executive Service, from his staff to the task force. Chris took his practical and meticulous talents to the tasks of managing the training contract, equipment procurement, and financial arrangements.[3]

Charles "Chuck" Franklin, who had recently retired from the US Navy, also came from the Pentagon to provide a professional public-affairs profile to a program that was a high-interest media topic in the United States and abroad. Raffi Gregorian later replaced Franklin when Franklin departed the team. Army major Stuart McFarren joined from the Defense Security Cooperation Agency to provide expertise on military assistance matters and remained with the program until its completion. Mark Sawoski, who had assisted me at Dayton during the proximity talks, also came aboard the T&E Program to help for a short period.

Holbrooke knew that we needed help within State and twisted Ambassador Darryl Johnson's arm to join the team briefly. Ambassador Jon D. Glassman soon replaced Johnson as the senior State Department representative during the critical period of diplomacy for the program. John Klekas, a Foreign Service officer who worked with me in the DOD Balkan Task Force, joined the team in the early stages. When Klekas moved on, Angel Rabasa replaced him. Glassman, Sawoski, Klekas, and Rabasa worked on the international side of the program and kept the non-State members straight on the intricacies of the State Department. The Central Intelligence Agency provided an officer to the task force to provide responsive intelligence input into the effort.

The White House announced that President Clinton accorded the personal rank of ambassador to the US special representative for military stabilization in the Balkans, James W. Pardew, on May 17, 1996. The Senate subsequently confirmed this rank on May 17, 1997.[4]

The White House Charter

The T&E Program required a White House charter to give it international stature and proper authority as a presidential priority within the US government. Just before Christmas in 1995, the T&E Task Force crafted a briefing with a set of principles to be considered by the Deputies Committee in the White House Situation Room on December 28, 1995.

The Situation Room in the West Wing of the White House is the nucleus of US national security decision making. A few steps from the Oval Office and the office of the national security adviser, the small and sparse Situation Room features a long conference table with seats for fourteen to sixteen people and about the same number of chairs for the backbenchers along the wall.

The national security adviser convenes the Principals Committee in the Situation Room. His deputy handles the Deputies Committee. Decisions made in that room are disseminated throughout the US government as national policy.

On December 28, 1995, Sandy Berger, the deputy national security adviser to President Clinton, chaired the Deputies Committee meeting that approved the T&E concept as presented. This decision served as the basic authority and the guiding principles for the T&E Program from start to finish.

The T&E charter approved by the deputies included the following components:

1. The United States would lead and coordinate an international program to train and equip the Bosnian army. The US contribution to the program would be leadership and coordination, advice to the Bosnian government authorities, and US military equipment. Necessary funding had to be found internationally.
2. The Interagency Task Force located in the State Department would lead the US program and report to the Deputies Committee.
3. The program would focus on defense and deterrence to promote regional military stability. Stability was to be achieved by assisting the Bosnians in creating sufficient military capability to respond effectively to regional military threats to the government and the people of Bosnia.
4. Military assistance would be designed to unify the Muslim-Croat Federation. The program was to promote maximum cooperation and integration of the separate military organizations into a unified Federation armed force within a single military command and single Ministry of Defense.
5. No uniformed US military personnel would participate in the T&E Program. The goal was to ensure that the US military was viewed as evenhanded in fulfilling its security responsibilities under the Dayton Agreement. Implementation in Bosnia would be accomplished through US contractors.
6. The Institute of Defense Analysis study of the Bosnian army would form the baseline for determining priority assistance requirements.
7. The program would be totally transparent. It would have no secret or covert components.
8. As conditions to start the T&E Program, the Bosniaks had to commit to a unified Federation military structure, cut their military ties to Iran, and expel Iranian Revolutionary Guards Corps personnel and other foreign fighters.

The early decision to make the program totally transparent was liberating. The best way to deal with skeptics and the conspiracy theorists was to hold the program up to public view. If the program developed as hoped, the transparency should have a deterrent effect on the Serbs as well. The only

serious downside to transparency was the possibility of scaring off potential donors to the program who would have preferred anonymity.

With the UN arms embargo on Bosnia lifted after Dayton, Congress
authorized the president to draw down and transfer $100 million in DOD
equipment and service to Bosnia to improve its self-defense and to create
stability in the region. The T&E Program managed that drawdown authority for the administration as part of its responsibilities.[5]

15

Getting Started

With a concept approved, an organization in place, and the drawdown of US equipment authorized, the T&E team left Washington for the former Yugoslavia region as the calendar turned to the new year. The first step was to explain the US program to the recipients, potential donors, and skeptics in Europe. The next priority was to find international donors to pay for training and for equipment not available from US stocks. These resources, we hoped, would give the US program the necessary leverage to break the linkages to Iran and extremists and to integrate the two Muslim-Croat Federation armies into one structure. These goals were lofty.

Zagreb was the first stop. Once again, Croatia was very important to US policy in Bosnia. Geographically, Croatia had a long border with Bosnia and was critical to the movement of people and equipment into the country. Most importantly, Croats in Bosnia looked to Zagreb for guidance on their activities. If there was to be any hope of bringing Croatian military forces into an integrated defense structure in the Federation, Zagreb had to cooperate.

Below Croatian president Franjo Tudjman, the most important figure in Croatia was Goiko Susak, the craggy, chain-smoking Croatian defense minister who had built the Croatian military into a capable fighting force. As an immigrant in Canada, Susak was rumored to have had great success in the pizza business, but after independence he returned to Croatia to help his homeland. He had been a critical figure in talks with the Croatians during the Dayton negotiations, and he became the central figure in Zagreb to make the Croatian component of the T&E Program work.

Susak was pleased that the United States had decided to make the T&E Program a program for the Federation as a whole instead of a Muslim-only effort. He understood that the condition for receiving the benefits of the T&E effort was cooperation from the Bosnian Croats in the integration of the Federation military into a single structure. Although Croatia had al-

lowed the Iranian arms to flow into Bosnia, the Croatians worried about
the link between Bosnia and extremist groups. Susak also liked the T&E
Program as leverage to break that link.

Susak made two important concessions in the first meeting. Croatia
would allow the Iranians and others to leave the region through Zagreb.
More importantly, he authorized the use of the Croatian port of Ploce on
the Adriatic Sea as a free port for the shipment of T&E equipment for Bosnia if the program fairly benefitted Croats in the Federation.

We took a ragged Ukrainian-operated UN charter flight, jammed in
with a frozen-food shipment, from Zagreb to Sarajevo. The Sarajevo airport was still operated by the UN and was a mess of makeshift sandbagged
and scarred buildings. The wreckage of a military transport aircraft sat just
off the runway.

In the evening, we joined Mo Sacirbey, the Bosnian foreign minister,
and Mabel Wisse-Smit for dinner at the Jez, the wartime restaurant that
had offered security from shelling in central Sarajevo. Over dinner, Sacirbey informed us that he would be the primary contact in the Bosnian government for the T&E Program.

President Alija Izetbegovic and other senior Bosniak and Croatian
leaders approved the US T&E concept in our meeting with them the next
day, January 6, 1996. Izetbegovic confirmed that Sacirbey would be the
primary Bosniak point of contact.

The two militaries in the Federation—the ABiH and the Croatian
Army in Bosnia (Hrvatsko Vijece Obrane, HVO) were separate forces under separate ministries of defense. In Sarajevo, General Rasim Delic of the
ABiH and General Zivko Budimir of the HVO listened to our presentation
on the T&E Program with obvious suspicion about its seriousness.

Carl Bildt, the EU representative at Dayton, had recently arrived in Sarajevo as the international high representative for Dayton implementation.
Like many others, Bildt was not enthusiastic about T&E, but he accepted
it as a fact of life. The transparency of the program helped eased his concerns, but he warned me that the British authorities were strongly opposed
to T&E and that I could expect serious problems from them. Bildt particularly noted the opposition by General Michael J. D. Walker, the senior British military officer in Bosnia.

This warning was of no concern at that point. I had attended a meeting between Secretary Perry and British defense minister Michael Portillo
in which Portillo had stated that the United Kingdom did not favor T&E

but would not cause difficulties in implementation. Unfortunately, the rest of the British government and the military did not seem to get the word. I never expected the Europeans to contribute significantly to the program. Neutrality toward T&E would be enough, but even that was not to be.

Milosevic

We left Sarajevo for Belgrade to present the T&E Program to Milosevic and General Momcilo Perisic, the chief of the Yugoslav army General Staff. After a warm greeting from the Serbian president, I explained the program and argued that in the end the Federation army would present no threat to Serbs. In fact, the United States would ultimately like to see all military forces in Bosnia brought into a single structure. Here again the transparency of the program was an important selling point.

"Jim, I'll have better arguments against your program the next time we meet. I wish you had not taken this particular job after Dayton," Milosevic said.

Milosevic dismissed the Bosnians' security interests and proposed instead that Bosnia be demilitarized. He believed that giving military capability to the Muslims was neither necessary nor wise.

Neocon Oversight

Back in Washington, T&E policy was now a hot topic, and the demand was high for briefings to the media, Congress, Contact Group embassies in Washington, and others.

The Bosniaks needed technical and political help in Washington and turned to sympathetic Americans who had helped them during the Dayton negotiations. Richard Perle was one such adviser. Perle, with his background in US national security and his experience at Dayton, was a natural fit.

Holbrooke had been cautious with Perle at Dayton, but I had worked through the military annex with Perle. His style was direct and intellectually tough. I found him difficult but not unreasonable or impractical in the T&E Program.

Early on, an influential group long sympathetic to the Bosnian Muslims and composed largely of national security hawks called on the T&E team to discuss its role in assisting the Bosniaks. The group constituted the brain trust of the neoconservatives in America—Richard Perle, Paul Wol-

fowitz, and Douglas J. Feith. Wolfowitz, a former State and Defense Department official, would become the deputy secretary of defense and Feith
the undersecretary of defense for policy in the George W. Bush administration. These men went on to become primary cheerleaders for the unnecessary war in Iraq in 2003.

The team's relationship with all of them was rocky and occasionally
adversarial. Perle made it clear that he did not believe the T&E team was
adequate for the job and criticized the effort as far too small and cheap. He
created a standing organization, the Acquisition Support Institute (ASI), to
handle daily business, and the ASI remained active throughout the T&E
Program. We rejected some of the institute's proposals, such as putting international donor money in the stock market and converting the US drawdown to an open-ended access to US equipment, but accepted the more
practical ones.

Overall, Perle and the ASI were helpful. They were tough and effective
negotiators on behalf of the Bosnians regarding the contract for military
training. They served as a double check on the program as it went forward,
and they put forth some sound proposals. Their pressure offset critics of the
program in the United States, and they were often helpful in explaining the
nature and rationale of US policy to their clients in Bosnia.

16

Two Conditions

The Institute of Defense Analysis study presented during the Dayton negotiations had concluded that training was needed throughout the Muslim-Croat Federation military structure, especially in the noncommissioned officer corps. Once the Federation leaders were convinced that modern training was a priority task, the next step was an agreement that the NATO standard was to be the benchmark for training and equipping the Federation force.

Military assistance by other nations was one potential source of training. But few nations were willing to help train the Federation. In the end, eleven countries in addition to the United States contributed. Turkey was an enthusiastic supporter, but its resources were limited. The only European country to participate was the Federal Republic of Germany. Bangladesh, Egypt, Indonesia, Jordan, Malaysia, Morocco, Pakistan, Qatar, and the United Arab Emirates (UAE) provided various specialty training.[1]

The other potential source of training was commercial contractors. In fact, they were the only option for developing a proper training system because no US uniformed personnel could be associated with the T&E Program.

The Bosnians had little experience in competitive contracting. Chris Lamb and his group took on the task of developing a training contract to start the bidding process, while the rest of the T&E team tried to raise international funding to pay for the training.

Lamb enlisted the professional acquisition staff in the DOD to help craft a draft contract. After a legal and policy review, Perle's group, the ASI, refined the draft, got approval from the Federation, and put it out for bidding by interested companies. The list of competitors was narrowed to three companies, who submitted formal proposals and made presentations to Federation representatives. The T&E team monitored the process but left the decision to the Federation, assisted by the ASI. At the conclusion of this bidding process, the Federation selected Military Professional Resources Incorporated (MPRI), a corporation in Alexandria, Virginia, as the training contractor on a one-year agreement.

No Stranger to the Region

A group of retired US Army general officers had created MPRI to provide military advice and training on a commercial basis. The company had a database of retired military personnel of virtually all ranks and skills who could be hired to fill contract requirements.

Bosnia was not MPRI's first experience in the Balkans. The Croatian defense minister, Goiko Susak, had previously hired MPRI to train the new Croatian army. This history created one more bit of controversy for the T&E Program.

While under contract to Croatia, MPRI was to teach leadership skills and provide advice on training and organizational modernization. The contract was in effect before and during the Croatian-Muslim military offensive in western Bosnia during the summer and fall of 1995. As the Croatian army offensive pushed forward, the media labeled MPRI the strategic planner of the offensive. MPRI denied the allegation, explaining that such advice was outside the scope of its contract.[2]

MPRI's vice president, General (ret.) Carl E. Vuono, a former chief of staff of the US Army, was the key corporate figure for the T&E Program in Bosnia. Vuono also had served as commander of the US Army Training and Doctrine Command. The chief of MPRI's European operation was General (ret.) Crosbie E. Saint, a former commander in chief of the US Army in Europe.

Vuono was well known as chief of staff of the army from 1987 to 1991. He had also been chief during the buildup and conduct of Operation Desert Storm against Iraqi forces in Kuwait in 1991. Saint carried an army-wide reputation as an exceptional leader and cavalry officer.

The contract between the Federation and MPRI was refined in the spring of 1996, but it could not be executed until the United States found the international money to fund the contract and worked out the procedures to handle international donor funding.

Although the United States had made the decision to go forward in supporting the contract, Washington required the Bosniaks to comply with the two conditions to start the T&E Program. First, Sarajevo must break its military ties to Iran and expel mujahedeen and other foreign fighters.

Second, the separate Muslim and Croatian forces in the Federation must be brought together into a single Ministry of Defense and military command. The instrument for this second condition was parliamentary and government approval of a Federation defense law.

Intelligence on the relationship with Iran and the movement of foreign fighters continued to show that the Bosniaks were dragging their feet in meeting this condition. The Izetbegovic government retained a cozy relationship with Iran through Tehran's embassy in Sarajevo, and in early March 1996 the press reported the continued training of Bosnian military personnel in Iran.[3] The United States pressed the Bosnian leadership at every opportunity to solve this problem or risk damaging the relationship with the United States, including its commitment to train and equip the Bosnian military.

The Bosnians were not the only problem holding back the program, though.

By early February 1996, the T&E Program was floundering. I told the Deputies Committee on February 2, 1996, that the program was a hollow shell. It had no funding and therefore no training and no equipment because the administration had not approved the US drawdown authority. Our efforts to raise international funding, training, and equipment donations had faltered. In short order, the deputies approved the T&E Program's use of the $100 million in excess US military equipment and supported an international donors conference to raise money. A cable from the State Department containing a worldwide appeal for international funding, which had been dormant in the bureaucracy for weeks, also was released.

I immediately flew to Ankara to ask Turkey to host the donors' conference in March.

17

International Donors

I knew nothing about raising international donor money when the T&E Program started. In my ignorance, I believed that wealthy Muslim societies, outraged by the plight of Muslims in Bosnia during the war, would easily open their wallets for an American-run program to give the Bosnian Muslims a self-defense capability. After all, they had donated generously to Sarajevo's humanitarian and military needs during the war. I was naive.

The State Department's global appeal for donations to T&E was the first step. Prince Bandar, the Saudi ambassador in Washington since 1983, suggested a trip to his home country, followed by an international donors' conference, to get things rolling.

The Saudis have very effective ways to deflect a constant stream of hopefuls appealing for money for projects. A visit to Riyadh, Saudi Arabia, in late January produced meetings with senior government officials, who only passed the request for funding assistance to higher levels without success. State was simultaneously pushing the Bosnian government to use its channels to appeal for support for the T&E Program. By the end of February, the T&E collection plate was still empty. The international donors' conference in mid-March was the next hope for funding help.

On the way to Ankara, the T&E team stopped in Brussels and Vienna to explain T&E to NATO and the Organization for Security and Cooperation in Europe (OSCE).

The arguments in favor of the T&E Program were straightforward:

1. Bosnia as a sovereign nation with self-defense interests was a reality after Dayton. T&E would focus on self-defense.
2. T&E would be transparent, and the United States would control the flow of weapons and assistance into Bosnia.
3. In desperation, the Bosnian government had turned to extremists in some cases for self-preservation. T&E would break Bosnia's military

relationship with Iran and remove radical extremist influences from Bosnia.

4. T&E would foster unity between Muslims and Croats in the Muslim-Croat Federation and would serve as a standard to integrate all forces into a single Ministry of Defense and joint command in the future.

5. T&E was the best way to orient the new country to Europe, Western democracy, and NATO.

6. T&E would provide the military stability necessary to allow NATO forces to leave Bosnia in a responsible way.

In dozens of briefings and discussions in Europe over the course of two years, I never felt that I changed anyone's attitude, much less any government's policy. European governments had a blind spot when it came to national security for Muslims in Bosnia.

The Empty Collection Plate: March 15, 1996

US ambassador Marc Grossman in Ankara had worked out the arrangements for the conference with Turkish authorities. Meanwhile, Deputy Secretary of State Strobe Talbott agreed to chair the Ankara Donors Conference with his Turkish counterpart, Onur Oymen, undersecretary in the Turkish Ministry of Foreign Affairs.

The signs were negative on the eve of the conference. The Bosniaks preferred that their donors provide funds directly to them and not through a US program that included Croats. Muslim countries were also holding back, waiting to see what the Saudis and other big potential contributors would do. The Saudis were evasive on whether they would even attend the conference.

I tracked down Talbott at breakfast before the conference opened later in the day. "Strobe, this conference is likely to be a disaster. I can't confirm any serious commitments beyond what the United States and Turkey are prepared to provide. I can't even assure you that the Saudis will show up. If you want to pull out of this thing now, I wouldn't blame you," I said.

Talbott took the bad news in good humor. "We'll make the best of it. This is what we do," he said, and he followed through on chairing the meeting.

The Ankara Donors Conference was a bust as a fund-raising effort. Although the representatives of thirty countries showed up, the Saudis did

The United States and Turkey sponsor a donor conference in Ankara to raise international funding for the US-led military Train and Equip Program for Bosnia. (US Department of Defense)

not attend, and Organization of Islamic Conference countries decided to support Bosnia on a bilateral basis. The Europeans, led by the United Kingdom, lectured attendees on the need for arms reductions in Bosnia. Other than the US equipment donation, training funds from Turkey, and a few speeches of support, contributions were minimal. The international press publicly declared the conference a failure.

T&E critics in Europe and the United States delighted in the spectacle of the failure in Ankara. Those in Tehran and Bosnia who wanted to maintain close ties between Bosnia and Iran also must have been encouraged by the news.

After the Ankara conference, those of us on the T&E team retreated to Istanbul to lick our wounds and take stock of the situation in one of the world's great cities. Istanbul is layer upon layer of history, much of it tied to the Balkans. Byzantium and Ottoman rulers had controlled the Balkans from there for fifteen hundred years before that region had broken away.

I knew Istanbul from the time Kathy and I had lived in Izmir from 1979 to 1981. In the evening, I arranged for the hotel to book a restaurant on the Bosporus for a team dinner. The hotel put us in a taxi and dispatched it to a spot on the European side of the Bosporus to await a boat to take us to the restaurant on the Asian side.

Like so many things in Turkey, dinner was an adventure. After a lengthy cab ride, we were dumped out in a park along the Bosporus. Suddenly the potential for a second disaster in two days was becoming real. However, in a few minutes we heard the putt-putt sound of a small engine, and the lantern on the boat became visible. Our ride—a small open boat with seats and a Turkish driver who spoke no English—launched across the strategic waterway busy with large commercial ships.

The restaurant on the Asian side sat on the water with an outside dining area where we could see ships passing on the Bosporus and the lights of the European side of Istanbul in the distance. The menu was perfect—Turkish meze and fresh seafood washed down with local wine and raki, the national anise-based liquor. The boat ride back to the European side gave us a spectacular night view of the Galata Tower, the Topkapi Palace, the Hagia Sophia, and the grand mosques on the skyline. The overall experience was worth the adventure.

I reported to Washington that the failed donors conference had exhausted my potential to raise funding for the T&E Program. We needed a new approach.

The elusive Saudi ambassador, Prince Bandar, had said in one of our meetings that he had a close relationship with the former president George H. W. Bush and regretted that he did not have similar access to the current administration. Of course, the United States had deployed tens of thousands of troops to Saudi Arabia during Operation Desert Storm, and close coordination with the Saudi government had been necessary. From these discussions with Prince Bandar, though, I took it that President Clinton would need to be involved if serious contributions to the T&E Program were to be forthcoming.

Presidential Envoy to the Persian Gulf: April 12–16, 1996

The national security staff in the White House realized that only an appeal from the president had the potential to raise the funding essential to implementing the T&E commitment. The solution was to dispatch Counselor to the President Thomas F. "Mack" McLarty, former White House chief of staff and a lifelong friend of President Clinton, to Saudi Arabia, the UAE, and Kuwait to appeal for financial support as the personal representative of the president.

McLarty was skeptical that such a mission would succeed. He knew that the emir of Kuwait had declined a previous request from Vice President Al Gore, and he understood that the Saudis had turned down Secretary of Defense Perry. McLarty also was aware of the failed Ankara Donor Conference. When President Clinton personally asked him to make the effort, McLarty said he would, but he was reluctant to leave for Arab capitals without some assurance that the mission would be fruitful.

A positive signal from Saudi Arabia was essential if the mission were to succeed. Without Saudi support, others in the Persian Gulf were unlikely to contribute. At first, the White House tried to arrange a meeting with Crown Prince Abdullah through Prince Bandar, but the Saudi ambassador in Washington was not the answer. With the official aircraft waiting at Andrews Air Force Base on the day of our departure, Mark Parrish from the NSC Staff and I sat in the West Wing of the White House outside Sandy Berger's office waiting for a positive signal. After President Clinton intervened directly with Crown Prince Abdullah bin Abdulaziz al Saud to ensure the delegation would be received, the McLarty mission to raise donations for the T&E Program took off for Saudi Arabia.[1]

The first stop was Jeddah on the Red Sea to see Crown Prince Abdullah, who was handling the day-to-day business of the monarchy on behalf of the infirm King Fahd. We landed at Jeddah on April 13 in time to spend the night at the government guest house to rest up for our audience with the crown prince the following day. The "guest house" on the waterfront was in fact an Intercontinental Hotel operated on behalf of the kingdom.

Mo Sacirbey had joined the US group to represent the government of Bosnia in the appeal and to thank the leaders at every stop for their past support to Bosnia. In a dinner with the US ambassador to Saudi Arabia, McLarty was not encouraged by the embassy staff's negative evaluation of the mission.[2] The following morning, our motorcade proceeded to the royal palace, where we waited in a large marble hall with Saudi attendants and officials milling about dressed in their traditional loose robes and head coverings. One man was leaning on a large sword. It was a scene from an orientalist painting.

We were ushered into the meeting hall, where, after introductions, McLarty was seated next to Prince Abdullah, who was dressed in the more official *bisht,* a dark cloak with a gold border. The rest of us sat in chairs lined up next to McLarty. The meeting was very formal and was conducted through the Saudi translator.

After greetings, McLarty presented a letter from President Clinton and explained the T&E Program for Bosnia. He emphasized that President Clinton considered his commitment to provide Bosnia adequate security in the future a top foreign-policy priority. Prince Abdullah responded that the Saudi people were very troubled by the Muslims' tragic situation in Bosnia during the war. Many had donated personal funds to aid the Bosnians.

McLarty eventually came to the issue of a Saudi financial contribution to the president's T&E Program. He suggested that a Saudi contribution on the order of $50 million would be appreciated. Prince Abdullah seemed somewhat relieved after clarifying that the amount was $50 million with an *m*, not $50 billion with a *b*. More pleasantries were exchanged, and the meeting adjourned.

"Was that a yes?" McLarty asked the translator on the way out.

"That was a yes," he responded.

The first stop had achieved success. The Saudis agreed to contribute $50 million to the program.

The delegation flew east from Jeddah to the UAE, where the attitude toward women and non-Muslims was considerably more relaxed than in Saudi Arabia.

After the US delegation had dinner with Sheikh Mohammed, the UAE president's son, and spent a night in Abu Dhabi, embassy cars drove us out of the irrigated greenery and bright blue sea of the city and into the desert. President Sheikh Zayed bin Sultan Al Nahyan, the seventy-eight-year-old ruler, waited for us at the royal palace about thirty miles away in the stark landscape of the desert. Sheikh Zayed preferred the Bedouin culture in the desert to the capital whenever he could escape.

The desert residence was not as elaborate as the Saudi palace but was still impressive. Attendants escorted us to a room on an upper floor, where we sat in chairs along a wall. Glasses of strong tea were poured into small glasses for us. This meeting was more straightforward than the audience in Jeddah. Sheikh Zayed opened with a long speech on the need to put an end to the suffering in Bosnia.

"We are ready to help," he said. "It is our religious duty."

McLarty again emphasized President Clinton's prioritization of the T&E Program and requested a contribution of $30 million.

"We must fulfill our duty even if some of our own needs are unfulfilled," the sheikh responded.

The meeting with the sheikh had delayed the delegation's schedule, so a UAE helicopter flew us to an awaiting aircraft. From Kuwait, the word came that the emir's staff was offended by the delay and had postponed the meeting in Kuwait City. As we approached Kuwait, the staff relented, and we proceeded to the conference center to meet Emir Jaber III, Sheikh Jaber al Ahmed al Sabah.

This meeting, too, was straightforward. Unlike the other meetings, which had been more intimate, the emir was joined by senior members of the Kuwaiti cabinet. After introductions, the emir sat quietly, fingering the tassel on his gold-trimmed black outer cloak as President Clinton's letter was translated for him. McLarty reinforced the contents of the letter and requested a donation of $50 million. The emir made no commitment but was positive in his response.

"Helping Bosnia is a duty," the emir said. "We will do as much as we can, not because they are Muslims, but because they were a wronged people. We will do everything possible."

Suddenly, the emir posed the question that had hung in the air in all of these appeals: "How strong is the Federation [of Croats and Muslims]?" he asked Sacirbey.

"The money will not be given to anyone who does not support the Federation," Sacirbey responded. "The United States and friends like you will make sure the Federation survives and the money is used to promote peace."

"That is what we hope for," the emir said.

On the trip to the airport, senior Kuwaiti officials escorting us to our aircraft assured McLarty that the emir was committed to supporting the request.[3]

The McLarty trip to the three Gulf states on behalf of President Clinton was a success critical for the T&E Program, rendering commitments of $130 million, more than enough to fund the first year of the training contract and beyond. Combined with the US equipment donation, these donations meant that T&E was suddenly on the road to reality, a huge relief for those of us involved in it.

The UAE later reduced its financial support to $15 million and offset the rest with the transfer of equipment, including tanks, armored personnel carriers, and artillery.

The Sultan of Brunei: September 9, 1997

The final international donation to the program came from Southeast Asia in 1997. Ambassador Darryl Johnson's earlier visit to Kuala Lumpur produced a commitment of $10 million from Malaysia. In a subsequent trip,

Ambassador Jon Glassman obtained a donation of $17 million by Brunei, but we needed to increase the amount to cover T&E costs.

In September 1997, Chuck Franklin and I traveled to Bandar Seri Begawan, the capital of Brunei, to call on Sultan Hassanal Bolkiah, the Muslim ruler of this tiny, oil-rich country on the edge of the rain forests of Borneo. With a letter from President Clinton to the sultan in hand, I hoped to gain a commitment for an additional $13 million, raising the Brunei total to $30 million.

Bandar Seri Begawan was a small city caught somewhere between modernization produced by great oil wealth and the simpler life of a Southeast Asian fishing and agriculture society. Several international luxury merchants had stores in the shopping center in town. A grand new mosque reflected the sultan's commitment to Islam in society.

The Brunei experience had a "Wizard of Oz" character to it. Educated in the United Kingdom, the sultan enjoyed polo and had built a top-quality polo club and stadium outside the capital to indulge his hobby and provide a venue for socializing. He had also constructed a large Disneyland-style facility nearby, Jeradong Park, whose rides, games, and gardens were immaculately maintained and free. The park had originally been built for the royal children but was made available to everyone in Brunei.

After a lunch with Prince Mohammed, the foreign minister and the sultan's brother, we went to the palace to meet the sultan. The waiting room was opulent, outfitted with the finest in carpets, silk, marble, inlaid furniture, and lighting. The protocol chief briefed us on the seating for the meeting and the rules: there was to be no pointing with the index finger, no crossing of legs, no loud speech, and we were to back out of the meeting in order not to turn our backs on the sultan. Obviously, casual Americans unfamiliar with local protocol had passed this way before.

The protocol officer ushered us into a meeting room richly appointed, like the waiting room, where the wealthiest man in the world, the sultan of Brunei, dressed in a business suit, greeted us. A soft-spoken man with the gentle manner of Southeast Asia, the sultan listened to our appeal and read the president's letter, but he committed to no more than considering the request. He made it clear that he would like a meeting with the president at an upcoming international event.

We returned to the waiting room, where we were served tea and cakes before we departed the palace and began the long trip back to Washington.

Brunei ultimately raised its contribution from $17 million to $27 million.

Managing International Donor Money

As a result of our trip, the T&E Program received a total of $152 million in international financing.[4] Although this amount is large for many projects, it is a very modest sum in the world of military training and equipment. It gave T&E the means to fulfill the training contract for a few years and to purchase specialized equipment to fill in gaps in the equipment provided by the United States and other donors. With equipment donations, the funding was enough to create a capable small force but insufficient to build and sustain a fully modern army.

The limited amount of money required very careful management to ensure maximum impact. Further, mishandling the money would threaten the credibility of the program among donors and others. I did not know the Bosnians well enough to judge them, but I had seen American assistance programs in Vietnam and elsewhere compromised by local corruption, and I was determined to avoid this pitfall in the T&E Program.

Two T&E Program policy decisions protected the funding. First, I decided that no donor funds would be placed in the Federation Treasury for salaries. The T&E Program was responsible for training and equipping the military. The Federation was responsible for paying its forces and civilian authorities. Second, the United States would control the expenditure of the funds on behalf of the donors. The Federation would set priorities, make decisions, award contracts, and make other financial commitments, but the donors had to approve the Federation's expenditure decisions, and the T&E Program would make payments directly to venders.

The US legal regime for holding and spending donor money was complex. According to the Constitution, the president could not spend money unless authorized by Congress. Further, the attorneys in the State Department kept raising the Iran-Contra scandal of 1985–1987 as the example to avoid. No one wanted to repeat the mistakes of previous administrations in managing donor funding for this project.

Chris Lamb, working with the State Department legal staff, devised a special system for managing T&E donor funds that gave an appropriate amount of accountability and control without violating legal restrictions. Donor funds were held in trust in the US Treasury and invested in US Treasury instruments until committed. Authorities in the Federation would make written requests to donors to spend a certain amount to fulfill a specific contract or expenditure validated by the US T&E Program. Once the donors approved, the US Treasury, on behalf of the donors, would pay that amount to meet the contract or expenditure. A T&E-managed auditing system was put in place to ensure that the execution of payments complied with all requirements and approvals.[5]

Throughout the life of the T&E Program, international donors had final authority over their funds and were given full and detailed account-ability of each use of their donations. I know of no misuse of any T&E funding or equipment throughout the period in which the program was implemented.

18

Hard Choices

Removing Islamic Extremists from Bosnia

Oversight of international donor funding and control of the flow of military equipment and training gave the T&E Program powerful leverage over the Bosniak and Croatian authorities in the Federation. The T&E team used that leverage to pressure the two components of the Federation to meet the conditions that would allow the program to start.

The United States forced the Bosniak government to make a binary choice: a military relationship with the United States or a continued security relationship with Iran and groups the United States considered extremist. Bosnia could not have both.

The White House devoted the full range of US capabilities to determining if the Bosnians were complying—intelligence, military, and diplomatic sources. Some things, such as training camps and the presence of fighters in units, were easy to check. Other activities were more difficult to monitor.

On February 16, 1996, in a major embarrassment for the Sarajevo government, French SFOR troops raided an Iranian training center in Bosnia and detained five Iranians. The center had mock-up models of SFOR headquarters and the US embassy.

By the spring of 1996, the results of efforts to break the ties to foreign fighters were mixed. Many mujahedeen and Iranian Revolutionary Guards Corps advisers had left Bosnia. Others had stayed, and the close military and government relationship with Iran continued into 1996.

The process to certify Bosnian compliance on foreign forces required an interagency recommendation to the president. Every US meeting with Izetbegovic and his government at any level exerted pressure to fulfill that obligation. As of mid-May 1996, however, the intelligence community could not recommend certification in Deputies and Principals Committee meetings.

Bosnian newspaper cartoon depicting US pressure on the Izetbegovic government to break its military relationship with Iran and jihadist groups. The text on the rolling pin says, "Aid Blockade." (Cartoon by Bozo Stefanovic, *Oslobodjenje*, Sarajevo)

By June 1996, the T&E Program had equipment and international donor funding for the MPRI contract, and the contract had been negotiated and was ready for signature. What was missing was presidential certification on foreign forces and passage of the defense law. In frustration, I flew to Sarajevo to confront President Izetbegovic personally on the lack of progress.

The message in this private meeting with the Bosnian president in Sarajevo on June 14 was sharp. The United States was deeply disappointed that the relationship with Iran continued, that some foreign fighters remained, and that the Federation Parliament had adjourned without passing the defense law. The United States had acted in good faith, but Sarajevo had not fulfilled its commitments.

Hasan Cengic, the Bosniak minister of defense, was a serious problem. A trusted colleague of President Izetbegovic, he had arranged for foreign military assistance to the ABiH during the war.

"Cengic does not want our help. He wants to wreck a security relationship with the United States and kill the Federation. I do not believe he wants anything to do with multicultural democracy," I told Izetbegovic. "This is a path to isolation and partition, not a path to security for Bosnia," I added.

The Bosnian president was defensive in his reply. "We will resolve this," he asserted. He then went on to claim that he could not locate all the foreign fighters and to blame the Croats for the problems in passing the draft law.

The constant pressure worked. In late June, following a full interagency review in Washington, including a recommendation by the US embassy in Sarajevo, President Clinton certified to Congress that Bosnia was in compliance with the removal of Iranian and other foreign forces.[1]

Melding Two Armies into One

At the end of the war, the Muslim and Croat components of the Federation had kept separate and parallel Ministries of Defense and armies. Sarajevo was the headquarters of the ABiH. The HVO had its headquarters in Mostar, located in the Croatian region of the country. If Bosnia were to become a unified country, these independent military structures had to be integrated.

We obtained the service of James Locher, a consultant on defense structures, to advise the Federation on preparing a law to unify the two organizations. The primary negotiators for the Federation were the two defense ministers, Vladimir Soljic for the Croats and Hasan Cengic for the Bosniaks. Soljic was a lifelong friend of Croatian minister of defense Goiko Susak in Zagreb. Cengic was a wartime hero and close to Izetbegovic and the Iranians.

Neither of the two Federation defense ministers was eager to move forward on defense consolidation. The Bosniaks saw the T&E Program as the US commitment to them specifically, not to others, but they could not legitimately resist the idea of multicultural institutions if Bosnia were to become a real country. The Croats simply wanted to stay separate while receiving a cut of what the United States was offering. We would have none of that. T&E was not going to perpetuate the destructive ethnic segregation that was the root of most problems in the region.

As T&E fund-raising and equipment solicitations continued, Locher and others concentrated on negotiating a revised defense law for passage by the Federation Parliament. Without passage of an adequate law, the program would not go forward.

Pressed on the issue at a Washington forum convened at Blaire House in mid-May 1996, President Izetbegovic and Kresimir Zubak, the Croatian president of the Muslim-Croat Federation, agreed on the principles of the proposed defense law and committed to ensuring their passage into law.

The changes in the defense law would accomplish several important structural changes:

1. Create a single chain of military command from the president and vice president through the minister and deputy minister of defense to a single joint command of the Federation Armed Force.
2. Integrate the military command into a single system.
3. Unify training and logistics into a single system.
4. Create a professional military force committed to respect for individual religious beliefs.
5. Prohibit military officers from engaging in political activities.
6. Prohibit the organization of military units based on religion or ethnic identification.
7. Require common uniform insignia.

As normal as these changes seem to Americans, they were revolutionary in Bosnia, and getting them approved by Federation leaders and the Parliament was agonizing. Although two Federation presidents had approved the law in principle in Washington, by June 1996 the Parliament had still failed to approve the law. The T&E Program remained on hold.

Secretary of Defense Perry and the Central Intelligence Agency director John Deutch elevated the pressure to pass the defense law when they visited Sarajevo at the end of June.[2] After months of verbal wrangling and US pressure in Sarajevo and Zagreb, the defense law finally passed on July 9, 1996, removing the last obstacle to launching the Train and Equip Program in Bosnia.

Yet we were still not in the clear: passing the law was one thing; implementing it was something else. Implementation would eventually take more than two years of constant US pressure and negotiations.

The day the Federation defense law was passed by the Parliament, Bosniak defense minister Hasan Cengic, who had been one of the major obstacles to the law, asked for a meeting. Cengic was intense, aggressive, and manipulative. But, like Izetbegovic, he had been jailed for Muslim nationalist activities in the Communist period, and he was a hero to many for arranging the desperately needed military equipment shipped from Iran during the war. His ability to get things done had made him valuable to the Bosniak leaders. His links to Tehran were deep, and he was quick to criticize the United States while praising Iran.

"We will need $4 million to be transferred to us from the donor accounts to start the program," Cengic said as we sat across a table from each other. But I was not about to let donor money go to a structure that I was sure would misuse it.

"Minister, you should understand something," I replied. "Not one penny of donor money will pass through your hands, not one penny. All of it will go for training and equipment. You will make the decisions, but we will pay the bills in coordination with the donors. You supply the army; we will train and equip it."

At the end of this meeting, I concluded that Cengic was never going to accept the kind of unified, Western-oriented military structure intended by the T&E Program. He needed to be replaced, but removing him would not be easy.

With President Clinton's certification to Congress regarding the removal of foreign fighters and the passage of the Federation defense law, authorities in Sarajevo had met the basic conditions to begin implementation of the T&E Program. The White House promptly announced the beginning of the US-led program to train and equip the armed forces of the Muslim-Croat Federation.[3]

The next step in launching the program in Bosnia was putting MPRI in place to begin advising and training the Federation military forces.

19

No Easy Prey

US Trainers Deploy to Bosnia

Less than a week after the White House announced the beginning of the T&E Program, the Federation leaders signed the one-year commercial contract with MPRI to assist in training and advising the Federation. International donor funds paid the $40 million cost of the contract.

In a speech in Sarajevo to officially start the program, I emphasized that its purpose was to create a stable military balance that would deter future military aggression against the people of Bosnia.

The United States had two commitments in Bosnia. One was the even-handed implementation of the Dayton Agreement. SFOR and the Office of the High Representative in Bosnia were responsible for that task.

"The second commitment, separate from the first, is to create a military balance in Bosnia to secure a lasting peace after SFOR has departed. In that context, the United States is not neutral. This war had an aggressor, and it had a victim," I said during the ceremony to sign the contract. "The program started today is to ensure that there will be no future victims and no easy prey for partisans of war. . . . In the future, if someone wants a fight, it will be more than a fair fight."[1]

In short order, General Vuono and his team committed Major General (ret.) William M. Boice and, over time, 170 civilian veterans and retired or former US military personnel to Bosnia to fulfill the various tasks called for in the contract. The MPRI concentration of talent and experience was impressive. At one point, MPRI had thirty-six US War College graduates in Bosnia, including officers who had created the National Training Center in California.

MPRI proved adept at managing the many pressures on its operation in Bosnia. It gained the respect of its Bosniak and Croatian clients by successfully staying within its military tasks and avoiding political conflicts between the two parties. Although on contract to the Federation, MPRI was sensitive to US policy concerns and maintained close coordination with the T&E staff.

The company also dealt with accusations from critics that it was a group of "American mercenaries." MPRI personnel were unarmed and fulfilled no military functions except training, so they were not mercenaries.

The relationship with SFOR was a difficult one for MPRI, though. If anything, SFOR went overboard to be "neutral" in its treatment of Serbs, Bosniaks, and Croats in Bosnia once the T&E Program was started in earnest. In order to be seen as evenhanded, SFOR subjected MPRI, which advised only the Muslims and Croats, to constant petty harassment throughout its deployment, but MPRI handled each incident with professionalism.

I witnessed SFOR's treatment firsthand. On one trip I took early in the program to visit a Bosniak unit away from Sarajevo, Bosniak soldiers provided a security escort for my embassy vehicle. Just outside the city, the motorcade pulled over and stopped for a few minutes while the soldiers changed the patches on their shoulders.

"What is this all about?" I asked the escort officer.

"These guys are from the 'Black Swans,' and SFOR has prohibited them in Sarajevo. They change their patches when they go into the city and put them back on when they leave," he replied.

The Black Swans organization was an elite unit in the ABiH during the war. Rumors held that a soldier could join the unit only if he had lost an immediate member of his family during the war. They looked as tough as their reputation.

The harassment continued. SFOR forced MPRI to alter its field uniforms and continued to deal with the HVO and the ABiH separately instead of jointly in the new organization. It denied facilities, blocked training, and seized authorized and US-donated weapons and ammunition. I complained formally in September 1997, when the list of incidents ran to two pages. The harassment gradually subsided.[2]

MPRI wasted no time in getting started, and in two years its accomplishments were significant. It

1. advised the Federation on a strategic concept for defense of the territory;
2. established a combined Federation school;

3. helped create a professional noncommissioned officer structure;
4. installed a computer simulation center for command and staff training;
5. opened a combat-training center in the Livno Valley for tank, artillery, and maneuver training with modern training devices;
6. conducted initial field training for six brigades;
7. advised on new equipment training and integration into units;
8. assisted in integrating logistics, military training, and unit organization for the Federation army.
9. documented tactics, techniques, and procedures for the army.[3]

MPRI was well suited to the task of training the Federation Armed Force. The value for the cost was excellent. Conventional security assistance could not duplicate the level of US Army experience or continuity applied to the tasks in Bosnia.

MPRI was not the only source of international training, though. Turkey provided tank and artillery training for more than five hundred Bosnian Croat and Muslim personnel by 1998. Several other Muslim countries conducted bilateral training programs as well.

In a break with other countries in western Europe, the German government agreed in September 1996 to provide helicopter pilot and maintenance training in Germany for Federation personnel.[4]

German defense minister Volker Ruhe visited the new Federation training center in February 1997—the only senior European official to visit the T&E Program. On the way back to his helicopter after the briefing, I thanked Minister Ruhe for the unique German support in the face of serious European opposition elsewhere.

"I'm doing this all alone. Most object to my doing it," he replied.

"I know, but you are right," I said. I knew how he felt.

20

Wrestling an Alligator

Arms to Bosnia

The weapons necessary to properly equip a modest Federation Armed Force came from a variety of sources. The heart of the equipment program was the authority, approved by Congress, to transfer $100 million worth of excess US military equipment and services to Bosnia.

The US equipment donations to the Federation included 45 modern tanks, 80 armored personnel carriers, 15 helicopters, and 116 heavy artillery pieces, in addition to thousands of rifles, communications gear, trucks, and ammunition. Turkey and the UAE provided another 60 tanks, and Egypt and the UAE gave more artillery to the Federation.[1]

Delivering the weapons and equipment to Bosnia was another challenge. Immediately after inaugurating the program, we arranged to fly a small shipment of US equipment into the Sarajevo Airport as a symbol of equipment delivery to the Federation. We arrived in Sarajevo to discover that General Michael Walker, the British land-component commander in SFOR, had delayed the US shipment and denied press access to the airport to cover the delivery. With the assistance of Admiral Thomas J. Lopez, the senior SFOR commander, and Ambassador John Menzies from the US embassy in Bosnia, the obstructions were overturned. The first delivery of US military equipment to the Federation army took place in Sarajevo on August 29, 1996.

We also hoped that T&E Program funding could be used to create jobs in Bosnia. Construction of the various Federation military facilities was one way the T&E Program could help the economy. The program could also inject money into the economy through local production of military equipment. One of the glaring weaknesses of the local army was a lack of personal protective gear, in particular Kevlar helmets for the soldiers. After a competitive bidding process, the Federation selected a Bosnian company to be paid by donor funding to produce the helmets.

Artillery donated to the Muslim-Croat Federation of Bosnia under the US-led Train and Equip Program arrives at the port of Ploce, Croatia. (US Department of Defense)

The Devil Goes to Pale

The Bosnian Serb leadership accepted my offer to explain the T&E Program to them at their headquarters in the mountain town of Pale near Sarajevo. I used the trip to Sarajevo to witness the first US equipment delivery to Bosnia as an opportunity to visit the Serbs as well.

Two US embassy vehicles took us on the short trip to Pale from Sarajevo. The translator with us was a well-dressed young Bosnian who worked at the embassy. I asked him what he did during the war.

"I was in the market," he said.

I was puzzled. "Stock?" I asked.

"No, black," he replied.

Our embassy driver was a young Serb who had stayed in Sarajevo during the war and had served in the ABiH. I feared the staging of a provocation in Pale to embarrass us, so I asked the drivers and security people to stay together and to avoid any engagement that might lead to an incident.

The town of Pale seemed to know we were coming. People on the street gawked as we passed by and peered out the windows to watch as we drove into the headquarters compound.

My host was Momcilo Krajisnik, the most committed Bosnian Serb leader during the Holbrooke negotiations. At this point, Radovan Karadzic and General Ratko Mladic, under international indictment for war crimes, were in hiding. I had not seen Krajisnik since Dayton in November the previous year. He greeted me politely as a colleague who had shared a difficult experience and then pointed to a map behind his desk.

"Do you recognize this map?" he asked. "It is the map you delivered to Milosevic on the day the Dayton Agreement was signed," he said. "This map gave Sarajevo to the Muslims."

"Yes, I recognize it," I replied. It was the small official map finally agreed to by the parties at Dayton on the morning the agreement was complete. The Bosnian Serbs did not know that Milosevic had conceded Sarajevo until he showed them the map.

Krajisnik listened without comment to the presentation about the T&E Program. I offered full transparency to the Bosnian Serbs as the program went forward. I ended by stating the hope that someday soon Bosnia could have one integrated armed force.

He replied with one word: "Never."

The visit went without incident. I never returned to Pale, and I never saw Krajisnik again.

Equipment from Eastern Europe: Yes, No, Maybe

With donor money available, the T&E Program had funds to purchase equipment to fill gaps in the Federation inventory. The new democracies in eastern Europe were sinking under the weight of unneeded and costly Warsaw Pact equipment, so Jon Glassman, Chris Lamb, and others in the T&E Program fanned out across the region in search of equipment bargains.

In Prague, the Czechs wanted to help, but, like others, they did not want to step in front of the West Europeans. They would wait to see what others would do.

The Polish government was conflicted. Poland had massive amounts of excess equipment, but European political opposition to T&E had a real impact in Warsaw. Although Poland would consider the sale of other items, we left Warsaw convinced that further contact was not worth the trouble.

Even though the UN had lifted its arms embargo in 1996, the EU maintained its own embargo after Dayton, and it remained in effect until 2001. Poland aspired to be a member of the EU that year and so did not want to challenge EU policy. The representatives of several capitals told us privately that diplomats from EU countries were suggesting that cooperation with the T&E Program could affect their countries' future EU membership. The threats seemed hollow and impractical, but such pressure prevented open sales throughout eastern Europe. We never pursued covert sales, which violated the T&E transparency policy, although it would have been easy to do so.

Discussions with military-equipment executives in Bratislava, the capital of the Slovak Republic, were troubling beyond the scope of the T&E Program. Everything in the eastern European military inventory seemed to be for sale there.

In a meeting with one former Communist-era official in the Slovak Ministry of Defense, we inquired about the availability of man-portable air-defense weapons. These weapons are fired from the shoulder and are known as "manpads" in military parlance. The official said that we should talk to one of his contacts, a private arms merchant. He arranged a meeting later in the day.

The arms merchant was a young man with the attitude of an arrogant hustler. He offered the Soviet-made SA-13 system at a very reasonable price.

"Our technical experts must inspect them before we pay," I said.

"That's a problem," he replied. "I can deliver them to you after you pay, but an inspection before payment is not possible unless you people are prepared to go to Russia or other new countries to inspect them."

"We are in the market for legitimate arms sales according to international standards and US law," I replied. "We will not buy systems that do not have proper documentation."

"What documentation do you want? I will produce paperwork with Yeltsin's signature if that's what you want," he boasted. I declined and ended the meeting. But from that discussion I came to believe that in 1996, in the chaos of the collapse of the Soviet Empire, anything in the former Soviet arsenal was for sale if the money were available.

When we arrived in Bucharest, Romania, European diplomats already had warned the Romanians that their EU membership aspirations might be influenced if they violated the EU arms embargo by selling excess military equipment destined for Bosnia. The first visit yielded no sales. However, Romania later sold multiple rocket launchers to Bosnia through the T&E Program.

Other than a few Western-style advertising signs, the Ukrainian capital of Kiev seemed not to have changed much from the Communist days. The

Ukraine had many military items the Federation needed, but the government bureaucracy was in disarray regarding who oversaw military equipment. Nothing much came from the trip to the Ukraine.

Amsterdam was a more productive visit. The Federation desperately needed trucks to provide transportation for the army, and Jon Glassman found a suitable commercial supplier of used trucks in the Netherlands if the Dutch government would authorize the sale. The trucks were commercial ones, so the Dutch government agreed.

The Dutch merchant proved to be another story. After weeks of negotiations on every detail, Glassman and Lamb became convinced that the reputation of Dutch merchants as tough negotiators was fully justified. But in the end the Federation received the trucks.

Removing Defense Minister Cengic

The major shipment of US equipment was due to arrive in Bosnia in the autumn of 1996. That delivery became a crisis point that determined whether the T&E Program would meet its broader goals of reforming the military in Bosnia.

Hasan Cengic, to my surprise, accepted the position of deputy to a Croatian defense minister in the new consolidated Defense Ministry. Throughout the summer and fall, however, he caused trouble inside the Federation as both sides resisted implementation of the defense law. We also had information that Cengic continued to be engaged with Iran. He had to go if the program were to have any potential to succeed in breaking the link to Iran and unifying the Federation military.

By the end of August 1996, Assistant Secretary of State John Kornblum, Holbrooke's replacement in the State Department's European Bureau, joined me in advising President Izetbegovic that he should replace Cengic as deputy defense minister. Izetbegovic listened but took no action.

The Cengic problem continued into September as the major shipment of US equipment was making its way by sea for delivery to Bosnia. The *American Condor* was a huge ship designed to carry heavy US equipment to a war zone. Loaded with forty-five modern tanks and eighty armored personnel carriers from US stock, the *Condor* was sailing to the Croatian port of Ploce to deliver its cargo. There, the armored vehicles would be loaded on trains and shipped to Bosnia for Federation forces.

The cargo on the *American Condor* was the best possible leverage to force the removal of Cengic and to implement the defense law. However, engineering his removal from the Defense Ministry would require support from very high levels in Washington. The DOD and some senior levels at State agreed that Cengic had to go, especially after he continued to maintain his ties with Iran.

But Secretary of State Warren Christopher and his closest advisers did not agree; they weren't comfortable telling another sovereign government to fire a deputy minister of defense. I prepared a letter to President Izetbegovic and his Croatian counterpart in the Federation listing several actions required for implementation of the Federation defense effort, including the removal of Cengic from defense activities. The letter was to be signed by Secretary of Defense Perry and Secretary Christopher jointly.

Perry was at the State Department and signed the letter after a ceremony. "Jim, do we have to do this?" he asked.

"Yes. If Cengic stays, the whole program will be discredited," I said. Perry asked if Christopher would support the letter. I told him that I was uncertain.

"Come with me," Secretary Perry said. We headed down to the secretary of state's private office on the seventh floor, bypassing the gatekeepers in Christopher's outer office. Perry put the letter in front of Christopher.

"Chris, we need to remove this guy. Please sign the letter," Secretary Perry said.

After some discussion, Christopher signed the letter. I thanked the secretaries and bolted from the room, promising Christopher's grousing staff that a copy of the signed letter would be forthcoming.

I stopped in Zagreb to inform Croatian defense minister Susak that Washington was out of patience with the failure to implement the defense law in Bosnia and that the Bosnian Croats were much to blame.

I delivered the Christopher–Perry letter to President Izetbegovic in his office on September 21. He did not defend Cengic.

"America is like my wife," he said. "I love her deeply. I cannot survive without her. But sometimes she makes me furious."

During the months I had been in Bosnia, Izetbegovic had invited me to his home once. He and his wife lived simply in a modest apartment in the center of Sarajevo. I never saw Izetbegovic flaunt his religion, but the presence of an open Koran in a prominent place in the home showed his personal religious commitment. He displayed no interest in the grand trappings or ceremony of high office usually associated with a national president.

We were asking a great deal of Izetbegovic. Removing Cengic and breaking the security link with Iran meant rejecting a hero of the Bosnian Muslims' cause during the war and those who supported Sarajevo when others did not. It was a painful choice for the Bosnian president.

The next night while I was at dinner with some MPRI representatives, one of President Izetbegovic's assistants called to say that the president would remove Cengic if the Croats removed Vladimir Soljic, the Federation minister of defense. Because the Croats were not without blame in the failure to unify the defense establishment, I saw no problem with this request, but I needed clearance from Washington.

I broke into a conference call between Talbott, Kornblum, and Undersecretary of State Peter Tarnoff to explain the situation and to recommend that we accept the Izetbegovic proposal. They agreed. I called Izetbegovic's assistant and received a guarantee that if the Croats removed Soljic as minister of defense, Izetbegovic would remove Cengic.

The next morning Croat president Kresimir Zubak agreed to sack Soljic. I completed the deal with Minister Susak in Zagreb, who was not happy because he and Soljic were childhood friends, but he realized that the removal of his friend was the price of removing Cengic.

I returned to Zagreb and Sarajevo a week later to find that Cengic and Soljic remained in their positions. In response, I stopped the *American Condor*, loaded with armored vehicles to be delivered to the Federation, from docking in Ploce. I then instructed the ship to hold in the waters off Croatia until the conditions of the Christopher–Perry letter were satisfied.

The US Army had other tasks for the *American Condor*, and pressure was growing for me to release the ship by early October. The Deputies Committee decided to authorize the ship to dock in Ploce, but in a series of subsequent deliberations I convinced Washington that if the ship were to unload the US equipment, leverage on the Muslims and the Croats to remove Cengic and unify their forces would evaporate.

By the end of October, Izetbegovic still had not removed Cengic. I refused to authorize the ship to offload as the *American Condor* circled in the Adriatic, but pressure to bring the ship to port was intense. I reminded Izetbegovic and Zubak that $10,000 destined for their military was being burned each day the ship circled in the Adriatic Sea.

On November 15, after weeks of delay, Izetbegovic signed the necessary documents to remove Cengic and sent them to Zubak, his Croatian counterpart in the Federation. Zubak promptly disappeared. Finally,

Zubak, under pressure from Zagreb, completed the action on November 19. Cengic was replaced by Sakib Mahmuljan, a former ABiH corps commander. US intelligence agencies had no reason to oppose Mahmuljan.

Ante Jelavic, a former Croatian military logistics officer, replaced Soljic. Jelavic was a staunch Croat nationalist with political ambitions. He later caused constant problems in integrating the Bosnian and Croatian components of the Federation military, requiring us to engage Zagreb to pressure him to cooperate with the T&E Program.

Mahmuljan, in contrast, proved to be an exceptional defense leader. He was capable, practical, smart, but modest. I talked to him about the risks the United States was taking in supporting the Bosnian Muslims.

"If any of these weapons or this ammunition ever shows up in the wrong place and is used against Americans, everything that we have done here to help you will be discredited," I said. Mahmuljan understood the message and took care to ensure accountability of the materials, and none of it leaked into the wrong hands over the years.

The *Condor*

After twenty-seven days of treading water off the Croatian coast, the *American Condor* docked at Ploce on November 21. Controversy, however, continued even into the offloading of the ship.

Dutch military personnel happened to be aboard the ship as part of an exchange program with the United States. Because they were NATO soldiers, they were told not to participate in the offloading of the ship, and the transfer of equipment was halted. I was informed that the instruction originated with UK general Michael Walker, the long-standing nemesis of the T&E Program in SFOR. I asked Washington to intervene with The Hague and London to stop the obstruction to the delivery.

Later that day Walker tracked me down at the Jez restaurant to complain that he was falsely accused, and after a heated exchange we parted ways for good. His boss in SFOR, Admiral Lopez, later wrote a memo asserting that Walker had not been involved in the obstruction.[2] Walker retired in 2006 after serving as the British chief of the Defense Staff and receiving the US Legion of Merit military decoration. He retired as Baron Walker of Aldringham, no doubt an important position in Aldringham.

Walker was the most active opponent but not alone in harassing T&E implementation. SFOR never accepted the T&E Program. I met privately with virtually every US SFOR commander for three years to explain the

James Pardew (*left*), addressing the ceremony marking the arrival of US tanks and armored personnel carriers donated to the Federation under the T&E Program. Others present at the ceremony included (*left to right*) Croatian defense minister Goiko Susak (behind Pardew), Christopher Lamb, and the director of the Port of Ploce. (US Department of Defense)

program, its transparency, and the commitment not to cause problems for SFOR. However, low-level harassment and obstruction of new initiatives continued. Washington intelligence analysts were also skeptical of T&E, but their dire predictions that the Muslims would use their new military capacity to attack the Serbs never came true.

On Thanksgiving Day in 1996, a little more than a year after the Dayton Peace Agreement was completed, CNN and other international television outlets broadcast images of trains loaded with US tanks and armored personnel carriers rumbling from Ploce into central Bosnia. The Federation stored the tanks and armored vehicles in a common area in central Bosnia until they could be properly allocated to units.

A last heavy-weapons shipment from the United States would take place on May 9, 1997, when 116 heavy-artillery pieces were to be delivered to Bosnia. I thought that the international interest in the T&E training would wane after a year and a half of activity without incident. Not so. The press conference in Sarajevo announcing the delivery of the artillery was front-page news in the *New York Times* the next day.[3]

Once the equipment was on hand, the process of its allocation to units began. The United States distributed equipment based on standard organization and operational priority. The Federation wanted to allocate everything according to ethnic ratios without regard to practical requirements. We held up distribution until the two parts of the Federation had agreed on a combined force structure, but each decision was difficult.

Status Report

By the one-year point in 1997, the progress made in the T&E Program was having a serious psychological effect on the region and increasing the level of opposition elsewhere. It had achieved its objective of creating a credible deterrent to any Serbian plans to advance their separatist ideas by force. However, the improvements to the Federation military capacity also increased the level of opposition to T&E in Europe and in Washington.

Most of the fears and criticisms were unfounded, but I, too, had some concerns. In a one-year status report to Assistant Secretary of State Kornblum and others, I reported that T&E had fulfilled the basic commitment and had met many objectives. I also mentioned, however, my fear that the progress made on unifying and professionalizing the military in Bosnia might break down if the United States were to terminate the T&E Program prematurely.

"Today, the Train and Equip Program is like wrestling an alligator. We may have control, but we're afraid to turn it loose," I wrote in my report.[4]

The US military continued to oppose T&E and pressed for an interagency policy decision in early 1997 to cut back the program. Analysis within the intelligence community reinforced the military view with dire assessments that the T&E Program was destabilizing Bosnia and that the Muslims might use their new capability to seek revenge on the Serbs. The negative intelligence analysis disturbed me the most because I felt it did not reflect the reality of what was taking place in the Federation. The Muslims were not plotting to take revenge on the Serbs. They wanted to join NATO and the EU.

I was relieved when the Principals Committee, despite interagency concerns, reaffirmed support for the full T&E Program in early April 1997.

Intelligence and Policy

Although the negative intelligence assessment of the T&E Program disturbed me, it did not surprise me. From years in the business, I knew that the glass is always half empty in the intelligence world.

A skeptical intelligence community is, however, a national asset. US policy making benefits from a politically independent intelligence community with a professional commitment to objective analysis of the facts as it knows them. The intelligence community should look for trouble, fret over uncertainty, and worry about the possible negative implications of policy.

Intelligence professionals are responsible for preventing surprise, identifying risks, helping frame options, and projecting the consequences of policy decisions. Intelligence does not predict the future. Rather, it functions in a realm of uncertainty and misdirection. It can uncover important facts, provide unique insights, connect dots, and perform serious analysis of a sensitive situation. But in my experience with policy, diplomacy, and military operations, intelligence alone is rarely prescriptive. Rather, its primary value is to help reduce uncertainty and to help evaluate risk for the decision maker in each situation.

Intelligence is naturally skeptical because professionals in this field know the limitations of their information. They also know that to emphasize dangers and to be wrong is an embarrassment but to predict policy success and to be wrong can lead to disaster. A leader should view with deep suspicion any intelligence projection of certain policy success.

When well run, intelligence has the courage and credibility to take real and potential bad news to policy makers and others in positions of authority. Remaining fearlessly independent of political manipulation is critical for a competent national intelligence system. If intelligence becomes a political tool, it loses its value to national policy and can become a threat to democracy itself.

Intelligence can be a convenient scapegoat for scoundrels. Blaming policy problems on intelligence failure is easy: it can be claimed that better information might have produced better policy. But complete situational awareness almost never exists, and policy judgment is always the deciding factor. Unfortunately, the intelligence community has limited public defenses against shallow assertions of failure. Legitimate intelligence failures happen, but they are best determined by careful, independent evaluation and not by quick public declarations from those who have an interest in deflecting blame.

Negative intelligence assessments of the consequences of the T&E Program did not stop it from moving forward. They did, however, make the program sensitive to the projected consequences and take measures to ensure that those consequences did not happen.

The Federation Maneuver Training Center

The last major challenge in creating a capable Federation military was to build a maneuver-training area for heavy-weapons firing and large-unit maneuver training. Once the tanks, artillery, and armored personnel carriers arrived in Bosnia and were distributed to units, the Federation military needed a suitable training space adequate for unit maneuver and heavy-weapons firing.

In 1997, Federation leaders and MPRI settled on a training area in a remote, sparsely populated region of the Livno Valley in southwestern Bosnia. SFOR had originally suggested the location. The Federation, however, could not construct the center and begin training without the formal approval of both SFOR and the Office of the High Representative. This requirement gave opponents one last opportunity to block the T&E Program.

SFOR stalled on agreement for the center while continually interfering in routing Federation training. Because SFOR technically worked for him, General Wes Clark, by then the SACEUR, periodically stepped in to dislodge training obstructions, and SFOR ultimately allowed the center to move forward.

Jacques Klein, the American deputy in the Office of the High Representative, was a surprising opponent of the Livno center. Klein used a range of bureaucratic obstacles to impede construction of the center for months. When high-level officials in Washington became aware of his opposition and the press learned that an American official was blocking a major US program, pressure on Klein improved his attitude. By February 1998, obstruction to the center ended, and the Livno Training Center became operational.

After two years, the T&E Program had accomplished most of its primary goals. The Federation military was unified to the degree that it was possible to do so; major weapon systems and support equipment had been delivered; and quality training was ongoing at all levels. New training facilities were open and operating, and the influence of radical foreign forces in Bosnia was over. The T&E Program continued, but the remainder of the program was a process of refinement and sustainment.

Trainers from the military contractor MPRI conduct training for Federation soldiers on the M60 tanks donated to the Federation by the US government under the T&E Program. (Shutterstock.com)

Breakfast by the Waterfall

By 1998, the United States was trying to stop Milosevic from launching another harsh repression in the former Yugoslavia, this time against the Albanians in Kosovo, who were demanding independence from Serbia. T&E was winding down, and I was gradually shifting my focus to the Kosovo problem.

A visit to the Federation's Fifth Corps at Bihac in northwestern Bosnia in early October 1998 was one of my last actions in the T&E Program. We arrived at the corps headquarters in the early evening for a briefing by Lieutenant General Atif Dudakovic, reportedly the best operational general officer in the Bosniak inventory. The stocky and animated Dudakovic was the opposite of his boss, General Rasim Delic, the reserved and careful commander in Sarajevo. Dudakovic hosted a dinner that featured much food, drinking, war stories, and soulful singing of Balkan folk songs by a local group.

The next morning Dudakovic drove us to the Una River, which separates Bosnia from Croatia, where we stopped in a village and climbed a hill to a point overlooking a high waterfall that sent water crashing on the rocks below. On the way, we walked past the house of a young Serbian Orthodox priest, who was washing carrots in his yard. Near the bottom of the falls, cooks from the Fifth Corps had set up a breakfast of Bosnian bread, juice, fruit, meat, sliced vegetables, and coffee. Brandy and other drinks were available for those who wished.

When I inquired about Serbs who were returning to this area of Bosnia, Dudakovic sent for the priest we had seen earlier. The priest arrived with another young priest in a few minutes. The two men seemed at ease with the Muslim generals and soldiers. They laughed and talked easily about the local community as I watched for signs of tension. I saw none. This brief encounter gave me some hope for the future.

General Dudakovic subsequently replaced General Delic as commander of the Federation Armed Force.

By the end of 1998, after two years, the T&E Program had developed a slow and sometimes frustrating routine. The last major shipment of equipment, fifteen US helicopters, was made, but the integration of the two Federation armies, ABiH and HVO, was a constant struggle. The Bosniaks were incredibly generous toward the Croats in sharing the benefits of the US effort. The unappreciative Croat leadership in Bosnia, however, resisted force integration at every step. The HVO was a hollow force, more political than military. Ante Jelavic, the senior Croat in the Federation Defense Ministry, was using the HVO for his increasingly nationalist political ambitions. Meanwhile, the Croats made constant petty demands to irritate their Bosniak partners and to emphasize separation.

Privately, I consoled myself that at least President Clinton's commitment had been fulfilled, and T&E had given the Bosniaks the means to defend themselves if this whole international adventure were to fall apart and fighting were to resume. If that happened, the fight would be a very different conflict.

The T&E Program continued until October 2002, when the State Department announced its termination.[5]

21

Impact

As Yugoslavia fractured, the Serbs tried and failed to kill, drive away, or subjugate millions of largely secular Muslims in Bosnia and later in Kosovo. In confronting Serbian war crimes, the United States and its allies had two choices in dealing with the Muslim victims in the Balkans. They could engage them, recognize their interests, and encourage them to adopt democratic values as fully accepted citizens of European nations, or they could isolate or ignore them, with a virtual guarantee that extremist leaders elsewhere would exploit such isolation to oppose Western democratic interests. The choice for me was easy, but this argument won few converts for the T&E Program.

Despite the dire warnings about its consequences and the obstacles to implementation, the T&E Program fulfilled the US commitment made in 1995 to assist the Bosnian government with its future military capability. Through the T&E Program, an effective military balance was achieved in Bosnia, and a Muslim war of revenge against Serbs and Croats, which some had predicted, never took place. The T&E Program also exposed the Bosnians to high-quality military training, NATO standard equipment, modern defense structures, and practices appropriate to national security organizations in a democracy.

Sufficient military stabilization was achieved in Bosnia to allow NATO to reduce the number of its troops in Bosnia from 60,000 soldiers in 1996 to 7,000 and then to shut down SFOR in 2004, leaving the security mission to the EU. Nine years from NATO's deployment to its withdrawal is an extremely brief period for the presence of an international security force.

Bosnia did not become a haven for Muslim extremists. None of the attacks on the United States or in Europe in subsequent years originated in Bosnia, and none of the attackers were recruited from there. They instead came through central Europe.

By 1999, the separate armies in the Republika Srpska and the Muslim-

Croat Federation began to deteriorate. After Tudjman and Milosevic lost power in Croatia and Serbia, the external influence on Croats and Serbs in Bosnia began to decline, and the military assistance from Zagreb and Belgrade to clients in Bosnia dwindled. With the decline in tensions, a sense of military urgency and confrontation inside Bosnia withered as well. Local corruption in defense expenditures outside the T&E Program also began to drain resources for military readiness as maintenance and training standards slipped.[1]

Raffi Gregorian, an alumnus of the T&E Program, and James Locher, who worked on the original Federation defense law, took the unification of the militaries in Bosnia to the next logical steps in 2004–2005.

Gregorian left the T&E Program to become the political adviser to SFOR in 2004–2006. Jeremy J. D. "Paddy" Ashdown from the United Kingdom, who was then the high representative in Bosnia, later appointed Gregorian to cochair the Defense Reform Commission in Bosnia. The commission negotiated a law to consolidate and elevate the separate defense ministries and military commands of the Republika Srpska and the Federation into one national-level structure. In 2003, the Bosnia defense law integrated the Defense Ministry at the national level and created one command above the two entity armies.

That law was replaced in 2005 with a new defense law that took the integration of the armies to the ultimate level. On January 1, 2006, the two armies of the Federation and the Republika Srpska ceased to exist, and a new integrated armed force for Bosnia was created. The president of Bosnia, in coordination with the two deputies, became supreme commander of the unified armed forces. A single multiethnic Bosnian army subordinate to a single military chain of command, reporting through the national Ministry of Defense to the president of the republic, became the national security force for Bosnia. Its active-duty strength by law is 10,000 personnel, with a reserve component of 5,000.[2] In 2006, Bosnia became a member of NATO's Partnership for Peace Program, the first step toward eventual NATO membership.

This level of integration might have taken place without the T&E Program, but the latter effort gave the bitter and battered Muslim population in Bosnia confidence that their security would be in their hands. It also strengthened their negotiating position with Serbs and Croats in Bosnia, Serbia, and Croatia.

"The US T&E Program was messy at times, often difficult, but it achieved its strategic objectives in Bosnia, including regional stability," Gregorian said.[3]

In 2013, the government of Bosnia dispatched a contingent of Bosnian army troops to join the NATO International Security Assistance Force in Afghanistan. The Bosnian troops provided convoy and installation for NATO forces.[4]

Part 4

Kosovo
War and Independence

Overview of Prizren, Kosovo. (iStock)

22

A Land of Violence and Fear

Shaun Byrnes, chief of the US Kosovo Diplomatic Observer Mission (KDOM), led the first of two armored US embassy sports utility vehicles out of Pristina and into the countryside on January 19, 1999. Byrnes was taking me to meet members of the Kosovo Liberation Army (KLA), the independence movement fighting an increasingly repressive Serbian military and police presence in Kosovo.

We meandered around a bit to ensure that Serbian police and intelligence were not trailing us. They weren't, but a *BBC News* crew was. Near the small town of Malishevo, we encountered a KLA checkpoint as we left the main road. Proceeding into a village, Byrnes asked the KLA guards at the checkpoint to block the BBC crew for fear that the crew might later compromise the location of the KLA safe house.

The United States and the Contact Group were struggling to end the crackdown on civilians and to avoid another military clash with Milosevic and Serbia, this time over Kosovo. The security situation for Albanians in Kosovo was ominous, and the dangers were increasing. A KLA guard waved our vehicles into an enclosed compound in the village. The clan is the center of Albanian culture, and these family compounds were a mainstay of the Albanian villages in Kosovo. Surrounded by a high wall, each compound usually contained the family home, barn, and outbuildings. It provided privacy and a modest amount of security for an extended family.

I was not the first official American diplomat to engage the KLA; Richard Holbrooke and others had met with its leaders in recent months. For this meeting, our hosts were members of the KLA political directorate. Three young men in fresh military field uniforms escorted us to the second floor of the house, where they took off their weapons as we sat on cushions along the walls of a large room. A wood stove in the center of the room provided heat. After greeting us, our hosts brought out beer, peanuts, and bananas to munch on as we talked.

The KLA uniforms looked new, and the officers did not have the hardened look of combat veterans. I noticed that one of them was armed with a shiny, new, stainless steel Smith & Wesson .44 Magnum revolver. I mentioned the pistol, and he handed the loaded weapon to me to admire.

The discussion, conducted through a translator, lasted about two hours. The KLA people did not strike me as zealots. Rather, they were modest and open. My message to them was simple: restraint—do nothing that could get them labeled as terrorists. I urged them to negotiate with Ambassador Chris Hill from the Dayton team, whom Holbrooke had positioned as the regional US negotiator for Kosovo.

We left the compound and spent the rest of the day touring Kosovo to give me a feel for the area. We drove in a clockwise direction southwest out of Pristina to Malishevo, then up to Peja in the West, then north to Mitrovica before returning to the capital.

A day trip around Kosovo was possible because it is a small country, slightly smaller than Delaware, and about one-fifth the size of Bosnia. The population is about 1.8 million people, 90 percent of them Muslims.[1] The land is used primarily for farming and grazing, although a few areas, notably in the North, have some mining.

The largest number of Serbs live north of the Ibar River, which runs through the town of Mitrovica, although very important pockets of Serbs are located throughout Kosovo in communities near Orthodox churches and monasteries.

Byrnes's tour went to Mitrovica, a future international flashpoint in Kosovo. In addition to the ethnic division of the city north and south, the largest nonagriculture economic asset in the country, the Trepca Mine, was located just north of the city in the predominately Serb area.

A menacing Serbian military and police presence was visible in towns and on the highways as we drove around Kosovo. I watched an armored unit prepare to go on patrol, and we passed Yugoslavian army tanks along the roads in violation of agreements Milosevic had made with international representatives. The notorious Federal Republic of Yugoslavia (FRY) Special Ministry of Interior Police (Ministarstvo Unutrasnjih Poslova), or MUP, armed with long rifles and wearing distinctive dark-blue-purple military-style uniforms, were present in towns and at checkpoints on the primary highways. These units were accused of torture and murder of civilians throughout Kosovo. After a quick drive through Mitrovica, Byrnes guided us back to Pristina.

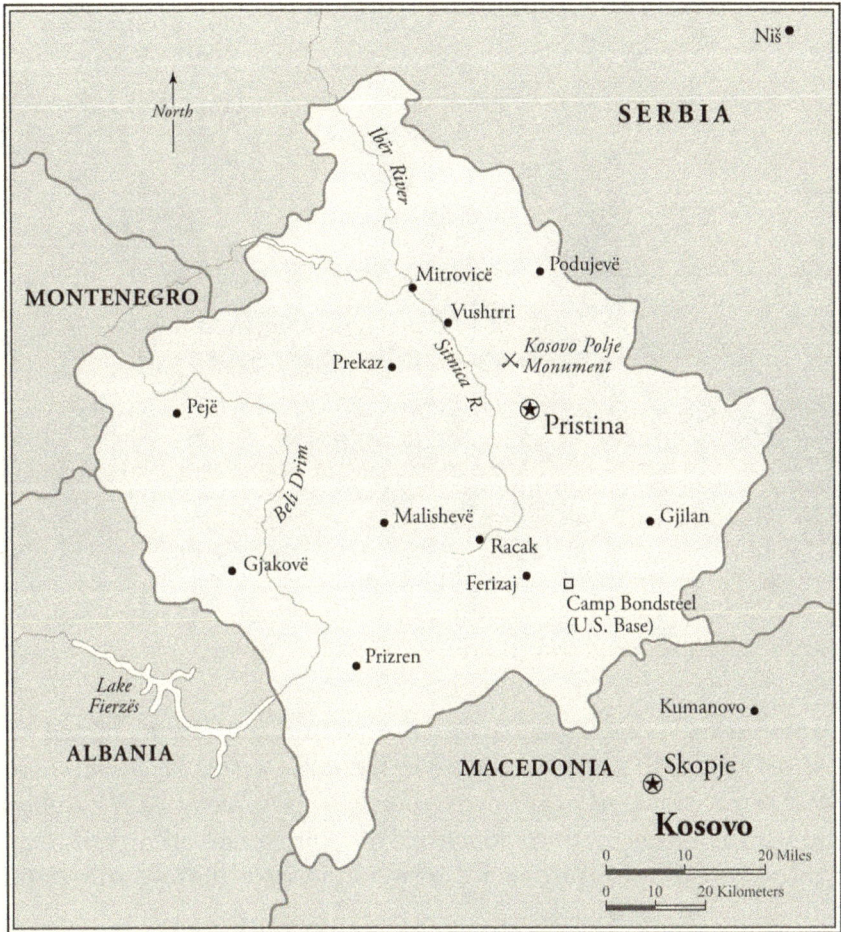

Pristina was a gloomy provincial capital consisting of large Soviet-era block apartments and bizarre Communist-modern architecture. Despite its determination to retain Kosovo as an integral part of Serbia, the Serbian government never invested heavily in the infrastructure of Kosovo or its capital. In fact, electricity was intermittent from a power-generating complex on the outskirts of Pristina, which pumped clouds of coal smoke into the air from the low-quality coal it burned. Water was also available only off and on.

The capital of Kosovo under Serbian military and police occupation was a city of fear. We arrived back in Pristina at dusk. By dark, the Alba-

A member of the Serbian Special Police on patrol in Kosovo, 1999. (Photograph by Arban Bujariu, *Koha Ditore*, Pristina, Kosovo)

nians were off the streets, and only a few internationals, the MUP, and the Pristina Municipal Police, dominated by the Serbs, were out and about. The MUP patrolled the city aggressively, rounding up suspected KLA members and supporters. But the Serbs dominated only the ground where they stood. Otherwise, they were surrounded by a hostile sea of Kosovo Albanians. This condition could not last.

After a night in the Grand Hotel, a Communist relic built for party visitors in the center of Pristina, I was off to Belgrade to talk to Slobodan Milosevic—who had easily transitioned from being the president of Serbia to being the president of the Federal Republic of Yugoslavia—about Kosovo.

"Kosovo Is the Heart of Serbia"

Most countries in post-Soviet eastern Europe in 1998–1999 were concentrating on the transition to democracy and a modern economy as they worked to qualify for NATO and EU membership. Not Serbia. The Serbs were obsessed with stopping the independence movement in Kosovo.

Kosovo held a special place in the Serbs' self-image, and they were not going to let it break away without a fight, even if that fight would retard

Serbia's future development. The dream of a "Greater Serbia"—control of large areas of Bosnia, Croatia, and Montenegro—had largely evaporated by 1998. Outside of Serbia, Belgrade technically controlled only Montenegro and Kosovo, the last provinces of the former Yugoslavia with significant numbers of Serbs.

Kosovo was deeply embedded in Serbian history and mythology, and independence for Kosovo was unacceptable to the Serbs. According to their history of the region, Kosovo fit into the mythology of the Balkans. Non-Muslims from Istanbul to Vienna saw themselves as the historic protectors of Western civilization against the Ottoman invaders. For the Serbs, one event—a battle near Pristina, Kosovo, in June 1389 between Serbian forces, led by Prince Lazar, and the forces of Ottoman sultan Murad I—is central to Serbian national identity. They continue to cling to the battle as a point of honor and sacrifice. Which side won is a matter of dispute, and both the prince and the sultan lost their lives as a consequence of the fighting.[2] The Serbs built a significant memorial to the battle, in which a stone tower overlooks the battlefield, which is known generally as Kosovo Polje, the "Field of Blackbirds."

Despite the national emotion over Kosovo, Serbia treated it more as a colony than as a treasure. Belgrade's commitment to the region was less than enthusiastic, and the Serb population in Kosovo was, in fact, relatively small. Belgrade did not invest heavily on developing Kosovo within the Yugoslav system, and Serbs were not eager to move there, despite continuous incentives to relocate. Kosovo was a backwater province of Yugoslavia, populated overwhelmingly by Albanians, and by 1998 the Albanians wanted independence from Belgrade.

In the autumn of 1998, three years removed from the Dayton Agreement, Milosevic became president of what was left of the FRY, now consisting only of Serbia, Montenegro, and Kosovo. His crony and loyal assistant, former foreign minister Milan Milutinovic, replaced him as president of Serbia in the same election. That election solved the problem of a constitutional term limit for Milosevic but in fact changed nothing in the country's leadership. Milosevic was still in complete control of the remains of Yugoslavia in 1998.

Kosovo was the political issue Milosevic had originally used to gain power in Serbia.[3] He could not politically or personally face the loss of Kosovo as the independence movement gained momentum among Kosovo Albanians in 1998 because it could destroy his political legitimacy among Serbs.

"Kosovo is the heart of Serbia. For every Serb, Kosovo is a holy thing," Milosevic told a delegation from the US Council on Foreign Relations in Belgrade shortly after the Dayton negotiations.[4]

Controlling Kosovo was an old problem for the Serbs. The major Western powers had included Kosovo as a component of the Kingdom of Serbs, Croats, and Slovenes during the Paris negotiations after World War I.[5] Serbian authorities thereafter repressed Albanian language and culture in Kosovo. At the end of World War II, the Communists killed thousands of Albanians in Kosovo to subdue the Albanian nationalists.[6] Tito annexed Kosovo into Yugoslavia after 1945, and the Yugoslav government later expelled thousands of Albanians to strengthen Yugoslav Communist control of the region.[7]

The Yugoslav Constitution of 1974 gave Kosovo the same autonomous status as other Yugoslav republics, except the right to secede. It also allowed Kosovo to have its own provincial constitution, deputies in the Serbian Parliament, its own judicial and education system, and a central bank.[8]

Serbian nationalists despised the Constitution of 1974, and after Tito died in 1980, they began to tighten control over Kosovo. In March 1989, three months before the grand celebration of the six hundredth anniversary of the battle at Kosovo Polje, Milosevic engineered a change to the Constitution to remove autonomy for Kosovo within Yugoslavia. The vote in the Kosovo Provincial Assembly took place in a hall surrounded by Serbian tanks and armored personnel carriers. Strikes and riots by Albanians followed the change in the province's status and generated organized political resistance.

Serbian repression of Albanians escalated after Milosevic removed autonomy and declared martial law in Kosovo. At the beginning, the Kosovo Albanians demanded that Belgrade restore autonomy. As the Kosovo Albanian protest movement grew stronger, Milosevic responded with increasingly harsh repressive measures throughout the 1990s.[9] By 1998, autonomy was no longer the primary objective for the Albanians. Local Albanian nationalists created an insurgent force, the KLA, to pursue independence. The KLA launched hit-and-run attacks as the security situation in Kosovo deteriorated into an armed insurrection against Serbian authorities.

The Armed Forces of the Republic of Yugoslavia (Vojska Jugoslavije, VJ) and MUP deployed in force to Kosovo in 1998. Reports of detentions, torture, summary executions, and massacres increased through 1998 and into 1999, and Arkan's Tigers and other paramilitary groups, who had raped and plundered in Bosnia before the Dayton Agreement was signed, now became active against civilians in Kosovo.

Robert Gelbard was the US special representative for Bosnia Implementation in the US State Department in 1998, but Gelbard saw his diplomatic portfolio more broadly, encompassing the increasingly tense situation in Kosovo.

During a meeting in Belgrade in February 1998, Milosevic maneuvered Gelbard into labeling the KLA as terrorists in a press conference. Shortly after the public designation of the KLA as a terrorist organization by a senior American envoy, Milosevic launched major military and MUP operations into Kosovo. He was finished with Gelbard, but the repression of Albanians in Kosovo and the KLA's response continued throughout 1998.[10] In this environment, international diplomacy was failing to bring the conflict in Kosovo to an end.

Special envoys are vulnerable to the negotiating parties' whims and will to negotiate. The parties must believe that an international envoy has the confidence of the highest authority of the government or of the international organization he or she represents. The envoy is less important than the negotiations, and major mistakes or signs of weakness can spell doom for the negotiator. In fact, envoys are disposable assets and can lose their mandate very quickly if the one or more parties to a negotiation refuse to deal with them for any number of reasons, including mistrust, personality clashes, or the simple desire not to negotiate.

The Albanians of Kosovo: Civil Disobedience versus Guerrilla War?

The ancestors of the modern Albanians probably lived in the region before the Slavs migrated to southeastern Europe. They converted to Islam under Ottoman rule.[11] Like the Bosnians, they were predominately secular Muslims after years of communism squeezed most of the religious fervor out of them. Just like Muslims in Bosnia and elsewhere in the Balkans, the Albanians saw themselves as Europeans. Albanians are the dominant ethnic group in Albania and Kosovo, and they are a growing minority in Macedonia, Montenegro, and southern Serbia. Some feared the threat of a "Greater Albania" movement in southeastern Europe, like the failed dream of a "Greater Serbia." Many expected the Albanians, with a common language and a common culture, to aspire to unify in the same way. However, I never found any convincing evidence of such a movement. The Albanians in each country were instead sympathetic but independent from Albanian movements in other countries. Each group would assist other Albanians in need, but they had no interest in granting local authority to a distant regional center.

New political resistance among Albanians escalated immediately after Milosevic removed autonomy and declared martial law in Kosovo in 1989. Dissidents created the Democratic League of Kosovo (Lidhja Demokratike e Kosoves, LDK) in late 1989 as the primary national party for Albanians. The LDK selected Ibrahim Rugova as its leader, and Albanians joined the party in droves, making the LDK the leading force for resistance.[12] Rugova was an intellectual, educated in philosophy and literature. He had been a journalist and the president of a writers' union, and he was an amateur geologist who collected stone samples from interesting geological sites in Kosovo.

Rugova was the most passive national political leader I had ever met. In 1998, when I first encountered him, I was fresh from the tough daily process of grinding through resistance to the T&E Program. In my initial meeting at his home in Pristina, I could not believe a man as outwardly docile as Rugova could be the Albanian leader to confront Milosevic. But Rugova was the face of resistance for the Albanians, and they showed deep and sincere loyalty toward him, despite his stoic approach to a ruthless bully like Milosevic.

Rugova's strategy for the LDK was one of civil disobedience and nonviolent resistance. The LDK urged Albanians to boycott Serbian institutions and to refuse to participate in Serbia's elections. It initially favored republic status for Kosovo on an equal level with the other remaining republics in Yugoslavia.

Each of my meetings with Rugova beginning in 1998 followed a similar pattern. An aid would escort me into the living room in his residence in Pristina, where he discussed the current situation in Kosovo over cups of Turkish coffee. Rugova, who usually wore an ascot with his suits, talked in an ambiguous style and never made a commitment. He would highlight Serbian offenses, call for Kosovo independence, and plead for international assistance. After the discussion, Rugova would invite me to an adjacent room, where he stored his special mineral collection. Before leaving, he offered the gift of a stone appropriate to the visitor's rank. In my first visit, he gave me a rock the size of a marble. In my last meeting with him in 2001, I noticed that my gift was a softball-size crystal. I took that as an elevation in my perceived status.

As Serbian repression increased in Kosovo, the Albanians grew disaffected with Rugova's nonviolent approach. Years of civil disobedience had failed to produce results for Kosovo, while other Yugoslav republics had successfully split from Serbia. In 1996, a second, more militant resistance movement emerged.

The appearance of the Kosovo Liberation Army was a turning point for the Albanian independence movement and for the stability of Kosovo. In 1996, the KLA declared itself a militant movement to liberate Kosovo, and KLA fighters began to attack Serb police and other targets. With the appearance of the KLA, Albanian resistance to Serbia had two tracks: Rugova and the LDK's civil disobedience movement and the KLA's militant approach.[13]

The KLA made clear that its goal was independence and that it was prepared to fight for it. The more aggressive KLA approach eroded the LDK's political authority, especially after Milosevic launched military and police operations in 1998. US diplomatic activity in Kosovo gradually expanded from engagement with Rugova and a few others to interaction with new leaders as the KLA gained political support. Hashim Thaci, who was an early opponent of Rugova's nonviolent approach, was the most well-known KLA political leader. After a confrontation with Rugova, Thaci left Kosovo for graduate studies in Switzerland and then returned to Kosovo to join the political leadership of the militant movement.[14] He became the KLA's primary political voice. After the war, Thaci created a formal political party, the Democratic Party of Kosovo, to provide a political alternative to the LDK.[15]

The KLA was a loose, decentralized organization without a clear organizational hierarchy. Of the many who fought with the KLA in the field, two became important national leaders. Agim Ceku had been a successful military officer in the Yugoslav army. When he became disgruntled with the Serbs in the conflict with Croatia, he switched sides. He rose to the rank of general in the new Croatian military but went home to Kosovo to join the KLA in 1998. Ceku, the most experienced senior military leader, brought improved organization and professionalism to the KLA. Although he refused a military title, he was the senior KLA military leader. Ramush Haradinaj was a tough and charismatic KLA commander and a national hero for the Albanians in Kosovo. He was legendary for carrying his dead brother, who was killed in action, for hours on his back so that his brother could be buried in his ancestral land.[16] After the war, Russian peacekeepers in Kosovo badly beat Haradinaj for mouthing off at a road block. He almost died in a separate incident involving a late-night confrontation with another Albanian clan. He was found in a barn the next morning, unconscious and dying from hand-grenade shrapnel in the head, and US medical treatment saved his life.[17]

Haradinaj lacked Thaci's polish but not his determination. Following the war, he formed his own political party and was prime minister in 2005 until a war crimes indictment interrupted his mandate. The ICTY in The Hague indicted the controversial Haradinaj, tried him twice, and acquitted him for war crimes against the Serbs in 1998–1999.[18] Veton Surroi was another important Albanian figure for US diplomacy in Kosovo. The son of a Yugoslav diplomat, Surroi was an intellectual, journalist, and publisher of the largest Albanian daily newspaper in Kosovo, *Koha Ditore*. He was not a member of the KLA but was influential within senior Albanian circles and important to Americans' understanding of the dynamics of Albanian political culture and its leadership. He also served as a senior adviser to Albanian delegations in several high-level international meetings. Surroi would later play a role in the Albanian negotiations in Macedonia.

The Albanian diaspora was a major source of political influence abroad and funding for the Albanian cause in Kosovo. The Albanian-American Civic League, centered in New York, rallied Albanian support for Kosovo in the United States. It raised money for programs in Kosovo and developed political relationships in Washington vital to keeping the cause of Albanians in Kosovo before leaders in the US Senate and House of Representatives and officials in the Clinton administration.[19]

The Kosovo Albanians gave the United States an unusual level of trust throughout the period of conflict with Serbia, the NATO air campaign, and the subsequent UN administration leading to independence in 2008. With that trust came a unique level of influence on Albanian authorities in Kosovo for years ahead.

Albright versus Milosevic

If the Albanian leadership in Kosovo was fragmented in 1998, so was the US diplomatic effort to deal with the growing crisis in Kosovo. Many members of the US national security structure who had managed the response to the conflict in Bosnia in 1995 were still on the Clinton team. Sandy Berger had been promoted to national security adviser in the White House after the departure of Anthony Lake. James Steinberg had moved from the State

Department to become Berger's deputy at the NSC. Former Republican congressman William Cohen had replaced Perry as secretary of defense in early 1997. In interagency policy debates on Kosovo, senior generals at the Pentagon resisted further military commitments in the Balkans. However, the success of NATO operations in Bosnia and Milosevic's continued brutality weakened their arguments and made their resistance less effective than before.

Madeleine Albright was sworn in as secretary of state in January 1997. I once noticed a little picture on a shelf in the secretary of state's small private office beyond the formal room for receiving official guests. In the picture, Albright is standing next to candidate Bill Clinton in the deep snow of the New Hampshire primary campaign in 1992, before Clinton became the official Democratic Party candidate for president. Early personal commitments like that build loyalties that are powerful currency in Washington, where loyalty can be fleeting. Albright had influence in the White House, and she used it.

Secretary Albright was a hard-liner on Kosovo. As US ambassador to the UN from 1993 to 1997, she had participated in policy decisions on Bosnia. Now, as secretary of state, she was determined that the United States "not stand by and watch Serbian authorities do in Kosovo what they can no longer get away with in Bosnia."[20]

Albright was not only the first woman to be secretary of state but also frequently the only woman in the White House Situation Room during Principals Committee discussions on Balkan policy. She also was usually the most militant person in the room. In a meeting in the White House in 1993, she famously challenged General Colin Powell, a national military icon, who was explaining why the use of force was not appropriate to stop Serbian atrocities in Bosnia, by asking, "What are you saving this superb military force for, Colin, if we can't use it?"[21] Albright wanted a credible military threat to reinforce diplomatic pressure on Milosevic over Kosovo. She believed from the beginning that only the threat or the use of force would cause him to negotiate seriously. She had been right in Bosnia, and she was convinced it was true in Kosovo. Diplomacy was her job, and she wanted to pursue every avenue to achieve a peaceful settlement, but she believed that a willingness to use military force was the best way to achieve a negotiated solution with Belgrade.

Kosovo in the autumn of 1998 was at the top of the international security agenda in Europe. The KLA was conducting hit-and-run raids against

Serbian targets in Kosovo. Milosevic, determined to destroy the independence movement in Kosovo, responded with a brutal military, MUP, and
paramilitary crackdown against Albanians across Kosovo.

US policy toward Kosovo in 1998 had two components. The first was
the diplomatic effort to stop the increasingly aggressive and heavy-handed
military and police repression of the Albanians that Milosevic had launched
in early spring. The first Bush administration had threatened Milosevic in
the "Christmas Warning" of December 25, 1992, asserting that the United
States was prepared to use force against Serbs if Serbia caused a conflict in
Kosovo. That threat remained in effect and had more credibility in 1998
after the NATO airstrikes in Bosnia in 1995.[22]

The second component of US policy was the goal to restore to Kosovo the status of autonomy that Milosevic had removed a decade earlier.
The United States initially did not pursue independence for Kosovo because
there was no hope that independence could be part of a negotiated solution with Milosevic. Albright was the central figure pushing aggressive US
policy on Kosovo in Washington. She maintained a constant international
dialog on Kosovo with her Contact Group colleagues in Europe and Russia throughout the crisis. Like Secretary Warren Christopher before her,
Albright had no interest in negotiating personally with Milosevic. But one
man was more than willing to engage him. Richard Holbrooke, technically
out of government, had access to Milosevic. Holbrooke was not without influence within the Clinton White House. In addition to being named a special envoy for Kosovo, Holbrooke was also the president's choice to replace
Albright as US ambassador to the UN.

The Kosovo policy stew at State had many cooks. Strobe Talbott, close
to Holbrooke, remained the deputy secretary of state. Within Albright's immediate policy circle, Assistant Secretary of State for Public Affairs James
T. "Jamie" Rubin and James C. O'Brien were senior advisers on Kosovo.
In addition to the normal organization at State, Special Envoy for Bosnia
Robert Gelbard also wanted a role in Kosovo. Ambassador Chris Hill took
on a negotiating role in the region from his embassy in Skopje, Macedonia.
Meanwhile, Holbrooke and others engaged Milosevic and leaders in Kosovo. Holbrooke had as early as the Dayton negotiations privately favored
independence for Kosovo. He thought it was inevitable and should happen
quickly. I agreed that independence was inevitable, but I disagreed with
him on timing. I questioned whether the Kosovo Albanians were prepared
to confront Serbia, as others had done. Even if they succeeded in breaking

free, I believed that they had very little capacity for self-governance. Marc Grossman, assistant secretary of state for European and Canadian affairs, accepted my offer to help with Kosovo in October 1998. With interagency concurrence, he designated me the US special representative for Kosovo Implementation, or the management of international programs on the ground in Kosovo as they monitored the increasingly deadly conflict between Serbian security forces and the Albanians.

The international Contact Group had evolved. Italy had joined as a new member. The Russian representative at Dayton, Igor Ivanov, had become foreign minister in Moscow, and the Russians were still reasonably cooperative on Balkan issues within the Contact Group. But Boris Yeltsin's power was waning as his behavior became increasingly erratic. Unlike in Bosnia, where Russia allowed UN authorization of military operations, Moscow opposed international military forces in Kosovo.

After the success of the Dayton negotiations, the Europeans were generally inclined to support US leadership in Kosovo, although they again were reluctant to confront Serbia directly with military force. They drew distinctions between Kosovo and Bosnia. Bosnia had declared independence from Yugoslavia and was recognized widely as an independent nation. Kosovo in 1998 appeared more like an internal rebellion within Yugoslavia. Further, the attacks by the KLA against Serbian targets in Kosovo were unsettling to other European countries that were struggling with their own separatist movements, such as Spain. The Europeans' determination to have any military actions in Kosovo validated by the UN Security Council was another difference with the Americans. Overall, Kosovo in late 1998 was another international contest between Milosevic in Belgrade and the United States with the support of the Contact Group. But it was unclear if Russia would join the consensus on Kosovo policy in the Contact Group if force were required to end the Serbian crackdown.

23

Prelude to War

Serbian military and MUP forces surrounded the Albanian village of Prekez early on the morning of March 5, 1998. The operation was in response to KLA attacks that had killed Serbian policemen days earlier. The goal was the capture of Adem Jashari, a known KLA leader. After the Jashari clan failed to respond to demands for Adem's surrender, Serbian forces, using artillery, tanks, small arms, and helicopter gunships, opened fire on the Jashari in their homes, indiscriminately killing at least fifty-eight Kosovo Albanians, including women and children.[1] Once news of the massacre spread in Kosovo, Albanians volunteered for the KLA by the thousands.

Credible reports of Serbian police detention, torture, summary executions, and massacres increased throughout 1998. After the Serbian crackdown in Kosovo, the Contact Group launched an intense international diplomatic effort to end the violence without international military intervention.[2]

US engagement with the Contact Group produced a limited set of economic sanctions on Serbia and two UNSCRs to pressure Belgrade to halt its excessive use of force in Kosovo. Contact Group economic sanctions blocked financing for export credits and money for privatization and denied visas authorizing travel by key Milosevic supporters.[3] The first UNSCR in March banned arms sales to Yugoslavia.[4] The second in September demanded a cease-fire, Serb withdrawal from Kosovo, and refugee returns.[5] By October 1998, UN secretary-general Kofi Annan reported that Belgrade was in violation of both resolutions.

At NATO, US pressure for action was also paying dividends. NATO's readiness to conduct operations in Kosovo improved in a step-by-step public process throughout the year. NATO flew eighty-five combat aircraft over Kosovo in a show of force in June 1998. By October, the alliance was in full preparations for a bombing campaign, and in November NATO troops deployed to neighboring Macedonia as a force to extract international observers if necessary.

Kosovo Verification Mission

One step short of military engagement was an increased international presence in Kosovo to serve as a neutral observer and local negotiating mission. The US embassy in Belgrade already had a presence in Kosovo in the US Information Service Office in Pristina, authorized by Milosevic in 1996.[6]

Milosevic, under international pressure, authorized the KDOM in June 1998. This mission, led by Shaun Byrnes, who had been detailed from the US embassy in Belgrade, consisted of about one hundred unarmed US and other international observers who would report on the activities of the combatant parties in Kosovo and actively negotiate cease-fire agreements when possible. Byrnes also maintained a degree of contact with the KLA that was not possible by other international observers.

In mid-October, Milosevic authorized the OSCE to deploy more unarmed international observers to Kosovo to verify Belgrade's compliance with international commitments and to serve a limited peacekeeping function when possible. Another American, Ambassador William G. Walker, led the OSCE Kosovo Verification Mission (KVM), which was envisioned to have a strength of about 2,000 unarmed observers in lightly armored utility vehicles painted bright orange. Walker's KVM never reached this number of observers.

Walker was a Foreign Service professional who had been US ambassador to El Salvador and had been impressive in Croatia in 1997 as head of the UN Transitional Authority in Eastern Slavonia.

I had responsibility for US support to the KDOM and KVM in my new position at State. Byrnes's KDOM was smaller than the KVM, but it had more experience on the ground and had excellent contacts in the KLA. In the KVM, Walker had a much larger organization and a stronger international mandate through the OSCE. Unfortunately, Kosovo was not big enough to hold both men. They refused to cooperate.

Walker was a courageous, if perpetually agitated, diplomat who pushed hard for required support. He expected the KDOM to be integrated into the KVM, which made organizational sense, but the understated and equally tough Byrnes simply refused to do it. I could not dictate the organizational marriage, and neither Ambassador Richard Miles in Belgrade

A patrol from the OSCE KVM enters an area occupied by the KLA in Kosovo in 1999. (Photograph by Arban Bujariu, *Koha Ditore,* Pristina, Kosovo)

nor the senior authorities at State were willing to force the issue. The two organizations remained separate despite Walker's constant objections, and I simply worked independently with both.

Structural integration was less important than the two missions' activities. Both the KDOM and the KVM provided valuable insights on the situation in Kosovo, and both inserted themselves into extremely dangerous positions between combatants in efforts to stop the fighting.

Throughout the summer and fall of 1998, Holbrooke, sometimes accompanied by SACEUR Wes Clark, came and went from Belgrade to press Milosevic to reduce the violence. Chris Hill and others frequented Pristina to push the Albanians to do the same. Various leaders from the Contact Group were also engaged. Yet the killing continued.

Holbrooke sent me to Belgrade on short notice just before Christmas to meet with Milosevic. I had a personal relationship with Milosevic from the Dayton talks, and Holbrooke was trying every possible option to push him to negotiate seriously on Kosovo. Milosevic agreed to see me, but the timing was uncertain.

New Palace, Same Milosevic: Belgrade, December 22, 1998

Engaging Milosevic was treacherous business for an American official. I accepted the diplomatic utility of a cordial personal relationship with a man like Milosevic, but I was never comfortable with it. He was a master of manipulation who, I knew, would use me for his bloody purposes and discard me without thought if I lost focus and gave him an advantage.

When my appointment with Milosevic was postponed, I used the extra time to have lunch with Wes Clark, who was in Belgrade to meet with the VJ chief. Bill Walker from KVM joined Clark and me for lunch in Belgrade. Clark was in a sour mood over the deteriorating situation on the ground in Kosovo. He told Walker not to expect much help from the NATO extraction force in Macedonia.

After the meeting, I traveled with Walker in his OSCE airplane to Pristina, where I met separately with the KVM and the KDOM that evening. My meeting with Milosevic was set for the next day.

I left Pristina with an embassy driver before daylight on December 22 to make the five-hour trip to Belgrade for the meeting. It was snowing in the Serbian capital when I arrived. As part of his transition from president of Serbia to president of the FRY, Milosevic had upgraded the venue he used for his official meetings, going from the drab Serbian presidential palace in central Belgrade to the Beli dvor, the White Palace, in a forested area of an exclusive area of the city. The Beli dvor, built for the sons of King Alexander of Yugoslavia in 1937, was an impressive structure of white stone with a grand hall, Louis XV–style furniture, and traditional European art. Tito had taken over the Beli dvor during the Communist period and used it for official meetings.

Goran Milinovic, the trusted *chef de cabinet,* greeted me and escorted me through the entrance hall to a large drawing room where Milosevic waited. Unlike the palace in Belgrade, this room featured large floor-to-ceiling windows, allowing natural light to flood the space. Joining him were two primary advisers: Nikola Sainovic, FRY vice prime minister and the special assistant for Kosovo, and Bojan Bugarcic, foreign-policy adviser. Sainovic would eventually be indicted by the ICTY in 1999 for his part in the Serbian actions in Kosovo. Bugarcic would become my contact with Belgrade during the NATO bombing campaign.

Milosevic, as always, offered brandy. I noticed that he was smoking again, but he claimed that he smoked very little anymore. He again recalled meeting Kathy at Dayton and inquired about our son, Paul, who had served in Bosnia, and other family members.

On substance, I told Milosevic that he had the right to conduct normal police and military operations, but the level of force and violence being employed by Serbs in Kosovo was excessive and unacceptable. I made the standard appeal for restraint and for the fulfillment of his international commitments. I also urged him to cooperate fully with the KVM.

Milosevic was coldly defiant. He expressed a deep dislike for Bill Walker at the KVM and accused the United States of supporting the KLA.

"Two years ago, the KLA was a handful of radicals. The brutality of Serb security forces in Kosovo—not American support—turned them into a powerful force," I responded, but he refused to engage further.

Milosevic ended the meeting with an invitation to return to Belgrade for further discussions. I would be back in the White Palace confronting him on Kosovo in less than a month.

On Christmas Day, three days after I called for restraint in my private meeting with Milosevic, Serbian police and military units launched a new wave of operations in Kosovo.

The Racak Massacre and Milosevic: Belgrade, January 21, 1999

The massacre in the village of Racak in Kosovo, like the massacre in Srebrenica in Bosnia, was the pivot point for international policy toward Kosovo.

The pattern of Serbian action at Racak was familiar. In retaliation for the killing of six Serbian teenagers in Peja and three Serbian policemen elsewhere, Serb police and military units engaged KLA fighters near Racak early on the morning of January 15, 1999. Serbian police first surrounded and then entered Racak around 7:00 a.m., as many local Albanian civilians attempted to flee into the countryside and others sought shelter in their homes. The police walked through Racak indiscriminately firing on people and wounding or killing many as they fled or attempted to hide. Males, including the elderly and boys as young as twelve, were rounded up, tortured, and summarily executed. By the time the KVM arrived in Racak late in the afternoon, the killing had ended.[7]

Bill Walker traveled to Racak the next morning after receiving overnight reports of the carnage from his observers. The Albanian bodies lying where they fell around the village told Walker all he needed to know. He found bodies of men in peasant clothing scattered about and others in groups. There was no evidence of a fight. Many of the dead were elderly

William Walker, chief of the OSCE KVM, observes the massacre of Albanian civilians by Serbian security forces in the village of Racak, Kosovo, on January 16, 1999. (Photograph by Arban Bujariu, *Koha Ditore,* Pristina, Kosovo)

men and boys who had been tortured and shot in the head. Walker was convinced that these deaths, which ultimately totaled more than forty, resulted from a massacre by Serbian special police, not from a military battle.

Walker raced back to Pristina to announce to the world that Serbian security forces had massacred civilians at Racak.[8] The reaction to his press conference was immediate. Washington and the OSCE stood behind him. Among the Albanians, Walker became an instant hero. Belgrade denounced him and claimed that the casualties had resulted from a legitimate military operation. Milosevic declared Walker persona non grata, an edict that the United States and the OSCE ignored. Serbia's supporters questioned Walker's assessment, and newspapers in France and Germany claimed that Walker had made a hasty judgment.

Walker's actions in going to Racak on January 16, 1999, and documenting what he observed as well as his decision to publicly announce the deaths there as a massacre of Albanians by Serb security forces were acts of professional courage by a seasoned diplomat. Sometimes a stark truth is uncomfortable and difficult in diplomatic circles. But Walker's actions forced the issue of Serbian atrocities in Kosovo with the international community and in my view shortened the overall length and limited the damage of the conflict.

I was in the region on other business when Washington again dispatched me to meet with Milosevic six days after the Racak massacre. Before returning to Belgrade on January 20, 1999, I spent a couple of days in Kosovo, where Walker briefed me in detail on Racak and gave me photos of the corpses of the old men and boys where they had fallen. I was convinced that the evidence of a massacre was overwhelming. I took the photos to Belgrade to use in the meeting with Milosevic in case they might make a difference in the discussion.

Milosevic invited me to lunch, and I spent the morning of January 21 in the US embassy preparing for the meeting. Washington had sent a cable with some vague instructions to guide my discussion. I was confident the meeting would be cordial, but circumstances were closing in on Milosevic, and I was determined not to be used to advance his agenda.

After Racak, Belgrade was swirling with diplomatic and press activity. Milosevic had just refused a Russian request for a meeting, and the Norwegian foreign minister was waiting to see him as well. Milosevic also was stonewalling Canadian judge Louise Arbour, chief prosecutor of the ICTY, who was demanding an international investigation of the events at Racak.

Goran again escorted me into the Beli dvor drawing room to see Milosevic. As in the past meeting, Milosevic was seated in a chair at one end of a marble coffee table. I sat on a couch to his right. Serbian president Milan Milutinovic and foreign-policy adviser Bojan Bugarcic sat in chairs across from me and to Milosevic's left.

I decided to open the meeting on a positive note because I knew the discussion was destined to become confrontational very quickly. Ambassador Miles had told me before the meeting that Milosevic was a new grandfather.

"Congratulations. I understand that your first grandchild was born last week," I began.

The tyrant beamed. He was clearly delighted to be a grandfather.

The meeting soon turned to substance, and I described the situation as I saw it. I reminded Milosevic that his forces had launched an offensive in December, two days after our previous discussion. I had just been in Kosovo, where Serbian police and military were an ominous presence in violation of agreements with Holbrooke and others. I told Milosevic that I had seen the KVM evidence on Racak and that Walker was right in describing it as a massacre by Serbian forces. With the disaster in Racak, the situation was rapidly approaching the point of no return.

"You have seen this [kind of situation] before. You know how this works," I said. "The United States, Wes Clark at NATO, the UN, OSCE, the Russians, Justice Arbour—all have come with serious messages. You have rejected them all. Your position is seen as confrontational and defiant, and the international community is becoming increasingly unified against you. The United States and NATO are not going to back down, and you can expect them to be tougher in the future, with more demands," I continued.

Milosevic listened carefully, but his mood darkened. He became increasingly assertive in rejecting every point.

"What do you want me to do?" he asked again and again. This was a rhetorical point. Milosevic knew exactly what was expected of his government. As to compliance with the agreement to pull his forces back from Kosovo, Milosevic said that he would comply soon "in a realistic way." He said that Justice Arbour had no jurisdiction in Yugoslavia and that the "inspections" were humiliating.

Milosevic was in total denial over Racak and presented his own version of what happened there. In his account, a battle between the army, police, and the KLA had occurred at Racak, and all the Albanians killed there were KLA fighters. He alleged that the KLA itself had shot its fighters in the head after they were dead and then had placed them in the trench. Milosevic spoke with the conviction of someone who believed what he was saying. Maybe he was delusional, but more likely he just thought I might be foolish enough to buy his story. He tested it on me, anyway, and I refuted his description in detail.

"If this is what your people are saying, they are lying to you," I told him, preferring to add some personal distance to the lies.

Milosevic continued with a vicious verbal attack on Bill Walker, the KVM chief. The Yugoslavian president was in a full fury at this point. I thought to myself that such an outburst must be terrifying to a subordinate or member of his government who was its target. I listened carefully and responded politely.

"I know you want an independent Kosovo," Milosevic stormed. "You are just putting out all of this bullshit about democratization in Yugoslavia. I am fed up with all these threats. Threats and aggression. Let NATO bomb us. Explain what you want. Is it independence for Kosovo?"

"Autonomy in Kosovo is the answer. Let people run their own affairs [within Yugoslavia]," I said. "Again, you know where this [situation] is going [if it stays on its present course]. Do you really want to take Serbia to war with NATO—the United States and the great democracies of western Europe?"

"Washington is a soft city," Milosevic said at one point.

Milosevic had a detailed knowledge of the procedural steps NATO must take to conduct combat operations and understood exactly where the process stood in Brussels at that moment.

I told him that I could explain in a few points what needed to be done to reduce tensions. He listened as I described these critical points:

1. Comply with existing agreements to withdraw forces to garrisons and stop the MUP repression in Kosovo.
2. On Racak, let Judge Arbour investigate the situation and bring any accused to justice.
3. Cooperate fully with the OSCE. Give the KVM full access within Kosovo, and withdraw the action against Walker.
4. Grant amnesty to political prisoners in Kosovo.
5. Agree to negotiate with Kosovo Albanians to reach an interim agreement.

We then adjourned to a nearby room for lunch. In addition to provid-ing Milosevic with a new official venue, his new status had improved his kitchen. The lunch featured much lighter fare, but Milosevic ate little.

We kept returning to the two versions of the Racak massacre. I told him that I had pictures if he wanted to see. He did not respond. At one point, Milutinovic pulled an article from the French newspaper *Le Figaro* from his briefcases to reinforce his point. "Milan is like a magician," Milosevic joked. "He pulls press items from his briefcase like rabbits from a hat."

Milosevic seemed to be probing to see if any argument on Racak would work to his advantage. I took a restroom break from the lunch to walk through the foyer, where I told the embassy officer to call Washington and inform them that I was getting nowhere with Milosevic.

"Jim, I will use your term. Walker is a horse's ass," Milosevic said after I returned to the table.

I drew on words attributed to various US presidents in the past: "Yes, Mr. President, he is a horse's ass, but he is our horse's ass. He called Racak as he saw it, and he cannot be removed [from Kosovo]."

I had become strangely accustomed to the surreal twists of conversa-tion with Milosevic. After hours of confrontation on massacres in Kosovo and potential for a NATO war with the Serbs, he turned to diplomatic gossip and Holbrooke. As the lunch ended, he asked about the problems Holbrooke was having with Senate confirmation of his appointment as am-bassador to the UN.

"I don't know the details, but not many people make money betting against Holbrooke," I said.

"He will get past these parking tickets," Milosevic said.

I left the Beli dvor after four hours of confrontational debate with Mi-losevic, convinced that he would not negotiate on Kosovo as he had done on Bosnia. On Bosnia, the Serbian leader had looked for ways to negotiate a way forward. In my discussions with him in late January 1999, I saw no inclination to compromise, no will to negotiate seriously. I left Milosevic that day certain that he was resigned to a major international confrontation over Kosovo, even if that meant war with NATO.[9]

Milosevic might have avoided independence for Kosovo, but he made a critical strategic miscalculation between October 1998 and March 1999. Had he cooperated with the international community, returned the level of security forces to normal levels, negotiated autonomy for Kosovo, and al-lowed international peacekeepers to monitor an agreement, he would have delayed Kosovo independence for certain, and he might have avoided independence as an outcome acceptable to the international community. Milosevic instead chose confrontation, virtually guaranteeing independence sooner rather than later.

Milosevic was no longer a cunning international figure with a negotiating plan. He knew that Russia would not save his policy in Kosovo. He also knew that war with NATO was rapidly approaching and that the Serbs could not win such a conflict, yet he did not have a strategy to prevent such a war. He was smart enough, though, to realize that the war would lead to independence for Kosovo.

By 1999, Milosevic could not avoid personal responsibility for the policy that had unleashed the brutal actions of his government's security forces in Kosovo. Perhaps he knew that the VJ, the MUP, and the paramilitaries had spilled so much blood that their actions could not stand international exposure. More likely, he decided to play to a domestic audience. He believed that he knew the Serbian people well. After all, he had risen to power on the nationalist passions regarding Kosovo, and he may have calculated that even a losing confrontation with NATO would solidify his position of power in Serbia and his legacy as a Serbian nationalist. Whatever the reason, the policy Milosevic adopted toward Kosovo became a disaster for the Serbs and led directly to Serbia's loss of Kosovo.

I never saw Milosevic again, but in 2001 I would have a hand in bringing him to justice.

At the same time that I was talking war and peace with Milosevic, a political scandal in Washington was emerging that would threaten to bring down the US president. I returned to Washington after filing a report from the embassy on the Milosevic meeting. When I arrived, Assistant Secretary Marc Grossman called me in to inform me that State and the White House had decided to appoint a "czar" for Kosovo. Ambassador James F. Dobbins from the NSC Staff would be named special adviser to the president and secretary of state for the Balkans. Grossman asked me to stay on as Dobbins's deputy in the Office of the Special Envoy for the Balkans at State, and I agreed.

Last Ditch Diplomacy: February–March 1999

The situation in Kosovo was moving quickly toward a decision to use NATO forces to stop the killing. The MUP and the VJ intensified their campaign of deadly collective punishment against the Albanians in Kosovo in the winter and spring of 1999. The KLA retaliated with local hit-and-run attacks against Serb security forces and Serb civilians. Meanwhile, international diplomacy failed to reverse the increasing violence; diplomatic threats and NATO demonstrations of force had not produced results, either. Instead of withdrawing forces from Kosovo as promised in 1998, Milosevic stepped up the violence.

A flurry of diplomatic activity followed the Racak massacre. Many argued that war was not inevitable and that every effort should be made to avoid it. Russia was particularly adamant that military force should not be used to compel Serbia to stop its brutality against the Albanians. In Washington, the administration worked on two tracks: a major diplomatic push for a peaceful settlement for Kosovo and preparations in NATO for war should the negotiations fail. Secretary Albright consistently pushed for a credible threat of force to back up the diplomatic effort.

American diplomacy centered on the Contact Group and the value of a unified international position, which included Russia. The primary mechanism for pursuing a peaceful settlement was an international peace conference hosted by the French government at Rambouillet, a historic chateau near Paris.

Albright threw her personal energy into the Rambouillet meeting in February 1999. Chris Hill, Jim Dobbins, and others who conducted the negotiations in France needed no help. I did not participate. The Dayton experience was enough for me. Further, after my meeting with Milosevic in January, I was convinced that an agreement at Rambouillet was not feasible. Milosevic did not attend the negotiations, sending Milutinovic in his stead. Without Milosevic at the meeting, no deal was possible, but the effort was important to international opinion.

The draft Contact Group peace settlement tabled at Rambouillet proposed autonomy for Kosovo and required that Yugoslav security forces be withdrawn from Kosovo and replaced by a NATO force. The meeting concluded near the end of February without agreement from either the Serbs or the Kosovo Albanians. But the Albanians subsequently accepted the Rambouillet plan.

The Rambouillet meeting elevated the international status of KLA leader Hasim Thaci. The Albright team at the conference judged Thaci, compared to the passive Rugova, to be the more capable Albanian leader. The United States continued to engage Rugova but gravitated toward Thaci as a leader with influence. This attention from the Americans also increased Thaci's status among the Albanians.

US secretary of state Madeleine Albright (*center*), in a press conference with KLA leader Hashim Thaci (*left*) and Kosovo Albanian political leader Ibrahim Rugova in June 1999. (Associated Press)

War with Serbia was fast approaching. Belgrade intensified operations in Kosovo following the breakdown of the Rambouillet talks. By mid-March, the dangers for unarmed international observers were too great for them to remain in Kosovo. Walker and Byrnes requested and received permission to withdraw, and both the KVM and the KDOM left Kosovo for Macedonia.

President Clinton participates in a briefing on Kosovo with Secretary of State Madeleine Albright, Secretary of Defense William Cohen, CJCS General Hugh Shelton, Central Intelligence Agency director George Tenet, White House chief of staff John Podesta, and others in the Oval Office, March 26, 1999. (William J. Clinton Presidential Library)

In Washington, as events made war over Kosovo ever more likely, a scandal involving improper sexual relations between a White House intern, Monica Lewinsky, and President Clinton had developed into a legal storm that dominated the US national political agenda. In coming months, this scandal would lead to measures to impeach the president. During the time that the Lewinsky scandal raged in Washington, I never saw anything from the scandal spilling over into US or international policy development for Kosovo.

The Clinton administration now faced both political opposition and a lack of public enthusiasm for another military operation in the Balkans, but its success in Bosnia helped deflect opposition to engagement in Kosovo. American leadership, including coercive military operations, had ended the genocide in Bosnia. In Kosovo, Milosevic was repeating the same strategies of collective punishment and ethnic cleansing he had used in Bosnia.

President Clinton therefore justified military operations in Kosovo on US national interests and on the moral and humanitarian imperatives to act. In a speech on May 13, 1999, he laid out a vision for Europe as a region "undivided, democratic and at peace." "In this age of growing international interdependence, America needs a strong and peaceful Europe more than ever as our partner for freedom and for economic progress, and our partner against terrorism, the spread of weapons of mass destruction, and instability," Clinton stated.[10]

Although a more controversial rationale for war, the moral and humanitarian case for action was easier to define. Clinton rejected the theory that wars in the Balkans were inevitable, and he justified military action to stop "tyrants who use racial and religious hatred to strengthen their grip and to justify mass killing."[11] Kosovo had all the characteristics of a sequel to the Serbian genocide in Bosnia. The evidence of the unfolding humanitarian tragedy was abundant and beyond dispute.

"If the European community and its American and Canadian allies were to turn away from and therefore reward ethnic cleansing in the Balkans, all we would do is to create for ourselves an environment where this sort of practice was sanctioned by other people who found it convenient," Clinton said.[12]

As the United States pressed for the use of force, Russia used its position in the Security Council to block UN authority for international military action in Kosovo.

The UN had authorized NATO operations in Bosnia, and the US and European governments planned for UN authorization for NATO operations in Kosovo as well. However, Russia, which had allowed the UN authorization for the use of force in Bosnia, was unyielding in opposition to it in Kosovo. As the situation shifted increasingly toward international military intervention, the Russians blocked a Contact Group proposal for a UNSCR authorizing the use of force.

With UN action blocked by Moscow, the United States took the issue to its European allies in NATO for a regional mandate. Secretary Albright convinced European governments that UN authority was desirable but that Russia could not be allowed to use the UN to veto legitimate NATO action. As a result, the North Atlantic Council authorized NATO operations in Kosovo without specific UN approval.

It was unclear if Russia believed it could prevent a NATO operation against Serbia or was just making a point of principle. Regardless, Russian action in New York weakened the role of the Security Council by forcing legitimate action to run around UN authority. Despite this difference between Russia and other members of the Contact Group, Russia continued to participate in the group and later joined the NATO-led Kosovo Force (KFOR) and supported the UNSCR authorizing international administration of Kosovo.

In a meeting in Belgrade on March 22, Holbrooke made one final attempt to convince Milosevic to avoid war. A defiant Milosevic rejected Holbrooke's appeal. Ambassador Miles closed the US embassy in Belgrade and departed the country on March 23. That same day NATO ordered the commencement of the air campaign against FRY military and police units in Kosovo.[13]

24

Madeleine's War

March 24–June 10, 1999

The NATO air campaign, Operation Allied Force, was authorized for humanitarian purposes in Kosovo. The stated objectives of the operation were to stop the violence, military actions, and repression; to remove Yugoslav security forces from Kosovo, enabling the deployment of an international military presence in Kosovo; and to promote the return of refugees.[1]

Secretary of State Madeleine Albright insisted from the beginning that diplomacy must be reinforced by the credible threat of force in Kosovo if it were to succeed in ending the violence. She cherished and cultivated her public image of toughness, and she was not inclined to compromise with Milosevic. Diplomacy had produced a relatively unified international position that FRY forces must leave Kosovo and that international civilian and military authorities should replace them in Kosovo. Once Milosevic rejected that outcome and launched a more intense crackdown in Kosovo, military action was the only option left other than backing down.

After the Contact Group exhausted the diplomatic options, Albright engaged her European Contact Group colleagues each day by telephone to keep the group together as the NATO military operation unfolded. During the NATO operation, both her critics and her supporters referred to it as "Madeleine's War."[2]

General Wes Clark, as SACEUR, commanded the NATO air operation against the Serbian forces of Slobodan Milosevic, a man Clark knew personally. The NATO operation started gradually with strikes against VJ and MUP facilities in Kosovo and then expanded to include infrastructure and command-and-control facilities in Serbia, including high-value military and police targets in Belgrade.

As the air campaign progressed, Washington began to debate proposals for ground combat forces. Clark's pressure for the use of attack helicopters

Destruction of the FRY Ministry of Defense building in Belgrade during NATO air strikes against Serbian military and police targets during the air campaign to expel Serbian security forces from Kosovo in 1999. (Shutterstock.com.)

in Kosovo created further tensions with Washington. In the end, neither a NATO land invasion nor the use of attack helicopters was necessary.

The VJ never committed its air force against NATO or presented an effective defense to the NATO attacks. Belgrade's primary response to NATO air operations was to launch a campaign to expel Albanians from Kosovo.

Throughout the air campaign, Serbian paramilitaries, MUP, and armed forces rampaged through Pristina and the countryside, turning Kosovo into a land of horror for the Albanians. Their strategy was simple: kill or expel every Albanian in Kosovo, and they went about their bloody business with savage enthusiasm. The Serbian security forces swept through towns and villages throughout Kosovo, expelling people from their homes and forcing them on to evacuation corridors leading to Macedonia and Albania. They burned homes and villages and slaughtered Albanians individually or in groups, sometimes as family units. Tens of thousands of Kosovo Albanian refugees flooded into Macedonia and Albania. During the air campaign, Kosovo was the Racak massacre on a grand scale.

No one knows the real number of dead, but one estimate places the number of Albanians killed by Serbian forces during the seventy-eight-day air campaign at 10,000.[3] Ninety percent of the Albanians in Kosovo became

Albanian refugees flee their homes as Serbian security forces attack Albanian communities in Kosovo during the NATO air campaign in 1999. (Photograph by Arban Bujariu, *Koha Ditore,* Pristina, Kosovo)

displaced persons or refugees of one kind or another. Estimates ran to about 800,000 refugees outside of Kosovo and 700,000 displaced in Kosovo.

The strategy of brutality and expulsion against the Albanians in Kosovo was a critical misjudgment by Milosevic. The images of thousands of desperate people fleeing their homes only strengthened US and European resolve in NATO and ensured that Kosovo would reject any future relationship with Serbia.

The NATO air campaign punished the Serbs and destroyed infrastructure but was not effective against the small formations of paramilitary and police units savaging Kosovo. NATO had no observers on the ground, and combat aircraft conducting their bombing raids above 15,000 feet for defensive reasons were not effective against these types of targets.

Russia reacted harshly to the NATO air campaign after its strategy to stop NATO action through the UN Security Council failed. The Russian prime minister abruptly cancelled a meeting with the US vice president; Russia called for UN Security Council meetings on the operation; Moscow withdrew temporarily from the Contact Group deliberations; and President Yeltsin rejected an invitation to attend the NATO summit in Washington.

Keeping Russia engaged in the international process on Kosovo was in everyone's interest. Moscow also risked becoming irrelevant to finding a suitable solution as long as it remained on the sidelines. For the West, future UN action on Kosovo was not possible without Russia; Russia still had influence in Belgrade, and hostility over Kosovo could reverse positive developments in the West's relationship with Russia.

Washington and Moscow needed a way to keep the Russians engaged in the diplomatic process to terminate the NATO air campaign on acceptable terms. Yeltsin made the first move by proposing to President Clinton that former Russian prime minister Viktor Chernomyrdin negotiate an end to the NATO operation. During a meeting in Washington, Chernomyrdin suggested an international negotiating partner, and at Secretary Albright's suggestion former president of Finland Martti Ahtisaari, an experienced UN official and international diplomat, was designated as Chernomyrdin's negotiating counterpart.[4] Chernomyrdin and Ahtisaari engaged extensively with Deputy Secretary of State Strobe Talbott to find a set of conditions necessary to terminate the air campaign.

Chernomyrdin, Ahtisaari, and Talbott hammered out an agreement on the set of NATO conditions for ending the air campaign. These conditions were accepted by the G8 foreign ministers, including Russia, at their meeting in Germany in early May. The conditions required that Belgrade remove all FRY military, police, and paramilitary forces from Kosovo; that the KLA demilitarize; and that an international civilian and military presence be deployed to administer and provide security for Kosovo.[5]

Chernomyrdin and Ahtisaari took the war-termination conditions to Belgrade for Milosevic to consider. Meanwhile, staffs in Brussels, New York, and Contact Group capitals were drafting military-technical agreements and a UNSCR that were consistent with the G8 principles.

Trouble mounted for Serbian leaders. On May 27, 1999, the ICTY issued indictments against FRY president Milosevic, Serbian president Milutinovic, FRY vice prime minister Sainovic, and two other senior officials in Belgrade, charging them with murder, persecution, and deportation in Kosovo.[6]

The Direct Washington–Belgrade Channel: May 31–June 10, 1999

Belgrade sent signals to the United States by the end of May 1999 that Milosevic wanted a direct link to Washington in addition to the international negotiations over the ongoing war with NATO. After Secretary Albright and National Security Adviser Sandy Berger approved such a link,

Jim Dobbins and I contacted an American leader of a nongovernmental organization who had high-level contacts in Belgrade to establish the link. The contact in Belgrade was Bojan Bugarcic, the foreign-policy adviser who had attended my meetings with Milosevic in Belgrade. Belgrade was given a choice of three contact names and numbers. As one of those names, I became the US contact in Washington.

A communication channel to one of the parties that occurs separately from the primary negotiation is always dangerous to the process and generally should be avoided. Each party in a negotiation always seeks soft spots, cracks, and opportunities in negotiating positions to promote its own position. In a negotiation, especially one separated by long distances, effective coordination between the primary and secondary channels can be very difficult and potentially disruptive. In this case, my conversations with Bugarcic were reported to Strobe Talbott at State and James Steinberg at the White house.

I decided that the best course for me would be to maintain a tough position toward any Belgrade proposal during the conversations. That was my personal inclination, anyway; higher levels and the primary negotiators could always be more flexible if they decided to do so.

Bugarcic called three times on the afternoon of May 31 to ensure that the channel was real and to invite me to Belgrade for direct talks. I relayed the invitation to the White House Situation Room, where the Deputies Committee was meeting. Clearly, Milosevic wanted to talk directly to the United States in addition to meeting with Chernomyrdin and Ahtisaari. The deputies decided against accepting the invitation, preferring to focus attention on the Chernomyrdin–Ahtisaari visit to Belgrade. However, they also wanted to keep the Bugarcic channel open for the time being.

The following day Bugarcic and I established a schedule for daily contact. He reiterated the invitation to come to Belgrade and told me that we would have good news soon. The good news turned out to be Belgrade's approval of the G8 conditions to end the air campaign. Bugarcic assured me that the agreement included the word *all*, which meant that Belgrade agreed to remove all police, military, and paramilitary forces from Kosovo. Compliance with this provision would effectively terminate Belgrade's control of Kosovo.

He also proposed a meeting between NATO and FRY security forces as soon as possible to work out the details of the withdrawal, and he reiterated the invitation to come to Belgrade.

Contact with Belgrade immediately shifted to Kumanovo, Macedonia, near the Kosovo border, where NATO, VJ, and MUP generals negotiated the military-technical agreement (MTA) that would be the basis for Serbian withdrawal and NATO deployment to Kosovo. The Kumanovo meeting on June 4 did not go well, however.

Milosevic was up to his old tricks. Bugarcic called me at home in the late evening of June 4. It was 4:00 a.m. in Belgrade. Bugarcic claimed that Belgrade had agreed to a force in Kosovo to be authorized by the UN. It did not agree to a NATO deployment without UN Security Council authorization. The FRY precondition for a UNSCR authorizing NATO deployment would shift leverage back to Russia to control the process. I told Bugarcic that a UNSCR was not possible until the air campaign ended and that a military agreement authorizing NATO deployment was required to stop the air campaign.

Bugarcic accused the United States of siding with the KLA and serving as its air force.

"Bojan, you must understand that no MTA with authority for NATO [to enter Kosovo] means the bombing will continue," I said.

"Jim, this is the raw use of power to intimidate us. It is not acceptable," he responded.

"Bojan, what message do you want me to pass? Are you going to sign the MTA?"

"We want a Security Council resolution first. We see this as two steps. We have sold the Chernomyrdin–Ahtisaari agreement to our people on the basis of a Security Council resolution for the force. We understand: NATO at the core. [There are] no games here," he said. "NATO is coming in. We want a purely military-technical agreement first, then a resolution before the force deploys."

"That could create a vacuum, and we do not accept a resolution first. It is not possible," I said, then paused. "Here is my message: sign the MTA with authority for NATO in Kosovo. If you do not, the bombing will continue."

"I understand," Bugarcic responded.

I reported the conversation to Dobbins and Steinberg at the NSC. They were getting a similar message from other channels and were working on revising the draft MTA. The Serbs, meanwhile, submitted their own revised MTA draft that weakened NATO authority.

The NSC instructed me to call Bugarcic on June 6, but he was difficult to reach. When he did call back, he was detached and did not want to engage on specifics. As instructed, I told him that Belgrade was walking back on the Chernomyrdin–Ahtisaari agreement, a position that was endangering the whole structure.

Related discussions were going on at the same time within the Contact Group and the G8 over the details of the future UNSCR on Kosovo. The Russians continued to object to the use of NATO as the KFOR and to the authority of that force.

The Belgrade strategy was clear by this point: get a pause in the bombing, then negotiate the NATO deployment and authority in the UNSCR before signing the MTA. Bugarcic was more upbeat in the next call on June 7. He expressed confidence about getting an agreement that would allow a UNSCR before an MTA, with conditions for the withdrawal agreed upon and the bombing suspended.

The problem continued to be agreement on the sequence of events. We would not stop the bombing until the required conditions were met. These conditions included the MTA, a cease-fire in Kosovo, and the beginning of the VJ and MUP withdrawal. The sequence that FRY wanted was a bombing pause, a UNSCR, an MTA, and then withdrawal. At Steinberg's direction, I called Bugarcic, but our discussion became circular arguments over positions. He continued to push for a pause in the bombing. I told him that a pause before the MTA was unacceptable.

"I know you are serious," he said. "You are bombing my town [Belgrade] tonight. I can hear them [the bombs]. This is an aggression."

"We do not want to open this discussion because it will not be productive," I said. He agreed.

A draft UNSCR was approved by the G8 on June 8 for consideration by the UN Security Council at the appropriate time. However, the MTA negotiations remained blocked.

On Talbott's instruction, I called Bugarcic on June 8 to stress that Belgrade must call off the Russian demand for a bombing pause before a UNSCR and that it must sign the MTA before the bombing ended. Belgrade wanted a bombing pause first, and so Bugarcic proposed another option: begin the force withdrawal, then pause the bombing.

In reporting the call, Talbott emphasized that Belgrade must meet all Chernomyrdin–Ahtisaari conditions, or minor movement of forces would not initiate a bombing pause. I called Bugarcic back to inform him that I had confirmed that Belgrade must meet all requirements of the Chernomyr-

din–Ahtisaari agreement—in other words, that just beginning a withdrawal would not be enough. The Serbs had to sign the MTA, or the bombing
would continue.

Bugarcic phoned back with a more formal proposal. Belgrade wanted
a purely technical military agreement without "broad political authorities"
for NATO. That agreement would contain language that Belgrade would
accept the mandate as authorized in a UNSCR. Serbian forces would begin
withdrawing immediately, NATO would pause the air campaign, and the
UNSCR would be passed in New York.

Steinberg and Talbott discussed Belgrade's proposal with Sandy Berger, Secretary of Defense Cohen, and General Hugh Shelton, the CJCS. They
rejected it and told me to push the Serbs back into the channel of negotiations at Kumanovo.

In another harsh conversation with Bugarcic, I passed on the rejection
of the Serbian offer.

"This channel is not working," Bugarcic said as we ended the call.

The ringing phone woke me up at 5:00 a.m. on June 9. Bugarcic was
calling with three points to be resolved. I could tell from his voice that
the Serbs were eager for a deal and that he was directly involved in the
negotiations.

I got a hostile Steinberg out of bed with the Serb proposal.

"I don't want you talking to Bugarcic anymore," Steinberg said. "We
can't have a separate channel. This must be worked out at the border."

"He called me. Do you want his message or not?" I said.

"Do you know they quoted you at the border yesterday as having proposed a pause in the air strikes based on a minimum withdrawal?" Steinberg asked.

"That doesn't surprise me. They will say anything to get their deal.
They are tricky. Do you want his message or not?" I said.

"Yes." I relayed the points to Steinberg.

"Do not call him [Bugarcic] back. No more contact," Steinberg said.

"OK."

Ten minutes later Steinberg called to say that Berger wanted me to call
Bugarcic and give him a reaction to the Serb proposal. The calls continued
for another hour or so, but events were moving too fast in the direct negotiations at Kumanovo to keep pace.

By midafternoon, I learned that the MTA was signed at Kumanovo.
The MTA gave KFOR the authority to occupy Kosovo to provide a secure

The NATO-led KFOR, including a large US military contingent, deploys to provide a secure environment for international governance of Kosovo under the authority of UNSCR 1244 and the MTA reached with Belgrade. (NATO Archive)

environment under UN auspices. KFOR also controlled the airspace above Kosovo. The MTA required hostilities to cease and all FRY forces to withdraw from Kosovo within eleven days.

The MTA referred only to the international KFOR. NATO was never specified in the document.[7]

The next day, June 10, NATO secretary-general Javier Solana announced in Brussels that the NATO air campaign against the FRY was suspended after seventy-eight days. A few hours later in New York, the UN Security Council passed UNSCR 1244, essentially transferring governance of Kosovo to international civilian and military authorities.[8]

Quick diplomatic action barely averted a military confrontation between NATO and Russia in the next few days as the Russian military raced to deploy forces to Kosovo ahead of NATO. Russia moved about 150 troops from their contingent in SFOR, the international force in Bosnia, to Kosovo, where they immediately occupied the airport near Pristina.

The deployment of Russian troops to the Pristina Airport triggered a serious clash between General Wes Clark, the SACEUR, and British general Michael Jackson, the NATO commander on the ground in Kosovo who had previously served in Bosnia. Clark ordered Jackson to deploy helicopters to block the runway at the airport after the Russians arrived.

"I will not start World War III for you," Jackson told Clark, refusing an order he considered a dangerous confrontation with the Russians.[9]

General Jackson's fear of calamity was unfounded. While a confrontation was brewing in Pristina, intelligence showed that Russian airborne forces were preparing to reinforce the unit at the airport from bases in Russia. Talbott immediately flew to Moscow to engage the Russian government. In Washington, the Dobbins team also acted. John Menzies, former ambassador to Bosnia, organized instructions to US embassies in countries between Russia and Kosovo to deny flight clearance for Russian military aircraft through national airspace, thereby creating a political barrier to the Russian deployment. Moscow stopped the reinforcement of Russian troops at Pristina, which could have created a dangerous military confrontation. Russian troops subsequently worked with NATO in Kosovo.

The combination of determined diplomacy and military coercion worked. All FRY forces were out of Kosovo by June 20. NATO forces deployed into Kosovo as thousands of Albanian refugees in Albania and Macedonia flooded home.

I received another early-morning phone call at home on June 14 from Neboysa Vujovic, deputy foreign minister in Belgrade and coordinator of the Serb withdrawal from Kosovo. Vujovic was frantic about the safety of Serbs in Kosovo and of Serb civilians fleeing Pristina. He pleaded for a statement from KFOR urging Serbs who lived in Kosovo to stay there. I passed the message to General Joseph W. Ralston at the Pentagon. KFOR quickly issued a statement urging Serb civilians to stay in Kosovo. Vujovic called back to say thanks for the statement. Serb officials showed no remorse for the crimes their government had committed or sanctioned in Kosovo, only concern for the safety of Serbs remaining there. Their arrogance was monumental.

Shortly after the NATO air campaign ended, Richard Holbrooke, after a year waiting for Senate confirmation, was sworn in as US ambassador to the United Nations on August 25, 1999. Three days later he traveled to Kosovo and Bosnia in his new capacity.

25

Midwife to a Nation

Kosovo was a wreck when Serbian security forces left in June 1999. Towns and villages were in shambles. Refugees were streaming back as international civilians and military forces were flowing into Kosovo. Serbian technicians and officials who worked in government agencies had fled. Kosovo had no government and no police, and the Kosovo Albanians had no experience in real self-governance. Electricity and water supplies were sporadic. Except for local farming, Kosovo had no economy, and the infrastructure was in a serious state of neglect.

Security was the priority issue. Kosovo was a land of the blood feud. Society centered on the clan and a code of honor that demanded vengeance for offenses against the clan. As the Serbs withdrew, Kosovo Albanians committed acts of local retribution and vengeance to settle scores. The first order of business for the international community as it deployed to Kosovo was to protect the local Serbs from revenge attacks.

The negotiated international documents—the MTA and UNSCR 1244—transferred sovereignty for the territory of Kosovo to the United Nations until an unspecified political process determined Kosovo's future status.[1]

UNSCR 1244 gave international organizations in Kosovo the authority to secure Kosovo under Chapter VII of the UN Charter. It authorized two independent international organizations in Kosovo to work in coordination with each other: an international civilian presence to be led by a UN special representative of the secretary-general (SRSG) and a separate international security presence. The civilian presence, known as the UN Mission in Kosovo (UNMIK), under the SRSG would have all executive, judicial, and legislative authority in Kosovo until local institutions were established. The security presence, KFOR, would be led by NATO but would include non-NATO partners. KFOR would be responsible for deterring external threats, demilitarizing the KLA, and creating a secure environment in Kosovo. It would support UNMIK but would not be subordinate to it. Political direction of KFOR would remain at the North Atlantic Council in Brussels, and command of KFOR would stay within NATO channels.

A senior UN official, Sergio de Mello, filled in as SRSG until Dr. Bernard Kouchner of France arrived as the first permanent SRSG on July 15, 1999. Kouchner was the founder of Medecins sans frontieres and had served in ministerial positions in the French government. An energetic and capable man, he charged into the tasks at hand as the organization formed.

Kouchner was essentially an international viceroy, governing a war-ravaged Kosovo. He needed to restore local order and create the conditions for local self-governance. He had to keep the UN bureaucracy in New York happy as he dealt with Paris and other Contact Group countries at various levels. Local Serbs also needed attention and support.

Kouchner faced the major task of coordinating the independent-minded international organizations in Kosovo that made up UNMIK; the UN managed the administration of Kosovo and necessary humanitarian assistance; the EU took responsibility for reconstruction and economic development; and the OSCE accepted the task of institution building. In addition to NATO, that made four major international organizations operating within Kosovo.

Bernard Kouchner proved to be an excellent first leader of this complicated and cumbersome organization. International organizations never act as efficiently or as quickly as the involved nations expect them to—even when these nations decline to take direct responsibility. UNMIK was no exception, but I came to respect Kouchner and appreciate both his passion for the job and his theatrical nature as I traveled in and out of Kosovo during his tenure as SRSG.

Kouchner understood the issues in Kosovo and looked for practical solutions. He was comfortable in the SRSG position and was not afraid to speak up about problems. He had authority, but he also had a gregarious demeanor and straightforward approach that won the Albanians' respect and helped him with the international organizations and the national capitals looking over his shoulder.

The international mandates caused thousands of foreign civilians and soldiers to deploy to Kosovo as part of UNMIK and KFOR. They came with money, equipment, and authority to a damaged area with virtually no economy and a growing population. International civilians are always very well paid and have exceptional benefits. Along with all the good they accomplish, they also have a serious impact on the local society. International institutions can hire the best local workers and rent the best facilities. A low-level employee in an international organization may have a greater income than the most senior local official. New businesses cater to their needs while pricing out local customers. They drive up prices for housing, food, and services and generally set up two economies—one for the foreigners and one for the locals. With all that international organizations accomplish, they often take on the aura of colonial paternalism over time, and they can make large segments of the economy dependent on their funding. Once these organizations are created, bureaucratic inertia and benefits can keep them larger or alive longer than necessary after their fundamental tasks are fulfilled.

As Yugoslavian security forces departed, KFOR's task shifted from protecting the Albanians from the Yugoslavs to protecting the Serbian enclaves in Kosovo from Albanian vengeance. It patrolled throughout Kosovo but concentrated its activities around Serbian communities and religious sites.

KFOR also pumped money into the Kosovo economy, but military personnel were largely isolated from the local population except when performing their official duties. To accommodate the American forces in KFOR, the United States constructed a major facility, Camp Bondsteel, in southeastern Kosovo.

KFOR consisted of a headquarters on a hilltop near Pristina known as "Film City," and 50,000 troops from more than thirty countries originally deployed around Kosovo. The force included 3,500 from Russia and 5,000 from the United States. That force gradually declined according to the security assessment. Russia's troops left on good terms in 2003. By 2009, the size of KFOR was down to 5,000, with 750 of them from the United States. The number of US troops in Kosovo seemed less important than their presence, which alone was enough to be a stabilizing influence on the Kosovo Albanians.

In Washington, when the air campaign ended, Jim Dobbins, the special adviser to the president and secretary of state on democracy in the Balkans, had a small staff assisting him. I was his deputy and was joined by Ambassador John Menzies and Laurel Miller, who had been a legal staff expert at Dayton during the Bosnia negotiations. This organization set about preparing US postwar policy in Kosovo.

Dobbins, a career Foreign Service officer, was a practical, strategic thinker who was an elite crisis-management adviser to the White House and secretary of state. He recently had been on the NSC Staff in the White House and had served at high levels in the State Department in the past, including as ambassador to the EU. Earlier in his career, Dobbins had a run-in with Senator Jesse Helms, the Republican chairman of the Senate Foreign Relations Committee, and Helm had blocked him from positions requiring Senate confirmation.

Dobbins had a reputation as a tough bureaucratic infighter in Washington. He believed that good ideas were the key to winning bureaucratic battles there, and he produced a steady stream of them. Unlike Holbrooke, he did not relish the public limelight, and his personal reserve could make him difficult to work for. But after a while I concluded that Dobbins was a brilliant loner who also was a very skilled operational diplomat in a crisis.

I spent the next year and a half working for Dobbins on Balkan policy, in particular the practical elements of US assistance programs for Kosovo, the Washington interagency process, engagement of Albanian leaders in Kosovo, and responses to congressional interests on Kosovo.

US civilian assistance to Kosovo was funded largely through an existing program, the Support for East European Democracy, to help East European countries transition to democracy. The United States spent $1 billion from 1999 to 2012 for development in Kosovo, primarily through the US Agency for International Development, in a variety of assistance projects, ranging from police training to media development.[2]

The US investment in Kosovo was serious, including assistance funding, civilian personnel, and the American component of KFOR. The United States held a special level of trust among the Albanians that went beyond the level of American financial commitment. Many factors created such trust. Among them were Secretary Albright's determination to end the Serbian repression in Kosovo, Walker's public stand after the Racak massacre, US leadership of the international effort to expel Serbian forces from Kosovo, and the support from Albanian Americans. This level of trust gave the United States significant influence among the Albanians in Kosovo.

In 1999, the State Department established a US Diplomatic Mission in Pristina very near the KFOR headquarters. It sent experienced Balkan hand Lawrence G. Rossin to open the office, but Christopher Dell arrived soon after the mission opened as the first long-term chief of mission from 2000 to 2001. Dell returned to Pristina in 2009 as the second US ambassador to Kosovo.

Law enforcement in Kosovo was an important early problem. The country had no police once the Serbs withdrew. KFOR was not ready to assume police functions and was eager for international police to deploy to fulfill law enforcement responsibility, a task that UNMIK took on until a Kosovo police force could be created.

UNMIK and the associated international and bilateral programs generally worked well from 1999 to independence in 2008. Kosovo produced a democratic constitution and chose government leaders at all levels through valid elections. UNMIK set up interim institutions of government and implemented rule-of-law structures supported by a professional Kosovo police force equipped and trained by the international community. Integration of Serbs into Kosovo institutions occurred to a degree, but Serbian resistance encouraged by Belgrade made full integration impossible. And UNMIK was never able to break the Serbian nationalist hold on Mitrovica or to stop Belgrade's interference in the affairs of Kosovo.

The biggest issue in Kosovo was economic development, with its associated problems of very high unemployment, corruption, and crime, but international economic-development programs in Kosovo performed poorly. In addition, UNMIK failed to complete major infrastructure projects. Electricity and water supplies were still sporadic in Pristina even after years of international assistance programs.

Army in Waiting

The UN mandate gave KFOR the responsibility for the demobilization of the Kosovo Liberation Army, and demobilizing it was a delicate issue. The KLA was a tough group of local militias, organized under a loose central structure. The Albanians considered the KLA their national army.

Dobbins recognized that simply collecting weapons from the KLA and sending the fighters home was not practical and could be dangerous. He also knew that the Kosovo economy could not absorb thousands of KLA fighters immediately. Without an alternative, they might simply go underground as a militant organization and a source of constant tension.

UNSCR 1244 required the demobilization of the KLA, but the creation of a new army by the international government would imply that the final status of Kosovo was predetermined. However, the dangers of a massive demobilization of KLA fighters into a jobless economy were obvious.

Dobbins hit upon the idea of a peacetime response force to deal with civil emergencies in Kosovo as an alternative to the KLA. This organization, named the Kosovo Protection Corps (KPC), was supplemented by an internationally sponsored demobilization program for former KLA fighters who did not participate in the KPC. Because of my military background and experience with the T&E Program in Bosnia, I spent a great deal of time working on KPC development.

Agim Ceku and other KLA leaders swallowed their pride and agreed to cooperate with the American idea of a national emergency response force. For the Albanians, this option preserved a structure organized generally along military lines with a mission roughly equating to national service. At least the KPC would give former KLA fighters an organization and allow them to operate openly. For the international community, such an organization absorbed much of the KLA structure, gave its former soldiers meaningful work to perform, and gave KFOR daily oversight over the organization and its activities.

The KPC, with General Agim Ceku as the first commander, was born as the peacetime alternative to the KLA soon after UNMIK and KFOR deployed. SRSG Kouchner authorized the KPC in an UNMIK regulation on September 20, 1999. The KPC was to perform only five civilian emergency functions: disaster response, search and rescue, humanitarian assistance, demining assistance, and infrastructure rebuilding. It was to have an authorized strength of 3,000 active duty personnel and 2,000 reservists. UNMIK would provide the resources for the KPC, and KFOR would provide day-to-day supervision.[3]

Ceku was a practical military officer with sound political judgment. He was straightforward with the international community, and his military bearing, effective command of English, and pragmatic nature made KFOR comfortable in dealing with him. Ceku had a keen sense of the KPC's limits, and he made the best use of it.

No matter how peaceful its mission or transparent its activities, the KPC made the international community very nervous. From 1999 until the declaration of independence in 2008, UNMIK and KFOR kept a wary eye on it. At the same time, Albanians saw the KPC as the linear descendant of the KLA and the nucleus of a future national army.

Flashpoint Mitrovica

The Serbs remaining in communities around Kosovo felt isolated and abandoned after Serbian security forces withdrew. They were justifiably fearful of violent Albanian retribution. As UNMIK and KFOR influence expanded, law and order were gradually restored around the Serbian enclaves. Under pressure from the international community, the Albanians began to realize that their interests were served by the inclusion of Serbs in the society of Kosovo and in local and national institutions.

Mitrovica, a town of about 100,000 people in the North, held the largest concentration of Serbs living close to the border with Serbia. Following the NATO air campaign, communities largely separated on ethnic lines. The Ibar River, running through the center of Mitrovica, became the dividing line between Serbs in the North and Albanians in the South.

Belgrade promoted ethnic separation in Kosovo, and Mitrovica became a symbol of that policy. It served as the center of Serbian rejection of every effort to promote ethnic cooperation in Kosovo. Serbs north of the Ibar routinely rejected offers to cooperate and refused to participate in Kosovo elections or to recognize Kosovo institutions of government. They did, however, participate in elections in Serbia and follow policies directed from Belgrade.

Belgrade used every opportunity to promote segregation in Mitrovica. The Belgrade government continued to pay Serbian officials in northern Kosovo and created parallel institutions not responsive to UNMIK or to the new government in Pristina. More importantly, police in civilian clothes from the Interior Ministry in Belgrade maintained an intimidating presence in northern Kosovo. They set up roadblocks and checkpoints in the North, responded to any event they considered a threat, and guarded the central bridge over the Ibar River connecting the North and South in central Mitrovica. Throughout the UN and NATO mandate, that bridge was the most volatile potential flashpoint in Kosovo.

The separatist Serbian enclave in the North encouraged a steady stream of proposals from some Americans and Europeans over the years to partition Kosovo by giving the territory north of the Ibar River to Serbia as a solution to the lack of cooperation from Belgrade on Kosovo. Partition of Kosovo would not address the fundamental problems, however, and would create a whole series of new ones. Partitioning the North would ignore many smaller Serb communities elsewhere in Kosovo. It also would encourage Serbian or other ethnic extremists elsewhere in the region and raise the potential to partition Bosnia.

In addition, the Albanians in Kosovo would not accept partition and might well fight to retain territory. They considered the North to be within the territory of Kosovo and the mining industry in the North to be a potential source of economic development in the future. Certainly, the sizeable Albanian population in the Presevo Valley in southern Serbia had the capacity to cause considerable parallel trouble in Serbia if any partition proposal became serious in Kosovo. US policy wisely rejected any suggestion of partition.

Serious violence flared twice in Mitrovica. The most dangerous incident happened in March 2004 after a teenage Serb was wounded in a drive-by shooting and three Albanian children drowned in the Ibar River trying to escape Serbs who were chasing them. French KFOR troops guarding the bridge stood between the Albanians and Serbs when angry Albanians gathered in southern Mitrovica and attempted to cross the bridge to engage Serbs. Gunfire broke out in the melee before KFOR gained control of the situation. Six Albanians and two Serbs were killed, and eleven French peacekeepers were wounded in the fighting. These events in Mitrovica triggered angry attacks against Serbian communities in other parts of Kosovo.[4]

Four years later, in March 2008, shortly after Kosovo declared independence, UNMIK police reinforced by KFOR troops fought to reclaim a courthouse that Serbian protestors had stormed and occupied days earlier. The operation succeeded, but brief, intense fighting between Serbian Interior Ministry security forces and UNMIK police and KFOR killed one Ukrainian policeman and wounded around sixty UNMIK and KFOR personnel.[5]

Milosevic Falls from Power: October 2000

Slobodan Milosevic knew how to manipulate and intimidate fellow Serbs to retain his power in Belgrade. I believed that the political opposition in Serbia was too weak to challenge him and that he would take all necessary measures to sustain his position in the FRY presidential elections to be held in Serbia and Montenegro in September 2000.

The Milosevic period of leadership had been a disaster for the Serbs. Unlike most of the countries of the region, Serbia was not moving toward democracy, EU and NATO memberships, or economic development. A defiant, inward-looking Serbia continued to be isolated internationally. Many of its leaders were indicted for war crimes, and the economy was a tangle of corruption and patronage. Serbian influence was in retreat everywhere in the former Yugoslavia, and Kosovo was on the road to independence.

But I thought that Milosevic had the capacity to hang on to power for a long while. His dependent cronies controlled the government, the courts,

242   *Kosovo: War and Independence*

and the economy, and he had the support of the security structure in the country. He had, after all, been a successful Communist. He knew how to run an autocratic government.

Jim Dobbins, however, questioned the depth of Milosevic's control. Dobbins believed in public-opinion polls and studied legitimate polling in Serbia, some conducted by private organizations, some by the US government. From those polls, Dobbins detected cracks in the popular support for the regime and became convinced that Milosevic was politically vulnerable. Because Albright despised Milosevic on many levels, Dobbins had no trouble convincing her that a concentrated effort to encourage political opposition in Serbia just might get the job done.

Dobbins directed a wide-ranging effort to assist the political opposition in Serbia months before the FRY presidential elections in September 2000. Throughout the year, the United States committed $25 million in assistance to Serbia's democratic opposition to Milosevic. That assistance was designed to provide grassroots political training for the opposition and to encourage opposition forces to unify and to pool their efforts. The funding also promoted independent media in Serbia and encouraged democratically oriented, nongovernmental organizations, youth groups, and trade unions to oppose Milosevic. European allies committed funding to enhance democracy programs in Serbia as well.[6]

Encouraging opposition in Serbia was no easy task. Serbia in 2000 was a country whose own public saw little hope for change. Milosevic had effectively neutralized and fragmented the political opposition. The public was passive, accustomed to powerful leaders, and fatalistic about the potential for change. One exception to this national political depression was Otpor! (Rebuff!), a civic youth movement committed to removing Milosevic from power. Otpor!, which also demanded democratic reforms and a fight against corruption, grew into a national movement that brought new energy to the political opposition in Serbia.

The United States and other countries encouraged Otpor!, meeting with its representatives and providing training and support. Two US nongovernmental organizations—the National Endowment for Democracy and the International Republican Institute—were particularly active in working with Otpor!. Using the enthusiasm of young people, Otpor! conducted nonviolent protests, staged rock concerts and street theater, and generally thumbed its nose at the Milosevic regime. Through its activities, it tapped into a deep-seated public disillusionment with the regime. As the

FRY elections approached, the opposition movement in Serbia gained unity and strength.[7]

To further encourage Serb voters, the United States and the EU announced before the vote that they were ready to lift recently imposed economic sanctions if voters in Serbia were to elect a candidate in opposition to Milosevic.[8]

Milosevic probably underestimated the opposition until it was too late. His measures to retain power were primitive. In August 2000, Ivan Stambolic, former president of Serbia and the man Milosevic had overthrown to come to power in Belgrade, disappeared. When his body was found later, Milosevic was alleged to have had him assassinated because Stambolic was a viable challenger in the elections to be held that year.[9]

Just before the election, the Milosevic government jammed through a series of constitutional amendments that structured the election process in his favor without any public debate. The government of Montenegro and UNMIK in Kosovo refused to participate in the election, yet voting was conducted in both places. Opposition voting monitors were denied access to voting areas or were intimidated. Ballots lacked security, and voting irregularities were reported as pervasive. The FRY also denied visas to the OCSE, which routinely monitors elections in the region. Nevertheless, the OSCE declared the election on September 24, 2000, to be fundamentally flawed.[10]

In the face of Milosevic's harassment of opponents, large sections of the public began to unify around the Democratic Opposition of Serbia Party and its leader, Vojislav Kostunica, a conservative lawyer. Serbian voters flocked to the polls on September 24, 2000, despite the massive manipulation of the vote. Two days later the Federal Election Commission announced that Kostunica had won the vote but had fallen short of the 50 percent required to win on the first vote. The commission declared that a second vote would be required even though it was clear that massive vote manipulation had denied Kostunica more than the essential 50 percent. Kostunica claimed victory and refused to participate in a runoff. The international community rallied around him and pressured Milosevic to accept defeat.

Milosevic continued to maneuver. On October 4, the FRY Constitutional Court announced a judgment that a second election should occur in mid-2001, the end of the existing Milosevic term as FRY president. The opposition responded by taking to the streets in massive demonstrations in Belgrade. Demonstrators seized control of the Parliament building and state broadcasting facilities on October 5.

The next day, in front of the marble fireplace in the foyer of the Beli dvor, Slobodan Milosevic resigned as president of Yugoslavia and accepted the election of Kostunica as his replacement. Kostunica was sworn in on October 7, and two days later the United States and the EU lifted the remaining economic sanctions on the country.

The Milosevic era of murder, corruption, and manipulation in the Balkans was over. He suddenly went from national leader to major liability for the Serbs as international pressure for his rendition to the ICTY increased.

Kostunica favored the rule of law and democratic practices. Otherwise, the best that could be said of him was that he was not Milosevic. The new FRY president refused to cooperate with the ICTY on war crimes indictments. He was not eager to pursue EU membership, much less membership in NATO. For Kostunica, Serbian nationalism was not just a political expedient. He was a true believer, a dedicated, conservative Serbian nationalist who made no effort to improve the relationship with Kosovo, Bosnia, or the international community on regional issues.

In December, after parliamentary elections that same year, the Democratic Party and the Democratic Opposition Party formed a coalition government and selected Zoran Djindjic as prime minister of Serbia. Djindjic was more reform minded, favoring European integration, democratic reforms, and programs against organized crime and corruption.

Caging the Beast

US ambassador to Serbia William D. "Bill" Montgomery was on the phone from Belgrade when I arrived for work at the State Department on Thursday, June 28, 2001. Police from the Serbian government of Prime Minister Djindjic had surrounded the Milosevic residence in Belgrade and were in the final negotiations on the transfer of Milosevic to the ICTY in The Hague. The Serbs wanted international help.

Montgomery and I had been involved in the Balkans for years. In June 2001, he had been chief of mission and now was US ambassador in Belgrade. He and I had most recently worked together to stop Serb–Albanian violence in the Presevo Valley of southern Serbia. Montgomery had convinced the Djindjic government to act in the national interest by transferring Milosevic out of Serbia to The Hague to face international justice.

The new George W. Bush administration was still settling in after the transition to power the previous January. The Republicans generally pre-ferred to work within existing organizations rather than to create task forc-es and special envoys. By this point, Dobbins was gone from the Balkan account. I was the last senior Balkan hand still standing at State after the transition, and I was to be the last special envoy for the Balkans. Marc Grossman, the new undersecretary of state for political affairs, proposed that I be nominated as US ambassador to Bulgaria. I was pleased with the opportunity, but the job was not open until the summer of 2002.

The new Bush administration could not avoid the unfinished business in the Balkans. Action on ICTY indictments was one important leftover task in the region, and Milosevic was the most important fugitive to be de-livered to the court.

Montgomery called on June 28 to pass on the request by the Djindjic government in Belgrade that the United States or some other government transport Milosevic to The Hague after he surrendered. The Serbs could fly him by helicopter from Belgrade to the US base at Tuzla in Bosnia, but they needed someone to transport him from Tuzla to the Netherlands. Mont-gomery thought that the United States should do the job, and he pushed for an immediate response.

I did not have time to coordinate the request with the Pentagon and quickly called General Joe Ralston, who had replaced Wes Clark as SA-CEUR, at the NATO military headquarters in Mons, Belgium. He was reluctant to get involved in the Milosevic transfer and said that the US mili-tary would take a pass. I relayed the information to Montgomery, who said that the Serbs had already arranged for the British to take Milosevic from Tuzla to The Hague.

After a brief, ironic stop in Bosnia on the way, Milosevic was delivered to the International Court in The Hague, where he was to remain in cus-tody for the rest of his life.

I had discussed the ICTY with Milosevic several times in the past. He had nothing but contempt for it. He rejected its legitimacy. He saw it as purely a political institution, not a legal one. He considered the situation in the region a big international game and was convinced that the United States, specifically Madeleine Albright, had instigated the international in-dictment. While in power, Milosevic knew that the ICTY had marginal-ized Karadzic and Mladic, and he had to worry that the fear of indictment would further weaken his stable of cronies and have a corrosive effect on his public support.

Facing charges of genocide and crimes against humanity, former president of Yugoslavia Slobodan Milosevic (*center*), flanked by court security guards, appears before the UN ICTY in The Hague, Netherlands, July 2001. (Associated Press)

Nearly two years later, on March 12, 2003, as Prime Minister Zoran Djindjic, the leader who had turned Milosevic over to the ICTY, stepped out of a sedan to enter his office in central Belgrade, Zvezdan Jonanovic fired two shots from a high-velocity rifle into Djindjic's chest, killing him almost instantly.

The assassin was a former senior member of the Red Berets, an organization the Interior Ministry under Milosevic had created as an elite special-police unit with close ties to organized crime and paramilitary activities in Bosnia and Kosovo. Prosecutors claimed that Jonanovic was part of a conspiracy that acted to oppose the transfer of indicted Serbs to the ICTY and Djindjic's campaign against organized crime. In 2007, a Serbian court convicted Jonanovic and nine other men in the conspiracy to assassinate Djindjic.[11] The Red Berets were also associated with the assassination of former Serbian president Ivan Stambolic before the FRY election in 2000.[12]

In the end, Milosevic evaded international justice. He manipulated the court and turned his trial into theater. He represented himself before the court and effectively strung out the legal process, using the political and legal tricks that had brought him to power and kept him there for so long.

Milosevic died of a heart attack on March 11, 2006, at age sixty-four while in international custody in The Hague.[13] The man who was personally responsible for the death or misery of millions of people was never held legally accountable for his actions.

In separate trials, the ICTY first acquitted former Milosevic interior minister Jovica Stanisic and his subordinate, Franko Simatovic, the founders and supervisors of Arkan's Tigers and the Red Berets, of all charges in 2013 and then ordered their retrial. The Trial Chamber ruled that the two men could not be held criminally responsible for the crimes committed by Serb paramilitaries in Bosnia because prosecutors had not proved personal intent at the trial.[14]

26

Independence

The Ahtisaari Process

The UN Security Council Resolution authorizing UN administration of Kosovo called for a political process to determine Kosovo's future status. After years of international governance of Kosovo, pressure was building in the summer of 2005 to start defining Kosovo's future.

KFOR stabilized and restored relative peace throughout Kosovo after 1999. During its years of governance, UNMIK assisted Kosovo authorities in creating provisional institutions of self-government. Kosovo had a provisional constitution and executive, legislative, and judicial branches of government. Internationally trained police were operational, and local municipal institutions were working. This progress made the Albanians more committed to independence and increasingly anxious for final status to be determined.

Within the United States, Richard Holbrooke, again out of government, and members of Congress were pushing US leaders for a process to determine Kosovo's future status. At the State Department, R. Nicholas Burns, the undersecretary for political affairs, took on the task of moving the Kosovo process forward with the Contact Group. Below Burns, Deputy Assistant Secretary for Europe Rosemary DiCarlo was the primary US representative in the Contact Group.

In the summer of 2005, the Contact Group agreed to begin measures to determine Kosovo's future status as called for in UNSCR 1244. The process would have two sequential steps. The first step would be an evaluation to determine if the Kosovo Albanians had sufficiently met international standards necessary to consider their future status. In the second, the UN secretary-general would appoint an international official to evaluate the options for Kosovo's status and to recommend a solution to the Security Council.

Independence for Kosovo was the inevitable outcome of this process. In the beginning of the Kosovo mission, independence from the FRY had not been any national capital's option, but anyone who had worked seriously on Kosovo by 2005 knew that returning its sovereignty back to Belgrade was not possible. After the brutality in 1998–1999 and after NATO had expelled Serbian security forces from Kosovo, restoring Serbian sovereignty in Kosovo simply was not feasible. When Montenegro broke away from Yugoslavia without issue in 2006, no other outcome was realistic. Independence for Kosovo would not come quickly, however. It would take almost three years of international negotiations before it became a reality in 2008.

By that time, I had become the deputy assistant secretary-general for operations on the NATO International Staff in 2005, after completing three years as US ambassador to Bulgaria. NATO was still engaged in Kosovo, but I was interested in Afghanistan, where NATO was becoming more involved. As I settled in at NATO, Secretary-General Jaap de Hoop Scheffer was eager to raise NATO's profile within the Contact Group. I could help, given my background.

The UN and Contact Group had a policy of "standards before status," and in 2003 UNMIK set out a list of seven standards with conditions that Kosovo had to address as part of the process to determine its status.[1]

The UN secretary-general appointed Ambassador Kai Eide, Norway's permanent representative to NATO, in 2005 to evaluate Kosovo's progress in meeting Contact Group standards as a prelude to status talks. I knew the capable Eide from his previous involvement in the Balkans. Like me, Eide was drawn to crisis management.

Eide's job was to evaluate whether the Contact Group standards had been met by the Albanian majority in Kosovo. Eide took his time, completing his report to Secretary-General Kofi Annan in October 2005. Although he found mixed results in the meeting of these standards, he assessed that the time had come to commence the status process.[2]

The next step was the appointment of a UN special envoy to consult with all parties involved in Kosovo, to seek a solution, and to make a recommendation to the UN Security Council. Selection of the international envoy was critical, and the Contact Group helped the UN select the best possible choice, Martti Ahtisaari. A former president of Finland, Ahtisaari had held several senior UN positions. He had the full confidence of Washington and European capitals, and, importantly, he had Russia's support

because of his experience with Viktor Chernomyrdin during the negotiations to end the NATO air campaign in Kosovo in 1999.

Holbrooke asked me to become Ahtisaari's US partner in the Kosovo
status negotiations. Holbrooke, Undersecretary Burns, and others at State
approached me that summer of 2005 to take the position, but I turned it
down. I confided to Holbrooke that I disagreed with the Bush administration's national security policy and did not want to be a high-profile senior
official for it again. In my view, the administration had badly bungled the
national response to the attacks on the United States on September 11,
2001, and I considered its policy decisions after that to have been reckless.
They had violated basic American values, undermined the Constitution,
and damaged American credibility everywhere. Further, I did not see the
Bush government as serious on the Balkans.

In 2005, cooperation on Kosovo policy generally continued within the
Contact Group despite the strained US relationship with its European allies created by the Bush administration's unilateralist approach to foreign
policy and by the controversy over the US war in Iraq.

Ahtisaari was officially appointed as UN special envoy for Kosovo status in mid-November 2005. He began consultations while he established
a support organization in Vienna, the UN Office of the Special Envoy on
Kosovo. His US negotiating colleague was Frank Wisner, a former senior
US diplomat and defense official.

Ahtisaari knew that the Contact Group was the driving force in the
Kosovo deliberations and stayed very close to it as he proceeded. The Contact Group and the UN Security Council had worked in tandem on Kosovo
ever since the NATO air campaign in 1999. The Security Council looked
to the Contact Group for steerage on the Kosovo process, and the Contact
Group pursued international authority for Kosovo policy from Security
Council deliberations.

NATO and the EU were adjunct members of the Contact Group because of the level of institutional engagement in Kosovo. Some European
members preferred to keep the EU as the primary partner, to the exclusion
of NATO, but the United States insisted that NATO have a coequal seat at
the Contact Group table. I represented NATO in the Contact Group at the
political director and staff levels from 2005 until Kosovo declared independence in 2008.

The Contact Group issued a set of guiding principles for Ahtisaari to
use in developing his recommendation on Kosovo's future status.[3] He was

UN special envoy
Martti Ahtisaari
led the international
negotiations to
determine Kosovo's
future status.
Kosovo declared
independence
under international
supervision in 2008.
(United Nations
Photo Library)

to consult with the parties and develop a proposal for settlement of Kosovo's status consistent within the guiding principles. The principles gave Ahtisaari much latitude for negotiating with the parties, and he used it.

Ahtisaari's personal style was important to the negotiations. He showed the confidence of experience and success, but without the sharp edges of some negotiators in high positions. Personally, Ahtisaari was disarming. He came across as a decent, thoughtful, and fair person who understood the importance of his task and was doing his best to find the right solution. He was careful to be inclusive and patient in listening to all sides, but he also kept the deliberations focused and moving forward to conclusion.

Underneath his open and inclusive demeanor, Ahtisaari was a crafty negotiator. He was a realist, determined to find a practical solution to Kosovo's status. He set the agenda for the negotiations and drew proposed practical solutions from his consultations with the parties and the Contact Group. In doing so, he refused to allow his process to be derailed or marginalized.

After a few weeks of consultations, Ahtisaari admitted privately that he saw no solution other than independence. All Contact Group capitals except Moscow agreed informally with that assessment. For Washington, London, Paris, Berlin, and Rome, the five Contact Group capitals favoring independence, the question was a matter of form, timing, and level of international involvement. Moscow was the real issue, and Russian opposition was a serious problem because Russia could use its veto in the Security Council to block official UN support to any outcome.

In the Contact Group deliberations on Kosovo in 2005–2008, Russia was not the same cooperative member that it had been on Bosnia and Kosovo in 1995–1999. Its continued participation in the Contact Group caused many in Washington and European capitals to believe that it would eventually come around to the solution that the others in the group supported. That assessment underestimated Vladimir Putin's determination to express Russia's power and independence from the West on Kosovo and other issues.

In 2005, the principal Russian diplomats on Kosovo included Sergey Lavrov, a longtime senior diplomat who had replaced Igor Ivanov as foreign minister. I had observed Lavrov many times, and he could be a difficult adversary. Deputy Foreign Minister Vladimir Titov, who had been the Russian ambassador to Bulgaria when I was there, attended some Contact Group meetings at the political director level. A constant presence in every Kosovo discussion was Alexander Botsan-Kharchenko, "Sasha," as his Contact Group associates called him informally. Sasha and I knew each other from interaction in previous Balkan issues. His Contact Group colleagues liked and respected him personally. He was not confrontational, but he laid out in a straightforward manner Russia's opposition to independence for Kosovo.

Ahtisaari met frequently with the Contact Group to provide updates on the parties' positions, to present his views on the way forward, and to hear the Contact Group capitals' reactions. The Contact Group was content to follow his lead on the negotiating process. But Ahtisaari was unable to reconcile the two parties' positions: the Albanians demanded independence, and the Serbs rejected it. Ahtisaari and the Contact Group did not have sufficient leverage to shift the parties' positions one way or the other.

Inside the Contact Group, Russia would not agree to any proposal that called for or implied independence for Kosovo. Although the Europeans realized that independence was the only practical outcome, they were not enthusiastic about an independent Kosovo. They favored independence, but with extensive, long-term international supervision.

Russia and Serbia played diplomatic defense. Their negotiating strategy was the same one that had failed to prevent the NATO air campaign in 1999—demand that the status of Kosovo be decided in the UN Security Council, where Russia would be able to block independence. By insisting on a UN process, Putin and Lavrov also exploited the Europeans' concerns about recent US actions to bypass the UN to conduct the war in Iraq. If independence were to be the outcome, Russia would force the United States to go around the UN again.

At several points, Ahtisaari called together the Kosovo Albanians and the Serbs, including Serbs from Kosovo, to discuss several areas of possible compromise. Without exception, these meetings were an honest effort at negotiations, but they made no headway on substance.

Ahtisaari tried unsuccessfully to elevate the direct talks to the level of presidents and prime ministers in July 2006. As at Dayton, these direct talks produced little more than aggressive posturing for the delegations but no substantive shifts in position.

Ahtisaari presented his final recommendations to the Contact Group and the parties in February 2007. The Ahtisaari plan recommended a period of international supervision leading to independence for Kosovo. The plan of fifteen articles and twelve annexes called for a constitution recognizing a multiethnic society and based on democratic principles, rule of law, and international norms of humanitarian rights and freedoms.

UNMIK would be replaced with an international civilian representative from the EU. The representative would not have executive authority but would assist in the transition to independence. KFOR remained in a more limited role as well.

The Ahtisaari proposal replaced the KPC with the Kosovo Security Force, made up of 3,300 personnel. The Contact Group, however, could not face the creation of an armed force, a component of almost every independent country, so the plan instead gave the new Kosovo Security Force the awkward task of "security functions not appropriate for police or other law enforcement organizations."[4]

Ahtisaari's consultation with the parties on his draft proposal produced the predictable hostile responses. After sixteen months of meetings with representatives of Pristina and Belgrade failed to produce an agreement, Ahtisaari completed his task by submitting his proposal to the Security Council on April 3, 2007. As expected, Belgrade completely rejected the Ahtisaari plan, and Russia blocked all efforts to gain a Security Council endorsement for the plan.

Late in 2007, after months of US and European efforts failed to convince Moscow to accept the Ahtisaari plan, the Bush administration decided to move independence for Kosovo forward and began to develop European endorsement for independence. I called on longtime Contact Group colleague Sasha Botsan-Kharchenko at the Foreign Ministry in Moscow near the end of 2007.

"Jim, you know how much we oppose independence for Kosovo. We probably are not able to stop it if the US is determined. But the price you will pay for that is in Georgia," Sasha said.

Kosovo declared independence on February 17, 2008, with the support of France, the United Kingdom, Germany, Italy, and the United States. The United States and Costa Rica recognized Kosovo as a sovereign nation the next day.[5] Shortly thereafter, the United Kingdom, France, Albania, Germany, Turkey, and other countries followed. After five years, more than one hundred nations recognized Kosovo. Greece and Cyprus, with sympathies toward Serbia, and several European countries, such as Spain because of issues with its own domestic independence movements, did not recognize Kosovo.

Ibrahim Rugova, who had led the political resistance to Milosevic in 1998, died in January 2006, two years short of Kosovo's independence. Today Rugova is considered the father of that independence.

In April 2008, separatists in South Ossetia declared independence from Georgia. Fighting soon broke out between Russian and Georgian military forces. In August 2008, Russia settled into a long-term occupation of "independent" South Ossetia and Abkhazia.

Independence of Kosovo was the last act in the dismemberment of Yugoslavia, eighteen years after it had begun in Slovenia and Croatia. However, Serbia continued to oppose independence, and an international presence, including the EU and NATO, remained in Kosovo to ensure stability.

Part 5

Macedonia
The Ohrid Agreement

Lake Ohrid, Macedonia (Shutterstock.com)

27

A War or a Nation?

War again threatened the people of the Balkans, this time in Macedonia, less than two years after the NATO bombing campaign in Serbia and Kosovo in 1999. For six weeks in the summer of 2001, American and European diplomats struggled through fragile and stormy negotiations, riots, threats, and cease-fire violations to reach an agreement that prevented a civil war in Macedonia.

The George W. Bush administration, as it assumed power in January 2001, assembled a national security team with remarkable experience at the top. Vice President Richard Cheney, Secretary of State Colin Powell, and Secretary of Defense Donald Rumsfeld potentially formed one of the strongest national security teams in US history. Yet this group quickly deteriorated into bitter turf fights and leaped to ideological approaches to foreign and national security policy. Rumsfeld in particular wanted to pull out of the Balkans, including an end to the US military commitment to KFOR, the lynchpin of stability in Kosovo. Despite the constant pressure he applied, Rumsfeld ultimately failed to end the US participation in KFOR.

A new war in the Balkans was the last problem the new Bush administration wanted. In its officials' minds, Bosnia and the Balkans were carryover issues from the Clinton presidency, but Balkan conflicts did not end on inauguration day. Insurgent attacks began early in the new administration, and fighting between Macedonian government troops and the Albanian insurgents escalated through the winter and spring of 2001. As the situation deteriorated, the administration fell back on the previous Bush policy of transferring responsibility for the problems in the Balkans to the Europeans. But in 2001 the US investment in the former Yugoslavia was too large and the American engagement too important to stay on the sidelines. To prevent war in Macedonia, the new administration could not avoid American participation in the peace effort.

Laurel Miller and I were all that remained of the Office of the Special Envoy for the Balkans at the State Department after Jim Dobbins moved on with the change of government.

The early international efforts to stop the fighting in Macedonia were failing. The Macedonian strategy was reliant on military solutions and lacked any serious political process to settle the issues. In addition, KFOR and UNMIK refused to act against the National Liberation Army (NLA), an Albanian insurgent group operating from Kosovo, thus giving the NLA a haven in an internationally controlled area. Without a serious political process and with the military situation deteriorating, the conflict in Macedonia could only grow worse.[1]

My assignment to go to Macedonia came quickly in June 2001. Two days before I left for Macedonia, I was coordinating the rendition of Milosevic to the ICTY in The Hague. As I worked on the Milosevic transfer, Jim Hooper, a longtime Balkan activist and one of the originators of the dissent letter to the secretary of state in 1993 protesting the lack of US action to defend Bosnia, called to say that I would be asked to be the US envoy on a joint US-EU diplomatic effort to try to prevent a war in Macedonia. Unknown to me, Hooper had recommended me to the White House through Robin Cleveland at the Office of Management and Budget.[2] Cleveland knew me from her time on the Senate staff. Shortly after the call from Hooper, a senior official at State asked if I would take on the job, and I said yes. Two days later I was on a plane to Macedonia's capital, Skopje, to join François Leotard, former minister of defense of France, as the two international envoys in Macedonia. Our job was to help Macedonian president Boris Trajkovski reach a settlement between the major political parties.

"Pardew will stay until a deal is made," President Bush told British prime minister Tony Blair, according to a member of the White House staff. The Europeans, I was told, were frustrated and wanted to move fast to an agreement.

The potential war in Macedonia was a major international issue for the first eight months of the new Bush administration. I left Washington for Skopje on June 30, 2001, as part of the latest international effort to stop or prevent a Balkan war. On the flight, I wondered if the parties to the conflict in Macedonia—the Slavic Macedonian majority and the Albanian minority—wanted a nation or a war. Macedonia was too fragile to accommodate both.

Alexander's Legacy

People who live in modern Macedonia struggle with the same questions that others in the Balkans worry over: Who are we, and where do we fit in this region? They chose the legacy of ancient Macedonia and its historic leaders, Philip and his son, Alexander, as the foundation of their cultural heritage. But history overlaps modern borders, and Greece also staked a claim to the ancient Macedonians. The resulting controversy between neighbors over the legacy of a lost civilization influenced domestic and international relationships in Macedonia as this new country struggled with the challenges of creating a new democracy in the twenty-first century.

The Macedonia of Philip and Alexander in the fourth century BCE encompassed the area of modern Macedonia, eastern Greece along the Aegean coast, a corner of southwestern Bulgaria, and a sliver of eastern Albania.[3] Alexander and the ancient Macedonians were long gone by the time the Slavic tribes entered this area. The Greek claim also was a stretch because Macedonia was on the periphery of ancient Greece, and the ancient Macedonians did not consider themselves Greeks.[4]

Like other nations of the region, Macedonia experienced the coming and going of empires over the centuries. The Slavic tribes came south of the Danube and occupied the area of modern Bulgaria, Macedonia, and Serbia in the sixth century CE. All three Slavic nations are linked by the Orthodox Christianity of Byzantium and by the Cyrillic alphabet developed in the area to spread the faith. Bulgaria and Macedonian nationalists claimed some of the same heroes from the fighting that ended Ottoman occupation and gave them independence in the nineteenth century. In the twentieth century, both Bulgaria and Serbia dominated the region of modern Macedonia for a period.[5]

As Yugoslavia broke apart, Macedonia, which had been part of the Socialist Republic of Yugoslavia, became independent by referendum in 1991. Belgrade did not contest the break.

The "Apple of Discord"

Macedonia was admitted to the UN in 1993 with the awkward designation "the former Yugoslav Republic of Macedonia" as a compromise with Greece over the country's official name.[6] The name issue, as puzzling as it might seem to anyone outside the region, has been a damaging international obstacle for Macedonia, delaying its membership in NATO and the

EU. The lack of a suitable, internationally accepted name for the country also was a blow to the collective national confidence and a major source of insecurity for the country's Slavic population.

Macedonia is a small, landlocked country about the size of Vermont. The population is around 2 million, split largely between the ethnic Macedonian Slavs (64 percent) and the Albanians (25 percent). Turks, Vlachs, and Roma make up the remaining population.[7]

The ethnic Slavs in Macedonia bristled when I referred to them as "Macedonian Slavs" to distinguish them from Macedonian Albanians. In their minds and in their constitution after independence, Macedonia was a nation-state of ethnic Macedonian (Slavic) people in which Albanians and other minorities had rights. The minorities, however, resented the implied and real discrimination contained in this concept. To the consternation of its neighbors, Macedonia also declared official concern regarding the status and rights of ethnic Macedonians living in nearby countries.[8]

The Macedonian obsession with its national identity was deep. Based on a history of struggling for identity and cultural survival, Macedonians saw themselves as surrounded by potential enemies: Bulgaria, Serbia, Greece, and Albania. The ethnic Macedonians also felt threatened by the nation's large Albanian minority, who demanded rights and had links to Kosovo and Albania on Macedonia's border.

I saw Macedonia as the epicenter of ethnic insecurity in the region in 2001. In *Who Are the Macedonians?* Hugh Poulton calls Macedonia "the apple of discord in the Balkans."[9]

28

Pop-up Insurgency

The Albanians in Kosovo were secure by early 2001. Kosovo was stable and governed by the UN, but Albanian trouble was brewing again elsewhere in the Balkans. A new threat to peace—the National Liberation Army—appeared in Macedonia in January when its fighters attacked a police station in the village of Tearce near the Kosovo border. In February, the NLA and government forces again clashed near the village of Tanusevac. Within weeks, the NLA was a national Albanian rebellion that threatened to destabilize Macedonia.[1]

The NLA insurgency followed the general pattern of the KLA insurgency in Kosovo. The recognized political parties were having little or no success in resolving issues important to the Albanian population. Albanian militants seized the initiative from them and used force to pressure the government to address the Albanians' demands. The government, in turn, reacted with force to stifle the rebellion.

At first, the leaders of the recognized Albanian political parties in Skopje opposed the NLA. They viewed the movement as dangerous to the security of the Albanian community and a direct challenge to their personal political authority in Macedonia. But, just as in Kosovo, the conventional political leaders lost public support to the armed insurgents.

The nature of the NLA was vague. It was not a Kosovo movement, but Albanians from Kosovo were involved. Ali Ahmeti, born in Macedonia but educated in Pristina, was identified as the NLA commander and political chief. The NLA also maintained headquarters in Prizren, Kosovo. When the NLA first appeared, NATO noted that several senior officers in the KPC disappeared and were presumed to be involved in the NLA movement.

The NLA had some important advantages. Macedonia could not effectively control its borders with Albania and Kosovo, giving the NLA external havens and logistics routes into Macedonia. The NLA was lightly armed and could conduct high-profile hit-and-run attacks on Macedonian

Albanian fighters in the NLA, Macedonia. (Reuters)

security forces and infrastructure. The well-organized and sympathetic Albanian diaspora, which had assisted the KLA two years earlier, also was inclined to provide a range of support to the NLA if the conflict grew more intense.

If the NLA caused no trouble in Kosovo, KFOR was not a threat to it. KFOR had no mandate to engage in counterinsurgency activity in Kosovo on behalf of the Macedonian government. With no mandate, neither KFOR nor the international police in Kosovo were inclined to challenge the NLA in Kosovo with force, which was a constant source of irritation to Macedonian leaders and generated a range of conspiracy theories among the ethnic Macedonian population.

Defeating an insurgency can be the most difficult task for any government. In the Balkans, the Serbian campaign against the KLA had failed, even though the Serbs had a well-established police and military structure, training, and equipment. Milosevic's harsh repression of the Albanian population in Kosovo only strengthened support to the KLA. Macedonia, independent only since 1991, had only new, poorly trained, and poorly equipped police and military structures to deal with the problem. It lacked the capacity and experience to respond effectively to a serious insurgency. A military victory over the NLA in Macedonia was not feasible. The only practical solution was a political agreement between the ethnic Macedonians and the Albanians.

By March 2001, the NLA was a national movement that was fighting government forces around Tetovo, the city with the most Albanians in Macedonia. A concerned UN warned of a new refugee crisis in the Balkans if fighting between ethnic Albanian rebels and Macedonian security forces got worse.[2] In late March, President Boris Trajkovski announced a major military offensive involving armor, artillery, and attack helicopters near Tetovo. The offensive had little success, but the shelling of villages near Tetovo created thousands of Albanian refugees.

Nationalists and Moderates—the Macedonians

The war in Kosovo in 1999 had placed a heavy burden on the Macedonian government when at least 300,000 Albanians from Kosovo fled to Macedonia to avoid the fighting. National leaders felt underappreciated for their cooperation with NATO during this period and were not satisfied with the international support they received to help handle their domestic challenges.

As the Albanian insurgency grew stronger, most senior ethnic Macedonian leaders believed that the international community should endorse the government's aggressive use of the police and the army to defeat the NLA in the countryside. They resented international pressure to limit military operations and to negotiate with Albanian leaders. They wanted to crush the rebels by force.

The responsibility for finding a solution to the rebellion fell to Boris Trajkovski, the forty-five-year-old president of Macedonia. Before independence, as a lay minister in the Methodist Church, he had been confined by the Communists for his religious activities. After independence, he became politically active with the nationalist Internal Macedonian Revolutionary Organization–Democratic Party for Macedonian National Unity (Vatreshna Makedonska-Revolutsionerna Organizatsiya–Demokratska Partija za Makedonsko Nacionalno Edinstvo, VMRO-DPMNE Party). He also served as deputy foreign minister during the war in Kosovo.[3]

The burly and emotional Trajkovski continuously pursued international help to end the conflict in his country. He was a deeply religious man who felt that God had placed him in power at a critical moment in Macedonia's history.[4] His energy and commitment to negotiations established him as the focus of attention in Washington and Europe.

Trajkovski viewed himself as a neutral arbitrator between the government and the Albanian parties. The US and EU envoys were to be facilitators, working on a settlement on behalf of the president of the country. Unfortunately, the Albanians never saw him as an unbiased arbitrator. To them, Trajkovski was not in a strong position, and he was heavily influenced by the Macedonian nationalists.

In the negotiations, Trajkovski's constitutional position was weak. He had the limited authority of a president in a parliamentary democracy. He was commander in chief of the Macedonian Armed Forces and president of the Security Council for National Defense. Otherwise, the prime minister and the government constitutionally held most executive power in the country.[5] The government of Macedonia was controlled by Macedonian nationalists, and they wanted to physically destroy the Albanian rebels. They were not interested in negotiations.

Throughout the winter and spring of 2001, limited battlefield success caused the government of Macedonia to vacillate between military action, negotiation, and reconciliation. The government's military offensive near Tetovo in March stalled.[6] President Trajkovski subsequently met with President Bush in Washington and then led a national prayer dinner in Skopje as part of a reconciliation policy.[7] Near the end of May, Trajkovski authorized a second government military offensive, which again failed to disrupt the NLA.[8]

Ljubco Georgievski, a thirty-five-year-old poet and political party leader, was prime minister of Macedonia in 2001. Years earlier Georgievski had founded the VMRO-DPMNE with the goal of unifying Macedonians in a Macedonian state. He was a staunch Macedonian nationalist and a dedicated anti-Communist. His popular nationalist agenda propelled him to political prominence when the Socialist Democratic Union of Macedonia (Socijaldemokratski Sojuz na Makedonija, SDSM), composed mainly of converted Communists, floundered after independence from Yugoslavia.[9]

Georgievski became prime minister of a coalition government that included major Albanian parties in 1998. After fighting broke out with the NLA, he formed a national unity government of major Slavic and Albanian parties in February 2001.[10] His personal goal was to defeat the NLA by military and police action. If that were not possible, he would consider dividing the country along ethnic lines. To the often petulant and defiant Georgievski, Macedonia was for the ethnic Macedonians. Others could live there, but without equal status.

Ljube Boskovski, the government's interior minister, was the Macedonian leader most committed to a violent solution to the rebellion. A member of the VMRO-DPMNE and a former member of the National Assembly, Boskovski was appointed interior minister in the Georgievski government in May 2001, and he held that position until 2002, running the national police, the paramilitary forces, and the national intelligence organization.

I expected the defense minister to be a hard-line nationalist, but he was not. Vlado Buchkovski was a moderate in the government. He generally carried out the government's decisions, but he also understood the limitations of the armed forces and the dangers of the conflict. At least on one occasion, he refused to authorize the Macedonian army's participation in Interior Ministry operations.

The primary opposition party in Macedonia was the SDSM, led by Branko Cervenkovski. A former Communist who helped form the SDSM, Cervenkovski preceded Georgievski as prime minister from 1992 to 1998. During the fighting and the negotiations in 2001, he remained relatively passive toward the policies of the VMRO government.

Politicians and Rebels—the Albanians

The Albanians had reason to be dissatisfied with their status in Macedonia. The ethnic Macedonians running the government heavily discriminated against them. Albanians were not represented adequately in national institutions such as the military, the police, and the bureaucracy. They were alienated from the government and felt deprived of influence on local issues affecting their lives. They wanted the education system to include instruction in Albanian and to be recognized by the state, and they demanded that their language and cultural symbols be accepted as legitimate. As in Kosovo, I saw no inclination to create some form of "Greater Albania." The Albanian leaders I encountered in Macedonia saw no advantage to being subordinate to leaders in Albania or Kosovo and seemed content to be Macedonians if their rights, influence, and status could be improved.

The Macedonian government leaders considered only two Albanian political leaders—Arben Xheferi and Imer Imeri—as legitimate negotiators.

Xheferi was the most important recognized Albanian political figure in the talks with the ethnic Macedonian leaders in 2001. Age fifty-three and educated in Belgrade, he was an Albanian intellectual who had lived in Pristina for years as a journalist. He returned to Macedonia when Yugoslavia collapsed and became the leader of the Democratic Party for Albanians

(Demokratska Partija na Albancite, DPA), the largest Albanian political party at the time. Xheferi suffered from Parkinson's disease, which affected his speech and mannerisms but not his mind. He was an intelligent and crafty negotiator who understood the personalities and complexities of the process better than most. Xheferi's primary assistant in the DPA, Mendu Thaci, had a reputation for corruption and illicit activity.

Imeri and his party, the Party for Democratic Prosperity (Partija z Demokratski Prosperitet, PDP), were important but less influential in the negotiations than Xheferi. The PDP was a smaller party, and Imeri seemed focused on one issue—Albanian education—rather than on the larger set of issues. However, any peace agreement required his approval to be valid.

President Trajkovski and the Macedonian government were absolute in their refusal to include anyone from the NLA in the negotiation. To them, negotiating with the NLA would constitute dealing with "terrorists," but Ahmeti, as the commander of the NLA, held the keys to a peaceful settlement. I knew the political dangers of talking to the NLA and had no contact with any of its members before, during, or after the negotiations. In fact, I never met or talked to NLA leader Ali Ahmeti until ten years after the Ohrid Agreement was signed.

Born in Macedonia, Ahmeti attended university in Kosovo, where he became a student activist against the Yugoslav regime in the 1980s. After being arrested and jailed by the Serbs, Ahmeti fled Kosovo for political asylum in Switzerland. He returned to Kosovo to help found the KLA to fight against Serbian repression. He turned his attention to Macedonia after Serbia lost Kosovo in 1999. Ahmeti recruited KLA veterans and Albanian volunteers in Macedonia to join him in the mountains along the Kosovo–Macedonia border to begin an armed rebellion against the government of Macedonia.

The aims of the NLA at first ranged from secession to improved Albanian rights. By April 2001, the NLA had settled on the same demands for rights as those expressed by Xheferi, Imeri, and other conventional Albanian leaders. By that time, small-scale attacks had escalated into a national insurgency.[11] Despite several Macedonian army, police, and paramilitary attempts to defeat the NLA, the organization gained strength within the Albanian community as the fighting spread in the countryside.

The NLA strategy was extremely dangerous to the Albanian population. It employed provocative hit-and-run attacks against the government. These strikes risked igniting a bloody and destructive government campaign of repression against Macedonia's Albanian population. The NLA did not have the broad international sympathy that the KLA enjoyed during the Milosevic repression of Kosovo. Further, Washington and the European capitals, although favoring negotiations, also recognized the right of the Macedonian government to defend itself.

The NLA was not a large force, and it was armed primarily with light weapons. The maximum number of active combatants at its peak was estimated to be about 3,000. Others estimated its strength as fewer than 1,000. The NLA could not defeat the government in sustained combat, but it could conduct small attacks to demonstrate government weakness or to provoke a destructive overreaction.

Tough Realities

President Trajkovski and the ethnic Macedonian political leader in the government faced some hard realities in June 2001 as they reacted to the Albanian rebellion. The Macedonian government was in no condition to respond effectively to an armed Albanian rebellion. The country was struggling in every sector. The ongoing transition to democracy was spotty. Political experience was thin, and institutions of government were weak in most cases. The embargo on Serbia, corruption, and the war in Kosovo had damaged the economy. The unemployment rate was extreme.

Inside the Macedonian government, powerful voices favored aggressive, punitive military action against the Albanians, but the army was made up mostly of local remnants of the former Yugoslavian army. It was small, consisting of about 16,000 active-duty personnel, and equipped with old Soviet equipment, including tanks and artillery.[12] The army had the means to win a limited conventional battle, but it had neither the intelligence capability nor the strength to secure significant territory or to prevent hit-and-run attacks.

Although weak, the Macedonian military and police were capable of inflicting punishing destruction in Albanian communities, generating high civilian casualties and a new flow of Balkan refugees fleeing the fighting. Such punitive violence would only cause the fighting to escalate and place the existence of Macedonia as a country in question, with uncertain consequences for Albania, Kosovo, Bulgaria, Greece, and Serbia. This was the nightmare scenario Washington and Europe wanted to avoid.

The US and European capitals, although sympathetic to Macedonia, were not willing to intervene militarily in another Balkan war and were not offering military support to the government either directly or indirectly through NATO.

Despite the limitations on both sides, NLA attacks and punitive government responses intensified through the first six months of 2001. The potential for the conflict to expand into a full-blown civil war was increasing.

The EU and NATO—Solana and Robertson

Washington and the European capitals, weary after ten years of conflict in the Balkans, knew the dangers in Macedonia and wanted to move quickly to head off another war. Macedonia had the potential to seize the US security agenda for the Bush team, just as Bosnia and Kosovo had done for the Clinton administration.

When Secretary Rumsfeld in the Pentagon pushed to withdraw US troops from the Balkans in the early days of the Bush administration, the issue of US engagement in the region again became a point of tension between the United States and its allies in Europe. As Macedonia steadily moved toward a civil war, Secretary of State Colin Powell informed NATO members' foreign ministers meeting in Bucharest, Romania, on May 30, 2001, that President Bush had decided to remain engaged in the Balkans. "In together, out together" was a shorthand phrase for the US commitment.[13]

Leaders in European capitals had learned from their experience in Bosnia that the EU lacked an adequate structure to deal with common foreign-policy and security issues. In response, they created a proto–foreign ministry within the EU Commission. To lead the organization, the EU appointed Javier Solana of Spain as high representative for common foreign and security policy in 1999.

Solana had strong credentials on both sides of the Atlantic. He had earned a PhD in physics from the University of Virginia and spent years teaching in the United States. After serving as foreign minister of Spain, Solana was named secretary-general of NATO in 1995 and thus oversaw NATO policy in Bosnia and Kosovo. From NATO, Solana moved to the EU foreign-policy job.[14] When fighting started in Macedonia, he seized the opportunity to engage the EU directly in finding a negotiated solution.

NATO was another international organization searching for a peaceful end to the fighting in the early months of the Macedonian conflict. Solana's replacement as secretary-general at NATO, George Robertson of Great Britain, also saw a negotiating role for the North Atlantic Alliance and engaged personally in the problem.

EU foreign-policy chief Javier Solana (*left*) and NATO secretary-general George Robertson discuss the negotiations in Macedonia in 2001. (Associated Press)

Robertson and Solana were opposites in personality. Solana was a smooth conciliator and shrewd diplomat; the feisty Robertson was a gregarious and direct Scotsman. Robertson had been a Labour Party leader in Scotland and secretary of state for defense for two years in the Blair government before taking the NATO job in 1999.[15] He, too, was determined to use his office to prevent another war involving NATO in the Balkans.

Solana was an inside deal maker. Robertson wanted to tackle a problem head on and to make a decision. Both men helped reform the international institutions they represented into post–Cold War organizations. Solana was secretary-general of NATO at a transformative period from 1995 to 1999. Robertson continued the NATO-reform process as Solana moved across town to central Brussels, where he became the first official EU foreign-policy leader.

Both Solana and Robertson went often to Macedonia, usually in tandem, from January to June 2001 to stop the fighting. For Solana and the EU, Macedonia was the first opportunity to engage the EU as an institution in a serious European foreign-policy and security issue. For Robertson and NATO, the situation was particularly acute. NATO had 3,000 troops in Macedonia, providing logistics support to Kosovo, so the consequences to NATO of a war in Macedonia would be immediate and direct.

NATO and EU activities are tightly controlled by consensus decisions among the member nations. The secretary-general of NATO and the EU high representative normally operate under the precise instructions of their governing councils, but in the spring and summer of 2001 events required more speed and independence of action by the two senior representatives of these international institutions, which suited Solana and Robertson, who by nature were inclined to stretch their mandates to the fullest.

Both men urged restraint as the Macedonian government leaders vacillated between fighting and negotiating. The two men's engagement was particularly intensive after the government announced a national offensive in late March, and fighting, involving tanks and attack helicopters, broke out near the major Albanian population center of Tetovo.[16]

The Bread Factory

As Macedonia moved toward war in the spring of 2001, government action was ineffective, and military operations were making the situation worse. Meanwhile, the government's effort to negotiate with the Albanians was half-hearted, despite pressure from Solana, Robertson, and others.

In May, the Albanians offered a proposal to end the fighting in Macedonia. Two men—one American, one Kosovo Albanian—became the central figures in this drama. The American was Ambassador Robert Frowick, a career US Foreign Service officer with years of experience in the Balkans. The recent wars in the Balkan had drawn several Americans and Europeans to the region. Holbrooke was one; I was one; Frowick was another.

Frowick had retired from the Foreign Service in 1989 but had continued to accept diplomatic missions after he left the government. He was chief of the OSCE mission in Bosnia after the Dayton Agreement. As the conflict in Macedonia spread, the OSCE once again called on him to go to Skopje as its representative.[17]

Frowick was well respected in the State Department, where he was known for his personal decency and his unassuming yet effective diplomatic style. In May 2001, after he took up his OSCE duties in Skopje, he proposed to President Trajkovski that he be allowed to work with Albanian leaders in Albania, Kosovo, and Macedonia to pressure the NLA to stop fighting in favor of negotiating. Trajkovski supported Frowick's initiative, as did US ambassador to Macedonia M. Michael Einik; Ambassador Hans-Joerg Eiff, the senior NATO representative in Skopje; and UK ambassador Mark Dickinson. At every step, Frowick was careful to keep President Trajkovski and his US, UK, and NATO colleagues informed.

Veton Surroi, the Kosovo newspaper publisher in Pristina, was the Kosovo Albanian involved in the initiative. Every American diplomat engaged in Kosovo policy knew Surroi. He had been a member of the Kosovo delegation at the Rambouillet conference in 1999 and was a frequent contact of American diplomats in Kosovo. Surroi and Frowick had known each other for years.

In meetings in Pristina, Frowick urged the most senior Kosovo Albanian leaders to push the NLA to stop fighting in order to allow negotiations to go forward. While in Pristina, Surroi urged Frowick to include the NLA in any negotiations, but Frowick was convinced that its inclusion in peace talks was not feasible.[18]

Weeks later in Skopje, Frowick talked with Surroi about the potential for a settlement. Following this meeting and after consulting with international representatives, Frowick sent Surroi a letter setting out his understanding of what an intensified political dialog might address. Surroi was increasingly alarmed that the situation was spinning out of control.[19] Feeling he had gained some traction with Frowick, he took the initiative to engage Albanian leaders to develop a peace proposal. At a bakery in the industrial zone of Prizren, Surroi convinced Arben Xheferi, the recognized Albanian political party leader in Macedonia, and Ali Ahmeti, the NLA commander operating from Prizren in Kosovo, that the Albanians should develop a unified position to present to President Trajkovski through Frowick as the OSCE representative. The goal was to start a serious peace negotiation.

On May 20, Surroi sent Frowick an analysis on how to move to negotiations leading to disarmament of the NLA. On reading the paper, Frowick agreed to serve as the messenger to present to President Trajkovski a more detailed Albanian proposal.[20]

Surroi continued to push for Ahmeti to be part of the process, but Frowick did not believe that either the Macedonians or the international community would accept Ahmeti's participation. For Surroi, a negotiation was not possible without the NLA's acceptance. Surroi decided to personally pursue a unified Albanian negotiating position that would include Ahmeti, even if the NLA commander were not to take part in future negotiations. Frowick agreed to include the unified Albanian position in the package, which he would forward to the Macedonians as a potential starting point for a negotiation.[21]

Robert Frowick and President Trajkovski were personal friends from Frowick's earlier international mission in Macedonia. The two men attended the same church, and Frowick occasionally joined the Trajkovski family for Sunday lunch after church. Frowick informed the US and UK ambassadors, the NATO representative, and finally Trajkovski of the Albanian initiative, and the Macedonian president told Frowick that he would take the Albanian proposal to the government.[22]

Meanwhile, Surroi was back at the Prizren bread factory negotiating a unified Albanian position between the leaders of the two main Albanian political parties and the NLA. But word of the process was leaking out in Skopje. Christopher Dell, the US chief of mission in Pristina, notified Washington on June 23 that Surroi had reached an agreed Albanian proposal in a letter signed by the Albanian leaders, including Ali Ahmeti, the NLA commander. Details of the agreement were provided to London and the EU.[23]

At one point, a furious British ambassador Dickinson called Surroi complaining about the inclusion of Ahmeti in the internal Albanian discussions. By the time the Albanian position was agreed and signed by Arben Xheferi, Imer Imeri, and Ali Ahmeti, the document was in the press, including Surroi's own newspaper, *Koha Ditore,* in Pristina.[24] The secret internal Albanian bread factory negotiations were public, creating a political firestorm in Skopje because Ahmeti had signed the resulting document. Ambassador Frowick, who had never met or negotiated directly with the NLA, delivered the proposal to President Trajkovski. In so doing, he became the victim of the erratic, explosive, and divided decision-making process in the Macedonian political structure.

Frowick was in a weak position. He was on his own, and when he ran into trouble, he lacked the kind of high-level backing by Washington and the important European capitals needed to survive the volatile Macedonian political attacks against him.

Frowick became the target of Macedonian rage. The government denounced him for negotiating with "terrorists," and so the international representatives in Skopje abandoned him. Trajkovski informed Ambassador Einik in Skopje that Frowick "should leave Macedonia."[25] Both the US and the British embassies issued statements criticizing NLA participation in the development of an Albanian negotiating position.[26] Robert Frowick was left to the howling political wolves in Skopje. This incident ended his mission in Macedonia and his formal diplomatic career in the US government. Macedonian leaders immediately labeled the NLA "terrorists."

Terrorism is the tactic of brutal violence against civilians to incite fear, to provoke an overreaction, or to increase morale and recruitment by demonstrating the strength of the organization using it. It is a cheap alternative when conventional military options are not available, and it is costly for the target's security forces to defend against effectively. Leaders often find it easy to label enemies as terrorists, but the term is so laden with emotion that doing so can obscure the true nature of the conflict and the enemy they face. While defending aggressively against the threat of terrorist attacks, policy makers, if not careful, can play into the hands of the perpetrators or become confused over the causes and character of the core conflict as well as over the nature and goals of their enemy.

As unfair and painful as the Frowick experience was, it was valuable to the upcoming peace negotiations. First, the Surroi process forced the Albanian political and insurgent leaders to communicate with each other and to reach a set of common objectives for future negotiations. Second, it demonstrated to future negotiators like me just how divided and volatile the Macedonian leadership could be when confronted with new proposals. Third, it showed the limits of who could be included in future talks, at least in the short run.

The Brink of War

Fighting continued into the early summer, alternating between periods of combat and cease-fire agreements brokered by NATO between the NLA and government forces. In early June, the NLA seized the town of Aracinovo, about six miles from Skopje. The Bush administration continued to leave the crisis in Macedonia to the EU and NATO, but pressure was building on both sides of the Atlantic for Washington to engage.

As the fighting near Aracinovo grew more intense, Solana and Robertson flew to Macedonia in hopes of ending the fighting.

Robertson had developed a level of personal trust with President Trajkovski. As a result, Trajkovski accepted a NATO adviser, Mark Laity, as an unofficial political adviser on his staff. Robertson also convinced the Macedonian president to allow a small NATO team to contact the NLA.[27] When Macedonian forces failed to drive the NLA out of Aracinovo, Solana brokered a cease-fire, and, at the government's request, a small, unarmed NATO team negotiated the withdrawal of the NLA fighters from the town.[28]

As NATO soldiers escorted the armed NLA combatants away from Aracinovo, nationalist hard-liners in Skopje lashed out at the international assistance. The Macedonian government on June 24 accused NATO of siding with the NLA.[29] On June 26, several thousand nationalist demonstrators rallied outside the National Assembly to protest the international evacuation of the NLA.[30] Rioters at one point attacked Western media crews in Skopje.[31] In response to the violence in the Macedonian capital, the US State Department authorized the departure of embassy family members from Skopje on June 26.[32] As violence against internationals spread in Skopje, President Trajkovski wrote to the US secretary of state to say thanks for two executive orders directed at the NLA and its supporters: one prohibited US citizens from financing the NLA; the other restricted entry into the United States of those working against peace in Macedonia.[33] This pattern of ethnic Macedonian nationalists' attacks on international representatives and organizations when events did not go as they wished would continue throughout the negotiations and the implementation period.

The Solana–Robertson visits to Macedonia provided temporary relief, but periodic intervention at high levels had not arrested the momentum toward war. The situation called for a dedicated international negotiating presence in Macedonia to engage the parties continuously.

By the end of June 2001, Macedonia was on the brink of a nationwide civil war. On June 25, the EU appointed former French minister of defense François Leotard as the EU special representative to Macedonia to be resident in Skopje.[34]

The US government announced on June 30 my appointment as special envoy for Macedonia to work with Leotard in a joint effort to prevent the looming civil war. That same day I was on a plane to Skopje, where Leotard and I would devote six weeks to intensive daily peace negotiations.

In sending me to Macedonia, the Bush administration had picked regional and negotiating expertise, not lofty public stature. I did not come close to the high-level profile of François Leotard, my European counterpart.

29

Leo-Pard

Macedonian security forces were fighting the NLA near Tetovo, thirty miles from Skopje, as I arrived in the Macedonian capital on Sunday, July 1, 2001. I did not know how long this assignment would last, but I knew from past Balkan exploits that the situation was delicate and would require dedicated, hands-on attention. Leaving Macedonia, even for a short period, might not be an option.

The White House and the State Department gave me minimum guidance before I departed for Skopje and only rarely provided instructions throughout the negotiations. The White House was interested mainly in reaching an acceptable peace settlement and transferring responsibility to the Europeans as soon as possible. I sent in an occasional formal reporting cable during the negotiations, but I usually kept the State Department informed through secure daily one-page emails and phone calls. Whether based on confidence in me or a lack of interest, Washington's remote attitude was welcome and gave me wide latitude to do the job.

My arrival in Skopje signaled the direct engagement of the United States in the peace effort and was of high interest to the local and international media. The Europeans understood that American engagement was necessary to give the Albanians confidence in the negotiations as they moved forward.

Only five members of the international Contact Group were active in the Macedonia situation. Russia was on the sideline for this one. The "Quint," as the group called itself, consisting of representatives of the United States, the United Kingdom, France, Germany, and Italy, were frustrated by the situation in Macedonia. They wanted Leotard and me to be aggressive and to move quickly to an agreement. That attitude suited me fine.

Laurel Miller, my primary American associate throughout the negotiations, was already in Skopje. We had worked together in Washington throughout the war in Kosovo and its aftermath. She knew the region, the issues, and the culture of the State Department. I trusted her completely. Her European colleagues on Leotard's EU team soon came to respect her, and they all bonded as a unified team of "experts."

Over the next several days, the US team would expand to include essential expertise. Sam Laeuchli, a State Department political officer who spoke French, joined us, as did a public-affairs officer, Jan Edmonson, who helped with the media. We also had a representative from DOD and a security team for the delegation. Our group operated out of the US embassy in Skopje, and the EU team rented offices and a residence for Leotard in the city.

On arrival in Skopje, I dropped my bags at the Alexander Palace Hotel and went to work. Leotard joined me at the US ambassador's residence for our introductory discussion. The meeting that afternoon proved to be a crucial strategy session that would define our general approach to the negotiations.

I had heard of Leotard but knew little about him. I had no insight into his instructions from Paris or Brussels and no idea of what to expect from him. As a former minister of defense and minister of culture in France, he had held high positions and had more political experience than I did, although he lacked my background on the Balkans. My previous experience with French officials had been positive, although I knew they could be difficult for American representatives, seemingly as a matter of principle. After leading the T&E Program in Bosnia, which included all the difficulties I had with European governments, and after my role in the war in Kosovo, I could only imagine what Leotard had heard about me.

Language was a concern. My French-language skills consisted of a one-year college course years ago. Leotard grasped more English than I understood French, but we needed translation to ensure complete understanding. He made a serious effort to improve his English that summer, while I shamefully made little effort in French. Ultimately, the language difference was no real obstacle to our effort.

Both of us knew that unity of effort would be critical to success, and we agreed to work closely and openly as a joint negotiating team. Once the initial courtesy calls on Macedonian officials were completed, we agreed to conduct our meetings jointly with the parties. We understood that neither of us could interact with Ali Ahmeti or any member of the NLA as part of our negotiations.

We started with a blank sheet of paper. Neither of us had a precon-

Negotiating partners US special envoy James Pardew (*left*) and EU special envoy François Leotard during talks leading to the Ohrid Agreement in Macedonia. (Reuters)

ceived idea of what a final agreement might look like. Until our arrival, there was no draft settlement document for the parties to consider. I knew from experience that open-ended discussions with the parties usually led nowhere, and we could not rely on the parties to put forth a balanced proposal to be considered. We needed a plan on how to proceed; we needed something to negotiate.

I suggested that we get permission from President Trajkovski to jointly develop a draft paper with some proposals to get the process moving. Leotard agreed and recommended that we use a paper by French legal expert Robert Badinter as a place to begin drafting our paper. Badinter had presented to the Macedonians earlier some ideas on decentralization of government, and they had been received favorably. Once the parties began deliberating a draft document, we would have the beginnings of a negotiation. From our first meeting, Leotard and I had an agreement on a unified effort and a rudimentary negotiating strategy. We had a plan.

I came away from that meeting impressed. I expected Leotard to be gracious, and he was, but he also was thoughtful, open, practical, and willing to operate jointly. The meeting gave me early confidence that we could work together effectively. This was not to be a clash of egos between the two of us. Without close cooperation, I doubted that we could succeed. The difficult events in coming weeks reinforced these first impressions.

The success or failure of the US-EU negotiations would be determined in many ways by the relationship between Leotard and me. From the first day until the end, the two of us and our staffs worked in concert, developing and considering options, reaching common approaches to problems, and presenting a unified position to the parties. I could not have imagined a better negotiating arrangement.

Our relationship strengthened over the course of the summer to the point that the Albanians jokingly referred to us as "Leo-Pard."[1]

Rules of the Game

Skopje sits at the base of Mount Vodno in northern Macedonia. The Vardar River generally runs west to east through the city center. A provincial capital in the former Yugoslavia, Skopje had largely been rebuilt after an earthquake killed more than 1,000 people and destroyed much of the city in 1963, so it was a special combination of the old and the recent.

The major city square, commercial district, and government buildings constructed in the typical Communist style were on the south side of the Vardar. The old bazaar with small shops, cafés, the historic Mustafa Pasha Mosque, and the bulk of the Albanian population in the capital were on the northern side. A large stone *kale,* or Ottoman fortress, overlooked the city from the hill just north of the Vardar. The two banks of the river are connected by the Stone Bridge, a long and elegant structure built originally by Byzantine engineers and reconstructed later by Ottoman occupiers.

At the start of the first full week of talks, I began a round of courtesy calls on the parties to the negotiation. My first stop was with President Boris Trajkovski, a person I had met before. The Macedonian presidency and the National Assembly shared a building just south of the Vardar River near the center of Skopje. A large bronze equestrian statue stood in front of the building's modest exterior facade of tan stucco trimmed in brown stone. Across the street was a park that was to become the site of major demonstrations in weeks to come. Inside, the building was more impressive. A polished white-marble staircase led from the foyer to the president's office on the next floor. The president's office on the second floor overlooked the building's entrance.

A confident Macedonian president was upbeat about the new US-EU mission in our introductory meeting in his private office. Trajkovski made clear that he was the central negotiator in the process. Leotard and I were to be facilitators. We were not to be mediators in what Trajkovski saw as his negotiation, although in practice our influence increased as the negotiations progressed. Four additional Macedonia entities were to participate in the negotiations—the leaders of the four major political parties in the country: Ljubco Georgievski for VMRO-DPMNE, Branko Cervenkovski for the SDSM, Arben Xheferi for the DPA, and Imer Imeri for the PDP. As prime minister, Georgievski would represent the government. Trajkovski was adamant that the NLA could not participate in the talks or be a formal party to any settlement. He also rejected a British idea to move the negotiations to a site outside of Macedonia. I agreed. I did not come to Macedonia to negotiate a conference. Process was secondary.

Leotard and I recommended to Trajkovski that we start by giving him a draft international paper containing some ideas for a settlement built around the Badinter constitutional proposal. The president could then submit the draft to the parties for their consideration. The president liked the idea and agreed to proceed on that basis. I did not know if Trajkovski had the power to restrain the nationalist hard-liners, but from his demeanor in the first meeting he certainly seemed to feel that he was in charge.

In the first meetings with Leotard and me, Trajkovski was confident and positive; Prime Minister Georgievski took a hard, nationalist stance; and Cervenkovski, the opposition SDSM leader, was neutral. I was direct with the Albanian leaders: the NLA would not be a direct party in the talks; however, Xheferi and Imeri had to have the authority to speak for all Albanians. I asked for and received their assurance that their agreement would represent the position of the Albanian community, including the fighters. After separate introductory calls, with few exceptions, Leotard and I met jointly with the parties for the rest of the negotiations.

NATO Engages the NLA

That summer the negotiations in Macedonia had two very separate and distinct sets of talks. Leotard and I, representing the EU and the United States, were negotiating a national peace agreement between the recognized political leaders in the country. The NLA was not a direct party to those talks.

NATO maintained contact separately with the Macedonian army generals and the NLA leadership to achieve and maintain a cease-fire and to generally stifle the impulse to fight in the field. The NATO team did not negotiate the political aspects of the broader agreement.

Dutch diplomat Pieter Feith, who had led the NATO team at Aracinovo, would negotiate disarmament and potential amnesty terms with the NLA if a national settlement were achieved. During the political negotiations, Feith's job was to stop or reduce the fighting between the government and the NLA.[2]

Feith was NATO secretary-general Robertson's man on the ground. Officially, he was the director of operations on the NATO International Staff and director of the NATO Balkan Task Force in Brussels.[3] Feith proved to be a skilled and courageous negotiator over the summer.

Feith's effort was essential to a peace settlement, but he operated independently from the US-EU negotiations in Skopje. He officially reported directly to NATO and Secretary-General Robertson. Feith kept President Trajkovski informed of his talks with the NLA and maintained informal contact with Leotard and me throughout July, August, and September.

The Experts

Once Trajkovski approved the concept of an international draft, the international experts began preparing a document for the parties to consider.

The US-EU peace negotiations were conducted at two levels: principals and experts. To Leotard and me, the experts consisted of everyone in our staffs who worked on the negotiations. The parties also included experts who performed the detailed drafting and initial level of negotiation at a trusted level below Trajkovski and the four party leaders. Each of the Macedonian parties had its own set of experts. Some were policy advisers, some attorneys, and some technical experts on various areas under discussion.

Leotard had a staff of excellent young European diplomats and lawyers. Fernando Gentilini, a professional diplomat from Italy working within the EU, was Solana's man on the team and kept Solana informed of developments. Arnaud Barthelemy of France was a lawyer by training and a professional diplomat. Axel Dittmann, a German diplomat, and Thomas Markert, a German lawyer from the Council of Europe, rounded out Leotard's expert team. Like me, Leotard had a public-affairs officer and administrative assistants, plus a security detail from the French army.

My expert was Laurel Miller. Although I was the face of the US participation in the negotiations, Miller was an essential force for the international negotiators. She had a knack for detail and knew the legal danger and opportunities of agreement language. She immediately bonded with her EU counterparts and gained the early respect of her European, Macedonian, and Albanian colleagues. The Ohrid Agreement is a tribute to her talent as an international lawyer and a representative of the United States. Before the negotiations in Macedonia, Miller had worked on the Bosnian Constitution at Dayton. She was involved directly in the new Kosovo Constitution, and she influenced the Macedonian Constitution as well through the Ohrid Agreement. I can think of no person with more impact on more national constitutions in the Balkans than Laurel Miller.

This team of European and American professionals became a powerful force in the talks. The US and EU experts communicated often with staffs in Washington, Brussels, and Quint capitals as new positions were developed; but in Skopje they coalesced into a unified team and worked with a great deal of autonomy. The international experts also conducted the initial phase of talks with their counterparts in the parties to gather competing positions and to reduce to the most important those issues to be discussed with the primary negotiators. In general, the discussions between the experts were more substantive and avoided the verbal fireworks of the discussions between the negotiating principals.

International Leverage

Both the Macedonian and the Albanian parties seemed to have the will to negotiate seriously on a settlement agreement, but a positive outcome was not a sure bet. Whether the international community had sufficient leverage to entice the parties to overcome their differences also was unclear.

The party leaders in Macedonia, like those in virtually every other nation in the region, reflected the desire by the population to join the EU and NATO. The EU and the United States could offer significant reconstruction and development financial assistance, and NATO membership would guarantee the country's future security. I asked Washington to prepare a package of assistance incentives to offer and requested that Washington consider the sensitive option of offering US recognition of Macedonia's constitutional name: the Republic of Macedonia.

International development assistance was not a significant incentive during the negotiations, but foreign aid became important leverage in the implementation phase. In the negotiations, the parties were focused on the talks, not on the long-term or potential development benefits. This struggle was between two very different views of the country's future: Macedonia for ethnic Macedonians or a multicultural Macedonia. Each side was prepared to fight for its vision, but each also knew that war could destroy its own vision along with its country. War also would put both parties in conflict with the United States, the EU, and NATO.

NATO offered one incentive that both parties wanted—NATO troops on the ground in Macedonia as a peacekeeping force. The Macedonian government believed from the start that NATO owed it for cooperating during the war in Kosovo and was disappointed that NATO had not committed forces on the government's side when fighting with the NLA began. NATO was not about to intervene, though. The alliance was willing only to negotiate between the NLA and Macedonian security forces to stop or reduce the fighting and to help disarm the rebels if the parties were to reach a settlement.

The NLA held NATO in high regard after the air campaign against Serbia ended the repression of Albanians in Kosovo. NLA leaders wanted NATO on the ground to implement any political settlement or disarmament agreement because they had no confidence in the Macedonian government to implement security agreements without being monitored. Implementing a political settlement was not a task that NATO authorities favored, but the alliance would continue to negotiate and monitor cease-fire agreement, disarmament, and amnesty talks.

NATO responded favorably on June 20 to President Trajkovski's request for assistance in disarming and demilitarizing Albanian insurgents in Macedonia. However, it conditioned its support to the successful completion of a political settlement between the parties in the conflict.[4] This request and NATO's favorable response provided the alliance with authority to engage the NLA throughout the summer as it planned to assist in the disarmament.

30

Fury in Skopje

The talks started cordially. Beginnings are typically the happy times, but I knew from previous negotiations that the early stage was the most positive period, when all parties put forth their most cooperative and optimistic image to the international visitors. It would not last. It never does.

Trajkovski announced at a major press conference on July 4 that a negotiating process had been agreed. Behind the scenes, the international experts were busily drafting the initial negotiating paper to present to the parties. A day later Pieter Feith achieved a cease-fire commitment from the NLA and the Macedonian army.[1]

Arben Xheferi asked for a private meeting with me on July 5, but I refused unless Leotard was present. That evening I was linked by secure telephone into a Principals Committee meeting in the White House Situation Room. The US-EU team had written a four-page first-draft framework proposal and then sent it to Washington and the Quint capitals for review before it would be delivered to Trajkovski.[2] The US Principals Committee approved the approach Leotard and I proposed based on the draft framework paper. This principals meeting was to be my only participation in a high-level interagency discussion of the Macedonian crisis throughout the negotiations.

In the first few days, we brought another international figure into the negotiations. Maximilianus "Max" van der Stoel, a former foreign minister of the Netherlands and Dutch ambassador to the UN, had been in Macedonia for some time as the OSCE high commissioner for national minorities. Specifically, van der Stoel was working on the recognition of a multilingual university in the predominantly Albanian city of Tetovo. He was a gently determined personality. His continued pressure for minority rights and for a recognized multilanguage university in Tetovo put him in bad graces with ethnic Macedonian leaders, but such was the fate of any international figure who told them what they did not want to hear.

Van der Stoel, who was seventy-four years old at the time, became an éminence gris of the negotiations, especially after the talks moved from Skopje to Lake Ohrid. His unassuming manner and wise countenance brought a calming influence to the discussions, and both Leotard and I listened to his advice.

The Dark Force

When Macedonia mobilized its reserve security forces earlier in the year to deal with the insurgency, it gave legitimacy to some rough, undisciplined nationalist paramilitary troops who were causing trouble in the countryside. I decided to visit Minister of the Interior Ljube Boskovski, who had operational control over these paramilitaries. Boskovski provided me with an armed police officer in civilian clothes, who rode with me in an armored SUV for my security in the early weeks of the talks. He was a nice man, but I presumed that he was there as much to collect intelligence as to protect me.

The minister was late for the meeting. As I waited, I noted that his office was the nicest in the Macedonian government. After a while, his motorcade of Mercedes with blacked-out windows arrived. I also saw that he had the best cars in the government. These were bad signs, and I still had yet to meet the minister.

Boskovski, with crew-cut hair and a suit over a black T-shirt, swaggered confidently into the room. This cocky guy clearly was enjoying the high life of his position. He looked and acted like a composite of every Balkan thug I had ever met, and I had met more of them than I could count.

I complained that the police and paramilitary activities in Albanian communities were undermining the peace process. He protested and dismissed the complaint. I thanked him for the security officer he had provided to me and left. I noted in my journal later that night that Boskovski was going to be a problem. I did not realize then how much of a deadly threat to peace he would be.

Life in the Goldfish Bowl

Any US envoy in a crisis is the most important intelligence target for each of the parties in a negotiation. I knew that I had to be the top priority for the Macedonian government and others. I assumed that I lived in general transparency to them and that my hotel room, automobile, telephone, and other aspects of life were monitored. The only time I considered myself free from local monitoring was in the most secure areas of the US embassy.

Living in the transparency of a goldfish bowl can be liberating. It forces the envoy to be careful, but it also makes the reality of monitoring a useful tool. The negotiator can say things elsewhere that might not be suitable to say in direct meetings but in this way still get them to the recipient. Further, in being monitored, the negotiator can shape the atmosphere of the talks, send signals, and misdirect the opposition.

Knowing that I would be overheard, at points when I felt Minister of Interior Boskovski was out of control and disrupting the negotiations through violence, I called American colleagues and asked about the progress on indicting him for war crimes. There was no pending indictment at the time, and I had no authority or engagement in the ICTY whatsoever, but I calculated that even just this mention of an indictment might restrain Boskovski. The calls appeared to do so, although the effect wore off after a few days.

The Pot Starts to Boil

President Trajkovski approved the paper prepared by the US and EU experts and reviewed by Solana and the Quint capitals. We presented the paper on Trajkovski's behalf to the parties as a draft negotiating document on July 7. Early on, the parties agreed that English would be the official language of the negotiated documents. This decision made careful legal review of the texts much easier.

The Badinter proposals, which the Macedonian parties generally supported, contained a range of actions to strengthen minority rights and authorities. Among his proposals, Badinter recommended

1. stronger authority at the local level over education, language, culture, local finance, environmental protection, and urbanization;
2. a qualified majority vote at the national level on laws affecting local authority (a qualified majority is a European procedure that makes it easier for a minority to block legislation or constitutional amendments in areas specific to their interests);
3. expanded use of non-Macedonian languages in education and in public administration;
4. authority to display ethnic emblems at the local level;
5. measures to reduce discrimination and improve minority access to government hiring; and
6. expanded minority participation in the Constitutional Court.[3]

The Badinter proposals were general statements of principle. They did not provide the specific implementation actions that the experts defined in the framework paper and the annexes.

In a separate paper President Trajkovski provided to the international team, he generally agreed with the Badinter proposals and listed several areas where he felt Macedonia already had made progress. He also called for a new "Declaration of the National Assembly" to supplement the Constitution, which recognized the heritage of the Macedonian people and the Macedonian Orthodox Church. It also established Macedonia as a national state of the Macedonian people. His paper rejected a new Albanian channel on Macedonian television and "the van der Stoel University."[4]

Negotiations have an energy level that reflects the urgency of the situation, the will of the parties to talk, external pressure, and the viability of the negotiating strategy. The presentation of the international draft framework paper suddenly brought new vitality to the talks in Skopje.

In the meeting with the parties, we could feel the tension in the room increase as we described the paper to them. The Albanians were not happy with the draft. Imer Imeri, who had health issues, appeared on the verge of a heart attack. The Macedonians also were in a state of agitation. They liked the summary draft without the annexes and wanted to restrict any change to 5 percent of the document.

A few days later we distributed to the parties the draft annexes with constitutional and other implementation details. The US-EU annexes proposed for negotiation took the principles in the draft framework agreement and converted them into specific constitutional amendments, laws, and a schedule to implement the agreement. The details shocked the parties.

We left the paper with them to consider for the weekend as Leotard and I flew by helicopter to US Camp Bondsteel in Kosovo to get a US military assessment on the NLA. The US Army had concluded that the NLA was well organized, armed, and willing to take battle casualties. This was not good news for the negotiations.

The Albanian Priorities

The Albanians responded in short order to the international draft. Their paper, citing examples of minority rights in Bosnia and Kosovo, was polite but direct. The draft was not acceptable to them in several areas. They wanted Albanian to be an "official language" in Macedonia, and they wanted local community control of police. They proposed reform of the

Ministry of Interior, the Macedonian military, and the judiciary as well as disbandment of the paramilitaries. The Albanians, despite their objections, said they were ready to engage in detailed drafting sessions and to negotiate their positions.[5] Everything they submitted crossed red lines for the ethnic Macedonians. Leotard and I told Xheferi that we did not think many of their objectives could be achieved.

The next round started with all parties' international experts engaging their counterparts in separate, specific talks on the text of the framework and the annexes. As the talks progressed, Trajkovski became increasingly disgruntled. The talks were not going as he and the ethnic Macedonian parties expected. The ethnic Macedonian parties quickly suspended their engagement in the talks, although the Albanians continued to meet with the international team.

Presidential Outrage

Tensions between the parties were on the rise. Pieter Feith informed us that both sides were to blame for the fighting around Tetovo on July 9 that threatened the NATO cease-fire agreement.

Trajkovski summoned Leotard and me to his office on July 12 to demand that the framework document without the annexes be signed immediately. He declared that the expert discussions must stop and that the annexes with the specific implementation actions must be set aside. We told the Macedonian president that it was not possible to get the Albanians to sign the framework only. The annexes contained the precision and the detailed commitments required for a settlement. He sent us to see Prime Minister Ljubco Georgievski and SDSM leader Cervenkovski, who were exerting heavy pressure on him to get a quick deal on the general framework without the details.

Later that afternoon Trajkovski called a meeting in the large room paneled by brown Macedonian woodcarvings adjacent to his private office. His purpose was to bully Leotard and me in front of the four parties. The president attacked us harshly for the process so far. The prime minister jumped in to accuse the Americans and the Europeans of causing Macedonia's current woes. Meanwhile, the Albanians watched quietly as the US and EU representatives endured a sharp tongue-lashing from the ethnic Macedonian leaders. The Albanians had to think that such a hostile outburst would only improve their negotiating prospects.

Our relationship with Trajkovski grew progressively worse in the coming days as the ethnic Macedonian parties boycotted the talks. He was furious at us because the Albanians would not complete the framework without the annexes. Any small issue in a discussion would send him into a tirade.

Trajkovski was under enormous pressure from the ethnic Macedonian nationalists, and the stress made him erratic. He would declare himself a neutral party in the talks and then demand a constitutional declaration that was pure Macedonian chauvinism. In one private rant, he threatened to resign. But after the storm, the president recognized that the annexes must be included in any final agreement.

Bastille Day, July 14, was an especially difficult day. The Albanian leaders came to the EU office to present a new paper containing settlement demands—some old, some new. After listening to their extensive list, we ended the meeting on a sharp note, telling them to be more realistic and to come back the next day with their top two or three priority issues.

In a meeting with Leotard and me in the presidential office later that night, Trajkovski launched into yet another anti-US, anti-Albanian lecture.

"The United States created the NLA and Kosovo. You created Ali Ahmeti. The United States is destroying my country," Trajkovski said.

"US troops in this region have kept the area together. We are trying to help you, and we must be able to speak truthfully to you," I responded. He again threatened to resign.

The ethnic Macedonians' inclination to see the negotiations as talks only between themselves and Leotard and me was a serious problem in the first three weeks of the process. They simply tried to pressure us into adopting their position and forcing it upon the Albanians. They acted as if the Albanians' position did not exist, and when that position entered the discussions, they exploded.

The next day the Albanians returned with their two priorities. Albanian as an official language was at the top of their list; local control of the police was second—precisely the two nuclear issues for the Macedonian parties. We offered to take the language demand to the Macedonians if the Albanians would accept the rest of the agreement. They rejected that proposal, and Imer Imeri again became physically distressed and left the meeting. The content of this meeting was too explosive to even mention to the Macedonians.

A major breakthrough from our perspective occurred on July 16 in a very small meeting with Xheferi inside the French embassy. I expressed extreme US disappointment at the Albanians' position. Their demands were too unreasonable to achieve a settlement. Xheferi then told us that he could accept a weaker position on the Albanian language and drop their demand for total local control of the police.

The Albanians accepted a draft text that made Albanian a second—but not a primary—official language and that weakened their desire for total local control of police. I told Xheferi that if he could assure me that the new text would be accepted by all Albanian leaders, we would put the proposal forward to the president as the best chance for an agreement. A few hours later Xheferi called back with the assurance.

We prepared a paper with the new compromise language, reported to Washington and Brussels, and began to mobilize high-level calls from capitals to the ethnic Macedonian leaders to reinforce the proposal as the best hope for peace.

Leotard and I took the draft compromises on language and police to President Trajkovski on the evening of July 16. Leotard was perfect in his soft-spoken but firm presentation. He always had a better approach with the Macedonians. He typically calmed them down, whereas I usually agitated them. He emphasized to the president that the Albanians had dropped several previous demands, including veto rights, community control of local police, and a dedicated vice president position for an Albanian, and that they had accepted the concept of a unitary state. Leotard stressed that the Albanians had softened considerably their positions on language and police.

We then proposed that the ethnic Macedonians accept the Albanian language as a secondary official language. We showed Trajkovski a draft text and urged the Macedonians to agree to the proposed texts as the best chance for a settlement.[6]

Trajkovski was subdued. He said that he did not want to argue. He read the changes and declared them unacceptable, with no hope of passing Parliament, but he would present them to Georgievski and Cervenkovski anyway.

"Never Tire of Doing What Is Right"

The Macedonian president was under heavy pressure from all sides. The day we presented him with the Albanian proposals, Trajkovski sent a personal letter to President Bush complaining about the nature and direction of the negotiations. He quoted II Thessalonians 3:13, "And as for you, brothers, never tire of doing what is right," in contrasting himself with those who were pressuring him to compromise.[7]

Trajkovski told us again that he was considering resigning from the presidency and predicted that the Albanian concept of a binational state would lead to the eventual breakup of the country. He sent five letters to President Bush during July 2001, trying to influence the negotiations through Washington. None of these letters ever produced an administration instruction to me to change the direction of the negotiations on the ground.

Later that day Georgievski and Cervenkovski told us directly that the Albanian proposal was unacceptable. I pleaded with them to compromise for the sake of their country, but they were unbending.

"The NLA has never shelled your capital. The day the NLA shells Skopje, remember this night," a frustrated Leotard told Cervenkovski.

The next day, July 17, Solana, Robertson, and German foreign minister Joschka Fischer called Trajkovski to support the package Leotard and I had presented the previous evening. However, when Trajkovski talked to Secretary Powell by telephone, he pleaded for relief, and Powell agreed to see what could be done to modify the US-EU proposal. That was the opening Trajkovski needed, and all hell broke loose for Leotard and me in Skopje.

President Trajkovski went on national television that night to attack the US-EU proposal. The Macedonian press became hysterical over the language issue, accusing Leotard and me of destroying their country. We never presented the compromise as a "take it or leave it proposition," although they accused us of doing so. Even the Quint in Rome sent word that we should back off a bit and present no ultimatums.

Our experts folded our new language into the overall US-EU draft on July 17 and distributed it to the parties, to the ethnic Macedonians' dismay. Their verbal explosion was painful to endure, but it ultimately produced a real negotiating draft as the basis for subsequent talks.

Trajkovski called us to his conference room to rebuke us personally before an expanded meeting of the parties on July 18. Only Xheferi attended for the Albanians. The president attacked Leotard, me, and the Albanians in a rambling, emotional rant. I responded for us with my best conciliatory speech.

"So much has been accomplished," I said. "Do not let this moment go by without careful, thoughtful analysis. The future of your country is yours to decide. We hope we can be of help, but the responsibility is yours."

Leotard later congratulated me for the tone, but my softer approach made little difference.

Following the meeting, the Macedonian leaders again assailed us in public, accusing me personally of being a deceptive agent of NLA leader Ali Ahmeti. Prime Minister Georgievski was particularly vicious in his public personal attacks, which continued for days.[8]

These attacks felt like the treatment that Ambassador Frowick had received from the Macedonians in May. When I had first arrived in Skopje, the American ambassador at the time had privately told to me that I was just another guy traveling through Macedonia and would not succeed. He said that sooner or later I would get "Frowicked," referring to the way the Macedonians had discredited and then expelled Ambassador Robert Frowick. I told him that it might happen, but I was not as decent as Frowick and would not go quietly. If I went down, I would take a number of people with me, including him.

I could feel the international support for our effort slipping away. This was the lowest point in the negotiations. On the evening of July 18, I felt that I was finished in Macedonia. I began planning my departure, but I knew that Leotard's and my absence would produce more serious fighting.

Then suddenly international support for Leotard and me began to turn around.

"We asked them [the US-EU team] to be aggressive. They were, and now they will pull back a little," Secretary Powell told allies at the G8 Summit in Genoa, Italy, in a show of support on July 19.[9] Both Solana and Robertson, who had had their own experiences with the explosive political atmosphere in Skopje, issued statements condemning the public comments by the prime minister and others attacking Leotard and me.[10] Support for us quickly started flowing again from European capitals.

In my enthusiasm over the Albanian compromises, I had oversold the proposal to the Macedonians, and in so doing I had taken too much US and EU responsibility for it. The compromises were the Albanians', not ours, and I should have presented them just that way to avoid becoming the focus of Macedonian wrath. The eruption probably would have happened anyway, but it did show that the most sensitive issue for peace was the status of the Albanian language in Macedonia.

I was concerned personally about the notion of multiple official languages in a country. The Albanians argued, however, that giving legal status to their language would be a unifying force in society. That had not been my experience in other Balkan conflicts. In Bosnia, the Muslims and Croats spoke essentially the same language, but Croatian nationalists used the contention that their language was unique as an argument for separation. However, for the Albanians, the status of their language in Macedonia was the top priority—the "capital issue," as Xheferi described it.

In Europe, multiple official languages in a single nation are not unusual. In a study done by our staff, ten of fifty-one nations in Europe and North America at that time had multiple official languages. The US Constitution, in contrast, does not designate an official language.[11]

Washington instructed me to lower the political temperature and back off a bit in the negotiations, and I complied.

The Media

Not every negotiation is conducted in a public spotlight, but when it is, the negotiator must manage the public-media aspects of the process.

Media outlets in an international crisis have a responsibility to inform their publics and to report events as they unfold. When the negotiations are not secret, a negotiator cannot avoid the media in an ongoing crisis of high public interest. Helping the media accomplish their job without compromising the diplomatic process is an important function of a negotiator.

With all the attention peace negotiations can generate, the envoy can never forget that media attention is about the talks, not about the negotiator. When the envoy becomes the focus of the media, the negotiations are in trouble. A negotiator also should never try to manage media relations in a high-interest situation without the assistance of a public-affairs professional. Media relations are too important, too complex, and too time consuming to be a secondary task for the primary negotiator or for a nonprofessional on the staff. Even Richard Holbrooke, who was as experienced with the media as anyone, kept a public-affairs professional on his staff during the Bosnia negotiations.

A US envoy in an international crisis must contend with three levels of public media. The White House and the State Department care most about the US domestic media. It is important for the negotiator to be cautiously positive but to keep expectations modest in media interactions on this level. If the raising of expectations of success is followed by serious problems in the talks, the administration's confidence in the negotiator can be damaged. Washington also is interested, but to a lesser degree, in the second level, the international media, because of the image of the

United States that the negotiation projects to allies and to the attentive American audience.

The third level is the local (non-US) domestic media—which in this specific case were the domestic Macedonian television, radio, and print media. Blogging is also an element of this level today, although it wasn't a factor in 2001. The local media is most important to local officials and the negotiating parties, and it can be the most difficult for the negotiator because local media outlets can be controlled by political figures and can be sensationalist, and without professional standards. Ignoring the local media is tempting but not wise because it can affect the image of the process on the other two levels. As a minimum, the negotiator should engage the local media in a factual, objective way but not become overly concerned about their reporting if it is extreme or seriously inaccurate.

The best approaches to the media are straightforward update statements characterizing the general nature and status of the talks. Major announcements as the negotiations progress should be worked out with the parties beforehand whenever possible. Closing each meeting with an agreement among the parties on how the session will be portrayed in the media should always be a goal. Such agreements not only coordinate the image of the session but also can build confidence between the negotiator and the parties.

It is tempting to use the media to negotiate in public, to influence others in the talks, or to send subtler signals. Each of these strategies is risky and can damage the prospects for success if it fails. At multiple points in the negotiations in 2001, the Macedonians tried to influence Leotard and me through personal attacks in the press. This strategy completely failed and, if anything, damaged their relationship with us.

I could not effectively manage the flow of information from the negotiations to the Macedonian media. The Macedonian press outlets were sensationalist, and many of them were tied directly to the government or to a political party. Every senior Macedonian official in the talks had favorite reporters on speed dial on their cell phones and would define every meeting to suit their interest before Leotard and I were out of the building. Objective journalism was in short supply among local media outlets.

Marines to the US Embassy

As the ethnic Macedonian leaders started to calm down, our relationship with them improved. Trajkovski called me to a private fence-mending session to explain calmly why the Macedonians could not accept Albanian as an official language. He said that there were only one and a half issues to resolve: language and the nature and control of police.

Trajkovski invited me to a casual dinner with him and his wife, Vilma, at the presidential residence over the weekend. At dinner, both of us tried to avoid the subject of the draft agreement. Rather, we spent the evening in small talk and gossip about politics in the Balkans more broadly.

During the dinner, Trajkovski said that the United States owed him for his help on Kosovo, Serbia, and other issues. He told me that he had written four letters to President Bush over the past week. He may have been trying to impress me with his direct link to the White House. I saw only some of his letters, but I knew that he had damaged his image seriously with the White House by these continuous and direct personal appeals. The volume of the letters smacked of desperation. Three days after the dinner, President Bush visited Camp Bondsteel in Kosovo less than a hundred miles from Skopje but did not visit or call Trajkovski.

I had considerable sympathy for President Trajkovski despite his erratic style and swings of emotion. The responsibility for leading Macedonia in crisis weighed heavily on him. I felt that he was a decent man who wanted to do the right thing for his country, but he was under heavy pressure from the extreme nationalists in and out of government. His volatile nature did not help him deal with them. He wanted the United States, the EU, and NATO to do his bidding, but in his mind we were making his situation worse. I feared that he lacked the personal temperament and the political experience to deal with the challenges ahead.

While the talks were moving back on track, the political storm created by the recent public ethnic Macedonian tirades against the international diplomats continued to fuel public outrage.

By July 23, fighting around Tetovo had grown more intense. Leotard and I issued a joint statement condemning the violence and calling for a return to the cease-fire.[12] Despite the statement, media commentary continued to attack us, and riots broke out in the center of Skopje protesting the negotiations. Minister of Interior Boskovski made the outrageous public assertion that NATO was flying helicopters into Macedonia from Kosovo in support of the NLA.[13]

Veton Surroi called from Kosovo to tell me that the NLA planned to attack Skopje if the Macedonian paramilitaries attacked Albanian civilians around Tetovo. I told him to try to calm things down.

Ethnic Macedonian extremists were on a rampage in Skopje by July

Violent demonstrations in Skopje forced the peace negotiations in Macedonia to be moved out of the capital to a secure site on Lake Ohrid. (Reuters)

25. Demonstrations and periodic violent attacks continued to shatter windows and glass in the doors of the presidential building, and demonstrators threatened the US embassy, forcing it to close. Preparations were made to evacuate the US ambassador and his family to a NATO base. The United States dispatched a platoon of marines to reinforce the security at the embassy compound in Skopje as the demonstrations continued. The marine platoon remained at the embassy until September 1.[14]

The Macedonian Information Agency on July 25 published an open letter from Prime Minister Georgievski to President Trajkovski calling on the president to use his power as supreme commander of the armed forces and police to restore order in Macedonia. Georgievski's letter was a call to arms, not a call to negotiate.[15]

The demonstrators were so aggressive that Leotard and I had to enter the presidential building for meetings through a back entrance. We concluded that continuing the talks in the explosive environment of Skopje was impossible.

On July 25, Trajkovski tried to restore order, calling for public calm and stressing that Leotard and I were in Macedonia at his request to help find a solution.[16] He was clearly in another struggle with the prime minister and the nationalists. That day he asked Leotard and me to prepare a new draft paper on language for review by his experts.[17]

My days of taking long walks from the Alexander Palace Hotel were over. The ethnic Macedonian public's hostility toward the negotiators was intense; the Macedonian government had notified our security people of death threats against me, and my personal security detail had increased.

If I had not been restricted to my hotel room in my free time, I might never have discovered a unique Balkan form of reality TV while flipping through television channels—a fortune teller call-in show. In this prime-time program, a dour middle-aged female fortune teller sat at a table shuffling Tarot cards. She was accompanied at the table by another woman, a telephone sitting on the table in front of them. The two women chatted as they waited for the telephone to ring. The phone rarely rang, so I concluded that this show was not at the top of the TV ratings.

When a rare call came in, the fortune teller would shuffle her cards, draw from the deck, and place an individual Tarot card face up on the table. She then went on to explain what the cards were telling her about the caller's question. Since I didn't understand the language, my attention quickly drifted away. In watching this program in the boredom of my isolation, I was struck by the cultural differences that made such a prime-time TV show possible in the Balkans.

Solana, Robertson, and Mircea Geoana of Romania, the OSCE chairman in office, flew to Skopje on July 26 to help. The visit was a public circus, but it was critical to putting the talks back on track.

In their meeting with these primary leaders of international organizations in Europe, the ethnic Macedonians vented their anger at the international community and at Leotard, Feith, and me. They cited public opinion against compromise and a feeling of loss of dignity and humiliation in Skopje.

"We are not a party to the negotiations," Robertson told the negotiating parties. "We are here to help. If your country descends into civil war, and you are this close [to peace], you will never be forgiven."

At the end of the discussion, the senior international leaders achieved a commitment from the Macedonians to continue to negotiate and to move the venue of the talks from Skopje to Tetovo. This mostly Albanian city was not a feasible site for the talks, but the commitment to move the talks was important. The following day Trajkovski decided to host the talks at the presidential retreat on Lake Ohrid. NATO restored the cease-fire in the field on July 26 just as the negotiations got back on track.[18]

The peace talks left the volatile atmosphere of Skopje to resume on Saturday, July 28, in a more tranquil, isolated site on the banks of Lake Ohrid in southwestern Macedonia near the border with Albania.

31

On the Banks of an Ancient Lake

Lake Ohrid, its clear blue waters surrounded by natural forests and mountains, is the most beautiful freshwater lake in the Balkans. The lack of commercial development during the Communist period in a way helped protect its natural beauty from overdevelopment. The lake, fed by natural springs and almost 1,000 feet deep in places, is one of the most ancient lakes in the world. Age and isolation endowed Ohrid with several unique species of fish, including a particularly large and tasty variety of trout.[1] Human settlements in the area date to the Stone Age, and the town of Ohrid on the northeastern bank of the lake existed at the time of ancient Greece.

Historically, the lake is most associated with the Orthodox Church and the spread of the faith from Ohrid through the Slavic nations to the north, including Russia. In the ninth century, Saints Clement and Naum, two disciples of Brothers Cyril and Methodius, who invented the prototype of the Cyrillic alphabet, established a center of religious learning, literature, and culture on the lake. This center helped spread the Cyrillic alphabet and therefore Christianity throughout Slavic lands.[2] The small Orthodox Church of Saint John, jutting into the lake on a promontory just outside the town of Ohrid, is a picturesque symbol of the lake's link to the Orthodox faith.

The bright sun and dry heat of a Macedonian summer were at full strength as the negotiating parties gathered on the bank of the sparkling waters of Lake Ohrid at the end of July 2001. Normally, this was a time when Europeans were in the final preparations for their traditional vacation period in August. The August vacation period is sacrosanct in Europe, but not for political leaders in Macedonia, who were trying to prevent war in their country.

The new venue for the talks, the presidential retreat, was on a rocky point at the edge of the lake a short distance from the town of Ohrid. The retreat was one of several villas built for President Tito of Yugoslavia. Like the hunting lodge used by Milosevic in Serbia during the negotiations with Holbrooke, it was not grand or ornate. Rather, its design was comfortable and functional.

A winding driveway off the main highway around the lake led to the two-story structure. The exterior of the main building was of stone on the first floor and stucco on the second. A simple set of stairs led to the main entrance. The back of the building featured a large terrace with a grand view of the lake through the trees. Lunch and dinner buffets were served on the terrace, which functioned as a convenient, pleasant place to hold small meetings or to wait for others to complete their meetings elsewhere.

A large dining room, used for the rare plenary meetings, opened onto the terrace. Other rooms inside the building on the first floor were available for smaller meetings. The furnishings were simple and comfortable, and the staff served a tasty iced coffee as a treat between meetings. The gardens contained seating areas and walking paths through pine trees, large bushes of rosemary or lavender, and other flowers around the property. Peacocks browsed the gardens.

The selection of Lake Ohrid for the negotiations turned out to be perfect not just because of its serene beauty but because of its isolation, 113 miles away from the supercharged political environment of Skopje, thus concentrating the parties' attention on the matter at hand.

President Trajkovski generally stayed at the retreat. The internationals occupied the Hotel Inex Gorica, a Communist-era motel on the lake a short distance away. The Albanians came and went from Tetovo or other Albanian communities. The ethnic Macedonian party leaders came and went as well. At Ohrid, Max van der Stoel of the OSCE joined the talks on a full-time basis. He had a calming influence on the parties, and personally, Leotard and I enjoyed his company.

The talks resumed at noon on Saturday, July 28, 2001, in the large hall of the retreat. President Trajkovski chaired a plenary session of the four parties, Leotard, and me.

Achieving an agreement at Ohrid required the resolution of the two major issues: the official use of the Albanian language and the municipalities' authority over local police. Within those two main issues, many details needed definition. The talks also had to resolve a series of secondary problems, such as the president's proposed preamble to the Constitution and the display of cultural symbols.

To give the Macedonians some breathing space, the international proposal presented in the opening session at Ohrid backed down slightly from the Albanian proposal that had caused the furor in Skopje on July 16. At the opening plenary session, an exultant President Trajkovski chose to focus on language as the topic of the day. A positive opening negotiating atmosphere quickly turned sour with the Albanian negotiators' disappointment.

Both sides wanted significant changes to the language section. Arben Xheferi, normally thoughtful and composed, was visibly upset. As the Macedonians rejected the Albanians' proposals, a brooding Xheferi threatened to leave the talks. We calmed him down and kept the conversation moving, and by the end of the evening the Macedonians made a major concession by accepting the concept of Albanian as "an official language in Macedonia" for the first time. The debate centered on defining what was meant by an official language in the draft settlement.

The talks resumed the next day, Sunday, July 29. The wording on language in the draft agreement was the topic of the day. After giving in on the principle of an official language the previous night, the Macedonians turned aggressive. Leotard and I arranged a private meeting between Trajkovski and the Albanian party leaders. In that meeting, Xheferi and Imeri pleaded their case for Albanian as an official language. They explained that the recognition of the Albanian language was the primary condition required to disarm the NLA. Trajkovski listened but rejected their proposals.

During the delicate discussions on Lake Ohrid, Emira Mehmeti, a young woman who translated for the Albanians, was critical to their understanding of the subtleties of the international proposals and to our understanding of their position throughout the Ohrid period of negotiations. She was particularly important to our grasp of the Albanians' concerns.

The Albanians later in the day made a concession that Albanian could be given the status of an official language without specifying the word *Albanian* in the draft agreement text. In response, the ethnic Macedonians, instead of becoming more flexible, raised their negotiating demands on the Albanians. Outside the talks, Prime Minister Georgievski attacked the Ohrid negotiations in the press as Interior Minister Boskovski plotted mischief in the countryside.

"A Millimeter at a Time"

The talks went back and forth for the next three days, the Macedonians demanding strict limits to the use of the Albanian language, the Albanians demanding the expansion of the use of their language in official practices.

Our team worked to find adequate compromises between the two positions. Plenary meetings were ineffective, quickly deteriorating into verbal posturing and political theater. Most progress was achieved through separate talks between negotiators and the parties.

Solana dispatched an Austrian diplomat, Stefan Lehne, to join Leotard's staff in Ohrid. Lehne was capable and added some new input to the process, but it was clear he wanted to nudge the talk toward a position friendlier to the ethnic Macedonians. He privately told me that many European capitals viewed me as too pro-Albanian. I listened in amusement. I felt that he should endure the twists, turns, bluster, and attacks of these negotiations for a few days before he passed any judgment.

"Watch how they treat us," Xheferi said through his translator before the plenary discussion that day. He was right.

Before the meeting, I called the State Department on a cell phone to give Washington an update.

"We are making progress a millimeter at a time," I reported.

Trajkovski opened the plenary session on July 30 by expelling the US expert, Laurel Miller, from the meeting. The previous day Miller had represented the international negotiators in a legal debate with the Macedonian lawyers on a technical legal issue. She was well prepared and had clearly won the debate. Leotard and I responded immediately that Miller's expulsion was outrageous and unacceptable and demanded to know the reason for it.

Trajkovski immediately backed down, and Miller stayed in the meeting, but the tone had been set. The Macedonians proceeded to joke around and verbally humiliate the Albanian negotiators. As the meeting wore on, Xheferi's face grew darker. He tilted his head down, his dark eyes glaring up at them. I could cut the mutual contempt with a knife. Nothing was accomplished that day.

"We are making progress a millimeter at a time," Trajkovski said to me later in the day, using the precise wording I had used in my call to Washington.

The next day the Macedonians became more flexible, making enough compromises on the details of the language issue to cause Prime Minister Georgievski to threaten to leave the talks. That day Trajkovski told me privately that he was having great difficulty with Georgievski and Boskovski behind the scenes.

After negotiating most of the night with the Albanian leaders away from the talks, Xheferi returned to the presidential retreat at noon on August 1. The previous day's effort had settled the language issue as we reached the one-month point in the negotiations. But Leotard and I had to assure the parties that nothing is settled until everything is settled. We would then meet with the press to announce the progress we had made in the hope that such an announcement would freeze that portion of the final agreement. It allowed us to lock in the text and move on to other issues.[3]

The composition of the police and their control at the local level were the major remaining problems to resolve. The Macedonians wanted to retain national control of the police under the minister of interior and to delay and limit the expansion of Albanian participation in the police force. The Albanians demanded just the opposite.

Republic Day, Macedonia's major national holiday, is August 2. As the Macedonian leaders left Ohrid to participate in national ceremonies, we had a welcome day off. I took a long walk along the lake and then traveled several miles to the thousand-year-old Monastery of Saint Naum on Lake Ohrid. Near the monastery, I took a rowboat ride over a beautiful, protected lagoon of natural springs. I returned to the hotel for a swim in the lake before dinner in the town of Ohrid.

"Do not destroy my country!" a Macedonian man yelled at me across the restaurant that night. The volatile media coverage of the negotiations had raised the tension throughout the country.

For the next two days, the parties debated their positions on the future of the police but came to no agreement. During that period, I received a bit of good news when State called to let me know that it had forwarded my nomination as ambassador to Bulgaria to the White House for approval.

Javier Solana was coming to Ohrid on Sunday, August 5, and I had the feeling that the Macedonians were holding out until he arrived, expecting that the EU foreign-policy chief would be more sympathetic to their position.

I was concerned about Solana's visit. His man Lehne had been pushing for positions that I did not consider achievable, and I did not know Solana's personal attitude about the process. I was also troubled that Solana was flying in with the Ukrainian foreign minister on a Ukrainian aircraft. The Ukraine had been eager to offer heavy weapons to support Macedonian military operations against the NLA, and Solana's visit was widely covered in the Macedonian media as a positive development.

Before Solana arrived, Laurel Miller and the European experts drafted compromise international solutions to the unresolved issues and forwarded them to Quint capitals for review before presenting them to the parties.

Despite my anxiety, Solana was brilliant. He took control of the discussion and probed, prodded, cajoled, and pushed the parties to decisions. By 8:30 p.m. on August 5, he had an agreement that 1,000 Albanians would be added to the police by 2003 and that the police would be reformed by 2004. The parties also agreed that the composition of the police would reflect the population and that international observers would monitor the transition. The primary obstacles to an overall agreement—language and police—were resolved as Solana flew away that night. But I knew that bringing the process to closure could be a challenge. In the case of the Ohrid Agreement, it also would be bloody.

The success of the previous day quickly degenerated into blockage in the first meeting of the parties on August 6. Trajkovski wanted his constitutional preamble agreed to and some modifications to the process of changing the Constitution made. He also demanded that NATO disarm the NLA before implementation of the political agreement. Disarmament was a separate negotiation conducted by NATO, so we rejected it as a precondition for implementation of the political settlement. Otherwise, we set about finding some compromise text on the preamble and the constitutional change process.

Executions, Ambush, Agreement

We woke up on Tuesday, August 7, to news that could destroy the negotiations. Overnight, Macedonian security forces had shelled two Albanian villages and executed five NLA fighters who had returned to their homes in Skopje.[4] The minister of interior claimed that they were "terrorists" preparing for attacks in the capital.

The Interior Ministry could not conduct such an action without the prime minister's approval. As we approached completion of a peace agreement, these executions looked like a blatant attempt to wreck the Ohrid talks, and the NLA was almost certain to retaliate. I complained directly to the ethnic Macedonian leaders.

We spent the day developing compromises on the two constitutional issues President Trajkovski had raised, but the Albanians were furious about the overnight violence and were distracted. They suddenly wanted to reopen areas of the agreement that had been closed.

As we negotiated, the US embassy in Skopje cabled Washington that the constitutional changes in the draft agreement would not pass the National Assembly unless the hawkish prime minister imposed absolute party discipline on VMRO members.[5]

The talks were extremely close to an acceptable agreement, but tensions were very high. The angry Albanians committed only to returning to the talks the next day. Veton Surroi again called to express his concern about the consequences of the police killings of NLA fighters in Skopje. He said that the NLA had "sleepers" in Skopje ready to conduct urban guerrilla war in the capital. Once fighting broke out in Skopje, the peace talks would be useless.

"Tell your friends [in the NLA] that they will be completely isolated if a war starts in Skopje," I responded.[6] I had to make it clear that the United States would not accept an escalation of violence that killed the peace talks without serious consequences.

The situation grew worse. As we arrived at the presidential retreat on the morning of August 8, we learned that the NLA had ambushed a Macedonian army convoy on the road between Skopje and Tetovo and killed ten ethnic Macedonian soldiers. These killings over two days placed the negotiations to prevent a civil war in Macedonia on the brink of failure.

Prime Minister Georgievski issued a press statement saying that he had broken from the talks.

Trajkovski summoned Leotard and me to his private office on the second floor of the retreat. This was the most critical moment in the Macedonian crisis. The nationalist pressure for all-out war against the Albanians must have been extreme after the ambush. I expected the worst—ethnic Macedonian wrath and a complete breakdown in the peace talks. Instead, Trajkovski was somber. The death of the ten soldiers had affected him deeply, and he was resolute about finishing the agreement. He said that he had no time or flexibility. He wanted the peace agreement finished that day.

President Trajkovski had chosen peace. Others may have as well, but the burden of national leadership on that day rested on his shoulders. Trajkovski was the indispensable leader in saving his country. Leotard and I committed to doing everything we could to complete an agreement that day. We asked that it be initialed by all parties if we succeeded.

The process accelerated after our meeting with Trajkovski. We went straight to Xheferi and Imeri, who had arrived at the retreat about noon. The message to the two Albanian leaders was simple: the ambush had destroyed their negotiating leverage. We told them that there was no further negotiating flexibility, and they should sign the proposal as presented the previous night.

The Albanians requested five minutes to talk. In a few minutes, they returned to ask for the inclusion of public funding for their university. We rejected that request. Xheferi agreed to sign the settlement, but Imeri refused, holding out for university funding. I made clear to Imeri that he did not want to be personally responsible for the failure of the negotiations, and so he agreed to initial the draft.

Laurel Miller and the experts from all parties worked together for most of the afternoon reviewing the draft agreement line by line to make small technical fixes and to ensure we had a draft that was acceptable to all parties in detail. The experts initialed each page of the draft, and in the early evening each of the negotiating parties initialed the document. Leotard and I initialed as witnesses.

The parties set Monday, August 13, as the day for formal signature of the agreement in Skopje. As with the Dayton Agreement, I had no sense of major accomplishment. All I could think about were the coming five days, when this fragile agreement could be shattered before it was officially signed. Once all parties had initialed, I reported the completion of the agreement to Washington and to NATO secretary-general Robertson. Leotard took care of Solana and the Europeans.

The Macedonian leaders had done nothing to prepare the ethnic Macedonian population for a completed agreement. To the contrary, Prime Minister Georgievski had used every opportunity to incite nationalist outrage and to undermine the agreement in public. President Trajkovski asked that we make no public statement of the success of the talks, fearing a violent public reaction. We complied, but the talks held no secrets for long, and the completion of the negotiations was in the press by 10:00 p.m.

Leotard and I had one final trout dinner with our team on the lake away from the presidential retreat. Elsewhere in Macedonia, a demonstration broke out in Skopje, fighting took place near Tetovo, and a riot occurred in the hometown of the soldiers killed in the ambush earlier in the day.

The peace agreement was completed in draft, but two difficult steps lay ahead: first, the agreement must survive the five delicate days before it would be officially signed; and second, the most difficult part of any agreement is implementation, and months of difficult implementation lay ahead.

The Last Czar

Leotard remained in Skopje, but I wanted a break. The agreement belonged to the Macedonians and the Albanians, and if I stayed in Skopje, I would be a lightning rod for every nationalist crackpot who opposed the agreement. I decided to leave Macedonia on August 9 and spend the time before the signing ceremony in Sofia, Bulgaria, my next assignment, so I took my team to the Bulgarian capital.

Bulgaria was a welcome relief from the tension of the negotiations. It had its ethnic tensions but nothing like those in the former Yugoslavia. Bulgaria had been a sovereign country for one hundred years and therefore had a national confidence that many countries in the region lacked. The institutions of government were still in transition from communism, but they had organizational experience and a depth of professional talent. Bulgarians also looked to the future and were focused on NATO and EU membership and not on their internal squabbles.

Important to me in the current situation, the Bulgarians maintained a mature and responsible policy on the troubles in Macedonia. Bulgaria had a vital interest in stability in Macedonia and a strong cultural link to the Slavic community there. However, it wisely chose not to meddle in the crisis or to provoke the ethnic Macedonians.

Because of their long and sometimes troubled history with the Macedonians, the Bulgarians were keenly interested in the negotiations. They seemed genuinely pleased that I came to update them and received me at the highest levels.

Simeon Saxe-Coburg Gotha became Bulgaria's prime minister less than three weeks before we met in Sofia. Simeon, the boy czar deposed by the Communists in 1946, had returned from exile in Spain to lead a political movement that won parliamentary elections and made him prime minister in July 2001.

The last czar of the twentieth century was a trim, bald, and well-dressed man of sixty-four with the easy grace of the European aristocracy. Simeon represented the hope of the Bulgarian people for real change, and I would work closely with his government for three years once I became US ambassador to Bulgaria in 2002.

Signing in Skopje

Back in Macedonia, the security situation became more tenuous after a landmine killed eight government soldiers on August 10. Apparently in re-

Signing the Ohrid Agreement in Skopje on August 13, 2001, are (*seated left to right*) ethnic Albanian political leader Arben Xheferi, Prime Minister of Macedonia Ljubco Georgievski, and President of Macedonia Boris Trajkovski. (Macedonian Information Agency)

sponse, Interior Minister Boskovski unleashed police and irregular vigilantes on the predominantly Albanian town of Ljuboten. From August 10 to August 12, police and irregulars under Boskovski's control reportedly shelled the town, set fire to homes, indiscriminately fired on civilians, killing many of them, and arrested and brutally beat many others.[7] Several years later, in 2005, the ICTY indicted Boskovski for his role in the police brutality in Ljuboten.[8]

As my team and I returned to Skopje from Bulgaria on the evening of August 12, the Macedonian government declared a unilateral cease-fire. When I woke up on August 13, I feared the Ohrid Agreement would not be signed that day.

Solana, Robertson, Geoana, and Belgian foreign minister Louis Michel, also representing the EU, arrived for the signing ceremony. As these officials made their round of courtesy calls, the Macedonians pushed for linkage between implementation and NATO disarmament of the NLA, but no one was open to that option. The government scheduled the signing event for the presidential residence in Skopje but did not publicly announce the location for fear of demonstrations. Around 4:30 p.m., the parties signed the Ohrid Agreement in the dining room of the presidential residence, and Leotard and I witnessed it.

Speeches by the parties in the subsequent press conference at the residence were generally conciliatory until one of the journalists asked Imeri why he did not speak in Albanian since Albanian was authorized in the agreement. We rushed to find Emira Mehmeti to translate into Macedonian and English as Imeri and Xheferi began to speak in Albanian. At that point, Prime Minister Georgievski stormed off, and Trajkovski became furious, but the ice was broken on the use of the Albanian language in official settings in Macedonia.

Early in the evening as I made my way back to the room at the Alexander Palace Hotel, I encountered a senior Greek diplomat, who attacked me, as the representative of the United States, for signing a document that referred to the country's name as the "Republic of Macedonia."

I was too tired to be diplomatic. "We just prevented a war in a country bordering Greece, and you complain over the name issue?" I said as I walked away.

The next day, August 14, I flew home to Washington from Skopje, almost exactly six weeks after I had arrived in Macedonia. The Ohrid Agreement was finished. Now the difficult task of implementation was about to begin.

The Ohrid Agreement

The Ohrid Agreement ended ethnic fighting in 2001 and laid the groundwork for a democratic political system that protects minority rights and respects the cultural identity of the people.

Ohrid at its heart is a peace agreement that preserved Macedonia as a nation. It was a commitment by all parties to cease hostilities and for the NLA to disarm and return to civil society. With the assistance of NATO, Ohrid established peace and averted a tragic civil war in Macedonia.

The scope of the settlement is broad. The parties agreed to change the preamble and fifteen articles of their national constitution and to pass a range of laws fundamental to the governance of the country. They also set specific deadlines for accomplishing the agreed tasks.

The framework document also recognizes the sovereignty and territorial integrity of Macedonia as a nation. The large Albanian minority committed to live as citizens in a unified Macedonia, and the ethnic Macedonians agreed not to partition the country, politically or otherwise. Ohrid avoids territorial division as a solution to resolve ethnic problems. In fact, the text contains a clear declaration that "there are no territorial solutions to ethnic issues."

The agreement declares the equal rights of individual citizens while respecting the cultural identity of minorities within the state. In general, the document requires equal opportunity and treatment of all citizens regardless of ethnic affiliation. In this regard, the agreement separates religions from the state and guarantees the right of freedom of religious expression.

In addition to the general framework document, the Ohrid Agreement contains three annexes. One specifies changes to the Macedonian Constitution; one details that laws be changed or written with deadlines; and one describes implementation and confidence-building measures.

For the Albanians, recognition of their language was the top negotiating priority. The agreement makes Albanian an official language authorized for use in official meetings and documents from the national level to the local level. In addition, it authorizes the display of Albanian cultural symbols when used with Macedonia national symbols.

Ohrid defines a formula for power sharing between major ethnic groups. It strengthens the power of municipalities and increases local authority over police, while ensuring that minorities have a means to block actions that unfairly infringe on their rights. It includes the concept of a qualified majority used elsewhere in Europe to protect minority rights in specific areas.

The agreement commits the government to nondiscrimination and equitable representation of minority groups in the organizations of government, in particular legal and law enforcement institutions.

The Ohrid Agreement, like other such negotiated documents, is not perfect. It prevented a potentially devastating war and held the country together. In return for the Albanians' commitment to Macedonia as their nation, the ethnic Macedonians gave greater rights and authority to the Albanian citizens of the country.

Disarming the NLA

Once the parties signed the political settlement, pressure shifted immediately to NATO to disarm and disband the NLA—tasks closely linked to the political settlement. The NLA would not disarm until a political agreement was completed and a government amnesty was in place for NLA fighters.

The government would not sign the agreement without guarantees that the NLA would disarm. Robertson needed all of this wrapped up to secure the North Atlantic Council's approval for the deployment of NATO troops to Macedonia to assist in the disarmament process.

At the Ohrid signing ceremony at the presidential residence, Robertson cornered Trajkovski to get a signature on the amnesty agreement for the NLA. After some difficulty, Robertson flew back to Brussels for a late-night North Atlantic Council session with the assurance of amnesty from Trajkovski.[9] Now having the council's approval, NATO began to deploy to Macedonia in Operation Essential Harvest.

The Trajkovski letter offered immunity from penal proceedings for NLA members who voluntarily disarmed, except those suspected of committing crimes "for which the International Criminal Tribunal for the Former Yugoslavia is competent."[10] A Macedonian law in 2002 granted amnesty to the NLA except when the ICTY launched legal proceedings in criminal cases falling under its jurisdiction.[11]

NATO quickly began Operation Essential Harvest in Macedonia in late August. It consisted of about 3,500 NATO troops, lasted thirty days, and involved the disarmament of the NLA and the destruction of NLA weapons.[12]

The NATO operation completed its disarmament task, but not without difficulty. Robertson was constantly on the telephone to President Trajkovski and Defense Minister Vlado Buchkovski to keep the program on track. Along the way, Georgievski's government challenged the number of weapons collected, and at one point the interior minister accused the NATO secretary-general of directly backing terrorists and conspiring against Macedonia.[13]

Disbanding the NLA created a security vacuum in Albanian communities, and the Macedonian government was eager to return its unreformed national security forces to these areas. Because no one trusted the prime minister or the interior minister, the international negotiators objected to the return of security forces to these communities without careful planning and transparent implementation under international oversight. Premature deployment would be destabilizing and might derail everything that had been accomplished. The return of Macedonian security forces to sensitive areas became a constant source of controversy between the government and international community representatives monitoring Ohrid implementation throughout the autumn of 2001.

Once the NLA was disarmed, NATO maintained a smaller force of seven hundred troops on the ground in Macedonia to help protect OSCE and EU civilian monitors.[14] The presence of NATO troops, even in small numbers, gave confidence to the Albanian communities in the immediate post conflict period.

32

The Long Struggle

Peace agreements are just words on paper until they are implemented. Implementation is usually a struggle when agreements are reached in a confrontational negotiating atmosphere. After the signing of the Ohrid Agreement, Macedonia was no exception. Reaching the agreement took forty-four days from my arrival in Skopje on July 1, 2001, until it was signed on August 13. Full implementation, very intense in the beginning, could take decades, maybe generations, to be absorbed into Macedonian society.

Implementation of such agreements requires the full attention and support of the nations and international organizations with an interest in the outcome. Opponents of an agreement usually try to block or stall implementation unless the agreement's sponsors apply pressure to complete agreed actions. Further, implementation often is subject to interpretation of the agreement's language and intention, and the parties may not have the resources to carry out key aspects of the agreement without external help. In the case of Macedonia, the EU and its member nations, NATO, and OSCE were directly engaged in implementation. The United States also contributed significantly to Ohrid implementation, but events on September 11, 2001, jolted the nation's attention away from the Balkans.

Leotard remained in his residence in Skopje for a few months to assist with implementation for the EU. From August to November, I flew back and forth from Washington to help with implementation when required. These trips became increasingly confrontational with the Macedonian leaders as my obvious frustration with resistance to implementation by the prime minister and the minister of interior agitated them more with each visit.

The implementation tasks for the Ohrid Agreement required difficult political actions by the parties. The early burden of implementation fell to the Macedonian National Assembly, dominated by the nationalist VMRO coalition and led by Stojan Andov, Speaker of the Assembly. The National

Assembly was required to pass the amendments to the Macedonian Constitution and the laws agreed to in the settlement.

The Macedonian government tried to set conditions before advancing agreed parliamentary actions. It demanded the NLA be disarmed and withdrawn from sensitive areas, a durable cease-fire be in place, and displaced persons be allowed to return as preconditions for implementation.[1] The international parties involved in implementation never accepted these conditions, but we met them as implementation proceeded. Nonetheless, Prime Minister Georgievski and Speaker Andov continued to stall the parliamentary process.

The nature and timing of the return of government police into Albanian areas vacated by the NLA constituted the most delicate issues. The Albanians had no trust in the unreformed Macedonian police, but NATO had no mandate for a large security force to remain in Macedonia. In a cable sent to the State Department on September 2, I recommended an extension of a small NATO force to ensure security for implementation into 2002, but Washington did not support it.[2] Leotard pushed Brussels to create an EU security force to do the job, but he also ran into resistance.

A Terrible Day

The violent attacks on the United States on September 11, 2001, immediately concentrated US foreign and national security attention on the threat to the nation presented by al Qaeda. "A terrible day in American history. . . . This is one of those historic events which change the nature of our country in unforeseen directions," I wrote in my journal on the morning of September 11.

The surprise attacks by al Qaeda on the United States less than a month after the parties signed the Ohrid Agreement had a serious effect on the atmosphere for implementation of the agreement in Macedonia. Prime Minister Georgievski made public statements in Skopje that after the September 11 attacks, the United States would change its policy in Macedonia by opposing the Albanian terrorists. He wrote a letter to President Bush on September 12 expressing condolences for the September losses, but his letter also linked the attacks on the United States to Macedonia's experience with terrorism over the past several months.[3]

I raced to Skopje to bluntly tell Georgievski that the use of the attacks in the United States to further his political agenda in Macedonia and to undermine the agreement he had signed was unacceptable. I then made public statements to the Macedonian media that there was no change to US policy toward Macedonia based on the September 11 attacks. I made it clear that the United States stood completely behind the Ohrid Agreement and the peaceful resolution of disputes. I also said that the United States objected to the use of the tragic events in New York, Washington, and Pennsylvania to gain local political advantage and to disrupt the political process ongoing in Macedonia.[4] I then privately assured Arben Xheferi that the Albanians should not be concerned about any change in US policy toward the agreement.

As the United States prepared responses to the September 11 attacks, the Europeans successfully negotiated a UNSCR recognizing the Ohrid Agreement and authorizing international involvement in its implementation.[5] I continued to lobby Washington in favor of a substantial international monitoring presence in Macedonia, but the administration remained opposed. After much back and forth with Washington, NATO authorized on September 26 a small force to stay in Macedonia after KLA disarmament and monitor the cease-fire.

By October 1, the lack of progress on Ohrid implementation caused considerable frustration. The international community had helped negotiate the agreement, had deployed NATO, EU, and OSCE personnel to assist, had disarmed and disbanded the NLA, had passed a UNSCR, and had put considerable funding into a police academy. Yet the Macedonian National Assembly still stalled on passing the constitutional amendments or agreed laws and failed to grant amnesty as promised, and paramilitaries continued to cause trouble. With no progress on implementation in Macedonia, the international representatives were reluctant to move forward on major economic-development programs for Macedonia or to assist in the return of Macedonian security forces to sensitive areas.

Dining Hall Outrage

One critical element of the Ohrid Agreement was reform of the Macedonian police. The agreement called for the police to represent the ethnic composition of the population, and the low number of Albanians in the existing police force required that a significant police-training program be conducted for Albanians. The agreement required the Macedonian government to hire and train five hundred new Albanian police officers right away, with the assistance of the United States, the EU, and the OSCE. To support police reform, the United States committed $2.75 million for professional police training and facilities improvements at the Macedonian Police Academy.[6] An initial group of one hundred Albanian recruits, male and female, were selected for the first training session.

The US commitment to police training was on a collision course with the nationalist paramilitary, however. In early September, the minister of interior created a special paramilitary unit of loyal VMRO-DPMNE nationalists known as the "Lions." Ill trained and undisciplined, the Lions were visible around Skopje and were accused of abusing Albanians. Unfortunately, Interior Minister Boskovski also stationed a large number of Lions at the Police Academy, where the new Albanian recruits were training.[7]

Because the United States was a significant contributor to the training program, I wanted to see progress at the academy firsthand, but Macedonian authorities stalled in arranging the visit. I soon learned why. I decided to meet with the US trainers at the academy on October 3 whether the Macedonians invited me or not. When I arrived, I was told the academy's commandant was not available to see me.

The US trainers were regular American police officers from US cities and towns who had taken a leave of absence to help train new Macedonian police. They were shocked by the conditions at the academy. They told me that a contingent of Lions, whom they described as a rag-tag gang of armed, undisciplined, and unruly thugs, caused constant trouble with the Albanian police recruits. They reported that the Lions were often drunk and constantly harassed and intimidated the Albanians, including verbal sexual harassment of the female Albanian police cadets. The Lions also had threatened the US police trainers and restricted them to specific areas of the academy.

When the Albanian students first arrived, the Lions denied many of them mattresses, forcing them to sleep on the floor. The previous day, according to the police trainers, the eating utensils in the dining hall were removed before the Albanians arrived for a meal, so that they had either to skip the meal or to eat with their hands.

I had never seen this kind of contempt for a US international assistance program in my career. The American police trainers took me on a tour of the campus, where I talked to the cadets, who confirmed the stories of harassment and intimidation by the Lions. As we toured, some members of the Lions were seen strutting around the facilities.

My anger grew the more I saw and heard from the American trainers and their students. We went into the dining facility in midmorning, where a few Lions were sitting around smoking and joking. My anger boiled over. I went to the serving line where the eating utensils for the next meal were sitting in metal containers on a stainless-steel table. In the emotion of the moment, I committed a brazen public act of anger. I took a spoon from the container and then knocked the rest of the silverware out of the containers onto the steel serving table with a loud crash. I then stalked out of the dining hall to the surprise and shock of the people who worked there. As I left the academy, I told the US trainers that an American program would not be treated this way and that I would correct the situation immediately.

I returned to central Skopje and reported the events to Leotard and others and asked for urgent meetings with Prime Minister Georgievski and Branko Cervenkovski, the Macedonian opposition leader. Leotard and Max van der Stoel went with me in a show of solidarity. The first meeting was with Cervenkovski. I explained to the SDSM leader what I had found, and, waving the spoon from the dining hall for emphasis, I called the conditions at the academy "a disgrace to Macedonia." Cervenkovski was sympathetic.

"You don't have to tell me about the Lions. These people will show up at the polling places in the next election to support the nationalists," Cervenkovski said before we left.

"Are you going to give him the spoon?" Leotard asked later when the call came for the meeting with the prime minister.

"Absolutely," I said. By the time we arrived at Georgievski's office, rumors were flying about my outburst at the police academy.

After describing my experience at the academy, I told Georgievski that US funding was now halted and that the Macedonian government had forty-eight hours to get the Lions out of the academy. I complained that the government had done little in six weeks to implement the Ohrid Agreement and that we would not support the return of Macedonian security forces into sensitive areas until substantive progress was made in the country's implementation commitments.

Georgievski then became the second official to blow his stack on October 3. He charged me again with insulting the Macedonian people. He called me a terrorist and the "commander of the NLA" who had directed the killing of Macedonian people during the negotiations. He continued his rant by accusing the United States of state-sponsored terrorism in Macedonia and US soldiers of involvement in terrorism in his country.

"This is unacceptable," Leotard said to me. "Let's go."

"Your statements are outrageous. I will not accept such statements about my country," I said to Georgievski. Leotard, van der Stoel, and I then stood up and left the room. Georgievski was on the phone to the local press before we were out of his building, declaring that he had thrown us out of his office and blasting me for my behavior at the academy.[8]

We returned to the EU office and drafted a joint public statement that the United States and the EU did not support the return of security forces to contested areas until progress was made on the Constitution and on amnesty for the NLA and until a coordinated, transparent plan were considered.

Despite assurances from President Trajkovski that the situation would be corrected, the Lions remained at the academy. In response, I stopped funding and withdrew the American police trainers and the Albanian cadets from the academy. After Washington demanded an apology from the prime minister, Georgievski apologized to the United States but not to me.[9]

The Macedonians were furious. In a meeting with Leotard later in the week, Trajkovski said that he could stand no further pressure from the United States and once more threatened to resign. President Bush sent a personal letter to Trajkovski on October 12 urging Macedonian authorities to quickly implement the Ohrid Agreement. A US message through the embassy to Trajkovski and Georgievski made the American position more direct. They were informed that government actions that undermined the agreement would cost them US support. At the same time, a letter from Bush to European leaders expressed the importance of the Ohrid Agreement to future US commitments to Macedonia.

The Lions left the Police Academy by October 16, and so the US trainers, funding, and Albanian students returned. However, my personal influence and effectiveness in Macedonia had ended with the emotional rampage in the Police Academy dining hall.

In retrospect, I realize that my outburst in the dining hall was excessive. A public display of personal anger, no matter how justified, does not advance the agenda. But I never regretted the subsequent withdrawal of US assistance, the demands, the deadlines, and the actions I took to remove the nationalist irregulars and to improve the conditions for the recruits and trainers at the police academy.

Throughout the fall, the EU and NATO, with US support, exerted steady pressure on the Macedonian government for implementation of the Ohrid Agreement. International assistance to Macedonia became contingent on the passage of agreed constitutional amendments and laws. Solana and Robertson visited Skopje frequently to push the political process along and to resolve the very sensitive issues of amnesty for the NLA and the return of security forces to contested areas.

Leotard, like me, felt that his effectiveness in Macedonia had run its course, and so he departed Skopje on October 20 for his home in Frajus, originally an ancient Roman port, on France's Côte d'Azur. He left with my deepest respect and appreciation. François Leotard was a first-class person in every way—smart, mature, professional, and unflappable. In Macedonia, he had broken new ground for the EU and was an exceptional partner in a difficult situation. He left Skopje as a successful international envoy who created peace in a unified Macedonia in 2001.

Alain Le Roy, a rising professional in the French diplomatic service, replaced Leotard as the EU representative in Macedonia. Le Roy was a different personality from Leotard, but we worked well together. He was brash, aggressive, and highly energetic. Le Roy was also a skillful diplomat who saw the value in cooperation and was focused on the priority aspects of Ohrid implementation.

Return of Security Forces to Albanian Areas

Leotard and I had successfully blocked a provocative scheme by the interior minister on October 3 to return security forces to Albanian areas without any preparation or international coordination. In a joint public statement that day, we had objected to the return of forces without adequate planning and the presence of international monitors.[10]

Negotiations had gone back and forth on the deployment of Macedonian forces to Albanian areas. Leotard, van der Stoel, the NATO representative, and I had sent a letter to President Trajkovski on October 8 laying out international requirements for the return of security forces if the international community were to help with the process. In that letter, the international community had insisted on a transparent plan from the government, a pilot confidence-building project, and full coordination with international organizations. In addition, amnesty for the NLA as agreed had to be approved.[11]

Trajkovski ignored the international conditions when nationalist pressure convinced him to support Minister Boskovski's plan to send Macedonian forces into Albanian areas without international approval. On November 9, in a private meeting without an American in the room, Trajkovski tried to bully Le Roy, the new EU envoy, into agreeing to the Boskovski plan. He proclaimed the Macedonian right to act in the national security interest, and he ordered Minister Boskovski to conduct his planned operation. On Saturday, November 10, Boskovski informed the international community of his operation. After listening to the minister, the international representatives judged the plan to be provocative and refused to support it.

Despite international opposition, Boskovski issued a public statement following the meeting, falsely claiming that the international community representatives supported his plan.[12] The US embassy issued a press release the same day condemning it.[13]

At midnight on November 10, President Trajkovski called Le Roy in a rage over the international representatives' refusal to endorse the plan to deploy police into Albanian communities. Le Roy reminded Trajkovski that the Macedonians could do what they wanted, but other nations and international organizations had no obligation to support their actions.

The controversial operation began on November 11 and quickly became a disaster. Boskovski sent two hundred fully armed Macedonian police into the Albanian areas, even though the Macedonian Ministry of Defense and the army refused to participate. The police arrested seven Albanians, but three policemen were killed, and one hundred Macedonians were taken hostage.

Just as Leotard and I had experienced in similar situations earlier, the previously overbearing Trajkovski was distraught over the ongoing police disaster in Albanian communities. He pleaded with Le Roy for help, saying that Interior Minister Boskovski and Prime Minister Georgievski, who had remained out of sight, had refused his orders to stop the operation. Le Roy called Paris to mobilize high-level international pressure on the prime minister to stop the operation. It worked. NATO later negotiated the release of the Macedonian hostages.

On November 12, President Trajkovski signed the letter of amnesty for all former NLA fighters except those indicted for war crimes by the ICTY. The Macedonian National Assembly passed a new preamble and fifteen changes to articles in the Macedonian Constitution on November 16, 2001, and Macedonian security forces carefully returned later to sensitive areas under international supervision and without serious incident.

Le Roy was an energetic risk taker with good judgment, and I liked him very much. He came by the Alexander Palace Hotel at 11:00 p.m. the night before I departed to say good-bye. I wished him the best and told him that I would not be back in Macedonia.

The next day, Tuesday, November 13, 2001, I departed Macedonia as the local media blamed me personally for the death of the three policemen in the Boskovski operation. I did not return to Macedonia for ten years.

The Ohrid Agreement

The Ohrid Agreement was the most important foreign-policy achievement of the Bush administration from the president's inauguration in January until the period after the attacks on September 11, 2001. Despite those attacks, which turned national attention away from the Balkans, Washington continued active engagement in the implementation of the Ohrid Agreement.

In Macedonia, the agreement achieved peace, ensured the unity of Macedonia as a multicultural nation, and addressed the primary issues of the Albanian minority. Overall, it offered Macedonia the opportunity to develop as a successful and contributing democracy in Europe.

Many people contributed to the Ohrid Agreement, but Boris Trajkovski was the leader indispensable to achieving a negotiated peace in his country in 2001. As president, he was under constant pressure from officials in the Macedonian government to pursue a military defeat of the NLA. At the same time, he faced contradictory pressure from the United States, NATO, and the EU to find a peaceful solution. At his core, however, Trajkovski wanted peace, and he made the right decisions at the critical moments. The Ohrid Agreement is his legacy, and it will have a historic effect on the future of modern Macedonia and the region.

The ethnic Macedonian nationalists never fully accepted the compromises contained in the Ohrid Agreement. But with no acceptable alternative, they grudgingly implemented most of the written commitments in the agreement under considerable pressure from the United States and EU nations.

Ten years after the Ohrid Agreement was signed, the International Crisis Group concluded that much of the agreement had been implemented and that a resumption of armed conflict in Macedonia was unlikely.[14]

Separate from the Ohrid Agreement, one international problem continued to hinder Macedonia's development—the dispute between Macedonia and Greece over Macedonia's constitutional name. This destructive quarrel about heritage and national identity has prevented Macedonia's membership in important international organizations and delayed the economic integration vital to the successful development of the region. It also has distracted local political elites and the public from dealing with important domestic issues facing the two countries.

Greece has a major advantage in the name controversy. As a member of both the EU and NATO, it has vetoed Macedonian membership in those two international organizations until a solution acceptable to Athens is found. Creative legal and diplomatic compromises exist, but a solution requires a level of active, determined international diplomacy lacking so far. US and European nations should give the name issue a much higher international profile, present serious incentives and penalties to both parties, and raise the resolution of Macedonia's name to the top of the agenda, with both Athens and Skopje included in every discussion.

Resolving the problem of Macedonia's internationally accepted name is in everyone's interest. Until Macedonia is integrated into Euro-Atlantic institutions, its long-term stability will be in question, and the southeastern flank of the EU and NATO will not be unified.

33

Turning Point

American Leadership and the Balkans,
1995–2008

The breakup of Yugoslavia, the most violent episode in the collapse of communism in eastern Europe, was a sequence of humanitarian and military crises that became a turning point in international relations with consequences far beyond the region.

Restoring peace and stability in the Balkans forced the United States, its European allies, Russia, and international institutions to confront security challenges in Europe at a time when they also struggled to understand the full effects of the end of the Soviet Union and the international security order that had existed for fifty years. The crises and the international responses to them became a laboratory for change in the early post-Soviet international order.

Consequences Avoided

The destruction and repression instigated by Milosevic and his supporters created massive human misery and threatened to derail the expansion of democracy in southeastern Europe. As the champion of democracy and human rights and the leader of Western democracies, the United States could not turn its back on aggression and the deteriorating humanitarian conditions in Europe.

Had the United States failed to exert leadership in the Balkans, the consequences could have been disastrous. Human suffering in Bosnia, Kosovo, and Macedonia would have been far worse, deepening hatreds and creating millions more refugees throughout Europe. Genocide and other war crimes would have increased. Without peace, the conflict could have spread outside the former Yugoslavia. Beyond the human misery and destruction of continued war, the failure to intervene would have weakened NATO and created a strategic leadership vacuum in Europe. Inaction could have seriously delayed, if not halted, the process of expanded democracy into eastern Europe and greater European integration. Further, instability in southeastern Europe could have allowed jihadists to gain influence in the region as European Muslim communities turned where they could for aid to defend themselves.

The United States and Europe

Intervention in the former Yugoslavia was not an easy choice for the United States. Yet the decision to engage in 1995 was more than just a response to a humanitarian crisis. Fundamental US national security interests also were at stake in the Balkans as Yugoslavia disintegrated.

The United States has other important, even vital, relationships in the world, but none is as critical to its security as the bond with the democracies of Europe. In addition to values in common with the United States, Europe is the most powerful democratic region in the world outside of the United States. Since 1945, European security has been at the very core of US national security, and sustaining American leadership among the democracies of western Europe is an essential component of this interest. Any real separation of the United States from its European allies would put the security of all at great risk.

"History has proven that America is not secure without a stable Europe, and Europe is not stable if its southeastern corner is not at peace," I told the US House of Representatives Committee on International Relations in 2000.[1]

Ultimately, the Balkans became the issue that redefined America's role in Europe.[2] Beginning with the Holbrooke mission in Bosnia in the summer of 1995, America reassumed a leadership role. US diplomacy in the Balkans thereafter was activist and multidimensional.

Russia and the West

Bosnia in 1995–1996 was the high-water mark of cooperation between Russia and the West in the early post-Soviet era. Russia at first assisted the

United States and its European partners on Balkan security problems as one way to forge a new relationship with the West. This period of East–West unity would be fleeting.

The level of partnership achieved in Bosnia between Russia and the West would have been unthinkable only a few years earlier. Russia participated actively in the early days of the Contact Group and the negotiations reaching the Dayton Agreement. Despite initial resistance from its military, Russian leaders set up a liaison element at NATO military headquarters, established a process to discuss common political topics with NATO in Brussels, and sent troops to Bosnia to work with SFOR on the ground. Russia's close relationship with the Contact Group on Balkan issues before the UN Security Council was important to international progress in the region.

But Russia's relationship with the West began to deteriorate in 1999 with the change in Russia's political leadership. The historic disintegration of the Soviet political and economic structure of Russia after 1989 had failed to produce the immediate domestic prosperity expected by the Russian public. The nation instead stumbled into lawlessness, corruption, economic chaos, and perceived national humiliation. In the turmoil of a transition in disarray, Russian nationalism and the popular desire for order propelled Vladimir Putin to power in the Kremlin. Rather than moving closer to the West, Russia retreated to another period of authoritarian rule. Putin provided order but at a great cost to democracy and to Moscow's positive relationship with the West.

Beginning in 1999 with Kosovo, Russia's reduced cooperation with the United States and Europe made international policy toward the region more difficult, especially in the United Nations. Russia blocked a resolution authorizing the use of NATO force to end the growing Serbian repression in Kosovo in 1999. In so doing, it took the issue out of UN hands and reduced UN influence. With broad-based European backing for the air strikes in Kosovo and Serbia, the limited nature and success of the NATO air campaign gave precedent to NATO's use of force without UN authority. Russia later participated in KFOR and joined in the approval of the UN mandate in Kosovo under UNSCR 1244. It subsequently prevented Security Council endorsement of the Ahtisaari proposal for Kosovo independence, but that process went forward anyway in 2008 without formal UN approval.

Russian relations with the United States and Europe deteriorated further when Russian forces invaded Georgia in 2008, then annexed the Crimea, and supported pro-Russian militants who occupied eastern regions of the Ukraine in 2014. The Russian military intervention on behalf of the Assad regime in Syria in 2015 was a further source of friction. With the relationships increasingly antagonistic, the Balkans was an area where Moscow had the means and the opportunity to challenge US and European influence and to undercut the development of democracy and the expansion of NATO and the EU.

Russia has maintained a network of contacts in Balkan nations who miss the good old days and are happy to promote Russian objectives when encouraged and supported. The current Russian nationalist agenda also is compatible with the attitudes of extreme Balkan nationalists, and Russian money pumps up the influence of ethnic nationalist political movements that promote ethnic separation and hostility. Russia also exploits the weaknesses of the press in the region, which is often dependent on questionable financing and subject to heavy political influence. In this environment, Russian disinformation campaigns feed false news and conspiracy theories designed to sow ethnic discord and weaken US and European influence, particularly among ethnic Slavic populations in the Balkans.

International Organizations

The conflicts in the former Yugoslavia created or transformed several international organizations.

The Contact Group—the informal coordination mechanism among key Western nations—was the primary point for developing international policy on Bosnia, Kosovo, and Macedonia. Coordination of international policy among these key nations is nothing new, but modern communications technology and the ease of travel made interaction within the Contact Group more frequent, more intense, and more widely spread at various levels of government than before. The Contact Group also brought post-Soviet Russia into a partnership with the West on the Balkans and improved Western understanding of Russian concerns.

The Balkan experience transformed NATO as an international security alliance. At the end of the Cold War, NATO was struggling to find its identity in the new-world security environment. In the early days of the conflict, Yugoslavia was outside of NATO's declared area of responsibility. As events unfolded, though, NATO conducted air operations over Bosnia, Kosovo, and Serbia and deployed expeditionary combat forces to Bosnia and Kosovo.

From 1995 on, NATO was the primary instrument for military policy in the region. In Bosnia and Kosovo, it expanded its operational partnerships beyond its member states to include Russia and other non-NATO partners. It also refined its relationship with the UN and the EU through working technical arrangements with both organizations. These changes were revolutionary developments for the North Atlantic Alliance and a forerunner to subsequent NATO activities in Iraq, Afghanistan, and Libya.

In Macedonia, NATO secretary-general George Robertson and Pieter Feith of NATO's international staff negotiated separate cease-fire, disarmament, and amnesty agreements in Macedonia to complement the Ohrid settlement. In so doing, they stretched the functions of the NATO secretary-general and the international staff into new areas. By working closely with the United States and the EU, they also demonstrated the complementary value of NATO and the EU engagement on transatlantic security issues.

The United Nations is normally the first international institution engaged when conflicts emerge. The UNPROFOR period in Bosnia was a low point for the UN, but the UN remained important to the region. As an implementation organization, it recovered in Kosovo. UNMIK, reinforced by the EU, OSCE, and NATO, effectively governed the country under UNSCR 1244 after Serbia was forced to withdraw from Kosovo by the NATO air campaign. Later, the Ahtisaari negotiations on Kosovo's future status, conducted under UN auspices, set the conditions for national sovereignty and the independence of Kosovo in 2008.

The international judicial process that held national leaders and others accountable for war crimes is an important legacy of the international intervention in the former Yugoslavia from 1995 to 2008. The International Criminal Tribunal for the Former Yugoslavia, a court authorized by the UN, brought to justice scores of national and ethnic leaders who violated international standards of human rights by committing acts of genocide, crimes against humanity, and grave violations of the UN Convention on Genocide and the Geneva Convention. In doing so, the ICTY set a standard of international humanitarian justice that future leaders engaged in violent conflict must consider.

After the court was established in 1993, it indicted 161 individuals, sentencing 80 of them for punishment. Leaders from multiple ethnic groups in Bosnia, Serbia, Croatia, Kosovo, and Macedonia stood before the ICTY in The Hague. Those indicted included an elected national head of state and dozens of senior government, military, and political officials.[3]

Of those participating in the Dayton talks, Slobodan Milosevic was indicted for genocide and crimes against humanity but died in jail and escaped a formal court judgment. Former Bosnian Serb general Zdravko Tolimir was sentenced to life imprisonment for genocide and crimes against humanity at Srebrenica and elsewhere in Bosnia. Former Bosnian Serb leader Momcilo Krajisnik received a twenty-year prison sentence. The ICTY acquitted former president of Serbia Milan Milutinovic.

The ICTY found former Bosnian Serb leader Radovan Karadzic, who had evaded capture for years, guilty of genocide and crimes against humanity and sentenced him to prison for forty years. Former general Ratko Mladic is in custody awaiting trial by the ICTY.[4]

Before the breakup of Yugoslavia, the European Union had no real mechanism for developing and implementing a common foreign policy. By 2001, it had a recognized foreign-policy identity and had taken on primary nation-building responsibilities in Bosnia and Kosovo, including the deployment of military and international police forces to replace NATO in Bosnia and alongside NATO in Kosovo.

In the Ohrid Agreement, Javier Solana achieved a major foreign-policy success as the first EU high representative for foreign and security policy. With Leotard and me working as partners in Macedonia, the negotiations in 2001 also became a primary example of diplomatic cooperation between the EU and the United States in conflict resolution.

The OSCE was active in Bosnia, and its Kosovo Verification Mission was the international monitoring organization in Kosovo until its withdrawal in 1999. The OSCE promoted ethnic rights in Macedonia before the US-EU negotiations took place and helped in conducting the Ohrid negotiations and implementing the agreement.

The United States and Muslims in the Balkans

The official objective of the US engagement in the former Yugoslavia from 1995 to 2008 was not to help one group but to restore stability to southeastern Europe and to end a general humanitarian crisis. Nevertheless, the millions of Muslims living in the former Yugoslavia were the people who most benefited immediately from the US-led intervention in the Balkans. The US and international action to stop or prevent deadly conflicts saved countless Muslim lives, defended their independence, protected their cultural identity, and guaranteed their rights as citizens. It also gave Muslims in Bosnia the means to defend themselves against future attacks. Overall, the United States offered the new countries born of the former Yugoslavia the chance to draw on the multicultural strengths of their societies to create a modern democratic future.

The United States did not seek credit for this outcome among Muslims, nor did it receive much recognition from those outside the region. The relationship between the Western democracies and Muslim societies around the world is among the most important and most sensitive foreign-policy and national security challenges in the post–Cold War world. The United States succeeded with Muslims in the Balkans because the military and diplomatic intervention pursued a humanitarian purpose and aligned with the interests and the future vision of the people of the region. If the Balkan nations with large Muslim populations prosper and are accepted into the mainstream of Western democracies, they can be models for accommodating Islam and democratic governance. They can also serve as a counterweight to extremists who are actively promoting conflict between Islam and Western democracy.

The Former Yugoslavia

The American and allied intervention brought enduring changes to the region of the former Yugoslavia. Although serious problems remain, the Balkan wars at the end of the twentieth century are over, and a general peace has settled over the region. Seven new nations have emerged from the fragmentation of the former Yugoslavia. Their borders are set, and most nations of the world recognize them as sovereign states.

Democracy is in various stages of development throughout the region. Ethnic nationalism simmers beneath the surface, but nations have democratically elected, representative governments, and most seem generally committed to basic democratic values. The majority of nations of the region have used the past two decades to restructure their constitutions, their governments, their economies, their educational systems, their security, and other institutions. These changes continue in what has been a major transformation in the lives and the opportunities for the 22 million citizens living in the nations carved from the former Yugoslavia.

Leaders of Balkan nations have generally reoriented their nations' future to Europe and the West and to membership in NATO and the EU. This integration, however, is not yet complete. Five of these nations, including Slovenia and Croatia, have become members of NATO and have deployed forces in international security missions. Slovenia and Croatia have also joined Bulgaria and Romania as full members of the EU. Others aspire to

The Balkans - 2008

membership and are in various stages of the membership process. Membership in these organizations draws Balkan countries into the mainstream of the transatlantic community of nations, reinforces their commitment to democratic values, and provides them with economic and other assistance to help them develop.

Even with this progress, there is no guarantee that all of the new countries will remain peaceful or that ethnic relationships will be cooperative. Five nations from the former Yugoslavia without EU and NATO membership—Macedonia, Serbia, Kosovo, Montenegro, and Bosnia—remain most vulnerable to instability, ethnic tensions, and external manipulation.

Some national political leaders persist in using ethnic tensions for political advantage rather than address the serious economic and other problems facing their countries. In that regard, Serbia continues to be dominated by Serbian ethnic nationalists who continue to meddle in the ethnic relationships and seek to promote ethnic separation in Bosnia and Kosovo.

Many nations in the Balkans are still plagued by pervasive corruption, weakness in the rule of law, and government inefficiencies left over from their Communist past. Economic growth also has been slow in the region. Hit especially hard by the global economic recession of 2008, the area suffers from low investment, high levels of unemployment, and widespread poverty.[5] These problems compound ethnic tensions that might be reduced by jobs and economic growth, and they cause ambitious young people to leave their home countries to pursue opportunities elsewhere.

Major new challenges for these nations include the flood of refugees from the wars in Iraq and Syria, the uncertainty over the EU's future after the British decision to exit the EU, and the confusion over the Trump administration's commitment to NATO.

Macedonia's ethnic relationships are particularly fragile. The surge of Muslim refugees from Iraq and Syria into the region strains ethnic relations in the country. Leaders of the ethnic Macedonian political party that has dominated the government for years have never fully accepted important elements of the Ohrid Agreement and have used fear and confrontation to obstruct ethnic cooperation and promote the party's nationalist political agenda. Macedonia's national identity and its national confidence remain clouded by its dispute with Greece over its official name and prevent its membership in NATO and the EU, to the region's detriment. This issue deserves urgent international diplomatic intervention by the US and European nations.

The US and European commitment to Balkan peace, stability, and development has been significant, and the nations formed from the former Yugoslavia have made much progress. But continued international attention, investment, and further integration of the region into Western institutions will be necessary in future years if these nations are to achieve their potential and to avoid the mistakes of their troubled past.

The Great Experiment

The recent Balkan conflicts showed once again that hate and fear are no basis for building a modern nation. Partition and policies based on ethnic and religious hatred and segregation offer no hope for a positive future.

Those nations that cling to hate, fear, and confrontation are likely doomed to conflict and weakness.

Diversity is a fact of life in modern societies. With today's instantaneous flow of information, ease of travel, and economic globalization, nations can no longer live in the isolation of the past. In this age of diversity, the future unity and strength of democratic nations will be determined not by race and ethnicity but by shared political and social values and by the equality of justice and opportunity for their citizens. The challenge is how to recognize the unique features of ethnic identity while integrating diverse groups into a community of common core values and laws. Nations that draw on the positive aspects of all groups within generally accepted democratic values will in the long run have the greatest chance for future democratic development and stability.

The new democracies emerging from the former Yugoslavia represent a great experiment that could change southeastern Europe fundamentally. That experiment centers on the concept that the rights of the people are defined by an individual's citizenship and not by his or her race, religion, or ethnicity; that the merit of the individual's character, talent, willingness to work hard, and personal achievement define personal worth; and that all citizens—regardless of ethnicity—have the right to equal opportunity for prosperity, security, and protection under the law.

Given the history of the region, the experiment may be idealistic, but it is the best alternative to ethnic wars and boundaries constantly redrawn to separate hostile ethnic groups. Every modern democracy is engaged in this experiment. Democracies always are a work in progress, a job never fully completed. In the Balkans, where the history of ethnic conflict is long and painful, this concept is particularly important. To meet the expectations of their people, democratic nations of the region must create conditions in which diverse groups and individuals can retain their respective identities while cooperating for the common good if the society is to develop and prosper. The degree of success or failure in this endeavor will determine whether the region can break from its destructive past.

The international engagement in southeastern Europe from 1995 to 2008 created the conditions for this experiment, but future peace and democracy are not a certainty in the region. The nations of the Balkans face difficult problems that might derail their development if not addressed. The United States and European nations can and should help, but ultimate responsibility for meeting these challenges lies with the leaders and the people of the area.

International intervention in the Balkans has accomplished much since 1995. This latest wave of outside influence that swept over the area was not one of conquest and repression but one of democracy and freedom for Balkan nations to find their own way in the future. Forward-looking national leaders will be essential to the development of these new nations. With international help, these leaders should seize this opportunity and deliver on the promise of democracy for all citizens of their nations. If they do, they can change the direction of their nations' histories and improve the lives of tens of millions of people in the region.

34

Crisis Management

The Balkan Experience

America's commitment to peace in the former Yugoslavia beginning in 1995 demonstrated the value of US leadership in an international crisis. In addition to the military power, economic resources, and democratic values that the nation brings to any crisis, its leadership in the Balkans promoted a unified international response and provided energy and a sense of direction absent when the United States was on the sideline.

The American peacemakers in the Balkans from 1995 to 2008 were an eclectic group of pragmatic political leaders, determined diplomats, and prudent military professionals. They overcame their differences and pursued common national goals to end or prevent war, restore order, and set the conditions for successful national development of the new nations of the former Yugoslavia.

As they struggled with the crises before them, they employed a tough-minded American idealism. They used aggressive diplomacy to give structure, incentives, and momentum to the peace process. When necessary, they authorized the use of NATO military force to end the fighting.

The Americans and their allies pushed through tough political obstructions created by the parties to the conflicts. They focused on the future and refused to become bogged down in the various interpretations of the past or in local ethnic bigotry. Their negotiating approach was practical and based on common democratic values and standards of international human rights. The peace agreements they helped produce gave the people of the new nations created from the former Yugoslavia a historic chance for national development if they can take full advantage of the opportunities before them.

The Balkan crises from 1995 to 2008 were transforming experiences for me as I went from army colonel and intelligence professional to apprentice diplomat, leader of a controversial implementation program, and then principal US negotiator of an agreement that prevented a war. Along the way, I drew several conclusions about the use of force and diplomacy in crisis management.

NATO

The United States functions best in an international crisis when it upholds its national values and acts within a coalition of strong and committed democratic nations. The NATO operation in the former Yugoslavia fits that standard. America can always choose to use force unilaterally or to act with convenient but usually weak "coalitions of the willing." Those coalitions, however, often are the costliest and potentially the riskiest of options.

The strongest security coalition for the United States is with Canada and the major European democracies committed to NATO. The North Atlantic Alliance has the advantages of existing national forces with common doctrine, compatible equipment, a standing command structure, and an established policy-making apparatus. Today, NATO is the transatlantic political-military institution most critical to the defense of Western democracy.

The intervention in the Balkans reformed and reinvigorated NATO and opened it to a broader range of security missions and international partners. But its future is not guaranteed as the military capability of many individual member nations decreases. The percentage of national gross domestic product spent on defense by NATO partners has been inadequate for years. Only the United States, Poland, Great Britain, Greece, and Estonia in 2014 and 2015 met the North Atlantic Alliance goal of spending 2 percent of gross domestic product on defense despite the security guarantee and other advantages nations receive from membership in the alliance.[1] All recent US administrations have expressed their frustration to European leaders about the erosion of national defense spending and the corresponding reduction in military capability. Once lost, these capabilities are not easily or quickly recovered, and a serious reduction in overall NATO military strength will only encourage the cynics of transatlantic unity and misguided American unilateralists and give comfort to radical Russian nationalists in Moscow.

NATO draws scant public interest until it is needed, and differences will naturally exist over its political-military decisions in the future, but its member nations' basic commitment to the institution must not waver. Keeping the alliance vital and effective requires attention and commitment. Maintaining its military, economic, and political strength is among the most critical security interests of the United States, Canada, and Europe and is essential to international peace and security in the future.

UN Authority

Neoconservative hawks and other American unilateralists may scoff at the need for UN authority for military action, but the rest of the world does not. The UN is the primary institution to debate and justify international military operations, and the United States gains legitimacy when it presents compelling arguments in seeking UN authority for the use of military force. Given even a single nation's ability to block Security Council decisions, obtaining a formal UN mandate may not always be possible. The UN has its weaknesses, but the legitimacy gained by presenting convincing US justification for the use of force to the UN is very important to influencing international opinion, building coalitions, and encouraging allied nations.

Activist Diplomacy

National power has limits and is never in a static condition. Diplomacy is among the most important nonmilitary means to preserve and protect US national power.

Once the United States decided to engage in Bosnia, Richard Holbrooke took control of the negotiations through aggressive diplomacy and led the process to conclusion. Martti Ahtisaari also was aggressive in Kosovo. In Macedonia, sporadic international talks dragged on for six months before François Leotard and I arrived in Skopje to pursue a peace agreement on a full-time basis.

The activist diplomat in a conflict situation must have a plan for a realistic, lasting solution to the crisis and must aggressively use available leverage to secure a settlement. The plan is not something formal, with details of actions and milestones. Rather, it is a broad and often unwritten vision of the way forward. It should consist of a clear understanding of the objectives, the negotiating tasks, a negotiating structure to engage parties, available leverage, and a vision of the nature of a settlement. Any diplomatic plan must be flexible enough to adjust to new conditions and opportunities as they arise.

In Bosnia, Holbrooke focused on Slobodan Milosevic as the key to success. Holbrooke produced a set of preliminary agreements, a cease-fire, the end of the siege of Sarajevo, and proximity talks in the United States. The process in Kosovo was similar until Milosevic became inflexible and resigned to war. Multiple envoys, including me, shuttled around the region without success before the conflict. The United States and the Contact Group then put forth an international proposal with little hope of agreement in proximity talks in France. Only the subsequent NATO air campaign compelled Serbia to withdraw its security forces and accept UN supervision of Kosovo.

The plan in Macedonia concentrated on the national president and the leaders of the four recognized political parties. As a negotiator in Macedonia, I hoped to find practical, detailed solutions agreeable to the parties if they could be achieved within the context of American and Western democratic values and international standards of human rights. Leotard and I took the lead in the negotiating process by drafting a detailed proposal around existing agreed concepts and presenting it to the separate parties for consideration.

The envoy must determine the level of detail necessary for a sustainable agreement. Agreements on process or on principle alone may provide a framework for further work, but by themselves they are not sufficient for a sustainable settlement. Specific, measurable commitments are required.

Each of the separate Balkan agreements contained enough specific commitments to hold the parties accountable for detailed implementation. The Dayton Agreement signed by the parties in Paris filled a large three-ring binder with more than one hundred pages of precise agreements and implementing actions. The fifteen pages of the Ohrid Agreement committed Macedonian political leaders to specific actions and timelines, including constitutional changes and laws to secure peace. The Ahtisaari plan for Kosovo provided the basis for independence in Kosovo in sixty pages of principles and detailed annexes.[2]

Special Envoys

Rarely can a secretary of state dedicate full attention to a single issue, even an important one, and the local ambassador based in a national capital does not carry the interagency and international linkages often needed to coordinate policy in a crisis. The selection of a special envoy with the full backing of US national leadership provides dedicated attention to a difficult diplomatic problem and personal accountability regarding the outcome.

Choosing personnel is usually the most important decision to be made in any difficult situation. The selection of an envoy to represent the United States in a crisis can be critical to the prospects for success, but the pool of experienced personnel is limited. Not many officials with Richard Holbrooke's drive and experience are waiting in the wings to take on difficult national-crisis-management tasks when they arise.

Once the special envoy is appointed, his or her credibility rests on the perception that he or she has full presidential and interagency support. Without that full support, the parties to a conflict will seek ways around the envoy when negotiations become difficult. Allowing alternative channels outside the recognized negotiation can easily derail the process. The best model to ensure unity of effort behind the envoy is an interagency charter through the secretary of state, the national security adviser, and the Principals and Deputies Committees.

The special envoys in the Balkans were supported by small, dedicated, and often interagency task forces in the Department of State. Special task forces are always controversial because existing agencies frequently lose people and authority to them. For sure, they infringe on the authority of the standard organizations and take resources from that structure. However, they also place a singular organizational focus on a priority task and free the regular organizations to handle their broader functions. Task forces also centralize authority and responsibility for a specific problem.

Relationship to the Negotiating Parties

The ideal relationship between any envoy and the parties is straightforward, balanced, and respectful. Whenever possible, the relationship should create positive expectations, trust, and respect. It should also involve a healthy degree of independence.

Negotiations are very personal and can become highly emotional at times. Tempers inevitably flare, and personal hostility enters the process. The international envoy cannot allow those factors to obscure the task at hand. I learned from experience to stay calm, not to overreact to provocations, and to remain focused on the negotiating objective.

In dealing with the parties, the envoy should never confuse power with character, commitment, or statesmanship, even though he or she is obliged to treat parties to the negotiations according to the protocol of the parties' positions.

Once an agreement is reached, the parties, not the envoy or the facilitating nations, should hold primary responsibility for the settlement and its implementation.

Pressure

The United States can bring a formidable range of incentives and penalties to bear in a crisis. Except for purely humanitarian assistance, any US envoy in conflict resolution should use every piece of available leverage to advance the negotiations and the implementation of an agreement.

The first task is to determine what is important to the parties. What things will influence their decisions to compromise and negotiate seriously? Does the envoy have the means to satisfy the parties' goals? Once those means are determined, the envoy can link existing leverage to the priority tasks, reserving the most valuable for the most difficult negotiating points.

In Bosnia, Milosevic wanted the economic sanctions on Serbia lifted, a costly war terminated on conditions he could defend, and the restoration of his international personal respectability through high-profile meetings. Holbrooke understood Milosevic's goals and effectively modulated them to influence the Serbian leader on important issues.

The Train and Equip Program was sufficient leverage to cause Bosnian Muslim authorities to break their military linkages to radical Islamic forces and begin the process of integrating the Federation's two armed forces. In using the program as leverage, we set clear conditions for implementation, remained consistent with those conditions, and withheld delivery until the parties met them.

In Kosovo, economic and political pressure, visa restrictions on Milosevic's associates, and other sanctions failed to convince him to negotiate. Only a seventy-eight-day NATO air campaign ended Serbian occupation of Kosovo.

In Macedonia, the primary leverage with the ethnic Macedonians was the very survival of their country as they knew it. The Macedonian Albanians were influenced by the direct participation of the United States in the talks and by the promise of increased political power in government and legal acceptance of their culture.

Closing

Formally signing an agreement makes it real. Negotiations in a crisis are only an interesting political activity until an agreement is settled formally. Closing is the essential moment of commitment in a successful negotiation, but it can also be the most difficult point in the process. Successful closing requires courage, steady nerves, and full support from interested national capitals.

The stakes usually are higher for the parties to an agreement than for the international envoy. The people who must sign the deal know their political future and their place in history will be defined by the agreement. Could they have gotten more? Did they give away too much? These questions are impossible to answer completely in a stressful process, but the negotiator must try to give the parties assurance that the agreement is the best possible outcome. Closing is the time to bring maximum international pressure to bear on the parties. The highest levels of government supporting the negotiators must engage directly with the parties to stress the need to complete the agreement and to assure the parties that signing it is the best option for them and for their people.

The potential consequences of failing to complete the agreement may be the best leverage to achieve closure. The reluctant parties at Dayton could not afford to discard everything that had been accomplished in the negotiations from August to November 1995—an end to fighting, the opening of Sarajevo, a detailed settlement proposal—and walk away from Dayton empty-handed. To do so might well return them to conditions they could hardly imagine.

In Kosovo, Milosevic had no will to negotiate, and no amount of international diplomacy in 1999 could induce Belgrade to withdraw from Kosovo. The Contact Group, less Russia, simply went around Belgrade in 2008 and authorized independence based on UNSCR 1244 and Ahtisaari's proposal.

In Macedonia, the major issues were resolved by early August 2001, but the parties continued to quibble over the details of essential implementation actions. Strangely, the Macedonian interior minister's attempt to scuttle the talks by executing NLA fighters and shelling Albanian villages backfired when the NLA retaliated by ambushing a Macedonian military convoy. Instead of ending the Ohrid talks because of these actions, as I feared, the parties completed the agreement within hours. In the end, the political leaders judged the Ohrid Agreement the best alternative to war and national destruction.

The Military

The commitment of US combat forces to a conflict area carries enormous risks for the president and for the nation. Such decisions are the most important any American president can make. After a late and contentious start, the US leadership got it right by using aggressive diplomacy backed by military force to address the violent disintegration of Yugoslavia.

The United States and its allies could not have successfully ended the ethnic conflicts and restored peace and stability in the Balkans without the active engagement of US and NATO military forces. The US military, acting within NATO, first compelled Serbia to cease hostilities in Bosnia and Kosovo and then provided a secure environment for implementation of the peace agreements. Those operations were limited, precise, and professional at every level. The United States and NATO never found themselves caught in an intractable civil war in Bosnia or Kosovo, as some predicted. Looking back, the overall costs of these operations to the US and to NATO militaries, particularly in terms of casualties, were small relative to the success achieved.

Milosevic and the Serbs were not prepared to fight hard against NATO military operations in either Bosnia or Kosovo. After the peace agreements ended organized resistance in the region, NATO never encountered a serious military threat in its implementation security role.

The primary threats to America's national security and international commitments in Europe and Asia require the US military to be capable of high-intensity combat operations on a grand scale. Those strategic threats, although more dangerous, are less imminent and beyond the scope of current all-volunteer forces. In the future, the United States will likely face important security situations more often with limited objectives and with success less well defined. In those situations, as in the Balkans, the place to start in effective crisis management is activist diplomacy supported by credible multinational force.

Implementation

Implementation is the difficult, often grinding side of peacemaking. Any agreement with hope for success contains specific actions, measures, and responsibilities for the parties to undertake to implement the compromises they agreed to. In most cases, implementation tasks are far more difficult and always take much more time than the negotiation itself.

Each situation is special, and international organizations and the US government do not maintain standby organizations easily available for implementation of international agreements. Implementation generally requires tailored international structures such as the Office of the High

Representative in Bosnia, the Bosnia T&E Task Force, and UNMIK. International organizations have their weaknesses, but they broaden the support for the effort, and they spread the costs and responsibility for implementation.

In most cases, the international envoy of any peace agreement is not the right person to be responsible for its implementation. The negotiator can advise and assist, but the process is best served by fresh leadership for implementation. The parties to an agreement frequently feel buyer's remorse for what they have done and are often criticized by their constituents for the compromises they made. The international negotiator is a natural target to deflect criticism. The negotiator can also be too close to the document he or she worked so hard to achieve and may carry residual resentment toward the parties.

Absorption

Patience is not a characteristic of American policy, and that is certainly true in implementation and assistance programs. We usually have unrealistic expectations about how quickly a society can accommodate advice and assistance, and this lack of patience can waste or reduce the effectiveness of assistance resources.

In Bosnia, the recipients of the T&E Program—Muslim and Croat military forces—had an educated, technically proficient force and a cadre of professionals experienced in conventional military operations. They primarily needed modern training, organization, and upgraded weapons. Even with such capable clients, the program front-loaded more assistance than the clients could absorb. Stretching out the program and devoting more resources over a longer period would have been a better approach.

Building a democracy in a conflict area not accustomed to democratic values is a project that requires decades, not months or years, to complete. The recipient society's limitations in absorbing assistance should temper donor expectations so that programs can be scaled to projects and levels that can make a real impact with the time and resources available.

Corruption

National assistance programs to help with implementation often must be creative and flexible to be effective. But US assistance programs should not compromise on corruption. Corruption—the abuse of official position for personal gain—is the greatest threat to any democracy, including American democracy. It is especially destructive to crisis management and postcrisis development programs.

Corruption is the primary danger to new democracies and to areas with pervasive poverty. Tolerating it can destroy the credibility of US assistance programs and of the leaders and governments that allow it. Along the way, corruption makes a mockery of the rule of law and democratic values in general.

My concern is less with corruption among US persons administering foreign assistance because they are subject to US law and procedure. Most troubling to me are the foreign recipients of American assistance who have no such constraints. The United States should never turn a blind eye to corruption by foreign recipients as the cost of doing business, especially in broken, post-conflict societies.

From Vietnam to Iraq and Afghanistan, leaders who are corrupt or who accept corruption in their government have little public credibility outside their circle of supporters and offer little benefit to the United States in the long term. American officials may not have a say in the selection of national leaders, but that does not excuse failure to prevent corrupt practices in assistance programs the United States controls.

The methods to attack foreign corruption of US assistance programs are straightforward. First, the United States should put anticorruption measures at the top of the policy priorities of every US assistance program. Both the American officials responsible for assistance and the recipients should know that they will be held accountable if they allow programs to be plundered. Second, the United States should demand transparency and established competitive processes in procurement. Pouring cash into foreign institutions without full transparency and accountability simply on the theory of "capacity building" is a wasteful folly. Third, the United States should increase significantly its oversight of program implementation and financial controls at every level. Any investment in oversight will more than pay for itself. Finally, we should hold foreign officials accountable. If legal remedies are not available regarding their behavior, we can confront them directly and isolate them from further association with US programs.

The T&E Program in Bosnia applied these principles on a small scale to limit corruption and to account for donor funding. By necessity and by design, we carefully managed the funding and material assistance in the program. The financial management structure gave local officials decision authority, but the United States and the donors required competitive contracting and accountability, and they controlled the money. With these procedures in place, corrupt officials either were removed or faded away. Over time, the supported organizations accepted proper oversight.

It is naive to believe that assistance programs are making a real difference or are achieving national objectives when they are placed into corrupt institutions and governments. Tough anticorruption controls that stop the leakage of American resources into the pockets of corrupt officials are instead the best way to achieve assistance objectives.

American Leadership

Every commitment of US diplomatic and military power in a crisis abroad adds to the national security experience and to the maturity of the United States in international affairs. Although the war in Vietnam and the invasion of Iraq produced painful lessons on the limitations and unforeseen consequences of the use of military power, the US interventions in the former Yugoslavia provided positive examples of the effectiveness of multilateral cooperation, the value of international organizations, and the merits of activist diplomacy backed by military force.

The US responses to the crises in the former Yugoslavia were major foreign-policy and national security achievements for two consecutive US presidents. The Clinton administration produced the Dayton Agreement and the associated peace and stability in Bosnia. It ended the Serbian repression in Kosovo and engaged international organizations in the security and governance of Kosovo. The Ohrid Agreement in Macedonia and the independence of Kosovo were positive foreign-policy accomplishments for the George W. Bush presidency.

When the United States led the intervention in Bosnia in 1995, American power and influence were at their post–Cold War zenith. Since then, international events and domestic attitudes have made American intervention abroad far more complicated. In 2001, the attacks on the United States on September 11 immediately swung the focus of American national security policy to global counterterrorism. Since then, however, strained relationships with traditional allies, Russia's retreat into authoritarian rule and confrontation with the West, the global economic crisis, Europeans' uncertainty over the future of the EU, and Americans' weariness with the long and costly wars in Afghanistan and Iraq have affected America's policy options in international crisis management.

In that climate, the United States has assumed a more cautious approach to crisis management, concentrating on counterterrorism strikes against extremists but reluctant to assert leadership in other international situations. This period of US aversion to international leadership will not last. Important conditions and interests, such as the humanitarian disasters in Syria and Iraq, will cry out for American leadership, as they did in Bosnia in 1995.

With its historic level of national power, the United States constantly faces difficult choices on when, where, and how to respond to the variety of conflicts and humanitarian disasters constantly emerging around the world. These decisions are particularly challenging when no direct or immediate threats to American security or to its vital national interests are apparent. The United States cannot and should not attempt to solve every humanitarian crisis. But American values are consistent with humanitarian intervention abroad, and the levels of American national power and influence today give the United States a unique opportunity to lead or to mobilize international humanitarian interventions when national interests demand action or when other options are inadequate.

The human tragedies produced by the breakup of Yugoslavia presented just such a complicated set of policy choices. After a reluctant start, determined US engagement in 1995 filled an international leadership vacuum in the Balkans. Once engaged, the United States combined aggressive diplomacy, multilateral cooperation, and the selective use of military force to end the massive human suffering in the Balkans and to give the new nations of southeastern Europe the chance to develop as democracies in the European mainstream.

The experience in the Balkans from 1995 to 2008 showed how American leadership can achieve sustainable solutions to destabilizing international humanitarian and security challenges. It also demonstrated the importance of working with capable multinational coalitions and international organizations in response to a crisis. In doing so, the US-led intervention in the former Yugoslavia provided lasting examples of efficient and successful American engagement in world affairs.

Acknowledgments

My account of the US-led intervention in the former Yugoslavia would never have been possible without active support from many people. First, Secretary of Defense William Perry and Undersecretary for Policy Walt Slocombe launched me into the uncharted professional waters of international diplomacy by selecting me to represent their department in Richard Holbrooke's negotiating group. The experiences leading to the Dayton Agreement in 1995 that I shared with other members of the Holbrooke team—Brigadier General Don Kerrick, Lieutenant General Wes Clark, Roberts Owen, and Chris Hill—were unforgettable. During the Dayton talks, Mark Sawoski gave me valuable assistance on negotiations involving territory and the military annex of the agreement. Holbrooke, for his part, accepted me as an integral member of his team and then brought me over to the State Department, where I remained engaged in Balkans issues until 2008.

At the State Department, I particularly appreciated the guidance and help from Nick Burns, Jim Dobbins, Marc Grossman, John Kornblum, and Jim O'Brien at critical points along the way.

In the Train and Equip Task Force, I was fortunate to have support from an amazing group of creative and energetic people who worked through controversy and opposition to make possible the US commitment to help the Bosnian people with their future security. That group of professionals included Chuck Franklin, John Glassman, Raffi Gregorian, Chris Lamb, Stu McFarren, John Klekas, and Angel Rabassa as well as Richard McKrensky at the US embassy in Sarajevo.

In the field, Ambassadors Chris Dell, John Menzies, and Bill Montgomery became close colleagues as we wrestled with tough Balkan problems in Bosnia, Serbia, and Kosovo.

Two people were essential to negotiating the Ohrid Agreement in Macedonia: François Leotard and Laurel Miller. I could never have asked for a better EU negotiating partner than Leotard, who was a calming, thoughtful force throughout the negotiations. Miller's judgment and advice at critical moments led to the success of the negotiations. In addition to Miller,

Leotard and I were supported by an amazing group of young professional European diplomats and lawyers, including Fernando Gentilini, Arnaud Barthelemy, Axel Dittmann, and Thomas Markert. Credit for the Ohrid Agreement also belongs to Javier Solana of the EU and Lord George Robertson of NATO, who laid the groundwork for our negotiations and made personal interventions at decisive moments in the process.

At home, Kathy was wonderful as the first-cut reviewer, proofreader, and encourager in chief when the writing and the administration involved in preparing this book for publication stretched out longer than imagined. I also must give special thanks to George C. Herring, Don Kerrick, John Klekas, and Chris Lamb for their thoughtful review of important sections of the book. Angela Cannon at the European Division was especially helpful during my research at the Library of Congress.

At the University Press of Kentucky, Jonathan Allison, Allison Webster, and the rest of the team showed the kind of enthusiasm and encouragement that made the publishing process a positive and productive experience.

Finally, the success of the international intervention in the Balkans from 1995 to 2008 is a tribute to the thousands of US soldiers, diplomats, civilians, allies, international organizations, and people of the region who worked and continue to work tirelessly for peace and democracy in the new nations of the Balkans.

Appendix

Personalities

Ali Ahmeti	Albanian insurgent leader of the National Liberation Army in Macedonia, 2001
Martti Ahtisaari	Former president of Finland; special envoy of the UN secretary-general on the future status of Kosovo, 2005–2008
Yasushi Akashi	Senior UN envoy to the former Yugoslavia, 1993–1995
Sergei F. Akhromeyev	Marshall of the Soviet army; military adviser to Russian president Mikhail Gorbachev; former chief of the Soviet General Staff
Madeleine Albright	US secretary of state, 1997–2001
Kofi Annan	UN secretary-general, 1997–2006
Louise Arbour	Canadian lawyer; chief prosecutor for the International Criminal Tribunal for the Former Yugoslavia, 1996–1999
Jeremy J. D. "Paddy" Ashdown	British political leader; high representative in Bosnia, 2002–2006
Leslie "Les" Aspin	US secretary of defense, 1994–1995
Robert Badinter	Prominent French legal expert; adviser to the Macedonian government
James A. Baker III	US secretary of state, 1989–1992
Arnaud Barthelemy	French diplomat, member of the EU negotiating team in Macedonia, 2001
Samuel R. "Sandy" Berger	US deputy national security adviser to the president, 1993–1997; national security adviser, 1997–2001
Carl Bildt	EU envoy on Bosnia; high representative in Bosnia, 1995–1997

Jacques Blot	French political director and member of the Contact Group, 1995
Major General (ret.) William M. Boice	chief of Military Professional Resources Incorporated activities in Bosnia, 1996–1997
Hassan al Bolkiah	Sultan of Brunei, 1967–present
Ljube Boskovski	Minister of interior, government of Macedonia, 2001–2002
Alexander Botsan-Kharchenko	Russian diplomat; member of the Contact Group, 2005–2008
Vlado Buchkovski	Minister of defense, government of Macedonia, 2001
Zivko Budimir	Major general, Croatian army, 1995; colonel-general, Armed Forces of the Federation of Bosnia-Herzegovina, 1996–2001
Bojan Bugarcic	Foreign-policy adviser to Slobodan Milosevic, 1999
Aleksi Buha	Bosnian Serb foreign minister, 1995
R. Nicholas Burns	Spokesman, US State Department, 1995; undersecretary for political affairs, State Department, 2005–2008
George W. Bush	President of the United States, 2001–2009
Shaun Byrnes	Chief, US Diplomatic Observer Mission, Kosovo, 1998–1999
Agim Ceku	General, Kosovo Liberation Army, 1998–1999; chief, Kosovo Protection Force, 1999–2006; prime minister of Kosovo, 2006–2008
Hasan Cengic	Bosnian Muslim cominister of defense, Armed Forces of the Federation of Bosnia-Herzegovina, 1996
Branko Cervenkovski	Leader of the Socialist Democratic Union of Macedonia, 2001
Viktor Chernomyrdin	Prime minister of Russia, 1998; Russian negotiator on Kosovo, 1999
Jacques Chirac	President of France, 1995–2007
Warren Christopher	US secretary of state, 1993–1997
General Wesley K. Clark	Holbrooke negotiating team member; J-5 (Strategic Plans and Policy) of the Joint Staff, 1995; supreme Allied commander Europe, 1997–2000

Robin Cleveland   Associate director, US Office of Management and Budget, 2001-2005

William J. Clinton   President of the United States, 1993–2001

William Cohen   US secretary of defense, 1997–2001

General Rasim Delic   Chief of Staff, Army of the Republic of Bosnia-Herzegovinia, 1993–1996; commander, Armed Forces of the Federation of Bosnia-Herzegovina, 1996–2000

Christopher Dell   US chief of mission in Kosovo, 2000–2001; US ambassador to Kosovo, 2009–2012

John Deutch   Director of the US Central Intelligence Agency, 1995–1997

Rosemary DiCarlo   Deputy assistant secretary of state for European and Canadian affairs and US representative to the Contact Group, 2005–2008

Mark Dickinson   British ambassador to Macedonia, 2001

Axel Dittman   German diplomat, member of the EU negotiating team in Macedonia, 2001

Zoran Djindjic   Prime minister of Serbia, 2001–2003; assassinated 2003

James F. Dobbins   US special adviser to the president and secretary of state on the Balkans, 1999–2001

Colonel S. Nelson Drew   US Air Force, original Holbrooke team member; member of the National Security Council Staff, 1995

Lieutenant General Atif Dudakovic   Commander, Fifth Corps of the Army of the Republic of Bosnia-Herzegovina, 1991–1995; commander, Armed Forces of the Federation of Bosnia-Herzegovina, 1998

Kai Eide   Norwegian diplomat; special envoy of the UN secretary-general, 2005

Michael Einik   US ambassador to Macedonia, 1999–2002

Douglas J. Feith   American attorney, assisted Richard Perle in advising the Bosnians on the Train and Equip Program; undersecretary of defense for policy, 2001–2005

Pieter Feith   Dutch diplomat, deputy assistant secretary-general of NATO for operations and NATO negotiator in Kosovo, 2001

Charles "Chuck" Franklin	Chief of public affairs, interagency Train and Equip Task Force, 1996–1997
Robert C. Frasure	Deputy assistant secretary of state for European and Canadian affairs; original Holbrooke negotiating team member
Robert Frowick	Representative of the Organization for Security and Cooperation in Europe in the negotiations in Macedonia, 2001
Peter Galbraith	US ambassador to Croatia, 1993–1997
Robert L. Gallucci	Chief, US State Department task force for Dayton implementation, 1996
Robert Gelbard	US special representative for Dayton implementation, 1997–1998
Fernando Gentilini	Italian diplomat, member of the EU negotiating team in Macedonia, 2001
Mircea Geoana	Rumanian political leader; chairman in office, Organization for Security and Cooperation in Europe, 2001
Ljubco Georgievski	Prime minister of Macedonia, 1998–2002
Lieutenant Colonel Daniel Gerstein	Assistant to General Clark during Bosnia negotiations 1995
Jon D. Glassman	Former US ambassador, senior policy adviser, interagency Train and Equip Program, 1996–1998
Kiro Gligorov	President of Macedonia, 1991–1999
Pavel Sergeyevic Grachev	Russian minister of defense, 1992–1997
Raffi Gregorian	Policy adviser, Train and Equip Task Force, 1997–1998; chief of staff in the task force on Kosovo, 1999–2001; principal deputy high representative in Bosnia, 2007–2010
Marc Grossman	US ambassador to the Republic of Turkey, 1995–1997; assistant secretary of state for European and Canadian affairs, 1997–2000; undersecretary of state for political affairs, 2001–2005
Ramush Haradinaj	Kosovo Albanian insurgent leader, 1998–1999; prime minister of Kosovo, 2004–2005
Pamela Harriman	US ambassador to France, 1993–1997

Christopher R. Hill	Director, Office of South-Central European Affairs, US Department of State; member of Holbrooke's negotiating team for Bosnia, 1995; US ambassador to the Republic of Macedonia, 1996–1999; US negotiator on Kosovo, 1998–1999
Richard C. Holbrooke	Assistant secretary of state for European and Canadian affairs, 1994–1996; chief negotiator of the Dayton Agreement on Bosnia, 1995
James Hooper	Former US Foreign Service officer and activist on the conflicts in the Balkans
Imer Imeri	Albanian political leader in Macedonia; head of the Party for Democratic Prosperity, 2001
Wolfgang Ischinger	Political director, German Foreign Ministry, and member of the Contact Group, 1995
Igor Ivanov	Russian deputy foreign minister and member of the Contact Group, 1995
Alija Izetbegovic	President of Bosnia, 1992–2000
Jaber III	Sheikh Jaber al Ahmed al Sabah, emir of Kuwait, 1977–2006
Lieutenant General Bernard Janvier	French commander of all UN forces in the former Yugoslavia, 1995–1996
Adem Jashari	Kosovo Liberation Army leader killed, along with his extended family, by Serbian Special Police, 1998
Ante Jelavic	Croat cominister of defense of the Muslim-Croat Federation, 1996–1998; Croat president of Bosnia, 1998–2001
Darryl Johnson	Former US ambassador, policy adviser on the interagency Train and Equip Task Force, 1996
Zvezdan Jonanovic	Assassin of Prime Minister Zoran Djindjic, 2003
General George A. Joulwan	US general, supreme Allied commander Europe, 1993–1997
Radovan Karadzic	Bosnian Serb president and cofounder of the Serbian Democratic Party in Bosnia
Patrick F. Kennedy	Assistant secretary of state for administration, 1993–2001
Brigadier General Donald L. Kerrick	Representative of the National Security Council on the Holbrooke negotiating team on Bosnia, 1995

Ban Ki-moon	Secretary-general of the United Nations, 2007–2016
Jacques P. Klein	US Foreign Service officer; principal deputy high representative in Bosnia, 1998
John Klekas	Policy adviser, interagency Train and Equip Task Force, 1996–1997
Nikola Koljevic	Bosnian Serb vice president, 1995; signed the Dayton Agreement on behalf of the Bosnian Serbs, 1995
John Kornblum	Assistant secretary of state for European and Canadian affairs, 1995–1997
Vojislav Kostunica	Last president of the Federal Republic of Yugoslavia, 2000–2003
Bernard Kouchner	Special representative of the UN secretary-general in Kosovo, 1999–2001
Andrey Kozyrev	Russian foreign minister, 1992–1996
Momcilo Krajisnik	President of the Bosnian Serb National Assembly and cofounder of the Serbian Democratic Party in Bosnia
Joseph J. Kruzel	Deputy assistant secretary of defense for Europe and NATO, 1993–1995; original Holbrooke negotiating team member
Anthony Lake	US national security adviser to the president, 1993–1996
Christopher Lamb	Senior member of the interagency Train and Equip Task Force, 1995–2007
Sergei Lavrov	Russian foreign minister, 2005–present
Stefan Lehne	Austrian diplomat, EU assistant to Javier Solana during the Lake Ohrid negotiations, 2001
François Leotard	EU special envoy in Macedonia, 2001
Alain Le Roy	French diplomat, EU representative in Macedonia, 2001–2002
James Locher	US consultant on defense reform in Bosnia, 1996
Admiral Thomas J. Lopez	Commander, US Naval Forces in Europe; commander, Implementation Force in Bosnia, 1995–1996
Sakib Mahmuljan	Muslim cominister of defense, Armed Forces of the Federation of Bosnia-Herzegovina, 1996

Thomas Markert	German lawyer; legal adviser to EU special envoy François Leotard in Macedonia, 2001
Mirjana Markovic	Spouse of Slobodan Milosevic
Lieutenant General Barry R. McCaffrey	Special assistant to the chairman, Joint Chiefs of Staff, 1992–1994
Major Stuart McFarren	Security assistance adviser, interagency Train and Equip Task Force, 1996–2002
Thomas F. "Mack" McLarty	Counselor to President Bill Clinton, 2006
John K. Menzies	US ambassador to Bosnia-Herzegovina, 1996; member of the State Department Task Force on Kosovo, 1998–1999
Richard Miles	Chief of mission, US embassy, Belgrade, Federal Republic of Yugoslavia, 1998–1999
General Manojlo Milovanovic	Chief of staff, Bosnian Serb army, 1995
Goran Milinovic	*Chef de cabinet* for Slobodan Milosevic
Laurel Miller	Legal adviser to the US delegation during the Dayton negotiations on Bosnia, 1995; deputy US envoy in Macedonia, 2001
Slobodan Milosevic	President of the Republic of Serbia, 1989–1997; president of the Federal Republic of Yugoslavia, 1997–2000
Milan Milutinovic	Foreign minister of the Federal Republic of Yugoslavia, 1995–1998; president of the Republic of Serbia, 1997–2002
General Ratko Mladic	Commander, Bosnian Serb army, 1991–1995
William D. Montgomery	US ambassador to Serbia and Montenegro, 2000–2004; special adviser on peace implementation in Bosnia, 1996–1997
Sheikh Zayed bin Sultan Al Nahyan	President of the United Arab Emirates, 1971–2004
Major General William L. Nash	Commander, US First Armored Division deployed to Bosnia, 1995; international representative in Mitrovica, Kosovo, 2000–2001
Pauline Neville-Jones	Political director, British Foreign and Commonwealth Office; member of the Contact Group, 1995

James C. O'Brien	Special adviser to Secretary of State Madeleine Albright, 1998–2001
Roberts B. "Bob" Owen	Legal adviser to the secretary of state and member of the Holbrooke negotiating team for Bosnia, 1995; international arbiter on Brcko, Bosnia, 1996
Andreas G. Papandreau	Prime minister of Greece, 1993–1996
General Momcilo Perisic	Chief of the General Staff of the Federal Republic of Yugoslavia, 1995–1998
Richard N. Perle	American neoconservative policy adviser; assisted the Bosniak delegation during the Dayton negotiations, 1995; assisted the Muslim-Croat Federation during the US Train and Equip Program, 1996–1998
William J. Perry	US secretary of defense, 1994–1997
Thomas R. Pickering	US ambassador to Russia, 1993–1996
Michael Portillo	British secretary of state for defence, 1995–1996
General Colin Powell	Chairman of the Joint Chiefs of Staff, 1989–1993; US secretary of state, 2001–2005
Vladimir Putin	President of Russia, 2000–2008 and 2012–present; prime minister of Russia, 2008–2012
Angel M. Rabasa	Policy adviser, US Train and Equip Program for Bosnia, 1997–1998
General Joseph W. Ralston	Supreme Allied commander Europe, 2000–2003
Zeljko Raznatovic ("Arkan")	Serb leader of the paramilitary group known as the "Tigers"
George Robertson	Secretary-general of NATO, 1999–2003
Lawrence G. Rossin	US chief of mission in Kosovo, 1999; deputy special representative of the UN secretary-general in Kosovo, 2004–2006
James T. "Jamie" Rubin	Assistant secretary of state for public affairs, 1998–2000
Ibrahim Rugova	Albanian political leader; president of Kosovo, 1992–2006
Donald Rumsfeld	US secretary of defense, 2001–2006
Muhamed Sacirbey	Bosnian ambassador to the United Nations, 1992–1997; foreign minister of Bosnia, 1995

Nikola Sainovic	Vice prime minister and special adviser to President Slobodan Milosevic for Kosovo, 1998–2000
General (ret.) Crosbie E. Saint	Chief of the Military Professional Resources Incorporated, European operations, 1995–1998
Abdullah bin Abdulaziz al Saud	Crown prince of the Kingdom of Saudi Arabia, 2006
Prince Bandar bin Sultan al Saud	Saudi Arabian ambassador to the United States, 1983–2005
Mark Sawoski	Office of the Secretary of Defense, assistant to James Pardew during the Dayton negotiations, 1995, and in the Train and Equip Program, 1995–1996
Simeon Saxe-Coburg Gotha	Czar of Bulgaria, 1943–1946; prime minister of Bulgaria, 2001–2005
Jaap de Hoop Scheffer	Secretary-general of NATO, 2004–2009
General John Shalikashvili	Chairman of the US Joint Chiefs of Staff, 1993–1997
Haris Silajdzic	Prime minister of Bosnia, 1995
Walter B. Slocombe	US undersecretary defense for policy, 1994–2001
Lieutenant General Rupert Smith	British commander of UN forces in Bosnia-Herzegovina, 1994–1996
Javier Solana	Secretary-general of NATO, 1995–1999; EU high representative for common foreign and security policy, 1999–2009
Vladimir Soljic	Bosnian Croat cominister of defense, Army of the Republic of Bosnia-Herzegovina, 1996
Ivan Stambolic	President of Serbia, 1986–1987; assassinated 2000
Jovica Stanisic	Chief of state security, Ministry of the Interior, Serbia, 1991–1995
James Steinberg	Deputy national security adviser to the president, 1996–2000
Michael Steiner	Deputy German representative to the Contact Group, 1995; deputy high representative in Bosnia, 1996–1997
Veton Surroi	Kosovo Albanian publisher and intellectual

Goiko Susak	Minister of defense, Republic of Croatia, 1991–1998
Strobe Talbott	Deputy US secretary of state, 1994–2001
Peter Tarnoff	Undersecretary of state for political affairs, 1993–1997
Hashim Thaci	Kosovo Albanian insurgent leader, 1998–1999; prime minister of Kosovo, 2008–2014
Mendu Thaci	Albanian political leader in Macedonia; deputy to Arben Xheferi, 2001
Marshall Joseph B. Tito	President of the Socialist Federal Republic of Yugoslavia, 1953–1980
Vladimir Titov	Russian deputy foreign minister, 2005–2013
General Zdravko Tolimir	Chief of intelligence and security, Bosnian Serb army
Boris Trajkovski	President, Former Yugoslav Republic of Macedonia, 1999–2004
Franjo Tudjman	President, Republic of Croatia, 1990–1999
Maximilianus "Max" van der Stoel	Dutch diplomat, Organization for Security and Cooperation in Europe high representative for national minorities in Macedonia, 2001
Alexander Vershbow	Senior director for Europe, US National Security Council, 1994–1997
Neboysa Vujovic	Deputy foreign minister of Serbia, 1999
General (ret.) Carl E. Vuono	Vice president of Military Professional Resources Incorporated, 1996; former chief of staff, US Army, 1987–1991
Lieutenant General Michael J. D. Walker	British commander, NATO Land Component Force in Bosnia, 1995–1996
William G. Walker	Chief, Kosovo Verification Mission, Organization for Security and Cooperation in Europe, 1998–1999
Frank Wisner	Former senior State Department and Defense Department official; US representative to the UN negotiations to determine the final status of Kosovo, 2005–2008
Mabel Wisse-Smit	Humanitarian activist in Bosnia, 1995–1996
Paul Wolfowitz	Undersecretary of defense for policy, 1989–1993; neoconservative interested in the Train and Equip Program for Bosnia, 1996

Arben Xheferi	Albanian political leader in Macedonia; head of the Democratic Party for Albanians, 2001
Boris Yeltsin	President of Russia, 1991–1999
Jovan Zamititsa	Bosnian Serb public-affairs chief, 1995
Kresimir Zubak	President of the Muslim-Croat Federation, Bosnia, 1995

Notes

1. Welcome to the Balkans

1. Stephane Groueff, *Crown of Thorns* (Lanham, MD: Madison Books, 1987).

2. Margaret MacMillan, *Paris 1919* (New York: Random House, 2002), 109–42.

3. David Halberstam, *War in a Time of Peace: Bush, Clinton, and the Generals* (New York: Scribner's, 2001), 78–79.

4. George C. Herring, *From Colony to Superpower: US Foreign Relations since 1776* (New York: Oxford University Press, 2008), 92.

2. Fools and Madmen

1. Thucydides, *History of the Peloponnesian War,* trans. Rex Warner (London: Penguin Books, 1954), 106; Winston Churchill, *A Roving Commission: My Early Life* (London: Butterworth, 1930), 246; Robert M. Gates, *Duty: Memoirs of a Secretary at War* (New York: Knopf, 2014), 589–91.

2. Noel Malcolm, *Kosovo: A Short History* (New York: Harper Perennial, 1999), 341, 344.

3. MacMillan, *Paris 1919,* 112.

3. The Inconvenient War

1. Halberstam, *War in a Time of Peace,* 32–33.

2. Ibid., 41.

3. Ibid., 36.

4. Foreign Operations, Export Financing, and Related Programs Appropriations Act of 1996, H. R. 1868, 104th Cong., 1st sess., January 4, 1995.

5. Quoted in Halberstam, *War in a Time of Peace,* 46.

6. Herring, *From Colony to Superpower,* 924.

7. UN Department of Public Affairs, *Background Paper, UN Protection Force* (New York: UN, September 1996).

8. UN Office of the High Representative, "List of UN Security Council Resolutions on Bosnia and Herzegovina," Sarajevo, Bosnia, n.d., at http://www .ohr.int/?cat=236&paged=9 or at http://www.nato.int/ifor/un/un-resol.htm.

9. "Bosnia War Dead Figure Announced," *BBC News,* June 21, 2007.

10. UN Secretary General Report to the Security Council, S/1995/1031, December 13, 1995, para. 15.

11. Halberstam, *War in a Time of Peace,* 252.

12. Ibid., 167.

13. Herring, *From Colony to Superpower,* 325.

14. Halberstam, *War in a Time of Peace,* 196.

4. Genocide

1. Marlise Simons, "Court Declares Bosnia Killings Were Genocide," *New York Times,* February 27, 2007.

2. Scott Anderson, "Life in the Valley of Death," *New York Times Magazine,* June 1, 2014.

3. Halberstam, *War in a Time of Peace,* 291.

4. Ibid., 286.

5. Several biographic sources try to capture Holbrooke, including "Ambassador Richard Holbrooke, a Biography," *Frontline* website, n.d., http://www.pbs.org/wgbh/pages/frontline/shows/military/guys/hbio.html; Roger Cohen, "Back from the Brink," *New York Times Magazine,* December 17, 1995; and Michael Kelly, "The Negotiator," *New Yorker,* November 6, 1995.

6. Richard Holbrooke, "America, a European Power," *Foreign Affairs,* March–April 1995, 38–51.

5. Death on a Balkan Mountain

1. James Keagle, emailed comments on the draft text, Washington, DC, October 14, 2014.

2. Stanley Meisler, "Clinton Eulogizes Bosnia Envoys, Names New Team," *Los Angeles Times,* August 24, 1995.

3. David Binder, "US Aides Protest General's Meeting with Serb," *New York Times,* September 4, 1994.

6. The Godfather

1. Richard Holbrooke, *To End a War* (New York: Random House, 1998), 74.

2. MacMillan, *Paris 1919,* 109–24.

3. David Binder, "Alija Izetbegovic, Muslim Who Led Bosnia, Dies at 78," *New York Times,* October 20, 2003.

4. NATO, "Statement by the Secretary General," Press Release (95) 73, Brussels, Belgium, August 30, 1995.

5. Christopher S. Stewart, *Hunting the Tiger: The Fast Life and Violent Death of the Balkans' Most Dangerous Man* (New York: St. Martin's Press, 2007), 121.

6. Malcolm, *Kosovo,* 341.

7. Holbrooke, *To End a War,* 106.

8. Bob Woodward, *Obama's War* (New York: Simon and Schuster, 2010), 211.

9. "Agreed Basic Principles," Geneva, September 8, 1995, at https://www.liverpool.ac.uk/library/sca/colldescs/owen/boda/amer1.pdf.

10. Chris Hedges, "3 Enemies Agree to Serbian State as Part of Bosnia," *New York Times,* September 9, 1995.

7. Lifting the Siege

1. International Criminal Tribunal for the Former Yugoslavia (ICTY), Case Number IT-95–5-I, July 1995.

2. Holbrooke, *To End a War,* 151.

3. Elaine Sciolino, "Serbs, Complying with Deal Forged by US, Begin Moves to Lift Siege of Sarajevo," *New York Times,* September 16, 1995.

4. "Panel Voids Conviction of a Senior Serb General," *New York Times,* March 1, 2013.

5. Chris Hedges, "NATO Warns Serbs of Bombing If More Artillery Is Not Removed," *New York Times,* September 17, 1995.

8. A Certain Kind of Technology

1. "Further Agreed Principles," approved by Bosnia, Serbia, and Croatia, September 26, 1995, Office of the High Representative, Sarajevo, http://www.ohr.int/?ohr_archive=further-principles-new-york-26-sept-95.

9. Sarajevo

1. UN High Commissioner for Refugees, "Looking Back at the Siege of Sarajevo—20 Years After," briefing notes, April 3, 2012, at http://www.unhcr.org/en-us/news/briefing/2012/4/4f7acfb5c7/looking-siege-sarajevo-20-years.html.

2. "Empty Chairs Mark Bosnia Anniversary," *BBC News,* April 6, 2012.

3. "The Bosnia Cease-Fire," *Washington Post,* October 6, 1995.

4. Dana Priest, "In Shift, US Would Arm Bosnian Muslims," *Washington Post,* October 7, 1995.

10. The Last Shuttle

1. Dana Priest, "President Not 'Bound' by Hill on Deploying Troops, Christopher Says," *Washington Post,* October 18, 1995.

2. Stewart, *Hunting the Tiger,* 84, 101, 123.

3. Ibid., 225–27.

4. Slavoljub Djukic, *Milosevic and Markovic: A Lust for Power* (London: McGill-Queens University Press, 2001), 4–5, 159–69.

5. "Thousands Bid Farewell to Arkan," *BBC News,* January 20, 2000.

6. Stewart, *Hunting the Tiger,* 268.

7. Quoted in Michael Mandelbaum, "Coup de Grace: The End of the Soviet Union," *Foreign Affairs,* February 1, 1992, 164–83.

8. Jamie Shea, NATO International Staff, Brussels, Belgium, telephone interview by the author, March 5, 2013.

9. Carl M. Cannot, "Clinton Jogs with General Insulted at White House," *Baltimore Sun,* April 5, 1993.

10. Steven A. Holmes, "The Somalia Mission: Pentagon, Clinton Defend Aspin on Actions Regarding Request for US Tanks," *New York Times,* October 9, 1993.

11. Holbrooke, *To End a War,* 225.

11. High Stakes in Ohio

1. Holbrooke, *To End a War,* 232.

2. "Srebrenica: The Days of Slaughter," *New York Times,* October 29, 1995, and "New Proof Offered of Serb Atrocities," *Washington Post,* October 29, 1995.

3. Marlise Simmons, "Hague Court Orders Retrial for 2 Aides to Milosevic," *New York Times,* December 15, 2015.

4. Elaine Sciolino, "3 Balkan Presidents Meet in Ohio to Try to End War," *New York Times,* November 2, 1995.

12. Get an Agreement or Shut It Down

1. Richard Holbrooke, draft note to SACEUR and commander in chief, allied forces southern Europe, December 9, 1995, author's files.

2. Ibid.

3. Ibid.

4. James W. Pardew, "The War Is Over," note to Secretary William J. Perry, December 1, 1995, US Department of Defense, Washington, DC.

5. Ibid.

6. Michael Dobbs, "US Starts Process of Army Aid," *Washington Post,* December 21, 1995.

7. US Army Center for Military History, "Bosnia-Herzegovina: The US Army's Role in Peace Enforcement Operations, 1995–2004," updated December 23, 2013, at http://www.history.army.mil/html/books/070/70–97–1/index.html.

8. General Framework Agreement for Peace in Bosnia and Herzegovina, signed in Paris, December 14, 1995, at https://www.state.gov/p/eur/rls/or/dayton/52577.htm.

9. UNSCR 1031, December 15, 1995, at http://www.nato.int/ifor/un/u951215a.htm.

13. Richard Holbrooke

1. Michael Kelly, "The Negotiator," *New Yorker,* November 6, 1995.

2. Woodward, *Obama's War,* 227.

14. A President's Commitment

1. Quoted in Samir Huseinovic and Zoran Arbutina, "Burned Library Symbolized Multiethnic Sarajevo," *Deutsche-Welle,* August 25, 2012.

2. Daria Sito-Sucic, "Sarajevo Reopens Landmark City Hall and Library Destroyed in War," Reuters, May 9, 2014.

3. Christopher J. Lamb, *The Bosnia Train and Equip Program: A Lesson in Interagency Integration of Hard and Soft Power* (Washington, DC: National Defense University Press, 2014).

4. Office of the White House Press Secretary, "The President Accords Personal Rank of Ambassador to the US Special Representative for Military Stabilization in the Balkans," Washington, DC, May 17, 1997; White House, "President Clinton Names James W. Pardew as US Representative for Military Stabilization in the Balkans with the Rank of Ambassador," press release, May 20, 1997.

5. Foreign Operations, Export Financing, and Related Programs Appropriation Act of 1996, HR 44264426PP, 104th Cong., 2nd sess., January 4, 1996, sec. 540a, extended in 1997.

16. Two Conditions

1. Lamb, *The Bosnia Train and Equip Program*, 34–35.

2. Roger Cohen, "US Cooling Ties to Croatia after Winking at Its Buildup," *New York Times*, October 28, 1995.

3. Chris Hedges, "Bosnia Sends Soldiers to Iran for Infantry Training," *New York Times*, March 3, 1996.

17. International Donors

1. Mack McLarty and James Pardew, telephone conversation, May 24, 2013.

2. Ibid.

3. Ibid.

4. Lamb, *The Bosnia Train and Equip Program*, 26.

5. Ibid., 26–28.

18. Hard Choices

1. Michael Dobbs, "Last of Iran's Military Units out of Bosnia," *Washington Post*, June 27, 1996.

2. John Pomfret, "Bosnian Force Nears Approval of US Training," *Washington Post*, July 7, 1996.

3. White House Press Office, "Statement on the Program to Train and Equip the Bosnian Federation Armed Forces," press release, Washington, DC, July 9, 1996.

19. No Easy Prey

1. James W. Pardew, "Statement at the Federation–MPRI Contract Signing Ceremony," Sarajevo, July 16, 1996, author's files.

2. James W. Pardew, "SFOR Interference with the Train and Equip Program," unclassified memorandum, September 15, 1997, author's files.

3. "Train & Equip Program Update," June 26, 1997, US Department of State, Washington, DC.

4. Lamb, *Bosnia Train and Equip Program*, 38.

20. Wrestling an Alligator

1. Lamb, *Bosnia Train and Equip Program,* 26.
2. Admiral T. Joseph Lopez to James F. Pardew, October 29, 1996, author's files.
3. Mike O'Connor, "US Is Supplying Army in Sarajevo with 116 Big Guns," *New York Times,* May 10, 1997.
4. James W. Pardew, "Train and Equip—One Year Status Report," unclassified note to Assistant Secretary of State John Kornblum, December 5, 1996, US Department of State, Washington, DC.
5. Richard Boucher, "Bosnia-Herzegovina: Successful Completion of Military Train and Equip Program," statement by the US State Department spokesman, Washington, DC, October 30, 2002.

21. Impact

1. Raffi Gregorian, interviewed by the author, Washington, DC, May 31, 2013.
2. Ibid.
3. Ibid.
4. "Bosnia Sends First Combat Unit to Afghanistan," Agence France-Presse, Military.com, January 4, 2013, at http://www.military.com/daily-news/2013/01/04/bosnia-sends-first-combat-unit-to-afghanistan.html.

22. A Land of Violence and Fear

1. US Central Intelligence Agency, *World Fact Book* (Washington, DC: US Government Publishing Office, July 2013).
2. Judith Herrin, *Byzantium* (Princeton, NJ: Princeton University Press, 2008), 311.
3. Malcolm, *Kosovo,* 341.
4. Quoted in David Phillips, *Liberating Kosovo: Coercive Diplomacy and U.S. Intervention* (Cambridge, MA: MIT Press, 2012), 65.
5. MacMillan, *Paris 1919,* 361–62.
6. Malcolm, *Kosovo,* 312.
7. Phillips, *Liberating Kosovo,* 6.
8. Ibid., 7.
9. Ibid., 5–10, 13.
10. Ibid., 87–88.
11. Malcolm, *Kosovo,* 28.
12. Phillips, *Liberating Kosovo,* 13.
13. Ibid., 68.
14. Ibid., 82.
15. Ibid., 123.
16. Ibid., 82.

17. Christopher Dell, former US chief of mission, later ambassador to Kosovo, to James Pardew, email, September 21, 2014.

18. "Kosovo Ex-PM Ramush Haradinaj Cleared of War Crimes," *BBC News Europe,* November 29, 2012.

19. Phillips, *Liberating Kosovo,* 31–44.

20. Madeleine Albright, *Madam Secretary* (New York: Hyperion, 2003), 381.

21. Ibid., 182.

22. "Crisis in the Balkans, Statement of the U.S. Policy on Kosovo," *New York Times,* April 18, 1999.

23. Prelude to War

1. Human Rights Watch, *Humanitarian Law Violations in Kosovo* (New York: Human Rights Watch, 1998), 27–28.

2. NATO, "NATO's Role in Relation to Kosovo," fact sheet, Brussels, Belgium, July 15, 1999.

3. Steven Erlanger, "US and Allies Set Sanctions on Yugoslavia," *New York Times,* March 10, 1998.

4. UNSCR 1160, March 31, 1998, at http://www.un.org/en/ga/search/view_doc.asp?symbol=S/RES/1160(1998).

5. UNSCR 1199, September 23, 1998, at http://undocs.org/S/RES/1191 (1998).

6. Phillips, *Liberating Kosovo,* 66.

7. Human Rights Watch, *Yugoslav Government War Crimes in Racak* (New York: Human Rights Watch, July 15, 1999).

8. Ambassador William Walker, interview, *Frontline* website, PBS, n.d., at http://www.pbs.org/wgbh/pages/frontline/shows/kosovo/interviews/walker.html.

9. "Milosevic 'Inflexible' on Kosovo, Envoy Says," *International Herald Tribune,* January 22, 1999.

10. "Transcript: Clinton Justifies US Involvement in Kosovo," CNN, May 13, 1999.

11. Ibid.

12. Ibid.

13. NATO, "NATO's Role in Relation to the Conflict in Kosovo," historical overview, Brussels, July 15, 1999, 4.

24. Madeleine's War

1. NATO, "The Kosovo Air Campaign," fact sheet, Brussels, updated 2012.

2. Walter Isaacson, "Madeleine's War," *Time Magazine,* May 9, 1999.

3. John Daniszewski, "Evidence Details Systemic Plan of Killings in Kosovo," *Los Angeles Times,* August 8, 1999.

4. Deputy Secretary of State Strobe Talbott, interview, *Frontline* website,

PBS, n.d., at http://www.pbs.org/wgbh/pages/frontline//shows/yeltsin/interviews/talbott.html.

5. "Full Text of Peace Principles," BBC, May 6, 1999.

6. ICTY, "President Milosevic and Four Others Indicted for Murder, Persecution, and Deportation," press release, The Hague, Netherlands, May 27, 1999.

7. "The Military-Technical Agreement," NATO's Role in Kosovo, Basic Documents, June 9, 1999, at http://www.nato.int/kosovo/docu/a990609a.htm.

8. UNSCR 1244, June 10, 1999, at http://www.nato.int/kosovo/docu/u990610a.htm.

9. Michael Jackson, "My Clash with NATO Chief," *Telegraph,* September 4, 2007.

25. Midwife to a Nation

1. MTA signed by the international KFOR and the FRY and Serbian governments, June 9, 1999, at http://www.nato.int/kosovo/docu/a990609a.htm; UNSCR 1244, June 10, 1999, at http://www.nato.int/kosovo/docu/u990610a.htm.

2. US Department of State, "US Assistance to Kosovo," fact sheet, April 1, 2012.

3. UNMIK Regulation 1999/8, September 20, 1999, Pristina, Kosovo, at http://www.unmikonline.org/regulations/1999/reg24–99.htm.

4. "Many Die as Kosovo Clashes Spread," *BBC News,* March 17, 2004.

5. UN Headquarters, "Ban Ki-moon Deplores Attacks on UN Mission as It Retakes Courthouse," press release, New York, March 17, 2008.

6. James W. Pardew, Principal Deputy Special Adviser to the President and Secretary of State for Dayton and Kosovo Implementation, statement, *Hearing before the U.S. House of Representatives, Committee on International Relations, on U.S. Assistance Commitments in Southeastern Europe,* 106th Cong., 2nd sess., March 9, 2000.

7. Roger Cohen, "Who Really Brought Down Milosevic?" *New York Times,* November 26, 2000.

8. United Nations, *Yearbook of the United Nations 2000,* vol. 54 (New York: United Nations, 2000) ("Belgrade complained to the Security Council President about the US and E.U. statements" [385]).

9. Nicholas Woods, "Milosevic Aides Found Guilty of Yugoslav Political Assassinations," *New York Times,* July 19, 2005.

10. OSCE, "Election in the Federal Republic of Yugoslavia, Preliminary Findings and Conclusions," statement, Warsaw, September 24, 2000.

11. "12 Convicted in the Assassination of Serbian Prime Minister," *New York Times,* March 23, 2007.

12. Gabriel Partos, "Analysis: Stambolic Murder Trial," *BBC News,* February 23, 2004.

13. Marlise Simons and Gregory Crouch, "Milosevic Is Found Dead in Cell, UN Officials Say," *New York Times,* March 12, 2006.

14. Marlise Simons, "Hague Court Orders Retrial for 2 Aides to Milosevic," *New York Times,* December 15, 2015; ICTY, "Jovica Stanisic and Franko Simatovic Acquitted of All Charges," press release, The Hague, Netherlands, May 30, 2013.

26. Independence

1. UNMIK, "Standards for Kosovo," report to the UN Security Council, December 10, 2003, at http://www.esiweb.org/pdf/bridges/kosovo/1/25.pdf.

2. Kai Eide, "A Comprehensive Review of the Situation in Kosovo," report to the UN secretary-general, October 7, 2005, at http://www.fehe.org/index.php?id=473.

3. Contact Group, "Guiding Principles for a Settlement of the Status of Kosovo," October 7, 2005, at http://www.esiweb.org/pdf/kosovo_Contact%20Group%20-%20Ten%20Guiding%20principles%20for%20Ahtisaari.pdf.

4. UN Office of the Special Envoy of the Secretary-General for the Future Status Process for Kosovo, "Report of the Special Envoy of the Secretary-General on Kosovo's Future Status," February 2007, at http://www.refworld.org/docid/4a54bc380.html.

5. Phillips, *Liberating Kosovo,* 182.

27. A War or a Nation?

1. James W. Pardew, "A Tougher Line with Skopje," note to Assistant Secretary Beth Jones, June 1, 2001, Washington, DC, declassified July 29, 2014, US Department of State, Washington, DC.

2. James Hooper to James Pardew and James Pardew to James Hooper, email, October 7–8, 2013.

3. Hugh Poulton, *Who Are the Macedonians?* (Bloomington: Indiana University Press, 2000), xiii.

4. Ibid., 13.

5. Ibid., 18–25, 48–54, 72–172.

6. Ibid., 177.

7. US Central Intelligence Agency, "Macedonia," in *World Fact Book* (Washington, DC: US Government Publication Office, 2013), at http://www.geographic.org/world_fact_book_2013/macedonia/index.html .

8. Poulton, *Who Are the Macedonians?* 172.

9. Ibid., 218.

28. Pop-up Insurgency

1. Vasiliki P. Neofotistos, *The Risk of War* (Philadelphia: University of Pennsylvania Press, 2012), 37.

2. "Macedonia: Fears of a New Balkan Conflict," Timeline, *BBC News,* August 30, 2001, available at http://news.bbc.co.uk/2/hi/special_report/1400914.stm.

3. "Boris Trajkovski," *Encyclopedia of World Biographies,* n.d., at http://www.notablebiographies.com/newsmakers2/2005-Pu-Z/Trajkovski-Boris.html.

4. James W. Pardew, "Macedonia—so Far, so Good," July 4, 2001, US Embassy Skopje Cable 1545, declassified July 29, 2014, US Department of State, Washington, DC.

5. Constitution of Macedonia, 1991, art. 79, 84, 86, and 88.

6. "Macedonian Timeline," *Guardian,* August 22, 2001.

7. Brad Joseph, "The Macedonian National Prayer Dinner," *Religion in Eastern Europe,* June 2002, 54–56.

8. Nick Thorpe, "Rebels Withstand Skopje's Onslaught," *Guardian,* May 29, 2001.

9. "Macedonia Timeline, Key Dates in the Crisis," *Guardian,* August 22, 2001.

10. "Macedonia Announces New Government Coalition," Associated Press, Vaksince, Macedonia, February 2, 2001.

11. Pavlos-Ioannis Koktsidis and Caspar Dam, "A Success Story? Analyzing Albanian Ethno-nationalist Extremism in the Balkans," *East European Quarterly* 42, no. 2 (2008): 170.

12. "Military Forces in Macedonia," *BBC News,* March 26, 2001.

13. NATO, "Remarks to the Press, Secretary of State Colin L. Powell," press release, Bucharest, Romania, May 30, 2001.

14. Biography of Javier Solana, Brookings Institution, Washington, DC, at https://www.brookings.edu/experts/javier-solana/.

15. "Who Is Who in NATO," Brussels, Belgium, January 6, 2004, at http://www.nato.int/cv/secgen/robert-e.htm.

16. "Macedonian Government to Launch Military Offensive," Radio Free Europe, March 20, 2001.

17. OSCE, "Robert Frowick OSCE Representative on the Situation in the Former Yugoslav Republic of Macedonia," press release, March 21, 2001.

18. Veton Surroi, *The Book of Butterflies* (Pristina, Kosovo: Koha, 2011), 102–3.

19. Ibid., 107, 126.

20. Ibid., 110–11, 126–29.

21. Ibid., 131–32.

22. George Frowick to James W. Pardew, email, December 18, 2013.

23. US Office Pristina, "Macedonian Albanians Adopt United Stance, Letter to the Secretary," Cable 000913, May 23, 2001, declassified July 29, 2014, US Department of State, Washington, DC.

24. Surroi, *Book of Butterflies,* 147.

25. US Embassy Skopje, "Trajkovski's Outrage at Albanian Coalition Partners' Actions," Cable 001101, May 23, 2001, declassified July 29, 2014, US Department of State, Washington, DC.

26. Surroi, *Book of Butterflies,* 148.

27. Mark Laity, *Preventing War in Macedonia: Pre-emptive Diplomacy for the 21st Century*, Whitehall Paper no. 68 (London: Royal Services Institute, 2008), 20.

28. US Embassy Skopje, "Macedonian Update: Cease-Fire Reached in Aracinovo, NLA Withdrawal Phase Begins," Cable 1463, June 25, 2001, declassified July 29, 2014, US Department of State, Washington, DC.

29. "Macedonia Timeline."

30. "Macedonia: Fears of a New Balkan Conflict."

31. "NATO 'Error' Enrages Macedonians," *BBC News*, Skopje, June 29, 2001.

32. US State Department, "Authorized Departure from Embassy Skopje," cable, June 26, 2001, declassified July 29, 2014, US Department of State, Washington, DC.

33. Boris Trajkovski to Secretary of State Powell, Skopje, June 28, 2001, US Department of State, Washington, DC.

34. Official Journal of the European Community, Council Joint Action concerning the appointment of the special representative of the European Union to the former Yugoslav Republic of Macedonia, June 29, 2001, https://www.consilium.europa.eu/uedocs/cmsUpload/L180–3.7.2001.pdf.

29. Leo-Pard

1. Surroi, *Book of Butterflies*, 219.

2. Laity, *Preventing War in Macedonia*, 37.

3. Ibid., 20.

4. NATO, "Skopje Requests NATO Assistance," press release, Brussels, June 20, 2001.

30. Fury in Skopje

1. R. Jeffrey Smith, "Macedonian Cease-Fire Raises Hopes for Peace," *Washington Post*, July 6, 2001.

2. Draft Framework Document, Skopje, July 3, 2001, declassified July 29, 2014, US Department of State, Washington, DC.

3. Robert Badinter, paper describing points of agreement in discussions with Macedonian officials, June 28, 2001, informal English translation, government of Macedonia, Skopje.

4. Office of the President of Macedonia, "Political Dialogue Recommendations," July 2001.

5. Arben Xheferi, "Reply to July 7, 2001 US/EU Draft Framework Document," July 9, 2001, author's files.

6. James Pardew and François Leotard, "Speaking Points for President Trajkovski," July 16, 2001, author's files.

7. President Boris Trajkovski to President George Bush, Skopje, July 16, 2001, declassified July 29, 2014, US Department of State, Washington, DC.

8. Peter Finn, "Peace Talks in Macedonia Appear to Be Near Collapse; Mediators Accused of Acting on Ethnic Albanians' Behalf," *Washington Post,* July 19, 2001.

9. Assistant Secretary of State Beth Jones to James W. Pardew, telephone call, July 19, 2001.

10. "Joint Press Statement by the EU High Representative for Common Foreign and Security Policy, Dr. Javier Solana, and the NATO Secretary-General, George Robertson," July 19, 2001.

11. Negotiating Staff Paper, "Multi-lingual States in Europe," July 20, 2001, author's files.

12. François Leotard and James Pardew, joint press statement, July 23, 2001, Macedonia Information Agency, Skopje.

13. David Holley, "Fighting, Riots Add to Tension in Macedonia; Government Spokesman Accuses US, European Envoys of Bias toward Ethnic Albanian Rebels, Casting Doubt on West's Mediation Efforts," *Los Angeles Times,* July 25, 2001; "USA Has No Interest in Destabilizing Macedonia, Envoy Tells Minister," *BBC News,* July 25, 2001.

14. US Embassy Skopje, "Departure of FAST Marines from Embassy Skopje," Cable 2011, August 30, 2001, declassified July 29, 2014, US Department of State, Washington, DC.

15. Prime Minister Ljubco Georgievski to President Boris Trajkovski, July 25, 2001, Macedonia Information Agency, Skopje.

16. "Trajkovski Urges Citizens to Stay Calm, Stresses EU, US Envoys Invited to Former Yugoslavia Republic of Macedonia," Agence France-Presse, Skopje, July 25, 2001.

17. US Embassy, "Macedonian Tug-of-War over the Political Dialogue," Cable 1724, July 25, 2001, declassified July 29, 2014, US Department of State, Washington, DC.

18. John Ward Anderson, "New Cease-Fire Holding in Macedonia," *Washington Post,* July 27, 2001.

31. On the Banks of an Ancient Lake

1. "Lake Ohrid, Ancient Lakes of the World," n.d., at http://www.worldlakes.org/lakedetails.asp?lakeid=8770.

2. "Ohrid—the City of Centuries," Municipality of Ohrid, official website, 2013, at http://www.ohrid.com.mk/history/history.asp?ID=380.

3. Peter Finn, "Macedonia Agrees to Make Albanian Language Official," *Washington Post,* August 2, 2001.

4. Daniel Williams, "Evidence of a Macedonian Execution," *Washington Post,* August 8, 2001.

5. US Embassy Skopje, "Without 31 Votes, the Numbers Don't Add Up," Cable 1830, August 7, 2001, declassified July 29, 2014, US Department of State, Washington, DC.

6. Surroi, *Book of Butterflies,* 220.

7. Human Rights Watch, "Macedonian Troops Commit Grave Abuses: Role of Interior Minister in Ljuboten Abuses Must Be Investigated," September 5, 2001, at https://www.hrw.org/news/2001/09/04/macedonian-troops-commit-grave-abuses.

8. ICTY, "Indictment against Ljube Boskovski and Johan Tarculovski Made Public," press release, March 15, 2005.

9. Laity, *Preventing War in Macedonia,* 50.

10. President Boris Trajkovski to Lord George Robertson, secretary-general of NATO, Skopje, August 13, 2001, NATO Headquarters, Brussels, Belgium.

11. Law No. 07–117/1, "Ordinance for Proclaiming the Law on Amnesty," art. 1, Skopje, March 7, 2002.

12. NATO, "NATO's Role in the Former Yugoslavia Republic of Macedonia, Operation ESSENTIAL HARVIST, 27 August–26 September, 2001," Brussels, Belgium, December 9, 2002, at http://www.nato.int/fyrom/tfh/home.htm.

13. Laity, *Preventing War in Macedonia,* 68.

14. Ibid., 73.

32. The Long Struggle

1. "Constitutional Changes under Pressure of Military Aggression," report of a speech to the National Assembly by Prime Minister Georgievski, Antiwar .com, September 3, 2001, at http://www.antiwar.com/rep/georgievski1.html.

2. US Secretary of State, "Subject: Requirement for a Post-'Harvest' International Security Force," Cable 152097, Washington, DC, September 2, 2001, declassified July 29, 2014, US Department of State, Washington, DC.

3. Ljubco Georgievski to President George W. Bush, Skopje, September 12, 2001, declassified July 29, 2014, US Department of State, Washington, DC.

4. Mark Heinrich, "Peace Envoy Raps Macedonian 'Misuse' of US Attacks," Reuters, September 20, 2001.

5. UNSCR 1371, September 26, 2001, at https://en.wikisource.org/wiki/United_Nations_Security_Council_Resolution_1371.

6. US State Department, "US Support for a Durable Peace in Macedonia," Washington, DC, declassified July 29, 2014, US Department of State, Washington, DC.

7. US Embassy Skopje, "Lions Need to Be in Cages," Cable 2059, September 6, 2001, declassified July 29, 2014, US Department of State, Washington, DC.

8. "Georgievski Showed Perdew [*sic*] the Door," Macedonian Information Center, Daily News Service, Skopje, October 4, 2001.

9. US State Department, "Demanding Apology for Prime Minister Georgievski's October 3 Accusations," Cable 172243, October 3, 2001, declassified July 29, 2014, US Department of State, Washington, DC.

10. François Leotard for the EU, Max van der Stoel for OSCE, Ambassa-

dor Dan Speckhard for NATO, and James F. Pardew for the United States, Joint Statement, Skopje, October 3, 2001, US Department of State, Washington, DC.

11. James F. Pardew, François Leotard, Max van der Stoel, and Claus Vollers to President Boris Trajkovski, October 8, 2001, setting international standards for return of security forces to sensitive areas, author's file.

12. Minister of Interior Ljube Boskovski, statement, Skopje, November 12, 2001, Macedonia Information Agency, Skopje.

13. US Embassy Skopje, press release condemning violence resulting from return of security forces to sensitive areas, November 12, 2001, US Department of State, Washington, DC.

14. International Crisis Group, *Macedonia: Ten Years after the Conflict*, Report no. 212 (Brussels: International Crisis Group, August 11, 2011).

33. Turning Point

1. James W. Pardew, Principal Deputy Special Adviser to the President and Secretary of State for Dayton and Kosovo Implementation, statement, *Hearing before the U.S. House of Representatives, Committee on International Relations, on U.S. Assistance Commitments in Southeastern Europe*, 106th Cong., 2nd sess., March 9, 2000.

2. Holbrooke, *To End a War,* 358.

3. International Criminal Tribunal of the Former Yugoslavia, Judgment List, n.d., at http://www.icty.org/en/cases/judgement-list.

4. Brian Murphy, "Karadzic Convicted of Genocide in Bosnia War Massacres," *Washington Post,* March 25, 2016.

5. World Bank Group, *Country Program Snapshots* (Washington, DC: World Bank, April 2015), and Transparency International, *Corruption Perceptions Index* (Berlin: Transparency International, 2014).

34. Crisis Management

1. Naftali Bendavid, "Just Five of 28 NATO Members Meet Defense Spending Goal, Report Says," *Wall Street Journal,* June 22, 2015.

2. Ban Ki-moon to the UN Security Council president, "Comprehensive Proposal for the Kosovo Status Settlement," March 26, 2007, at http://reliefweb.int/report/serbia/comprehensive-proposal-kosovo-status-settlement-s2007168add1.

Bibliography

Albright, Madeleine. *Madam Secretary*. New York: Hyperion, 2003.

Churchill, Winston. *A Roving Commission: My Early Life*. London: Butterworth, 1930.

Djukic, Slavoljub. *Milosevic and Markovic: A Lust for Power*. London: McGill-Queens University Press, 2001.

Gates, Robert M. *Duty: Memoirs of a Secretary at War*. New York: Knopf, 2014.

Groueff, Stephane. *Crown of Thorns*. Lanham, MD: Madison Books, 1987.

Halberstam, David. *War in a Time of Peace: Bush, Clinton, and the Generals*. New York: Scribner's, 2001.

Herrin, Judith. *Byzantium*. Princeton, NJ: Princeton University Press, 2008.

Herring, George C. *From Colony to Superpower: US Foreign Relations since 1776*. New York: Oxford University Press, 2008.

Holbrooke, Richard. *To End a War*. New York: Random House, 1998.

Joseph, Brad. "The Macedonian National Prayer Dinner." *Religion in Eastern Europe*, June 2002, 54–56.

Koktsidis, Pavlos-Ioannis, and Caspar Dam. "A Success Story? Analyzing Albanian Ethno-nationalist Extremism in the Balkans." *East European Quarterly* 42, no. 2 (2008): 161–90.

Laity, Mark. *Preventing War in Macedonia: Pre-emptive Diplomacy for the 21st Century*. Whitehall Paper no. 68. London: Royal Services Institute, 2008.

Lamb, Christopher J. *The Bosnia Train and Equip Program: A Lesson in Interagency Integration of Hard and Soft Power*. Washington, DC: National Defense University Press, 2014.

MacMillan, Margaret. *Paris 1919*. New York: Random House, 2002.

Malcolm, Noel. *Kosovo: A Short History*. New York: Harper Perennial, 1999.

Neofotistos, Vasiliki P. *The Risk of War*. Philadelphia: University of Pennsylvania Press, 2012.

Phillips, David. *Liberating Kosovo: Coercive Diplomacy and U.S. Intervention*. Cambridge, MA: MIT Press, 2012.

Poulton, Hugh. *Who Are the Macedonians?* Bloomington: Indiana University Press, 2000.

Stewart, Christopher S. *Hunting the Tiger: The Fast Life and Violent Death of the Balkans' Most Dangerous Man*. New York: St. Martin's Press, 2007.

Surroi, Veton. *The Book of Butterflies*. Pristina, Kosovo: Koha, 2011.

Thucydides. *History of the Peloponnesian War*. Translated by Rex Warner. London: Penguin Books, 1954.

United Nations (UN), Department of Public Affairs. *Background Paper, UN Protection Force*. New York: UN, September 1996.

US Central Intelligence Agency. *World Fact Book*. Washington, DC: US Government Publication Office, July 2013.

Woodward, Bob. *Obama's War*. New York: Simon and Schuster, 2010.

Index

STUDIES IN CONFLICT, DIPLOMACY, AND PEACE

SERIES EDITORS: George C. Herring, Andrew L. Johns, and Kathryn C. Statler

This series focuses on key moments of conflict, diplomacy, and peace from
the eighteenth century to the present to explore their wider significance in the
development of US foreign relations. The series editors welcome new research
in the form of original monographs, interpretive studies, biographies, and
anthologies from historians, political scientists, journalists, and policy makers.
A primary goal of the series is to examine the US engagement with the world, its
evolving role in the international arena, and the ways in which the state, nonstate
actors, individuals, and ideas have shaped and continue to influence history, both
at home and abroad.

ADVISORY BOARD MEMBERS

David Anderson, California State University, Monterey Bay
Laura Belmonte, Oklahoma State University
Robert Brigham, Vassar College
Paul Chamberlin, University of Kentucky
Jessica Chapman, Williams College
Frank Costigliola, University of Connecticut
Michael C. Desch, University of Notre Dame
Kurk Dorsey, University of New Hampshire
John Ernst, Morehead State University
Joseph A. Fry, University of Nevada, Las Vegas
Ann Heiss, Kent State University
Sheyda Jahanbani, University of Kansas
Mark Lawrence, University of Texas
Mitchell Lerner, Ohio State University
Kyle Longley, Arizona State University
Robert McMahon, Ohio State University
Michaela Hoenicke Moore, University of Iowa
Lien-Hang T. Nguyen, University of Kentucky
Jason Parker, Texas A&M University
Andrew Preston, Cambridge University
Thomas Schwartz, Vanderbilt University
Salim Yaqub, University of California, Santa Barbara

BOOKS IN THE SERIES

Truman, Congress, and Korea: The Politics of America's First Undeclared War
Larry Blomstedt

The Gulf: The Bush Presidencies and the Middle East
Michael F. Cairo

Reagan and the World: Leadership and National Security, 1981–1989
Edited by Bradley Lynn Coleman and Kyle Longley

American Justice in Taiwan: The 1957 Riots and Cold War Foreign Policy
Stephen G. Craft

www.ingramcontent.com/pod-product-compliance
Lightning Source LLC
Chambersburg PA
CBHW020452100426
42813CB00031B/3342/J